THE
MOST
UNSORDID
ACT

Lend-Lease, 1939-1941

I described this to Parliament later as
"the most unsordid act in the history of any nation."

Winston Churchill, *Their Finest Hour*, page 569

THE
MOST
UNSORDID
ACT

Lend-Lease, 1939-1941

WARREN F. KIMBALL

THE JOHNS HOPKINS PRESS, BALTIMORE

PREFACE

On March 11, 1941, President Franklin D. Roosevelt signed into law H. R. 1776, popularly known as the Lend-Lease Act. The bill was an extraordinary grant of power to the executive branch of the United States government and made it possible for America to provide Great Britain with vast amounts of war materials, in spite of Britain's inability to pay for the goods. It was, in short, a subsidy. Although the act's provisions were later extended to all America's allies during World War II, its purpose in 1941 was to aid England. The primary focus of this study is on the development of that remarkable "common-law alliance," as Robert Sherwood called it. The story begins with the gradual depletion of Britain's dollars and gold between 1939 and 1941 and culminates in the drafting of the bill, the ensuing Congressional debate, and the political maneuvering required to get the legislation passed by Congress. In addition to a detailed presentation of the genesis of an important piece of legislation, this study also provides a glimpse into the formulation and operation of the foreign policy of Franklin Roosevelt. Thanks primarily to the remarkable amount of detail available in the Morgenthau Diaries, we are afforded an invaluable look at the give-and-take inside an administration which precedes any major policy decision but which is usually obscured by a facade of seemingly unanimous support once a policy is formally adopted.

Some are wont to dismiss the details of the development of American support for Britain between 1939 and 1941 as unimportant because such support was bound to come in time. Although it may look simple in retrospect, it was anything but a simple process to those who ran the American government. Franklin Roosevelt was firmly convinced that one wrong move might well jeopardize the entire aid to Britain program, and he acted accordingly. R. S. Sayers, one of the authors of the official British history of World War II, summed up this idea. After noting that Americans supported aid to Britain in spite of their disillusionment with World War I and all that had followed, he concluded: "In retrospect the historian may emphasize that American participation was sooner or later inevitable, . . . but a nation of millions of people is not brought readily to decisions of this kind." More than any other single event prior to the actual declaration of war against Germany, the Lend-Lease Act signalled that participation.

Acknowledgments are the happiest part of any author's job. Not only do they signal the end of the task, but they provide an opportunity to thank those whose assistance made this book possible. Professor Jules Davids of Georgetown University gave generously of his time and thorough knowledge of American foreign policy throughout the drafting of the manuscript. Whatever value this study has is due in great measure to his expert advice. Professor Thomas T. Helde, also of Georgetown, suggested a number of approaches which I found invaluable. I am grateful to Professor J. Joseph Huthmacher of Rutgers University, who suggested that an examination of the development of the Lend-Lease Act was needed. Professors Frank Freidel of Harvard University, Stephen Ambrose of Johns Hopkins University, and George Herring of Ohio University read the entire manuscript and proposed a number of useful revisions. I owe a particular debt of gratitude to two of my colleagues at The University of Georgia: Professor J. Chalmers Vinson meticulously examined the manuscript for both content and style, and Professor Joseph R. Berrigan tried his best to add form and logic to the introduction and conclusions. The Department of General Research at The University of Georgia generously supplied the funds I needed to complete my research.

The staffs of all the research libraries and archives that I utilized were invariably courteous and helpful, especially Miss Elizabeth Drewry and her staff at the Franklin D. Roosevelt Library. The late Dr. E. Taylor Parks and his successor in the Historical Office of the State Department, Dr. Arthur Kogan, plus Mrs. Patricia Dowling at the State Department's files in the National Archives, made my research in that department's files both effective and enjoyable. Miss Jane Cullen, in the Office of the Secretary of the Treasury, worked long and hard to open the Treasury materials to me; that there was little information in those files was not her fault. I am grateful to both the State and Treasury Departments for refusing to let red tape stand in their way and permitting me to use the records of the Foreign Economic Administration, in spite of some uncertainty as to just which department presently controls access to those records. My sincere thanks are extended to Dr. Thomas Morgan, Chairman of the House Foreign Affairs Committee, for permitting me to see his committee's files on the Lend-Lease hearings plus the minutes of the executive sessions of the Foreign Affairs Committee during its deliberations on the act. I would also like to thank the Yale University Library for permission to quote from the Stimson Diary and Papers.

The contribution of all those officials and ex-officials who consented to interviews was most valuable. Although no single interview provided any volume of data, the information was usually of real importance. This was particularly true of my interview with Speaker of the House John McCormack and the staff Administrator of the House Foreign Affairs Committee, Boyd Crawford.

The newspaper clipping file of the Council on Foreign Relations was made available to me through the courtesy of Donald Wasson. I am also thankful to Dr. Wayne S. Cole of the University of Maryland, Dr. Robert Divine of the University of Texas, Dr. John Morton Blum of Yale University, and S. Everett Gleason of the State Department's Historical Office, for their encouragement. I am likewise grateful to Mr. Eiraj Jalali for his technical assistance in preparing the final draft.

To my wife, Jacqueline—who thought she married a sailor, found she married a graduate student, and hopes she married a historian—this is lovingly dedicated.

The University of Georgia   WARREN F. KIMBALL

CONTENTS

INTRODUCTION

On March 19, 1920, the Treaty of Versailles failed to receive the necessary two-thirds majority in the United States Senate, signalling the official end to America's brief and frustrating "entanglement" in the affairs of Europe. In reality, American economic and political strength made full withdrawal from international affairs an impossibility, nor was that what most so-called isolationists intended. Essentially, American foreign policy during the twenties was one of unilateral internationalism, or what Charles Beard later called "fortress America." Self-righteously convinced of their own ability to treat all other nations justly and objectively, and equally certain of their capacity to handle any and all problems alone, Americans dipped in and out of the European scene seemingly at whim. Generally content to act like their Puritan forebears and lead by distant example instead of active commitment, the United States "observed" at the League of Nations, toyed with disarmament, and verbally outlawed war in that great "international kiss," the Kellogg-Briand Peace Pact.

For twelve years following the end of World War I, no major world crises threatened America's dream-world security, and the onset of the Great Depression in 1929 only reinforced the tendency of most Americans to leave the remainder of the world to its own devices. Then in 1931, Japan disturbed that sense of security by invading Manchuria, and Americans began to realize that power politics was not dead after all. Few in the United States were willing to accept the full implications of John Randolph's aphorism that "only power can limit power," and President Herbert Hoover limited to words attempts by Secretary of State Henry L. Stimson to organize some type of collective and meaningful response to the Japanese aggression. Two years later the disintegration of the Weimar Republic brought Hitler and the

1

Nazis to power, but most Americans, including the newly inaugurated president, Franklin D. Roosevelt, welcomed any sort of stability in Germany. Within a brief space of time, Hitler gave Roosevelt and the rest of the world cause to change their minds. Germany's withdrawal from the disarmament conference and the League in 1934, and her brazen and boastful rearmament after March, 1935, further destroyed the euphoria that had enveloped America.

As the tension in Europe mounted, Americans, influenced by revisionist histories of World War I which emphasized Allied guilt in the origins of the war, were ready to take steps to insure that the next war in Europe would not involve the United States. In 1935 a Mussolini-manufactured crisis developed between Italy and Ethiopia, while, at the same time, the Senate Munitions Committee (Nye Committee) held hearings that helped persuade many that wars were planned and started by businessmen hoping to profit from the sale of arms and munitions. The result was quite logical. In August, 1935, Congress passed the first of a series of neutrality acts. Reflecting the prevailing American view of Europe and European wars, the bill was designed to guarantee American non-involvement by two means. Once the President declared that a state of war existed between two foreign nations, Americans were forbidden to sell or transport arms or munitions to the belligerents. The law also permitted the President to warn Americans that they travelled on the ships of belligerent nations at their own personal risk—a provision directly descended from the World War I controversy over the travel rights of neutrals. This first Neutrality Act had a duration of only six months, but it was easily repassed at the end of that time, with additional provisions forbidding loans to belligerents. Though it hardly affected Hitler's plans, this new provision prevented the United States from providing financial aid to Germany's opponents since most of those countries had defaulted on their World War I war debts and were thus ineligible for private loans under the provisions of the Johnson Debt-Default Act of 1934.[1]

By 1937, with the neutrality legislation again due to expire, the Roosevelt Administration found itself in a dilemma. The Spanish Civil War, and the involvement of Germany and the Soviet Union in that unhappy conflict, raised the spectre of threats to American security and interests, yet impartial neutrality had the overwhelming support of the public and Congress. Equally troublesome was the obvious fact that any total embargo on the sale of war goods to belligerents would penalize the American economy more harshly than anyone desired. The solution was a curious compromise. The Neutrality Act of 1937 retained the main features of its predecessors but permitted the Presi-

---

[1]The Johnson Debt-Default Act was passed in an attempt to coerce the Allies into paying their debts. By June, 1934, all the European nations except Finland had defaulted on those debts.

dent some discretion in the form of the "cash and carry" plan. This allowed the President to authorize the cash sale of goods to belligerents, providing they were not shipped in American vessels. Long-term loans and arms shipments to belligerents were, of course, still prohibited. Thus the United States hoped to gain all and sacrifice nothing. National interest and profits could be preserved by the selective application of "cash and carry," yet restrictions on the sale of arms, long-term loans, and travel by American citizens on belligerent vessels would prevent the nation from becoming involved in war.

A rapid succession of events soon made it clear, at least to the Roosevelt Administration, that such dreams were hopelessly futile. When Japan attacked China in July, 1937, without a declaration of war, President Roosevelt did not apply the Neutrality Act so as to avoid cutting off American arms sales to China. Unfortunately for that policy, the arms and strategic materials trade with Japan also continued, thus completely negating the value of leaving the American market open to a China that did not have sufficient funds or credit to buy what she needed. More ominous was the expansion of Nazi Germany. The unification of Austria and Germany in March, 1938, appeared logical, if unnecessarily abrupt, but the German pressure in Czechoslovakia, the Munich crisis, and the Nazi violation of that pact, convinced Roosevelt that neutrality could prove dangerous. It took only common sense to know that in the event of war with Germany, the Western democracies would have to buy arms and borrow large sums of money from the United States if they were to survive. The problem was how and when could that be arranged.

To a significant degree, Roosevelt's awkward position in 1938 was of his own making. Twice elected almost exclusively on domestic issues, he appears to have made no attempt to think out systematically a logical and realistic foreign policy. Just as in his handling of the depression, Roosevelt tended to deal with international affairs on an *ad hoc* basis. The President himself admitted in September, 1937, that American reaction to foreign problems was on a "24-hour basis."[2] Roosevelt's style of leadership added to the general uncertainty of his foreign policy. His initial response to a difficult problem was to sweep it under the rug in the hope that it would solve itself in time, and he proved particularly reluctant to make any frontal assault on the prevailing public support for impartial neutrality. At times one detects the outlines of a broad, if vague, plan—such as his unwillingness to permit any meaningful debate over foreign policy until after the election of 1940—but he rarely took his advisers into his confidence. Whether his aversion to any systematic approach to foreign policy was

---

[2] As quoted in A. Whitney Griswold, *The Far Eastern Policy of the United States* (New Haven: Yale University Press, 1962), p. 456.

conscious or habitual is hard to say, although his Secretary of War, Henry L. Stimson, favored the latter view when he characterized his contacts with Roosevelt: "His mind does not follow easily a consecutive chain of thought but he is full of stories and incidents and hops about in his discussions from suggestion to suggestion and it is very much like chasing a vagrant beam of sunshine around a vacant room."[3]

Roosevelt's administrative technique only added to the confusion. Overly sensitive to the possible political repercussions of almost every move he made, the President took great pains to avoid friction and open conflict with anyone. In short, he rarely said no to anything, and we can determine what he truly supported only by his actions. In the case of the British financial crisis during 1940, vague promises to both the English and the Administration supporters of aid to Britain flowed constantly from the White House, but obviously Roosevelt saw no real urgency regarding money for Britain until very late in the year.

Determining Roosevelt's intentions is made more difficult by his admitted desire to eliminate from the public record any revelations concerning his personal decision-making process. On one occasion when his daughter Anna temporarily took over as White House hostess, she told her father she had decided against keeping a diary during the period of her quasi-official status. Roosevelt expressed pleasure and commented that he really did not want people to know every little thing that went on. Treasury Secretary Henry Morgenthau, Jr., received a similar reply when he asked permission for his private secretary to take notes during cabinet meetings. The papers in the various archives reflect this attitude, making the task of analysis both challenging and treacherous.[4]

The President's sympathies became evident when he willingly cooperated with a French mission under Jean Monnet sent in October, 1938, to discuss purchases of aircraft and supporting equipment. Roosevelt's designation on December 17, 1938, of Treasury Secretary Henry Morgenthau, Jr., to co-ordinate American aid to the Allies further indicated the President's desire to build up western Europe's defenses against Nazi Germany. Henry Morgenthau, Jr., had repeatedly suggested that the American government supervise foreign arms purchases. Morgenthau himself later claimed that he was given the job because Roosevelt believed that the Treasury Department would be less "parochial" than the Departments of War and Navy, since the Army and the Navy appeared to be more concerned with arming the

---

[3]Henry L. Stimson Diary (Sterling Memorial Library, Yale University, New Haven, Conn.), Dec. 18, 1940.

[4]This complaint is echoed by most historians. For example, see William L. Langer and S. Everett Gleason, *The Challenge to Isolation*, 2 vols. (New York: Harper and Row, Torchbook ed., 1964, originally published for the Council on Foreign Relations, 1952), I, 3.

United States than with helping France and Britain prepare for attack.[5] The President's choice of Morgenthau to supervise the Allied purchasing program in America indicated Roosevelt's desire to make certain they would be able to buy what they needed. More frequently than any other Cabinet member, Morgenthau had warned of the potential threat to America posed by Nazi Germany and had long advised Roosevelt to adopt a tougher policy.[6]

In picking his Secretary of the Treasury for the job, Roosevelt also chose a close personal friend and adviser. Although Morgenthau's public image has been blurred by some historic mistakes, such as the dropping of the gold standard and the Morgenthau Plan for Germany, he was one of Roosevelt's key counselors. The President trusted Morgenthau's common sense and logic, though he often made him the butt of public jokes. It was not so much Morgenthau's expertise that Roosevelt looked for, but rather the intuitive guess. One of the Secretary's subordinates summed it up by noting that Morgenthau could be right more often for the wrong reasons than anyone he knew. In addition, Morgenthau was not a "yes" man. His arguments with Roosevelt were frequent and heated, although once the President came to a decision Morgenthau could be counted on to carry it out in both letter and spirit, regardless of his own views. At times their disputes became so vigorous that the two Eleanors, Roosevelt and Morgenthau, were forced to play the role of peacemakers.[7]

Morgenthau possessed the one type of expertise most desperately needed for this assignment. For all his naïveté in economics, he had done a superb job of administering the Treasury Department. He suffered from a generally weak constitution, and to conserve his strength he adhered to a rigid schedule, transferring his own highly ordered life to the Treasury Department. He was a firm believer in delegating authority, and his staunch loyalty to his subordinates quickly developed a high degree of *esprit de corps* within the Department. He held the so-called group meetings with top staff members almost every

[5]Henry Morgenthau, Jr., "The Morgenthau Diaries: IV–The Story Behind Lend-Lease," *Collier's*, CXX (Oct. 18, 1947), 17; Henry Morgenthau, Jr., "Summary Report of the Secretary of the Treasury, 1945" (photocopy of typed original, Washington, U.S., Treasury Dept., July 21, 1945), pp. 76-77; Langer and Gleason, *The Challenge to Isolation*, I, 46; John Morton Blum, *From the Morgenthau Diaries*, 3 vols. (Boston: Houghton Mifflin Co., 1959-68), Vol. II, *Years of Urgency, 1938-1941*, p. 65.

[6]Blum, *From the Morgenthau Diaries*, vol. I, *Years of Crisis, 1928-1938, passim*, especially p. 467. There is evidence that Morgenthau was more than merely an anti-Nazi, but tended toward Germanophobia as well. See *ibid.*, p. 7. Be that as it may, his opposition to Hitler was open and far more than just a vague psychological inclination.

[7]Interview with Edward Foley, General Counsel, U.S. Treasury Dept., 1939-42 (Washington, Nov. 3, 1966). Morgenthau's willingness to stand up to Roosevelt is brought out in all the memoirs of the day. For some good examples see Blum, *From the Morgenthau Diaries*, II, 13-42; and Grace Tully, *F.D.R. My Boss* (New York: Charles Scribner's Sons, 1949), p. 193. Mrs. Morgenthau's name was spelled Elinor.

working morning and remained on top of his Department without letting it become a one-man show. Thus Morgenthau's appointment to the job of supervising Allied purchases in America was significant. The task was largely an administrative one, and the President took care to select his top Administrator.[8]

Morgenthau's concern for aiding France and Britain against Hitler did not blind him to his sworn duty as a member of the President's Cabinet. He was conscious of the bias toward Germany inherent in his being a Jew and told Undersecretary of State Sumner Welles that he would resign if he found himself looking at the European problems as a Jew. He may not have been completely successful, but the effort was there. This concern for American interests was reflected in other areas as well. Morgenthau continually tried to find a satisfactory balance between American and Allied defense needs and steadfastly refused to countenance subterfuges designed to get around the Johnson Debt-Default Act, which prohibited private loans to nations that had defaulted on their World War I debts. In fact, in March, 1939, he promised Congress that it was the spirit not the letter of that law that he would obey.[9]

This concern for enforcing the true intent of the law was demonstrated late in 1938 when Morgenthau questioned France's ability to pay for arms, and Monnet responded by proposing the establishment of a dummy corporation in Canada. Since the Canadians had not defaulted on their World War I debts, that would enable the French to obtain credit. Morgenthau warned Monnet the dodge would do no good. His suspicions about French solvency aroused, the Secretary told William Bullitt, the American Ambassador in Paris, a staunch advocate of aid to France, that the French would have to come up with some cash before they could go any further, and he suggested to Monnet that a deposit of ten million dollars would do a world of good. Influenced by New Deal philosophy and the "merchants of death" thesis presented by the Nye Committee, Morgenthau's position indicated his distrust of bankers and private war financing, an uneasiness heightened by the French choice of legal advisers—Sullivan and Cromwell, who also represented Fascist Spain.[10] Thus, a year before war began in Europe and over two years before a solution was offered, the problem of ready cash had already made its appearance.

On January 23, 1939, the nation was shocked to learn of the crash of one of the new American bombers during a test flight on the West Coast. It was not the crash but the news that members of the French

[8]Foley interview, Nov. 3, 1966. Blum, *From the Morgenthau Diaries*, II, 1-4.

[9]*Ibid.*, pp. 81, 111; Morgenthau, *Collier's*, CXX, 17; H. Duncan Hall, *North American Supply*, History of the Second World War: United Kingdom Civil Series, ed. Sir Keith Hancock (London: Her Majesty's Stationery Office and Longmans, Green and Co., 1955). p. 244.

[10]Blum, *From the Morgenthau Diaries*, II, 67-68; Morgenthau, *Collier's*, CXX, 17.

Air Ministry were aboard the plane that aroused public opinion. This ultimately forced Roosevelt to state publicly that he personally had given permission for the sale of the planes to France. Actually, his public commitment to aid the Allies had come earlier that month. [11] The *Anschluss* and the German violation of the Munich pact were accomplished facts, and in his State of the Union Address of January 4, 1939, the President indicated his impatience with the existing neutrality legislation, which he believed might be of aid to the "aggressor." He suggested that there were methods "short of war" which could make it clear that America would not stop with a mere verbal condemnation of such nations. Thus America was publicly pledged to provide some degree of material aid to the Allies. [12]

The British had some premonitions of their financial shortcomings even before the shooting war broke out. They had begun to rearm before the Munich crisis, and Hitler's violation of those agreements had convinced Prime Minister Neville Chamberlain that negotiations would be possible only from a position of strength. [13] Arms purchases by the British were small in comparison to the period following the fall of France in 1940, but even limited buying brought home the fact that British gold and dollar reserves would have to be carefully husbanded. In April, 1939, the British Treasury informed the American government that it intended to take control of all its gold resources, as well as all foreign securities and dollar balances held by British nationals. They promised that they would consult the United States authorities before forcing the sale of any of their American securities, but obviously His Majesty's Government was well aware of potential dollar shortages. [14]

Even more significant was the mission of Lord Riverdale of Sheffield to the United States in July, 1939. The Roosevelt Administration had made clear its willingness to receive an official purchasing mission from Britain; Morgenthau, as a matter of principle, in fact preferred to deal with the British government rather than private business in such

[11]Blum, *From the Morgenthau Diaries*, II, 71-78, contains the best treatment of the French purchases of American aircraft outside the Morgenthau Diaries themselves. See also Langer and Gleason, *The Challenge to Isolation*, I, 48-49.

[12]Franklin D. Roosevelt, *The Public Papers and Addresses of Franklin D. Roosevelt*, Comp. Samuel I. Rosenman, 13 vols. (London: Macmillan and Co., 1938-50), VIII (1939), 1-12. Hereafter cited as Roosevelt, *Papers and Addresses*, plus appropriate year.

[13]British rearmament at this stage was more verbal than actual, but even that necessitated examining the financial situation. See Gen. Sir William Edmund Ironside, *Time Unguarded: The Ironside Diaries, 1937-1940*, ed. Col. R. MacLeod and Denis Kelly (New York: David McKay Co., 1962), pp. 21-56. See also Keith Feiling, *The Life of Neville Chamberlain* (London: Macmillan and Co., 1946).

[14]Blum, *From the Morgenthau Diaries*, II, 92. For a full discussion of the development of exchange controls by the United Kingdom, see R. S. Sayers, *Financial Policy, 1939-1945*, History of the Second World War: United Kingdom Civil Series, ed. Sir Keith Hancock (London: Her Majesty's Stationery Office and Longmans, Green and Co., 1956), pp. 226-51.

matters. Riverdale reported that Roosevelt was "100 percent in favor" of such a mission and believed the British representative should have direct access to the heads of the Executive departments. Even more heartening, the President promised to share American production at a ratio of around three to five. Because of the problem of public opinion in America, they decided to delay the formal establishment of such a mission until the war actually broke out.[15]

Lord Riverdale's conclusions in his report to the British government are most revealing. In general, they boil down to a conditional phrase: British requirements for the next two years could be met *if* the United States were not at war and United Kingdom dollar reserves held out. The implications were apparent. Should America enter the war, her military needs would leave little for England to purchase, and even that possibility would be a moot point without credit. [16]

As the crisis deepened during the summer of 1939, the British took further steps to prepare for increased purchases in America and to organize their domestic economy. Sir Josiah Stamp, as chairman of a subcommittee of the Economic Advisory Council, began an extensive survey of the economic and financial plans that had been prepared. In spite of the excellent work done by the Stamp Survey, Churchill complained later that when he became First Lord of the Admiralty in September, 1939, there was still no central government statistical organization; instead, each ministry used its own system. Considering this and similar problems, it is not surprising that Britain was hard pressed to come up with meaningful purchasing plans, particularly until the expected war became a reality. The fears expressed by Lord Riverdale all too quickly became fact. In the tense period just prior to the outbreak of war, the British gold reserve dipped alarmingly. Between August 15 and 24, 1939, overseas buying caused Britain to lose about sixty-five million pounds sterling of those precious reserves.[17]

The Roosevelt Administration was likewise dependent upon the turn of events in Europe. Although the President had informed Morgenthau that he would not be overly strict about lending money to the Allies so long as it was not for munitions,[18] for the government

[15] Hall, *North American Supply*, pp. 60-71. Much of the information gleaned from the various volumes of the official British History of the Second World War is not available or verifiable elsewhere at present. The authors had access to the British records, which are still closed. The volume by Hall, cited above, is the most valuable of any of the series for matters of diplomatic relations between the United States and Great Britain, although that was not its primary purpose.

[16] *Ibid.*, p. 67.

[17] W. K. Hancock and M. M. Gowing, *British War Economy*, History of the Second World War: United Kingdom Civil Series, ed. Sir Keith Hancock (London: His Majesty's Stationery Office, 1949), pp. 47, 221; Winston S. Churchill, *The Second World War*, 6 vols. (Boston: Houghton Mifflin, 1948-53), vol. I, *The Gathering Storm*, p. 468. Blum, *From the Morgenthau Diaries*, II, 92.

[18] Blum, *From the Morgenthau Diaries*, II, 90.

to go further and extend substantial credits would have required equally extensive Congressional appropriations, and the isolationists in that body, with strong support from the general public, could block that move. That power was amply demonstrated when the Administration failed to obtain the revision of the neutrality legislation it desired in June, 1939.[19] If that were not enough, the American military establishment expressed increasing anxiety about the state of American preparedness. Even though a military leader like General Malin Craig, Army Chief of Staff, approved of aircraft sales to the Allies as a means of increasing the production potential of American industry, it was a different matter when it came to most other items.[20]

Thus, in spite of a desire on the part of the British to buy, and a willingness on the part of the Roosevelt Administration to provide aid, neither side was a free agent. Fiscal responsibility on the one hand and public opinion on the other left the initiative to German Chancellor Adolf Hitler. The resolution of these conflicting desires within the Administration is the story of the genesis of the Lend-Lease Act of March, 1941.

The Lend-Lease Act marked the point of no return for American policy regarding Hitler's Germany, and that alone justifies an examination of its origins. But far more significant are the questions that story poses—both about Roosevelt's true motives and about the conduct of international relations within a democracy. Once war began in Europe, certain policy assumptions are apparent throughout the development of the Lend-Lease program. First and foremost, Roosevelt clearly believed that the defeat of Britain at the hands of Nazi Germany posed a very real threat to the national security and interests of the United States. The question was not whether America would aid Britain and the Allies, but to what degree.

In spite of this general if ill-defined agreement within the Administration to aid Great Britain, attitudes that militated against such support persisted. Most dangerous for the British was their inability to convince Roosevelt of the urgency of their financial problem. Throughout 1940, the President repeatedly made private comments indicating his belief that there was no need to deal immediately with Britain's money problem. His attitude logically followed from the persistent American conviction that the wealth of the British Empire was inexhaustible. Not until late in 1940 was Roosevelt finally dis-

[19]This unsuccessful attempt to revise the Neutrality Act of 1937 is fully discussed in Robert A. Divine, *The Illusion of Neutrality* (Chicago: The University of Chicago Press, 1962), pp. 229-85.

[20]Mark S. Watson, *Chief of Staff: Prewar Plans and Preparations*, United States Army in World War II: The War Department, ed. Kent Roberts Greenfield (Washington: Historical Division, Department of the Army, 1950), pp. 301-2. The details of this ever-present conflict between Allied and American needs are beyond the scope of this study. The most convenient treatment of the problem is in the book by Watson just cited.

abused of that notion, and some members of the Administration, like Secretary of State Cordell Hull, held firm to that position until long after Lend-Lease became law. Although Anglophobia contributed to this problem, its basic cause was ignorance concerning the nature of international economics. Most Americans could not understand how Britain could need American dollars and still have ample supplies of British currency.

It appears possible that the delay in finding a solution to Britain's dollar shortage was caused by more than just a lack of understanding about currency exchange. Throughout the pre-Lend-Lease period there appear pieces of circumstantial evidence which indicate an inclination on the part of the American government to take economic advantage of the United Kingdom's plight. From the onset of war, the basic policy of the Roosevelt Administration, particularly Henry Morgenthau, was to demand that Britain take meaningful steps to sell her business investments in America. This was followed by forcing England to buy dollars with gold and finally by suggestions that British investments in Latin America be sold for cash or at least posted as collateral for Lend-Lease aid.

Had the Administration pushed these ideas to their logical conclusion, it would have been a blatant example of economic imperialism. Britain had no choice but to yield to such demands if she wanted to resist Hitler. Nevertheless, although the inclination to expand America's economic holdings at Britain's expense repeatedly cropped up, little was done to implement it. In reality, few of Britain's holdings in the United States were ever sold, and none of her economic investments in Latin America went on the block because of pressure from the Roosevelt Administration. The British did transfer sizeable quantities of gold in return for dollars, but that had relatively little effect on her overseas investments. The Roosevelt Administration was aware of Britain's fears and repeatedly assured English diplomats that domestic politics necessitated taking such a hard line. Morgenthau insisted that Congress would never approve any meaningful financial aid to Britain unless it were convinced that the United Kingdom had utilized all available resources, and British representatives generally agreed. Certainly such strategy worked, for when the Lend-Lease bill came before Congress, no one effectively challenged Morgenthau when he presented figures showing Britain had used up its dollar resources. Considering this political problem and the failure of the Roosevelt Administration to do much more than just talk about forcing Britain to transfer her overseas holdings, it appears that economic imperialism was a subconscious temptation rather than an actual policy.

The Roosevelt Administration's decision to aid the Allies is far less controversial than the means used to accomplish that end. Looking particularly at the Lend-Lease Act, which committed the United States to total economic support for Britain's war effort against Germany, Roosevelt's critics have implied the full range of possible motives on Roosevelt's part. The harshest accusations have come from certain historians, particularly those who view World War II from the vantage point of the Cold War. These so-called revisionists have bluntly stated that the President consciously deceived the American people by calling the Lend-Lease Bill "aid short of war" while he knew full well that it would inevitably bring the country into the war. Some have accused Roosevelt of trying to put America on a war footing in order to pull the nation out of the depression; others picture his principal war aim as the extension of the New Deal to the rest of the world. Virtually all the revisionists are bitter critics of Roosevelt's domestic policies, and most infer that he had socialistic leanings that made him dangerously sympathetic to the Soviet Union.[21] Even some of the Lend-Lease Act's strongest supporters expressed concern over what they felt was a deceptive approach on the part of the Roosevelt Administration. News analyst Eric Sevareid wondered if the act did not involve a fundamental dishonesty, and Herbert Agar bluntly wrote in October, 1941, that the notion that the bill was designed to keep America out of war was sheer "bunk."[22] Charles A. Beard, who supported the New Deal, spoke for that group of domestic reformers who feared that international entanglements would mean the end of internal reform. Although he never went so far as to accuse the Roosevelt Administration of consciously lying, his testimony before the Senate Foreign Relations Committee made it clear that such was his belief.[23] He continued to develop that theme in his study, *President Roosevelt and the Coming of the War,* published in 1948.

On the other side of the coin, two of Franklin Roosevelt's most ardent apologists, Basil Rauch and Walter Johnson, found little to criticize in the President's actions. They placed the primary blame on the isolationists who so deluded the American public about the ability of the United States to insulate itself from European problems that the nation was placed in a position of great danger. Rauch claimed that the basic nature of the Lend-Lease debate was determined by the

[21]William H. Chamberlin, *America's Second Crusade* (Chicago: Henry Regnery Co., 1950), p. 350; Frederic R. Sanborn, *Design for War: A Study of Secret Power Politics, 1937-1941* (New York: The Devin-Adair Co., 1951), p. 233; Charles C. Tansill, *Back Door to War: The Roosevelt Foreign Policy, 1933-1941* (Chicago: Henry Regnery Co., 1952).

[22]As quoted in Sanborn, *Design For War*, pp. 249-50.

[23]U.S., Senate, 77th Cong., 1st sess., Committee on Foreign Relations, *Hearings on S. 275: A Bill Further to Promote the Defense of the United States, and for Other Purposes,* Jan. 27, 1941-Feb. 11, 1941 (Washington: U.S. Government Printing Office, 1941), pp. 307-17. Hereafter cited as SFRC, *Hearings.*

isolationists who chose to concentrate on the extensive powers granted the President by the bill instead of on the broad question of collective security; Johnson fell into a semantic defense by saying the legislation moved the United States into a status of "nonbelligerency," but not war. Rauch went even further in surmising that Roosevelt fully intended to create "a world system of collective security."[24] Thomas A. Bailey attempted to find a sort of middle ground by pointing out that the dangers of acting contrary to public opinion have often forced American presidents into using deceit, and labelled the Lend-Lease Act as such a case. He then mitigated his criticism of Roosevelt by implying that posterity would thank him for his action.[25] William Langer and S. Everett Gleason admitted that the Administration avoided any discussion of the long-term ramifications of the Lend-Lease Act but denied that Roosevelt was "either cynical or dishonest" in doing so since he and his advisers believed it was the best chance, "such as it was," of staying out of the war.[26]

The evidence concerning Roosevelt's motives is, at best, inconclusive. There is no doubt that he was resigned to the fact that American planes and ships would have to see active combat against the Germans, but nowhere can the historian find any clear statement, public or private, which indicates a similar belief regarding the use of the Army.[27] He told the Ambassador from the Polish government-in-exile, Jan Ciechanowski, that he hoped Lend-Lease was the only price Americans would have to pay in order to defend democratic principles but went on to admit that no one could tell if that would be enough. In a 1940 New Year's Eve letter to Francis B. Sayre, United States High Commissioner in the Philippines, he said much the same thing

---

[24]Basil Rauch, *Roosevelt: From Munich to Pearl Harbor* (New York: Creative Age Press, 1950), pp. 304, 312-13; Walter Johnson, *The Battle Against Isolation* (Chicago: University of Chicago Press, 1944), p. 210.

[25]Thomas A. Bailey, *The Man on the Street: The Impact of American Public Opinion on Foreign Policy* (New York: The Macmillan Co., 1948), p. 13.

[26]Langer and Gleason, *The Undeclared War*, pp. 267-68.

[27]On June 30, 1940, Roosevelt sent the Army planners a set of assumptions from which they were to draw up long-range plans. One of these was that the United States was actively engaged in the war by 1941, but only via air and naval forces. See Maurice Matloff and Edwin M. Snell, *Strategic Planning for Coalition Warfare, 1941-1942*, United States Army in World War II: The War Department, ed. Kent Roberts Greenfield (Washington: Office of the Chief of Military History, 1955), pp. 13-14. A month earlier he had told Lord Lothian that the United States would probably enter the war should a "catastrophe" occur, but that is hardly the type of commitment the revisionists accuse him of making. See J. R. M. Butler, *Grand Strategy*, vol. II, *September 1939-June 1941*, History of the Second World War: United Kingdom Military Series, ed. J. R. M. Butler (London: Her Majesty's Stationery Office, 1957), pp. 241-42. Further indications of Roosevelt's willingness to commit the Navy and Air Force can be found in J. W. Pickersgill, *The Mackenzie King Record*, 1 vol. (Toronto: University of Chicago Press and University of Toronto Press, 1960), I (1939-44), 120-21. See also, Watson, *Chief of Staff*, p. 380.

and further claimed that war depended upon Germany more than the United States.[28]

The entire scope of speculation regarding Roosevelt's over-all motives raises questions of immense significance about the responsibilities of leadership in a representative system. To what degree must an elected official follow his own conscience, even if it violates the desires of his constituents? Is it legitimate for a democratic leader to "educate" the public by only revealing portions of policy, or do democratic principles require complete candor, regardless of the possible consequences for national security? The development of the Lend-Lease concept and the Great Debate over the bill afford a case study in those questions which is quite limited in the scope of time involved but comprehensive in terms of the broadest questions of government and society.

---

[28]Jan Ciechanowski, *Defeat in Victory* (Garden City: Doubleday and Co., 1947), pp. 5-6; Franklin D. Roosevelt, *F.D.R.: His Personal Letters, 1928-1945*, ed. Elliott Roosevelt (New York: Duell, Sloan and Pearce, 1950), II, 1093-95.

PART *ONE*

THE CRISIS DEVELOPS
SEPTEMBER 1939 – NOVEMBER 1940

CHAPTER I

"A TERRIBLE, STULTIFYING VACUUM"

Hitler's invasion of Poland on September 1, 1939, and the British and French declarations of war on Germany which followed, temporarily ended the period of suspended animation which had followed the Munich crisis—although it was soon to set in again when the expected German march to the west did not materialize. The immediate problem facing the Roosevelt Administration was its inability, because of existing American law, to provide aid to Great Britain and France in their new status as belligerents. The President carefully followed the letter of the law and issued the neutrality proclamations that were called for, but at the same time he began the steps that ultimately led to the passage of the Neutrality Act of 1939. The revision of the neutrality legislation was the first major attempt by the Roosevelt Administration to provide meaningful assistance to the British against Hitler. Submitted to Congress late in September, 1939, the changes would permit belligerent nations to purchase war materials in the United States on a "cash and carry" basis.[1]

Senator William E. Borah of Idaho, in a speech on October 2, 1939, which opened the isolationists' attack on the proposed changes in America's neutrality laws, warned darkly of the consequences of the "cash and carry" concept. "We cannot stand up before the world and say, 'We will help to save democracy, we will help to save civilization,' and in the next breath say, 'We will do so only provided you pay cash.' "[2] Borah, who had not won any recent awards as a crystal ball gazer—it was he who had informed Roosevelt and Secretary of

---

[1] The story of the successful attempt to revise the neutrality laws in the fall of 1939 is well told by Divine, *The Illusion of Neutrality*, pp. 286-335.

[2] U.S., *Congressional Record*, 76th Cong., 2d sess., LXXXV, pt. 1, Oct. 2, 1939, p. 73. (Hereafter cited as *CR*.)

State Cordell Hull in July, 1939, that his unimpeachable sources predicted that there would be no war in Europe that year[3] —this time had hit the nail on the head. Those exact words might well have been spoken by President Roosevelt fifteen months later when he proposed the Lend-Lease Act to Congress, but in the fall of 1939, the Administration asked only that Britain be permitted to buy war goods on a cash basis. Borah mocked the notion that countries already experiencing financial problems and unable to pay even the interest on their World War I debt would be able to pay cash for any length of time. Time and again he asserted one of his central themes: once the United States departed from its neutral stance and began selling arms to England, America would not have the heart to refuse the British merely because they no longer had the ready cash. Sarcastically, he relabelled the proposed Neutrality Act the "credit and carry law." Savagely, he scorned those who would measure in dollars and cents the contribution of America toward what they considered the salvation of democracy.[4]

If the Administration had the data needed to refute Borah, Senator Tom Connally of Texas, a firm supporter of the Neutrality Act of 1939, was not privy to the secret. Given the job of answering Borah's speech, Connally made no reference at all to the isolationist's prediction but instead concentrated on demonstrating how unneutral the earlier neutrality legislation had really been.[5] In fact, the legislative strategy adopted by the Administration called for avoiding any admission that the purpose of the proposed bill was to aid Great Britain and France. Instead, the changes were defended as being the only means of establishing true neutrality and thus keeping America from being dragged into war.[6] This disingenuous tactic of letting the obvious speak for itself was used again by Roosevelt during the Lend-Lease debate.

The reason that the Administration made no attempt to defend the Allies' ability to pay cash indefinitely was that it actually knew very little about the financial future of Britain and France. This is hardly surprising; the Allies knew very little about it themselves. Financial predictions by both sides during World War I had proven notoriously incorrect, particularly in the matter of supply requirements, and the British were leery of repeating their mistake. Yet just such a journey into what one participant turned historian called "the misty uplands

[3]Cordell Hull, *The Memoirs of Cordell Hull*, 2 vols. (New York: The Macmillan Co., 1948), I, 649-50; Joseph Alsop and Robert Kintner, *American White Paper: The Story of American Diplomacy and the Second World War* (New York: Simon and Schuster, 1940), pp. 45-46.

[4]*CR*, 76th Cong., 2d sess., LXXXV, pt. 1, Oct. 4, 1939, pp. 72-74.

[5]*Ibid.*, pp. 83-95.

[6]Divine, *The Illusion of Neutrality*, pp. 297, 317-18.

of prophecy" was an absolute prerequisite to any semblance of Anglo-American co-ordination in the purchase of war materials.[7]

In drafting the proposed revision of the neutrality legislation, there seems to have been no opposition at all on the part of the Administration to either the "cash" or the "carry" concept.[8] Although the British had begun to concern themselves with the possibility of a shortage of dollars, there is nothing to indicate that any attempt was made to transmit this concern to Roosevelt or his advisers. In requesting Congress to revise the existing neutrality law, which forbade any arms trade with nations at war, the President clearly stated that American citizens should not be permitted to extend credits to belligerents. Although no one in the Administration seems to have foreseen any immediate financial problems arising from the "cash and carry" proposal, there was general agreement that the Johnson Act did not forbid government-to-government loans. This possibility apparently eliminated much of the potential worry over British finances. In addition, Roosevelt was primarily concerned with the broader question of "educating" public opinion to permit all necessary aid to the Allies. This may well have tended to obscure the more specific problems, for there seems to have been little thought given by American officials to the state of Allied finances. Yet, at the same time, the United States was putting itself into the position of becoming their major source of war materials—for cash on the barrelhead.[9]

The British were acutely aware of the potential problems involved in having to pay cash. Between August 24 and September 3, a set of currency and securities regulations was put into effect. These rules were the result of discussions between the Bank of England and the British Treasury which had begun back in the summer of 1937. They made all dealings in gold and foreign currencies a Treasury monopoly, required all gold and certain foreign currencies to be sold to the Treasury, and set up a system of registration for all securities marketable abroad—eventually leading to purchase and sale by the Treasury. Clearly a key theme behind all this was the desire to obtain and conserve U.S. dollars.[10]

[7]Hall, *North American Supply*, p. 169.

[8]Alsop and Kintner, *American White Paper*, pp. 72-77; Hull, *Memoirs*, I, 682; Divine, *The Illusion of Neutrality*, pp. 290-95. Langer and Gleason, *The Challenge to Isolation*, I, 222, imply that Roosevelt opposed the "cash" concept. Unless they cited something in the Berle Diaries, which are not available to scholars, none of the other sources they cite bear out this implication.

[9]Roosevelt, *Papers and Addresses* (1939), p. 519; Langer and Gleason, *The Challenge to Isolation*, I, 232; Ironside, *Time Unguarded*, p. 128, tells of the American military attaché in London, Gen. R. E. Lee, confiding that although Roosevelt wanted to aid Great Britain, he could do so only gradually as he educated the general public.

[10]Hancock and Gowing, *British War Economy*, p. 109.

When the Roosevelt Administration began to receive some reports giving the amount of gold and dollar reserves Britain had available as of September, 1939, the figures proved relatively accurate. A report on the British financial situation dated October 26, 1939, stated that they had $4,522,000,000 in gold reserves, and foreign investments added to dollar reserves totalled almost five and one-half billion dollars. In reality Great Britain had between $2.8 and $2.9 billion in gold and negotiable dollar resources combined, with the remaining $1.3 billion labelled as potential assets.[11] It is not surprising that Montague Norman, Governor of the Bank of England, characterized that situation as "worse than tragic," while the American Ambassador in Great Britain, Joseph P. Kennedy, commented that "England is busted now."[12]

Ambassador Kennedy's position in the Roosevelt Administration was an awkward and difficult one. He had an overpowering desire to insure that America avoided war, for he was certain that the next major armed conflict would destroy the economic and democratic institutions he cherished. This drive made him most sympathetic to the Clividen Set of Prime Minister Neville Chamberlain and even brought on the rather absurd assumption by the Nazis that he was anti-Semitic and pro-German.[13] He held highly erratic ideas of what should be the American approach to the crisis. Early in March, 1939, when it became apparent that the Munich Agreements were to be short-lived, Kennedy sent a long and detailed summary of the European situation to Washington. In it he concluded that Great Britain and France were no longer powerful enough to maintain the balance of power and that the United States should face up to the possibility of a totalitarian-dominated Europe. He warned that the burden of rearmament for America would be heavy and that civil liberties would have to be sharply restricted in the interest of national security. He closed with a statement with which the President must have fully agreed: "In short, America, alone in a jealous and hostile world, would find that the effort and cost of maintaining 'splendid isolation' would be such as to bring about the destruction of all those

[11]Harry L. Hopkins Papers (Franklin D. Roosevelt Library, Hyde Park, New York), box 300, "Book II: Economic Effects of Europe War," confidential report, Oct. 26, 1939, table IV, unsigned, no addressee. Hall, *North American Supply*, p. 245. The figures on British assets as of September 1, 1939, as submitted by the British Treasury to Morgenthau for presentation to the Senate and House committees holding hearings on the Lend-Lease Bill, roughly correspond to Hall's later and presumably more accurate statistics. SFRC, *Hearings*, p. 81.

[12]As quoted in Blum, *From the Morgenthau Diaries*, II, 104. Blum cites *North American Supply* by Hall as the source of these comments, but gives no page number. I have been unable to locate these statements in Hall's book.

[13]Dirksen to Weizsäcker, June 13, 1938, Germany, Auswärtiges Amt, *Documents on German Foreign Policy: 1918-1945*, Series D (1937-45), 13 vols. (Washington: U.S. Government Printing Office, 1949-64), vol. I, no. 457, pp. 713-18. Hereafter cited as *DGFP* plus volume number.

values which the isolation policy had been designed to preserve." [14] His preoccupation with avoiding war, however, prevented him from even considering the logical follow-up to this concept—actively aiding the democracies. Thus Kennedy was consistently pessimistic about the chances of the Allies and continually found himself in the position of seemingly supporting appeasement. A traditional belief in non-involvement in Europe, Allied military weakness, and a compulsion to avoid war approaching pacifism, left him little room in which to maneuver. His dilemma was increased by his intense fear of the communists in the Soviet Union. Thus it is hardly surprising to see him advocate a hands-off policy in the wishful and desperate hope of seeing the Nazis and the Soviets destroy each other. Roosevelt was fully aware that his Ambassador was increasingly out of step with Administration policies, and on October 3, 1939, he told Morgenthau that Kennedy was an appeaser who would put pressure on everyone from the King on down "if Germany or Italy made a good peace offer tomorrow." The President labelled him "a pain in the neck" but in typical Roosevelt fashion did nothing about it. Thus the United States was represented at the Court of St. James by a man who found it increasingly difficult to support the Administration's policies. [15]

When Kennedy bluntly characterized England as "busted," it is not clear just where he got his information. A recent biographer states that Chamberlain and Chancellor of the Exchequer Sir John Simon disclosed England's secret financial statistics to the Ambassador, but he gives no evidence for this. [16] At any rate, the Roosevelt Administration was inclined to concentrate on one problem at a time, and the firm position of the policy-makers was that "carry" was enough of a mouthful.

The battle over revision of the Neutrality Act was long and bitter. The isolationists and anti-interventionists seemed to sense that this first battle was a key one. All the traditional distaste and fear of

[14]"Summary of Strategic Situation," March 3, 1939, Franklin D. Roosevelt Papers, President's Secretary's File, Gt. Britain, Kennedy (Franklin D. Roosevelt Library, Hyde Park, N.Y.). The Presidential papers are divided into three groups: Official File, President's Personal File, and President's Secretary's File. These will be cited as Roosevelt Papers, plus either OF, PPF, or PSF to indicate the file. The papers also contain press conference transcripts, which will be cited as such.

[15]Blum, *From the Morgenthau Diaries*, II, 103. Roosevelt probably left Kennedy in London because of the political repercussions that his recall would have caused at home. This brief summary of Ambassador Kennedy's position is largely taken from two sources: William W. Kaufmann, "Two American Ambassadors: Bullitt and Kennedy," *The Diplomats, 1919-1939*, ed. Gordon Craig and Felix Gilbert, 2 vols. (New York: Atheneum, 1963), II, 649-81, which is an incisive interpretive study. Richard J. Whalen, *The Founding Father: The Story of Joseph P. Kennedy* (New York: New American Library, Signet Book, 1964), pp. 202-64, draws somewhat the same picture, although from a different perspective.

[16]Whalen, *The Founding Father*, p. 268. Whalen does cite a secondary source at the end of that paragraph, but that footnote does not pertain to the disclosure of such data.

Europe bubbled to the surface as Congress fought to resolve the question of America's position in world affairs.[17] Long-winded harangues regarding the United States position under international law were made by both sides, but these only served to camouflage the real issue—was it in America's national interest to aid the Allies? The new neutrality legislation that President Roosevelt signed into law on November 4, 1939, made two basic changes in America's neutrality stance. War materials could now be sold to belligerents, but they had to be purchased in the United States and shipped on foreign vessels. Travel in war zones was forbidden, and the general tenor of the previous neutrality legislation was maintained. Short-term credits might still be extended through the Reconstruction Finance Corporation or the Export-Import Bank, but it was long-range financing that Britain had to arrange.[18]

In addition to a shortage of dollars and a virtual total denial of credit in America, United Kingdom finances were also hurt by an unfavorable balance of trade with the United States plus a decline in dollar-earning exports from the entire sterling bloc. In short, the area serviced by the British pound sterling was losing dollars desperately needed by the English to purchase goods in America.[19]

Obviously this required careful rationing of dollars and a severe limit on imports from the United States. As many businessmen in America had feared, exports to Britain were shaved down to about two million dollars' worth per month, which Secretary of State Hull accurately termed "comparatively negligible." In addition, the Neutrality Act set up some artificial barriers to trade since it required a transfer of title before any war goods left American ports.[20]

In handling trade with the United States, the British government was concerned with more than just the legal aspects. American public opinion was of much greater ultimate significance and had to be carefully cultivated. Fully aware that the political effect of every step had to be fully evaluated so as not to deter further aid, the British Ministry

[17]Cushing Strout, *The American Image of the Old World* (New York: Harper & Row, 1963), is a provocative study of America's traditional image of Europe and its effect on our international position. See pp. 196-219 for a brief discussion of this during the years 1930-41.

[18]The minor loophole on short-term credit in government-to-government loans is best explained in Hall, *North American Supply*, pp. 55-56. The legality of even those type loans was challenged when Senators George and Pittman, during the course of the debate over the Neutrality Act, stated that the bill was intended to prohibit loans by any person, including corporate persons. *CR*, 76th Cong., 2d sess., LXXXV, pt. 1, Oct. 27. 1939, pp. 1017-18.

[19]Hall, *North American Supply*, p. 55. Hancock and Gowing, *British War Economy*, p. 107.

[20]Hull, *Memoirs*, I, 700; Hall, *North American Supply*, pp. 56-57. Business views on the Neutrality Act are discussed by Divine, *The Illusion of Neutrality*, pp. 319-23. See also Roland N. Stromberg, "American Business and the Approach of War, 1935-1941," *The Journal of Economic History*, XIII, no. 1 (Winter, 1953), 70-71.

consistently consulted with American officials before taking any major steps. Unhappily, the British found themselves unable to satisfy everyone. Americans were shocked when a nation supposedly preparing for war continued to produce and export luxury goods such as Scotch whiskey and fine woolens, not realizing these constituted Britain's prime source of dollars.[21]

The wisdom of British caution was borne out by the public-opinion polls of the day. Questions that offered an opportunity to support either directly or indirectly the position of the Allies showed Americans were most reluctant to get involved. Belief in eventual Allied victory made a sharp decline, while the per cent who disapproved of American entry into World War I rose. Those who favored intervention in case of apparent Allied defeat remained below 30 per cent, as did the number of those supporting the lending of money to Britain and France.[22]

When the British Ambassador in the United States, Lord Lothian (Philip Kerr), characterized "cash and carry" as a "makeshift arrangement," he was accepting a political fact of life, though one that Englishmen found difficult to comprehend. America felt no real sense of urgency about the European war, and the Allies had to realize that the American government moved in leisurely fashion in coping with each new crisis.

In the same speech, given on October 25, 1939, before the Pilgrims of the United States, a society dedicated to promoting good Anglo-American relations, Lothian warned that "even our cash will not carry us far, and your mission—the greatest any man can have today—is ultimately to carry our dear friends into the war."[23] He was well suited for a public relations job, and convincing American public opinion of the wisdom of backing Great Britain was just that. Lothian's biographer often criticized his judgment but noted that he was thoroughly knowledgeable of American politics and the delicacy with which he would have to operate. He lacked the class-consciousness of most of the British Establishment, and he demonstrated a knack for the common touch when he hoisted a black cat to his shoulders while coming out of the White House after his first

[21]Hall, *North American Supply*, pp. 57-59. Hancock and Gowing, *British War Economy*, p. 108; Stettinius, *Lend-Lease*, pp. 57-58.

[22]Frederic J. Fleron, Jr., "The Isolationists and the Foreign Policy of FDR: A Study in Executive Leadership" (Master's thesis, Brown University, 1961), pp. 224-29. Roosevelt's concern for public opinion is indicated by the fact that he arranged for some questions to be asked by the Gallup poll. See Manfred Landecker, *The President and Public Opinion* (Washington, D.C.: Public Affairs Press, 1968), p. 123, n. 7.

[23]J. R. M. Butler, *Lord Lothian (Philip Kerr), 1882-1940* (London: Macmillan & Co., 1960), pp. 266-67.

meeting with Roosevelt in August, 1939. Thus he combined tact with a good image.[24]

With the passage of the new neutrality legislation, the British established a formal organization designed to co-ordinate the purchase of war supplies in the United States. This group, known as the British Purchasing Commission (B.P.C.), was officially a branch of another operation, the British Supply Board in Canada and the United States, which was located in Ottawa, Canada. Although the British were fully aware that the major job of the B.P.C. would be in America, the facade of a Canadian headquarters was erected in deference to American neutrality sentiments. The B.P.C. was officially opened on November 7, 1939, in an office in the Cunard Building on Broadway in New York City, by its Director-General, Arthur Purvis.[25]

Estimates of Arthur Purvis, whether by contemporaries or historians, have been unanimously enthusiastic. Churchill described him as "highly competent and devoted" and of "outstanding ability." Stettinius called him "remarkably able and vigorous," and Morgenthau stated he was "the ablest British representative in Washington" as well as "one of the rarest persons I have ever known."[26] Morgenthau had been somewhat leery of Monnet because of the Frenchman's connections with the Wall Street bankers, but Purvis suffered no such taint. Purvis was a Scots-Canadian who had had brief experience in British government supply matters during World War I and had subsequently moved to Canada where he became a leading industrialist. As head of the British Purchasing Mission he was a "dollar-a-year man" in a job that required enormous energy and effort. One of his superiors in the Treasury classified him as an "Economic Ambassador, handling the major policy as well as the details of all questions except those which are definitely political in nature."[27] As a quasi-ambassador, Purvis was cognizant of the need to work closely and harmoniously with American officials, and Morgenthau—his key contact—found himself in a

[24]Butler, *Lord Lothian*, pp. 257-61. For another character sketch of Lothian, see Philip Goodhart, *Fifty Ships That Saved the World: The Foundation of the Anglo-American Alliance* (Garden City: Doubleday & Co., 1965), pp. 49-50. Lothian was also a staunch supporter of Neville Chamberlain's appeasement policy, and as late as July, 1940, tried to persuade the British Cabinet to listen to Hitler's peace terms, claiming he knew they were "most satisfactory." Harold Nicolson, *The War Years, 1939-1945*, vol. II of *Diaries and Letters*, ed. Nigel Nicolson (New York: Atheneum, 1967), p. 104. I have found no evidence whatsoever to indicate that Lothian made any attempt to promote such policies in the United States, nor does his biographer, J. R. M. Butler, find any.

[25]Hall, *North American Supply*, pp. 59-60, 70-71. The diplomatic correspondence which preceded the establishment of the B.P.C. is in U.S., Dept. of State, *Foreign Relations of the United States* (Washington: U.S. Government Printing Office, 1862——), 1939, I, 565-72. (Hereafter cited as *FR* plus the year and volume number.)

[26]Churchill, *Their Finest Hour*, pp. 25, 555; Stettinius, *Lend-Lease*, p. 21; Morgenthau, *Collier's*, CXX, 71-72.

[27]Sir Arthur Salter as quoted by Hall, *North American Supply*, p. 75.

closer working relationship to Purvis than to any other man except the President. What one historian calls the "Morgenthau-Purvis Channel" and another the "Morgenthau-Purvis Axis" became one of the key personal relationships of World War II.[28] Conveniently, the French counterpart of the B.P.C. was in the same building, and the two soon formed a co-ordinating body, the Anglo-French Purchasing Board. Each retained its own separate nature, but regular meetings were held to exchange information and avoid mutual competition. In addition, Purvis and his French counterpart, Jean Bloch-Laine, met informally each day for the same purposes. The initial onslaught of frauds, crackpots, and high-powered salesmen gave the offices of the two purchasing commissions a bizarre air. One old duffer wandered around trying to sell a lone mule that he labelled "a great bargain," while another hopeful swore he had invented an airplane that became invisible at 300 yards.[29]

As unofficial chief co-ordinator of American aid to Britain, Morgenthau had been requesting purchasing and financial data from the British since October,[30] but once the Allies formalized their purchasing organization the Secretary desired equivalent status. On his recommendation, President Roosevelt, on December 6, 1939, signed a memo creating what became known as the President's Liaison Committee. The group was assigned the job of "exclusive liaison" in procurement for foreign governments in the United States. In effect, Morgenthau retained over-all authority since Roosevelt named the Director of Procurement in the Treasury Department, then Captain Harry Collins, the chairman of the committee. The two other committee members were to be the Quartermaster General of the Army and the Paymaster General of the Navy. The Liaison Committee publicly stated, in an article in *Fortune* magazine, that its prime functions were to insure American security by seeing that Allied purchases did not interfere with Army and Navy rearmament programs and to prevent domestic prices from being driven up so high that United States military programs would be crippled.[31] Privately, it was clear an additional goal was to increase and improve aid to Britain. Sec-

---

[28]Hall has a chapter entitled "The Morgenthau-Purvis Channel," *ibid*, p. 72. Goodhart, *Fifty Ships*, p. vii, dedicates his book to "the Morgenthau-Purvis Axis." Biographical data on Purvis is taken from Hall, *North American Supply*, pp. 72-80; Blum, *From the Morgenthau Diaries*, II, 110; [Charles J. V. Murphy], "Allied Purchasing: 'The Best Bargain We Can Jolly Well Make,' " *Fortune*, XXI, no. 4 (April, 1940), 134; Hall, "Purvis, Arthur Blaikie," *Dictionary of National Biography, 1941-1950*, eds. I. G. Wickham, E. T. Wickham, and E. T. Williams (Oxford: Oxford University Press, 1959), pp. 700-702.

[29][Murphy], *Fortune*, XXI, 134.

[30]Hall, *North American Supply*, p. 96.

[31]Roosevelt to Morgenthau, Dec. 6, 1939, Henry Morgenthau, Jr., Diary (Franklin D. Roosevelt Library, Hyde Park, N.Y.) 228:44. Hereafter cited as Morgenthau Diary, with volume and page numbers. [Murphy], *Fortune*, XXI, 137.

retary of War Harry H. Woodring vigorously protested the establishment of the committee. Woodring's opposition typified the struggle that would go on until the Pearl Harbor attack. He strongly favored rearming America first—a task that could easily absorb every shred of America's arms production, particularly since the military had, in October, adopted an over-all contingency plan envisaging a multi-front war.[32] Roosevelt, fully aware of Woodring's lack of sympathy for his policies, had intentionally left the Secretary off the Liaison Committee. In fact, Woodring's attitude had been partially responsible for the creation of the new organization. In July, 1939, the Joint Army and Navy Munitions Board, which handled logistics planning for the military, had been given the authority to establish the Clearance Committee, which would co-ordinate foreign purchases in America and assist the Allies in placing orders. Although it is not clear just how this jibed with Morgenthau's appointment to the same basic task in December, 1938, the President's Liaison Committee made the conflict a moot point.

When the Army and Navy Munitions Board protested the formation of the Liaison Committee, Roosevelt claimed he was overruling their objections because the Procurement Division of the Treasury had more experience in purchasing and because over 50 per cent of the purchases would be of non-military goods. He also noted that the military services would have representation on the committee. The real reason for the new setup was apparent. The Clearance Committee had worked through the military secretaries, and by December this had forced Roosevelt to find some way to prevent Woodring from hindering Allied purchasing. Since a feud within the War Department was going on between Woodring and Assistant Secretary Louis Johnson, the President kept out of the battle by appointing neither to the Liaison Committee.[33]

The reports that Morgenthau received from the British provided a small window into Britain's finances, but for the first seven months of

---

[32]Watson, *Chief of Staff*, p. 103. This was Joint Army-Navy Plan 1, the first of the *RAINBOW* plans.

[33]Roosevelt to the Assistant Secretaries of War and Navy (Co-chairmen of the Army and Navy Munitions Board), Dec. 14, 1939, U.S., Dept. of the Army, ASF-International Aid Division Files, National Archives, Washington, D.C. (Hereafter cited as ASF files.) Richard M. Leighton and Robert W. Coakley, *Global Logistics and Strategy, 1940-1943*, United States Army in World War II: The War Department, ed. Kent Roberts Greenfield (Washington: Office of the Chief of Military History, 1955), pp. 30-31. Leighton and Coakley do not mention the apparent conflict between Morgenthau's authority and the Clearance Committee. Such jurisdictional redundancy was typical of the Roosevelt approach to administration. A good secondary source of information on the Woodring-Johnson controversy is Langer and Gleason, *The Challenge to Isolation*, I, 291; II, 510, 674. Documentary material on the dispute is found in all the primary sources for the period. Unhappily, no one has pulled them all together into a complete study of the episode. As with similar cases, Roosevelt avoided firing Woodring in order to avoid domestic political repercussions. Blum, *From the Morgenthau Diaries*, II, 118.

the war that glimpse was somewhat misleading. Until the German attack on Norway and Denmark on April 9, 1940, the British purchasing policy emphasized conservation of dollars and concentrated on building up her own production by buying machine tools. The shift to purchasing finished war materials did not begin until April, 1940, and when the Low Countries were invaded in May, the acquisition of finished war goods became paramount.[34]

A relatively clear indication of the financial problems to come showed up in the question of stock vesting orders by the British Treasury. Vesting was designed to give the British government control over English-owned American securities, making it possible for private individuals to sell them when there was need for American dollars. To avoid any weakening of the position of gold as the linchpin of international finance, the Treasury Department favored British sales of stocks rather than extensive gold transfers, but in December, 1939, private sales of stocks had fallen off so badly that Britain sold the United States $50 million of gold. Although one might suspect certain persons of hoping to see Britain forced to sell her American assets, thus eliminating the influence of British finance from the United States, there is no concrete evidence of such anti-British sentiments having any influence on the American government's policies. The only thing that even vaguely resembled an official attempt to take advantage of the Allied dilemma was the ludicrous proposal that the United States purchase the *Queen Mary* from England and the *Normandie* from France on the naïve rationale that they would be liabilities. The idea was preremptorily dismissed by the Allies.[35]

The continued gold drain, plus the failure of private sales of securities to pick up, caused the British Treasury to issue its first vesting order on February 17, 1940, covering some thirty million pounds sterling of American securities. The price for these securities held up until military reverses in April and May, 1940, caused it to drop drastically, as investors greedily waited for increased British dollar requirements to force them to sell below the market value. Although the vesting orders continued, the contribution of security sales to Britain's dollar reserves never really achieved its potential since policy was not to sell below the vesting price, that is, the market price when they were vested.[36]

---

[34]Hall, *North American Supply*, pp. 112-13. The main exception to that policy was the constant Allied demand for airplane engines and frames.

[35]Blum, *From the Morgenthau Diaries*, II, 96, 104, 106; Langer and Gleason, *The Challenge to Isolation*, I, 288. It was official New Deal policy to buy all gold offered for sale. In 1934 the price had been set at $35 per ounce.

[36]There is substantial material on the vesting question in Blum, *From the Morgenthau Diaries*, II, 103-9. The best summary of this problem is Sayers, *Financial Policy*, pp. 364-66.

Since it was obvious that by December, 1939, Britain would suffer from financial limitations even under a carefully restricted buying policy, Arthur Purvis brought up the question of capital assistance in conversations with Roosevelt and Morgenthau. Under existing policies, the British government was required to pay in advance for any plant expansion and other capital expenses involved in meeting British orders. Purvis hoped that the United States government could assume at least a portion of such capital costs. He argued that strategic production facilities would produce goods for both nations and suggested to the President that the United States might buy back the plants after the war. Roosevelt fended off the notion by saying he would not object if Purvis wanted to take it up with the Liaison Committee.[37] At the same conference Roosevelt mentioned the possibility of taking surplus TNT from the United States military and "diverting" it to the Allies, with replacement at a later date from current production. Exactly what sort of program the President had in mind is not clear. One historian finds in this the seed of Lend-Lease, but that would seem to be somewhat premature. The key word, quoted from a notation by Purvis, is "diverting." Roosevelt's meaning (or whether he actually used that word) is not recorded. Nevertheless, in a very limited way, Purvis had raised the question of Britain's shaky dollar situation.[38]

Regardless of the degree of Roosevelt's awareness of Britain's needs, there was little he could do without public and Congressional support. Roosevelt's awareness of the lack of that support was set forth in an exchange of letters with Colonel Frank Knox in December, 1939. Knox was the publisher of the *Chicago Daily News* and an avowed internationalist. Roosevelt wrote and offered him the post of Secretary of the Navy, but both Knox and the President agreed that the move would be interpreted as a political gimmick since the American public had no sense of real danger or crisis.[39] The public-opinion polls likewise indicated a strong desire to tread water. A Roper poll for *Fortune* magazine, published in November, 1939, showed the largest percentage (36.9 per cent) favoring neutrality and "cash and carry," whereas the next largest group (23.7 per cent) favored a refusal of aid to either side. Between the two they totalled 60.6 per cent of those polled. Late in December the American Institute of Public Opinion

---

[37] Memo for Morgenthau by Capt. Collins, Dec. 29, 1939, Morgenthau Diary, 232:316-17.

[38] *Ibid.* does not show that this was discussed. Hall, *North American Supply*, pp. 103-4, contains Purvis' remarks.

[39] Knox to Roosevelt, Dec. 15, 1939, Knox Papers (Library of Congress, Washington, D.C.). Roosevelt to Knox, Dec. 29, 1939, *ibid.* Secretary of the Interior Harold L. Ickes claimed in his diary that Knox's editorials frequently floated "trial balloons" for the President. See *The Lowering Clouds, 1939-1941*, vol. III of *The Secret Diary of Harold L. Ickes*, 3 vols. (New York: Simon and Schuster, 1954), p. 213.

(Gallup poll) reported that 82 per cent of those asked were opposed to lending money to either Britain or France. It seems doubtful that this sprang from a desire to save money since the number opposed dropped by only seven points when partial payment of World War I debts was made a precondition. In addition, 65 per cent favored lending money to Finland.[40] Finland's underdog position engendered great sympathy among Americans, but such figures also indicate that the public looked at aid to Finland as potentially less likely to drag the United States into war and feared lending money to the Allies because it appeared more likely to involve the United States.[41] In fact, Secretary of State Hull persuaded Roosevelt that to ask Congress for a loan to Finland would only further convince Congressional isolationists that he planned to do the same for Britain and France. This hardly gave Roosevelt, either from the public or his own Cabinet, a mandate to provide financial aid to the Allies.[42]

Following the establishment of the Liaison Committee, Roosevelt again lost the initiative to Hitler and the German Army. Hemmed in by public apathy, the coming Presidential election, and the absence of any novel ideas within his Administration, the President foundered in what Robert Sherwood called "a period of terrible, stultifying vacuum." Sherwood's belief that this was primarily due to election year pressures was borne out by Purvis' report to London, in March, 1940, that Morgenthau would be of little help until after that election.[43]

Roosevelt remained personally dedicated to aiding the Allies. Frances Perkins, his Secretary of Labor, pointed out his interest in the most picayune of ideas: Roosevelt suggested to the Cabinet that they ship to Great Britain anything that would shoot and was even desperate enough to suggest sending binoculars and opera glasses for use by their home guard. But any meaningful increase in aid to England was limited by two seemingly insurmountable barriers: extremely limited

[40]Hadley Cantril, ed., *Public Opinion, 1935-1946* (Princeton: Princeton University Press, 1951), pp. 969, 1101.

[41]Lord Beaverbrook, later Churchill's Minister for Aircraft Production but at the time a private citizen, made the intriguing suggestion to Churchill in December, 1939, that the Ministry take advantage of America's sympathy for Finland's gallant struggle by sending an agitator and publicist to America to drum up public support for fuller aid to Finland. He apparently was looking for some sort of "back door" to get the United States actively on England's side. Kenneth Young, *Churchill and Beaverbrook* (London: Eyre & Spottiswoode, 1966), pp. 134-35.

[42]Blum, *From the Morgenthau Diaries*, II, 130-31. Langer and Gleason, *The Challenge to Isolation*, I, 321-42, contains an excellent summary of the Administration's position on aid to Finland.

[43]Robert E. Sherwood, *Roosevelt and Hopkins: An Intimate History*, rev. ed. (New York: Harper & Brothers, 1950), pp. 123, 136. Sherwood's comment is made more interesting by the fact that he was not only the author of Hopkins' memoirs but was a speechwriter for Roosevelt as well. Hall, *North American Supply*, p. 92.

American production facilities and Britain's lack of dollars. Although the polls show that Americans were worried about the former, few guessed that it would be British orders—regardless of their ability to pay—that would play a critical role in the initial growth of America's wartime production machine.[44]

The calm before the storm, dubbed by Senator Borah the "phony war," also largely determined Allied purchasing policy. Arthur Purvis told a reporter doing a study of the British Purchasing Commission in February, 1940, that "because our funds are limited, we are trying to act as if we were on a desert island—on short rations, which we must stretch out as far as we can."[45] The American public, deceived by the inaction on Germany's western front, displayed more concern with the Russo-Finnish War than with any possible German intentions in the west. Anne Morrow Lindbergh summed up the feelings of many when she asked who was the greatest threat to European civilization—Russia or Germany—and concluded it was Russia.[46]

The Roosevelt Administration, convinced that naziism was a far more immediate and powerful threat to the United States but without any workable new ideas for assisting the Allies, concentrated on making more efficient those aid methods which were available. A long and complicated series of negotiations effectively denied Germany and her allies access to American strategic natural resources, such as copper, iron ores, and molybdenum; valuable as these arrangements were to the British war plan, they also further drained England of additional dollar resources since ultimately Great Britain had to pay cash for the goods. Morgenthau worked assiduously to prevent profiteering by American firms, something the Treasury Department was admirably equipped to do because of its vast experience on tax cases. At his request, the French and English voluntarily submitted every contract to the Treasury officials, who examined it and provided full information on depreciation and obsolescence. This was of great help to the Allies, who were investing huge sums for plant expansion. By February, co-operation between the United States, Britain, and France had

[44]Frances Perkins, *The Roosevelt I Knew* (New York: The Viking Press, 1946), p. 353. Fleron, "The Isolationists and the Foreign Policy of FDR," pp. 224-29, graph 3. The per cent of Americans willing to pay higher taxes to get a larger army always remained about 50 per cent.

[45][Murphy], *Fortune*, XXI, 134. Morgenthau's approval of the article was passed on to Capt. Harry Collins in a letter from the Director of Public Relations in the Treasury Department (Charles Schwarz) to Collins, Feb. 28, 1940, Records of the Foreign Economic Administration (under the custody of the Department of State), Files of the President's Liaison Committee, box 1, "Capt. Collins, Treasury Procurement, 1939-1940," file AO 4/5, "Publications and Periodicals," National Archives, Washington, D.C. (Hereafter Foreign Economic Administration records will be abbreviated as FEA records, but the other extensive identification is necessary as those files are not indexed and are poorly arranged.)

[46]Anne Morrow Lindbergh in *Reader's Digest*, as quoted in Chamberlin, *America's Second Crusade*, p. 116.

grown so close that the phrase "combined action" was in use. On January 23, the same day the formation of the President's Liaison Committee was formally announced, the French and British Purchasing Commissions held a press conference to declare the formation of the Anglo-French Purchasing Board. Thus the informal co-ordination between the Allies and the United States was put on an official basis in accordance with the express desires of the Roosevelt Administration.[47]

The apparent closeness of the co-operation caused some fears. The *American Aviation Daily* on January 27 expressed concern that Morgenthau's interest in the aircraft industry was a preliminary to a government takeover and predicted that Roosevelt would get around the spirit of the Johnson Act by some devious means and extend commercial credits to Britain and France. Britain's desire to wait until delivery before assuming the cost of plant expansion was interpreted as proof of her scheme to gain financial control over the industry. [48]

Morgenthau tried to combat such rumors in various ways. In a press conference on January 22 he admitted that Great Britain did have problems obtaining enough American dollars, but he flatly asserted that he knew of no discussions regarding either a direct or an indirect loan to England and further noted that if such talks were taking place, he would surely know of them. He then refused to elaborate any further even though the reporters protested that they were under the impression some sort of special relationship existed between the United Kingdom and the United States regarding finances. A month later he told reporters that he was convinced the Allies had the cash to pay for their purchases, and more besides.[49]

The Secretary of the Treasury also attempted to create some favorable press comment by permitting a writer from *Fortune* magazine, Charles J. V. Murphy, to do a feature article on the British Purchasing Commission.[50] Although the article admitted that Britain had adopted a policy of caution on dollar expenditures, the main thrust of the piece was optimism regarding British financial resources. It noted that Allied purchases to date had amounted to less than 1 per cent of their total war expense. The article brought up one fact that many Americans, particularly certain congressmen during the debate over

[47]Blum, *From the Morgenthau Diaries*, II, 113-14. Hall, *North American Supply*, pp. 71, 83, 86-93.

[48]*American Aviation Daily*, VII, no. 23 (Jan. 27, 1940), 114-16, found in FEA records, Files of the President's Liaison Committee, box 1, "Capt. Collins, Treasury Procurement, 1939-1940," file AO 4/5, "Publications and Periodicals."

[49]Morgenthau Press Conferences, vol. 14, conference of Jan. 22, 1940 (Franklin D. Roosevelt Library, Hyde Park, New York), pp. 47-54, and *ibid.*, conference of Feb. 26, 1940, p. 126.

[50]See n. 45.

Lend-Lease, never really grasped: Britain was not broke and could count on enormous overseas assets, including $750,000,000 in gold from mines throughout the Empire. Empire assets probably totalled something around $14,000,000,000. The immediate problem was not wealth—but dollars. To buy goods in the United States, England had to pay American dollars, and these dollars could be obtained only by selling English goods to the United States. Preferably this meant the sale of finished goods, but it also could mean the sale of gold and British-owned securities. The discussion of British wealth closed on what proved to be a wishful note when it mentioned that the British Empire was moving toward a pooling of its resources, which would make the question of the dollar supply a secondary problem. Prophetically, the entire treatment of British and French finances was qualified by the condition that this was true only so long as the war continued at its present pace.[51]

English spending estimates were based on the same short-lived assumption. In January, 1940, Lord Stamp estimated that at the planned rate of spending, the United Kingdom would suffer an unfavorable balance of trade for the first year of war exceeding £400 million.[52] The British Treasury estimated that the entire sterling area would run up an adverse balance of trade of about the same amount. In both of these separately conducted studies it was clear that Britain could not spend more than about £150 million per year of gold, although there was the possibility of increasing that by £70 to £80 million through sales of dollar securities. Since the government estimate, as of January 30, 1940, of purchases in the United States totalled £197 million for the first war year, the slightest intensification of the war, with the corresponding increase in spending that it would cause, would quickly put the British in the position of being unable to pay cash for American goods.[53]

[51]The phrase "total war expense" is ambiguous enough to include the entire wartime budget, and it is never clearly defined. Equally misleading is the fact that the article was published in April, 1940, but had been written in February. The gap covers a period during which significant purchases were made. The statement is rendered even more meaningless because the author limited himself to actual purchases, not the total of orders which had been placed. [Murphy], *Fortune*, XXI, 130, 132.

[52]The exchange rate of pounds sterling to dollars throughout World War II was £1=$4.06+. Sayers, *Financial Policy*, p. 324n.

[53]Hancock and Gowing, *British War Economy*, pp. 106n., 115. Hall, *North American Supply*, p. 114, gives an entirely different set of figures for the government estimate of spending in America for the first war year. Since these statistics are still in the closed files in Great Britain, it is impossible to compare them satisfactorily. Knowing the multitude of ways in which budgets and expenditures can be computed, one suspects the difference is due primarily to the inclusion or exclusion of various items. For example, it appears that Hall included payments due on previous orders, whereas Hancock and Gowing did not. However, from the material available one cannot be sure. In one sense it is a moot point since both books draw the same conclusion: that Great Britain could expect to run out of dollars within two years, even under restricted purchasing programs.

Desperate to save every possible dollar, the British government concentrated on buying only indispensable items from America and purchased such things as food from within the sterling area, even though the price was higher. In spite of their desire to avoid antagonizing the American public, the British government considered such export/import controls an absolute necessity since imports of luxury items caused an unnecessary drain on precious dollars. With tobacco one of the chief restricted items, it is hardly surprising that the Secretary of State, who was not only from the South but a convinced advocate of free trade, spent an inordinate amount of time protesting such limits. Restrictions on the import of other items, such as apples and pears, became major issues for Americans, while a prohibition on the importing of American movies was interpreted as a virtual insult to American culture. England may have been at war, but the State Department hardly seemed aware of it.[54]

The primary stumbling block was the universally accepted image of British opulence. Even Secretary of State Hull, supposedly close to the situation, found it impossible to believe Britain could not pay cash indefinitely. In fact, Hull remained skeptical right up to the passage of the Lend-Lease Act. In late February, 1940, after disputing some unofficial financial estimates given him by Lord Lothian, Hull obtusely griped that the British restrictions on agricultural imports made no sense because the cost of buying food from other countries still had to come out of British resources. He went on to complain about British dollar loans to other countries for "'imperative political considerations,'" even though he admitted seeing the necessity for such actions. Hull conveniently ignored the fact that the exchange of sterling for dollars was the problem, not over-all British wealth. Ambassador Lothian's reply cut to the quick of the matter. He dismissed Hull's complaints as not being the key issue and boldly presented the broader picture. Regardless of whose figures and statistics one used, the inescapable truth was that Great Britain could not indefinitely pay cash. He also tried to explain something Americans understood only partially, and Britons believed they never understood even slightly—that the constant drain on British assets in order to come up with dollars would ultimately ruin Great Britain and thus adversely affect the postwar economy of the United States, something America apparently did not accept until the Marshall Plan in 1947. The unspoken accusation was that the United States was using the wartime situation—as in World War I—to challenge Britain's overseas trade position. As an example of the permanent type of damage the

[54]The details of this silly episode can be found in *FR*, 1939, II, 213-33; and *FR*, 1940, III, 89-118. For a classic example of Hull's annoyance, see memo of conversation between Hull and Lothian, Jan. 22, 1940, *ibid.*, pp. 89-90. The British position is well outlined in Hancock and Gowing, *British War Economy*, pp. 112-14.

American demands could cause, Lothian pointed out that if the war went on for more than two years, Britain would have transferred almost all its gold and negotiable securities, plus a good portion of its foreign assets. All this would permanently reduce England's ability to purchase agricultural goods.[55] Although Lothian did not pass on any specific statistics to the American government, the figures were ominous. In one typical week during January, 1940, the British dollar reserves dipped by almost 4 per cent, from $360 million to $346 million. And that was under a limited spending policy![56]

The difference in approach between the State Department and Morgenthau was striking. Although Roosevelt did not publicly commit himself on such questions, his support for Morgenthau hardly rates as a vote of confidence for Hull's position. In truth, the role of the State Department under Franklin Roosevelt was a constant source of annoyance to Secretary Hull, since the President consistently acted as his own Secretary of State or bypassed Hull and delegated the conduct of specific foreign affairs to men like Under Secretary of State Sumner Welles or Morgenthau. It seems clear that Hull's political influence with Congress was the real reason he remained in the Cabinet, for he did not faithfully reflect all the nuances of the Roosevelt foreign policy.[57]

Cash was not the only problem that frustrated the Allies. American production capabilities were unable to meet even a limited demand. This inability to satisfy even current orders caused many British planners to view the United States as a marginal source of supplies, hence the emphasis on acquiring machine tools to increase the output of British factories. Although Edward Stettinius, later head of the Lend-Lease program, wrote that Britain believed it was necessary to get American production facilities operating at full potential, Morgenthau's attempts to increase Allied spending in the area of plant expansion were often like pulling teeth. In March, the British Minister of Supply, Dr. Leslie Burgin, expressed the hope that Britain would be required to spend less and less abroad as her own production increased, although he did admit the need for heavy buying in the United States, particularly of machine tools, for the following six months. As *Fortune* magazine pointed out in April, there was nothing

[55] Memo from Hull to the British Embassy, Feb. 21, 1940, *FR* 1940, III, 96-100; memo from Lothian to Hull, March 1, 1940, *ibid.*, 101-07. Lothian's pessimism was not reflected in a pamphlet written by England's most famous economist, John Maynard Keynes. Entitled *How to Pay for the War* (London: Macmillan and Co., 1940), the paper breathed an air of confidence, but nowhere did Keynes adequately treat the problem of exchanging sterling for dollars. The pamphlet can be found in U.S., Dept. of State, Official Archives, 841.51/1571. (Cited hereafter as State Dept., followed by the file number.)

[56] Hall, *North American Supply*, p. 233.

[57] All the major studies of Roosevelt's foreign policy make this point. It becomes strikingly evident during the Lend-Lease debate, discussed below.

even resembling a munitions industry in the United States, so British pessimism was justified. Even in the area of aircraft where the policy of limited purchasing was less stringent, England and France were forced to place orders with companies that had current production available instead of being selective and ordering only the latest models.[58]

The English desire to conserve dollars prevented British capital from playing a role in the expansion of American industrial production during the first eight months of the war, except for the aircraft industry, but that was minor compared to the domestic problem standing in the way of all-out defense production. Much to the frustration of men like General George C. Marshall, the Army Chief of Staff, Congress stubbornly refused to appropriate the huge sums for military purchasing which would stimulate industrial expansion. Although Marshall blamed this on pressures from the public, the opinion polls show that Congress consistently lagged behind its constituents in such matters.[59]

This problem of Congressional and public support, particularly in an election year, continued to limit the Administration's response to British attempts to find some way out of their dilemma. King George VI, who was on relatively close personal terms with the President, talked with Sumner Welles in March during Welles's peace mission to Europe. He asked the Under Secretary of State to carry a personal letter to Roosevelt. When Welles refused, the King noted disgustedly in his diary that the refusal stemmed from one passage in the letter which referred to Anglo-American collaboration. He interpreted Welles's action to mean "that the U.S. Administration & the U.S.A. are going to do nothing until after the Presidential election."[60] The same problem was behind Purvis' report to London late in March averring that he had found it impossible to get American officials to agree on broad policy and that it would be wiser to concentrate instead upon specific problems.[61] Consistently close co-ordination would have to await a solution to Roosevelt's political problems.

[58]Blum, *From the Morgenthau Diaries*, II, 115; Hall, *North American Supply*, pp. 114-15; [Murphy], *Fortune*, XXI, 68; Edward R. Stettinius, Jr., *Lend-Lease: Weapon for Victory* (New York: The Macmillan Co., 1944), p. 21.

[59]Forrest Pogue, *George C. Marshall: Ordeal and Hope, 1939-1943*, 2 vols. (New York: Viking Press, 1963-66), II, 17. In June, 1947, Dr. George Gallup of the American Institute of Public Opinion told an audience at the Industrial College of the Armed Forces that from 1935 on, the public favored more money for the Army and Navy while Congress moved in the other direction. He noted that during the war years the public always supported such appropriations long before Congress acted. Watson, *Chief of Staff*, pp. 15-16. General Marshall took the oath as Chief of Staff on September 1, 1939.

[60]As quoted in John W. Wheeler-Bennett, *King George VI: His Life and Reign* (London: Macmillan & Co., 1958), p. 506. The letter was sent anyway in April via diplomatic channels.

[61]Hall, *North American Supply*, pp. 91-92.

There was also opposition to Roosevelt's aid policies from within his Administration, centering in the War Department. When Woodring and Johnson—for once working together—and General Henry "Hap" Arnold, head of the Army Air Force, refused to release some classified data on airplane superchargers and engines, the President had had enough. At a March 12 White House conference he laid down the law, causing Morgenthau to exult, "Oh boy, did General Arnold get it!" Roosevelt warned the three to stop their resistance to the aid program, ordered them to stop leaking information to the isolationist press, and threatened unco-operative officers with duty in Guam. Uncharacteristically firm and uncompromising, Roosevelt instructed Johnson to announce publicly his support for the Liaison Committee and Morgenthau, and told Arnold to keep quiet. When Woodring continued to resist, Roosevelt told him either to toe the line or resign. Morgenthau, obviously elated, told Purvis they had just won the "battle of Washington."[62]

As the "Sitzkrieg" wore on, Washington and London became increasingly aware that although the immediate needs of the British could be met via "cash and carry," the long-range question of how to pay the bills would have to be faced. Extensive new aircraft contracts were signed early in April, which brought the total French and British commitment in the United States to about one billion dollars. Even more foreboding was the need for England to turn to America for small-arms ammunition since Commonwealth production could not meet demand. This necessitated large new outlays for capital assistance and indicated a developing trend.[63]

Breckinridge Long noted in his diary late in April that credit would have to be extended by the next session of Congress, if not sooner, while in the *American White Paper,* Alsop and Kintner, probably reflecting Administration sentiment—or at least what Roosevelt wanted the public to hear—stated that in two or two and one-half years Britain would have no dollars or convertible assets left. They wrote that at that time we would have to choose between credit, gifts of supplies, or a German victory. As Long accurately commented, a policy change was in the making—albeit "perhaps not entirely open and honestly expressed."[64]

Although the *White Paper* had been written in March, the attitudes of Long and others in the Administration were influenced by the German invasion of Denmark and Norway on April 9, 1940. Not only

[62]Blum, *From the Morgenthau Diaries*, II, 117-20.

[63]*Ibid.*, p. 120. Hall, *North American Supply*, p. 198.

[64]Breckinridge Long, *The War Diary of Breckinridge Long, 1939-1944*, ed. Fred Israel (Lincoln: University of Nebraska Press, 1966), entry for April 28, 1940, p. 86; Alsop and Kintner, *American White Paper*, p. 81.

did the ease of the German victory frighten many, but now the "phony war" in the west showed signs of becoming the real thing. Frantically searching for ways to help England before the beginning of the onslaught he was sure would come, Roosevelt raised the suggestion of the sale of British holdings in Latin America to American business interests. He made special reference to Argentine railways.[65] Although the British were never willing to take such measures, the idea continually cropped up until the Lend-Lease Act was safely signed into law.

Fortunately, in terms of propaganda, Roosevelt's notion was not public knowledge, for the Germans would have been quick to take advantage of it. They had already made effective propaganda use of "cash and carry," claiming it was an American attempt to drain Britain of all her gold, an approach in which they persisted until after the passage of the Lend-Lease Act. It was this sort of accusation which prompted Morgenthau to ask Canadian Prime Minister Mackenzie King to put pressure on the Chamberlain Ministry to make available fuller figures on British purchases in America. Morgenthau was convinced that something had to be done to demonstrate to the British that they were getting their money's worth.[66] In fact, the British press had been criticizing the United States for stockpiling gold, claiming that it had accumulated about 70 per cent of the world supply. Ambassador Kennedy, fearful that foreign nations might repudiate gold as an international standard, recommended to the President that the Administration drop its gold-purchasing policy, but his suggestion was coolly received. Morgenthau resented his interference and asked Prime Minister King to suggest to the British Treasury that they send a man to discuss the gold question, thus effectively bypassing Kennedy. Roosevelt also wrote the Ambassador and flatly told him that no change in American policy was contemplated.[67]

Britain's increasing need for dollars and the desire to indicate to the United States that His Majesty's Government would make the maximum effort to obtain sufficient dollars resulted in a continuation of the vesting of securities. Begun in February, 1940, a second vesting order was issued in April, with the two orders covering a total of £56 million, or about $310 million.[68] Vesting was one thing, and selling another. Morgenthau received weekly summaries of the sales of British-owned American securities under vesting orders, and these

[65] Hall, *North American Supply*, p. 249n.

[66] J. W. Pickersgill, *The Mackenzie King Record*, I (1939-44), 113-14.

[67] May 1-3, 1940, Morgenthau Diary, 259:401-9. The diary includes a copy of Kennedy's letter to Roosevelt and the President's answer, as well as Morgenthau's draft of a reply for Roosevelt. See also, Blum, *From the Morgenthau Diaries*, II, 109.

[68] Sayers, *Financial Policy*, p. 365.

showed that even by August, 1940, Great Britain had realized only some $51,500,000 through vesting.[69]

The steady drain on gold, the failure of the vesting orders to provide an adequate dollar supply, and the tentative increase in the scale of the war, all combined to cause Purvis to complain to Morgenthau that plant expansion costs were too much of a dollar drain. At a meeting held on April 12, Morgenthau clarified the American position for Purvis and René Pleven, in charge of aircraft purchases for the French. The Secretary pointed out that the political facts of life in the United States required that the War Department, Congress, and the nation as a whole had to be convinced that the aid program was not seriously interfering with American preparedness at home, therefore Allied aviation purchases had to be limited and the Allies also had to foot the bill for capital assistance.[70] There was no question of the American intention to help, but they—not Britain and France—would choose the time.

A pamphlet entitled *Paying for the War,* published by the British Labour Party in April, made no mention of credit or foreign borrowing as a means of financing the war, but that certainly did not reflect the hopes of the Ministry. The broader English hopes were expressed in a letter Ambassador Lothian sent to a friend in England in April, 1940. He commented that he did not expect the United States ever actually to declare war and openly join sides with Britain, but he believed rather that American participation in the war would come via a series of small steps, probably in the Pacific. Regardless of location, it would come as a result of Axis not Allied actions.[71] It was clear to the British that time and timing were of the essence. Up to the end of April, 1940, American aid had been of some help, but in general, Britain had been forced to rely on other sources for immediate aid. The key contribution of the United States to the British war effort was an intangible—but an essential—one. The slow but steady development of what is generally called "non-belligerency," and the growing awareness that the Roosevelt Administration could increase that aid when the situation worsened, stimulated that most precious of wartime commodities—hope.

---

[69]Aug. 13, 1940, Morgenthau Diary, 292:281. The weekly summaries of such security sales are found throughout the Diary.

[70]Blum, *From the Morgenthau Diaries*, II, 120-22.

[71]Douglas Jay, *Paying for the War* (n.p.: Labour Party, April, 1940), in Johnson to Hull, May 10, 1940, State Dept., 841.51/1571. Lothian to Sir Alan Lascelles (Assistant Private Secretary to the King), April 22, 1940, as quoted in Butler, *Lord Lothian*, p. 278.

CHAPTER II

"GOD, LOVE AND ANGLO-AMERICAN RELATIONS":
THE FRENCH CRISIS

On May 4, 1940, six days before Hitler unleashed his armies on the Low Countries, the British Chiefs of Staff Committee recommended that "financial consideration should not be allowed to stand in the way" of preparing to withstand the expected German offensive in 1940, for they believed Hitler would try to achieve a final decision by the end of the year. After an investigation of the shipping problem that had begun before the German offensive of May 10, the British government's examination of wartime economics, the Stamp Survey,[1] concluded in a report six days later that there was little sense in strictly conserving British gold and dollar reserves. Thus even before the invasion of France, elements of both the civil and military in the British government had taken a seat at what Churchill called "the hungry table."[2] Ironically, on the same day the British Committee of the Chiefs of Staff submitted its report, the American State Department dispatched a strong protest against British limits on agricultural imports from the United States, as the United States continued its naïve attempt to maintain normal peacetime trade relations.[3]

In England the immediate political effect of the German attack was the resignation of Prime Minister Neville Chamberlain and his replacement by the First Lord of the Admiralty, Winston Churchill. For years Churchill had been a staunch supporter of all-out preparedness and close ties with the United States. The anecdote about the British Foreign Office candidate who, when asked to name the three most

[1]See the Introduction, p. 8.

[2]Sayers, *Financial Policy*, pp. 366-67; Pogue, *Marshall*, p. 48.

[3]Memo of the Dept. of State to the British Embassy, May 4, 1940, *FR*, 1940, III, 115-16.

important things in the world, answered "God, love and Anglo-American relations,"[4] aptly describes Churchill's views, although he might have preferred to substitute the British Empire for love. He and Roosevelt had carried on a personal correspondence since November, 1939, so that an effective, if highly informal, relationship had already been established between the two leaders.

In the area of Anglo-American affairs, Churchill's Foreign Secretary, Lord Halifax, found himself in a position much the same as that of Secretary of State Hull. In fact, Churchill handled American affairs even after Anthony Eden replaced Halifax in January, 1941, in spite of an earlier comment by the Prime Minister that he wished he could put Eden in the Foreign Office to help with the United States.[5] Too much depended upon the Americans to leave things to subordinates.

The Roosevelt-Churchill correspondence that occurred before May, 1940, inspired an unusual episode. Tyler G. Kent, a code clerk at the American Embassy in London, personally decided that the messages exchanged between the two men had illegally bound the United States to a policy of intervention and aid to Britain. He secreted copies of some fifteen hundred documents in his apartment. After his arrest he stated that he had intended disclosing their contents to the American Congress and public. Kent attempted to justify his actions by asserting that Roosevelt was misleading the American public with half-truths. He was prosecuted under British law, after Ambassador Kennedy waived Kent's diplomatic immunity, and jailed until after the war.[6] Just what the documents contained is not clear, for they are still not available to scholars. In an article in the *Washington Times-Herald* on November 12, 1941, reporter Arthur Sears Henning said that one version of the story had this correspondence outlining the Lend-Lease concept as a means of getting around the Neutrality and Johnson Debt-Default Acts.[7] The only official answer to this accusation came in response to an inquiry made about Kent in 1944. At that time Roosevelt approved a letter written in the State Department which dodged the question by warning that any allegation that the President of the United States engaged in actions contrary to the declared policy

[4]Hall, *North American Supply*, p. 60.

[5]Anthony Eden, Earl of Avon, *The Reckoning*, vol. II of *The Memoirs of Anthony Eden, Earl of Avon*, 3 vols. (Boston: Houghton Mifflin, 1960-65), *passim*. Churchill's comment is in *ibid*., p. 168.

[6]The best treatment of the Kent affair is in Whalen, *The Founding Father*, pp. 303-14. Whalen is clearly sympathetic to Kent.

[7]Roosevelt Papers, OF 5613, "Tyler Kent." A reprint of the Henning article is contained in this file. Kent's mother claimed the article was suppressed after the first edition of the paper, but the last edition (the five-star edition) for that day still contained Henning's story. *Washington Times-Herald* (five-star ed.), Nov. 12, 1941, p. 5.

of the country could only cause doubts about the motives of the alleger. The Kent case itself was not discussed.[8] Regardless of the unusual circumstances of Kent's trial, which involved what seems now to be very shaky evidence of collusion with German agents, it seems highly unlikely that the Lend-Lease concept was discussed this early since later events show that Roosevelt had not worked out a solution to the money problem as late as December, 1940. It would have required truly herculean efforts to have hidden such data for over eight months. Breckinridge Long's impression, that the messages related to helping American shipping avoid the "danger zones," appears more likely.[9] Either way, the fact remains that the relationship between President Roosevelt and the new Prime Minister of Great Britain was unusually close.

Once in the Prime Minister's seat, Churchill was quick to act. On May 13, Ambassador Kennedy cabled the State Department that he had repeatedly been contacted by persons close to Churchill who suggested that the time had come for the United States to consider credits since Britain would have to build up its war efforts. Kennedy believed the hints had been prompted by a statement from Senator Carter Glass to the effect that the United States was contemplating such action. The Ambassador reported that he had brought up the subject of the four or five billion dollars worth of assets Britain still had available and that in view of America's experience with World War I debts, further credits could hardly be in the public interest.[10]

On the same day reporters tried to get Morgenthau to comment on the same question at a press conference. When one reporter pointed out that there were a number of moves being made on Capitol Hill to relax the provisions of the Johnson Debt-Default Act, Morgenthau merely commented that the Treasury was doing nothing to promote such action. Asked about the confused situation regarding short-term (90-day) credits, which had been permitted in the earlier Neutrality Acts but struck out of the "cash and carry" act, the Secretary said he had not been giving it any thought nor had anyone else. He gave the

[8]State Dept. to A. J. Muste, Oct. 1944, Roosevelt Papers, OF 5613, "Tyler Kent."

[9]Long, *War Diary*, entry for May 22, 1940, p. 97. The whole Kent story cannot be satisfactorily resolved until the actual documents Kent stole become available. I was informed by the staff at the Franklin Roosevelt Library that although they do have those documents, they are closed because of restrictions placed on them by the British government and the Churchill heirs. Further information on the Kent case can be found in an article by Whalen, "The Strange Case of Tyler Kent," *Diplomat*, (Nov., 1965), pp. 17ff. Harry Elmer Barnes, in an article "Revisionism: A Key to Peace," *Rampart Journal*, II, no. 1 (Spring, 1966), 46-47, claims he was told by a student of William Langer's (apparently David L. Hoggan) that Churchill threatened court action against Langer and Gleason if they used the "Kent documents" in their study, *The Challenge to Isolation*. True or not, they do not refer to the episode in any way. To date, the only examinations of the Kent affair have been by historians and journalists who were bitterly critical of Roosevelt.

[10]Kennedy to Hull, May 13, 1940, State Dept., 740.00111A-Financial 141.

same response to a question about providing dollars by purchasing raw and strategic materials from the sterling area. When the correspondents returned to the question of repeal of the Johnson Act, Morgenthau replied with double-talk. Exasperated, one newsman posed the key question pointblank:

Newsman: "Mr. Secretary, when do you expect the allied cash funds to be exhausted?
Morgenthau: "How old is Anne?
Newsman: "I don't know her.
Morgenthau: "Well, I don't know the answer to yours, either."[11]

The Secretary's humor may not have brought on any belly laughs, but his point was clear. There would be no denials along the lines of Kennedy's response to the English, for the Roosevelt Administration was examining the problem. On the day of the press conference, Morgenthau had telephoned Ambassador Lothian and requested that the British Treasury send over their Under Secretary, Sir Frederick Phillips, to discuss financial matters; the British agreed.[12]

Churchill adopted the direct approach on May 15 and in conversations with Kennedy made it crystal clear that he needed help from the United States. Kennedy asked what sort of help America could give "that would not leave the United States holding the bag for a war in which the Allies expected to be beaten." He added that Britain did not need money or credits at the time and in the short war Churchill kept predicting American aid could contribute little.[13] No retort from Churchill was reported by Kennedy, although if the Prime Minister made none, it must have been at the expense of almost biting off his tongue. With the Ambassador so completely out of step with Roosevelt's foreign policy, it is little wonder that Roosevelt and Churchill depended so heavily upon private communications. As Robert Sherwood confidently points out, with the attack on France, Roosevelt became positive "and this is not speculation—that if Britain fell a disastrous war for the United States would be inevitable."[14]

The British intensified their efforts to prevent the loss of dollars and dollar assets and on May 12 blocked the transfer of foreign-owned securities. Such sales had previously not been controlled, and this had resulted in discount selling of sterling and a drop on the world market

[11]Morgenthau Press Conferences, vol. 15, May 13, 1940, pp. 18-24.

[12]Memo of telephone conversation between Lothian and Morgenthau, May 13, 1940, Morgenthau Diary, 262:110-11. Memo of call from British Embassy, May 13, 1940, *ibid.*, 262:80. Morgenthau requested Phillips by name since they had had earlier dealings together.

[13]Kennedy to Roosevelt and Hull, May 15, 1940 (received May 14, 1940, Washington time), *FR*, 1940, III, 29-30.

[14]Sherwood, *Roosevelt and Hopkins*, pp. 125-26.

in the value of the pound.[15] What little was saved by such steps was discounted by the fall in sales of British-owned American securities. As the First Secretary of the British Embassy pointed out to the State Department on May 25, because of the German successes the price being offered for such securities had dropped so low that Britain had stopped liquidating them. He went on to raise the question of what would happen if further gold shipments should become impractical, particularly if Congress were not in session. He did not press for an answer, and the State Department offered none.[16]

Churchill's unsuccessful attempt to enlist Kennedy's support did not daunt him, for on the same day he sent his first letter as Prime Minister to Roosevelt. The Englishman adopted a tone and approach to which he adhered consistently until after the passage of the Lend-Lease Act. He specifically asked that the President proclaim a status of non-belligerency for the United States and bring to bear all aid short of sending armed forces. He warned that although Britain would fight on alone if necessary, a Nazi conquest of Europe would probably place America in an impossible situation. After mentioning a few specific items that England desperately needed, including aircraft and destroyers, Churchill lightly touched on the financial question in one concise sentence: "We shall go on paying dollars for as long as we can, but I should like to feel reasonably sure that when we can pay no more, you will give us the stuff all the same."[17] The Prime Minister's plea for what amounted to a war subsidy was the only direct one he made in the pre-Lend-Lease period.

Roosevelt's answer, sent the following day, discussed Churchill's specific requests but avoided any commitment on the money dilemma. The President did promise to discuss such matters when he felt he could make a decision on them.[18] For the remainder of the

[15]Hancock and Gowing, *British War Economy*, p. 109n. By March 27, 1940, the unofficial value of the pound had dropped to $3.48. The British continued to take similar actions, such as requiring that all exports from the sterling area had to be paid for in dollars, but these moves were minor compared to the size of the dollar drain. See Morgenthau Diary, 266:64, 162-64; 267:116-17, 437-41.

[16]Memo of conversation between F. R. Hoyer Millar and J. Pierrepont Moffat, May 25, 1940, State Dept., 841.51/1573.

[17]Churchill, *Their Finest Hour*, pp. 24-25.

[18]Roosevelt to Churchill, May 16, 1940, *FR*, 1940, III, 49-50. Such messages were actually sent via Hull and Kennedy and addressed internally to Roosevelt and Churchill. In addition, Roosevelt was usually referred to by a code name, such as SYLVIA, while Churchill was—by his own choice—labelled FORMER NAVAL PERSON. For the sake of clarity I have omitted such information from the citations. In addition, unless otherwise noted, the date used is the date on the document itself, which usually refers to the transmittal date. It should be kept in mind that London is five hours ahead of Washington, so that very often the same document will be referred to by two different days, depending on which government mentions it. This date difference was made more common by Churchill's habit of working long past midnight and then sleeping late in the morning.

period of the crisis in France, Churchill stuck to the matter of immediate material aid and left the financial problem alone.

In his cable to Churchill, Roosevelt suggested that if Purvis were given immediate details on what sort of "anti-aircraft, equipment and ammunition" Britain desired, he would do his best to help out.[19] From this commitment came the discussions and negotiations that ultimately resulted during the summer of 1940 in the transfer of a significant amount of "surplus" arms and ammunition. Although the arrangements were not completed for this until June 22, the day after the Franco-German armistice was signed, its birth belongs to the period of the French crisis. From the beginning it was strictly a cash deal, but it is still highly significant for the development of the Lend-Lease concept. In addition to demonstrating Roosevelt's desire to aid England, the awkwardness of the entire deal convinced many that truly effective aid would require Congressional action so that such legalistic gyrations could be avoided in the future. Since the actual aid that could be sent was small compared to British production,[20] domestic political pressures could temporarily take precedence, but it was increasingly obvious that new procedures were needed.

Roosevelt's request to Congress on May 16 for an additional appropriation for national defense made no mention of Churchill's message, and the only reference to the aid program was the plea that Congress do nothing to hinder the supplying of aircraft to the Allies.[21] Still, the expansion of American military purchases was a necessary prerequisite to the "surplus arms" arrangement since that deal was based on the principle of selling arms to Britain and replacing them out of current production.

On the evening of the same day, the President reviewed the British requests along with some additional ones which the French had made and told Morgenthau to work with General Marshall and find out how much could be transferred. Marshall found himself in a dilemma. Drawing up a list was easy, but designating the items on it as surplus was something else. Considering the sad state of American military preparedness virtually anything that would shoot could be considered necessary for the national defense. After wrestling with his conflicting loyalties for a few days, Marshall submitted a list to Morgenthau and the President. The items were, for the most part, World War I arms, but even those would help in the expected defense of the British Isles. Since delivery on purchases from American factories was months away, they had to do.

[19]*Ibid.*, p. 50.

[20]Hall, *North American Supply*, p. 134, gives the total of the "surplus" sales from June to September, 1940.

[21]Roosevelt, *Papers and Addresses (1940)*, pp. 198-205.

General Marshall was not the only one on the horns of a dilemma. The Johnson Debt-Default Act and the Neutrality Act made the proposed transfer highly questionable from a legal standpoint, and from the time Roosevelt approved the initial list until June 3, the swap was postponed as the Administration frantically searched for some sort of legal subterfuge. Under Secretary of State Sumner Welles and teams of lawyers from the Treasury, Justice, War, and Navy Departments finally exhumed long-forgotten statutes which made the deal possible. Not surprisingly, Arthur Purvis commented that the entire operation reminded him of a famous American Army officer's comment that "regulations are made for damned fools and second lieutenants." [22] Even a blatantly pro-Administration official history of Lend-Lease written late in the war admitted that the "surplus" goods swap created "a curious legal situation" that evaded the normal due process of law.[23]

With the legalities brushed aside, the Administration moved swiftly to get the goods shipped across the Atlantic. The United States Steel Corporation was cast in a supporting role as the private purchaser, and on the afternoon of June 11 it purchased from the Army and immediately sold for the exact same price to the Anglo-French Purchasing Commission $37,619,556.60 worth of "surplus" guns and ammunition. Although the firm received payment for any freight and storage expenses it incurred during its few hours of ownership, the deal hardly enriched its stockholders. With remarkable efficiency the first ship was loaded in two days and underway by June 13.[24]

Only the daily fears of waking to find German soldiers on the beaches of Kent had provided the rationale for the "surplus" arms deal, and even then Marshall and his Navy counterpart, Admiral "Betty" Stark, Chief of Naval Operations, were most reluctant to provide the necessary certification for any further transfers. For example, there was some artillery included in the first transfer, but General Marshall categorically refused to certify more heavy guns as "surplus" until February, 1941, when deliveries from American

---

[22]Hall, *North American Supply*, p. 137. Hall discusses the deal from the British viewpoint on pp. 131-38.

[23]FEA records, "History of Lend-Lease," Office of the Foreign Liquidation Commissioner, pt. 1, chap. 1: "Evolution of Lend-Lease," pp. 28, 38-39. (Hereafter cited as FEA records, "Evolution of Lend-Lease.") This summary of the "surplus" arms deal is drawn from the following sources: Blum, *From the Morgenthau Diaries*, II, 149-54; Stettinius, *Lend-Lease*, pp. 24-25; Langer and Gleason, *The Challenge to Isolation*, II, 481-88, 511-12; Watson, *Chief of Staff*, pp. 303-12; Pogue, *Marshall*, pp. 49-51; memo by Welles of conversation with Lothian, May 23, 1940, *FR*, 1940, III, 3-5; Hull, *Memoirs*, I, 770; Churchill, *Their Finest Hour*, pp. 142-43.

[24]Stettinius, *Lend-Lease*, pp. 26-28. Hall, *North American Supply*, pp. 136-38. A copy of the letter from Purvis and Bloch-Laine to the United States Steel Export Company in which the Anglo-French Purchasing Board agreed to buy the "surplus" goods, plus a list of the goods bought, is in *ibid.*, pp. 495-97.

sources could be assured.[25] The Army and the Navy consistently demanded the best of two possible worlds: both Marshall and Stark recognized the necessity of maintaining Great Britain as a bastion against Germany, but they insisted that this effort not interfere with American preparedness. They looked on support for England not as a solution to American national defense problems but as a temporary stopgap until the United States was rearmed. The National Defense Act, passed on June 28, 1940, specifically placed the onus on the military chiefs to certify such goods as not essential to the national defense.[26] Until the Lend-Lease Act, they remained in that dilemma of conscience.

The provision of the National Defense Act which inferentially permitted such transfers was foreshadowed in a set of resolutions introduced earlier by Senator Claude Pepper of Florida, one of Roosevelt's staunchest supporters. The resolutions themselves were relatively unimportant, but their story provides an interesting case study of Roosevelt's methodology and his problems with Congress. In a press conference late in May, Senator Pepper casually mentioned a possible solution to the question of how to provide immediate aid to Britain. He suggested that at the President's discretion, the United States might *give* Britain planes which it could replace from current orders. When the story hit the newspapers, Ben Cohen, one of the President's assistants and idea men, called Pepper and proposed the two of them draft a bill to that effect. They got together that evening, and after roughing out a resolution Cohen insisted they first call Roosevelt for his approval before introducing it. Pepper, fearing the President would disapprove, demurred, but Cohen said he would have nothing to do with it unless they checked with the White House. The next morning Pepper talked to "Missy" (Marguerite) LeHand, the President's personal secretary. He read her the resolution and said he would not introduce it if Roosevelt objected. Roosevelt never answered. Assuming this was tacit approval, Pepper introduced the resolution on May 21. Publicly, the President denied he had initiated the proposal.

At the request of Senator Hiram Johnson of California, a bitter opponent of any involvement in the European fracas, the resolution was taken up the very next day by the Senate Foreign Relations Committee. In the absence of instructions from the President, the State Department advised against passage since it would violate international law and the Neutrality Act of 1939. Similarly, staunch Administration supporters like Alben Barkley, the majority leader, asked

[25] Leighton and Coakley, *Global Logistics*, pp. 32-36.

[26] By inference, the bill permitted such transfers providing the goods were replaced from current production. For the text, see S. Shepard Jones and Denys P. Myers, eds., *Documents on American Foreign Relations* (Boston: World Peace Foundation, 1940), vol. II (July 1939-June 1940), 793-94.

Pepper to withdraw his resolution. After the original proposal and a reworded substitute were both roundly defeated in the Foreign Relations Committee, Pepper dropped the idea and instead introduced a resolution that would merely have put the Senate on record as supporting the exercise of existing Presidential power to sell or transfer war materials so long as it promoted the defense of the Western Hemisphere. Although Pepper did not mention the "surplus" arms deal which had been virtually consummated, this resolution directly supported that arrangement.

The brief debate that followed foreshadowed the bitter Lend-Lease debates eight months later. Senator Josiah Bailey of North Carolina denied any inference that the President could give away war goods, and Senator Homer Bone of Washington, who had been a member of the Nye Committee, asked if this meant the President could give away the fleet. Under questioning from Alben Barkley, Pepper made it clear that the President did not have the authority to give away any government property nor did his resolution propose granting new powers to the Executive. Told privately by the Senate leadership that to press such a resolution to a vote would only result in a repudiation of the President, Pepper dropped the idea.[27]

The details of this incident are far less important than the general atmosphere in which they took place. At this critical juncture, with the German sweep through France unimpeded and an invasion of the British Isles expected within the summer, Congress would not support even a mere expression of general support for the President's policies. Possibly some Senators, like Joseph Guffey of Pennsylvania, might have been influenced by an active campaign on the part of the White House, but Roosevelt was apparently unwilling to risk his prestige on such a gamble at that time. As he wrote to Grenville Clark, an active internationalist since World War I, the problem of steps "short of war" was political, that is, what he could get out of Congress.[28]

While the Administration frantically searched for some sort of legal justification for the "surplus" arms deal, and Congress just as franti-

[27]The story of the Pepper resolutions is taken from an interview with the Hon. Claude Pepper, M.C., Washington, D.C., March 6, 1967. Congressman Pepper was a senator from Florida and a member of the Senate Foreign Relations Committee during the period covered by this study. Even though the "surplus" goods deal was in the mill at the time Pepper introduced his resolutions, he claims his proposals were independently conceived. Additional details can be found in the *New York Times*, May 22, May 23, May 25, 1940; Pittman to Hull, May 21, 1940, and Hackworth to Hull, May 21, 1940, Cordell Hull Papers (Library of Congress, Washington, D.C.), Correspondence, box 47. The resolutions (S.J. Res. 259, S.J. Res. 263, S. Con, Res. 49) are in *CR*, 76th Cong., 3d sess., LXXXVI, pt. 6, pp. 6474, 6770, and 7649. The short debate on the concurrent resolution is on pp. 7649-70.

[28]On the wall of Pepper's office on Capitol Hill hangs a letter Roosevelt wrote in August, 1940, thanking Pepper for all the help he had given the President in the past few months. It does not mention the question of aid to Britain, but Pepper claims it did refer, among other things, to his resolutions; Pepper interview, March 6, 1967. Roosevelt's letter to Clark was dated May 18, 1940, and is in *F.D.R.: His Personal Letters, 1928-1945*, II, 1026.

cally avoided providing any solution to the President's dilemma, the recommendations of the United Kingdom's military and those of the Stamp Survey had filtered quickly through the British bureaucracy. Prompted by a recommendation from Jean Monnet, the French representative on the Anglo-French Purchasing Board, both the British and French governments decided to take their dollars out from under the mattress. On May 24 Purvis and Lothian were told that the War Cabinet would take steps to increase greatly American production capabilities for the benefit of the Allies, although the Foreign Office cautioned its Ambassador that the emphasis would have to be on obtaining the goods needed immediately to resist a German invasion. Churchill, as usual, put it more colorfully. "We followed a simpler plan, namely, to order everything we possibly could and leave future financial problems on the lap of the Eternal Gods." There was no sense in saving money and losing to Hitler, and the British knew it. If they continued to plan for a long war, it might well help to make it a short one. Even more, the thought of eventually taking the offensive against Germany could be entertained only if the American supply potential were fully realized. In Purvis' words, the time had come to "shoot the wad."[29]

In June, 1940, in one of the most remarkable feats of propaganda ever performed by a head of state, Winston Churchill, by his eloquence and bearing, turned a disastrous defeat in France into an inspiring boost for British morale. Churchill knew full well that the evacuation of Dunkirk was considered anything but a victory in the United States, thus his address to Parliament on the day the withdrawal was completed, June 4, closed with a passage aimed at influencing American opinion as much as that of the English. In forceful and flowing terms he vowed that Britain would never surrender:

We shall defend our island, whatever the cost may be, we shall fight on the beaches, we shall fight on the landing-grounds, we shall fight in the fields and in the streets, we shall fight in the hills; we shall never surrender, and even if, which I do not for a moment believe, this island or a large part of it were subjugated and starving, then our Empire . . . would carry on the struggle, until, in God's good time, the New World, with all its power and might, steps forth to the rescue and the liberation of the Old.[30]

Such emphatic words were intended to convince Americans that aid to Britain was not a case of pouring good money after bad, and they

[29]Hall, *North American Supply*, pp. 156, 159-60. Churchill's statement is from his book, *Their Finest Hour*, p. 557. Purvis is quoted by Langer and Gleason, *The Challenge to Isolation*, II, 714.

[30]Winston S. Churchill, *Blood, Sweat, and Tears*, comp. Randolph Churchill (New York: G. P. Putnam's Sons, 1941), p. 297.

were well timed, for Roosevelt needed all the help he could get. Senator Key Pittman, the Chairman of the Senate Foreign Relations Committee, publicly advised Churchill to abandon the British Isles since they obviously were unable to defend them and American aid would be wasted. Cordell Hull thought it necessary to warn Ambassador Lothian that England's friends expected her "to fight to the last dollar, to the last man and to the last ship, if necessary," while Breckinridge Long was convinced that Hitler would win within a few weeks and it would be foolhardy to antagonize the Germans until the United States was in a position to resist their military power. General Marshall and Admiral Stark signed a memorandum in mid-June which suggested that the President make "no further commitments for furnishing material to the Allies" since their planners believed Britain would soon be defeated.[31] With these men, all supporters of aid to Britain, believing England was doomed, Roosevelt's hopes of increasing the extent of that aid were little more than wishful thinking. This was especially true with public-opinion polls showing that only 30 per cent of those polled believed the Allies could win the war. The President's own views were not so pessimistic. On June 13 he instructed his military planners to assume that Britain would still be actively resisting Germany six months hence. Just how effective he expected that resistance to be is indicated by his further assumption that at the end of that six-month period, neither Russia nor the United States would have actively entered the war, although American ships and planes would be already participating.[32]

On June 10 Roosevelt gave his public answer to the defeatist sentiment that was so prevalent. In an address to the graduating class of the University of Virginia in Charlottesville, he committed the United States to a program of aid to the Allies. After first dismissing as deluded those who believed the United States could survive as "a lone island in a world dominated by the philosophy of force," he delivered his now famous condemnation of the jackal-like attack on France by Mussolini, saying: "the hand that held the dagger has stuck it into the back of its neighbor." With the justifications and accusations out of the way, Roosevelt closed with a brief but clear promise. "We will extend to the opponents of force the material resources of this nation." After following this with the statement that the second point of his program would be the preparation of America's own defense, the President went on to declare that there must be no obstacles to

[31]*Time*, June, 1940, as quoted in Goodhart, *Fifty Ships*, p. 83; memo by Hull of conversation with Lothian, June 11, 1940, *FR*, 1940, III, 36; Long, *War Diary*, entry for June 13, 1940, pp. 104-5; Matloff and Snell, *Strategic Planning for Coalition Warfare, 1941-1942*, pp. 19-20; Watson, *Chief of Staff*, p. 111.

[32]Matloff and Snell, *Strategic Planning for Coalition Warfare, 1941-1942*, pp. 13-14; Fleron, "The Isolationists and the Foreign Policy of FDR," pp. 224-29, graph 2.

those goals and that they had to be accomplished with "full speed ahead." As with most broad policy statements, the key to this speech was its interpretation. Roosevelt did not spell out when and what would be given, nor did he even allude to the financial problem. Yet he did use the extremely broad term "resources of this nation" with no qualifying adjectives. He did use the phrase "full speed ahead" without disclaimers, which was anything but ambiguous. He did speak of extending, not selling aid. Most important of all, he placed aid to the Allies and America's own military buildup on a par with each other. Neither was given precedence. Rather he spoke of aid, "and, at the same time" strengthening the national defenses.[33]

The prevailing state of opinion, within and outside the Administration, mitigated against any early moves to cope with the money question. Although Purvis had been instructed on May 24 to disclose the new British purchasing policy, it was extremely difficult to disabuse people of the image that the British Empire had an inexhaustible supply of wealth. There is no evidence to show that Roosevelt even considered it an immediate problem at the time of the Charlottesville speech, yet Churchill, Purvis, and other Britishers had clearly warned that the day of financial reckoning was drawing near. Having this inkling of an approaching money problem, yet faced with a Congress that had preremptorily dismissed the Pepper resolutions, Roosevelt acted as most presidents would have—he avoided the issue. His reluctance to face up to the coming crisis openly was made more certain by the hazy state of public opinion. Although the number of those favoring more aid to the Allies rose sharply and continually after the invasion of Norway and Denmark in April, the per cent of those willing to lend money to Britain and France rose far more slowly and was still below 50 per cent even after the fall of Paris, four days after Roosevelt's speech.[34] The President feared that if he asked Congress and the public to make a decision, they might make the wrong one.

Before President Roosevelt can be fully condemned for a lack of faith in the democratic system, one must understand that he had available to him data that indicated the degree of Britain's military and financial problems. Yet, at this point, he was not permitted to disclose such information, nor would he necessarily have wanted to even if Churchill had been willing. To have painted the picture in its true colors would have provided ammunition for those who believed England could not survive the summer, yet the actual events have

[33]The entire text of Roosevelt's Charlottesville speech is in Roosevelt, *Papers and Addresses* (1940), pp. 259-64. A stickler for proper naval terminology might point out that "all ahead flank" or "all ahead emergency" call for even more speed, but I doubt Roosevelt even thought of that, although he was not above playing with semantics.

[34]Hall, *North American Supply*, p. 160; Fleron, "The Isolationists and the Foreign Policy of FDR," pp. 224-29, graph 3.

shown how mistaken that position was. In addition, as Sherwood pointed out regarding the "phony war," the election was but a few months away, and a politician out of office is among the world's most useless objects.

The full extent of Roosevelt's commitment can be understood only in the light of the diplomatic correspondence that was exchanged at the time of Charlottesville speech. When the French, backed up by Churchill, asked for a public statement of American support, Roosevelt promised support but refused permission to publish his message. In response to a message from Prime Minister Robert Menzies of Australia, begging Roosevelt to make all of America's financial and material resources available to Britain and France, the President privately committed his Administration to provide aid "in ever increasing quantities and kinds." Both of these promises were clear, strong, and unequivocal. Neither touched on the financial questions involved, but their tone indicated that money would not be the problem.[35] Yet at the same time, at a press conference on June 11, Roosevelt flatly denied that his Charlottesville speech would mean any modification of "cash and carry." At the same conference reporters gave Roosevelt a chance to support various Congressional moves to repeal the Johnson Debt-Default Act and the neutrality legislation, but the President pleaded ignorance of such proposals and dodged the issue.[36]

Despite Roosevelt's refusal to amplify his Charlottesville commitment, the English press interpreted it broadly. A report sent from London to Secretary Morgenthau quoted from the *Financial News* the typical response:

The United States Administration has shown clearly that Britain and France *need no longer be deterred by consideration of available gold and exchange resources.* They may buy every scrap of available material, safe in the knowledge that a President and an administration which had taken every risk in assisting the Allies *will not now be satisfied to abandon the European "frontier" merely because of inability to pay.*[37]

The schizophrenia of Roosevelt's private and public policies surfaced again within a few days after his address at the University of Virginia. When a British feeler made on May 30 proposing dollar loans using British-owned American securities as collateral got nowhere,

[35]Menzies to Roosevelt, June 14, 1940, *FR*, 1940, III, 11-12; Roosevelt to Menzies, June 20, 1940, *ibid.*, pp. 12-13. The correspondence on the French requests is in *ibid.*, 247-55.

[36]Roosevelt Papers, PPF 1-P, vol. 15, press conference of June 11, 1940, pp. 556-58. File PPF 1-P consists of bound volumes of transcripts of Roosevelt's press conferences. It is far more complete than the selections printed in Roosevelt, *Papers and Addresses.*

[37]*Financial News* (London), as quoted in message from Butterworth to Treasury Dept., June 15, 1940, Morgenthau Diary, 273:38-40. The italicized portions were underlined in red pencil, probably by someone in the Treasury Department.

Purvis requested some sort of relief from the expense of paying for plant expansion, and Morgenthau agreed the time had come for the United States to share the load. Shortly after the Charlottesville address, Purvis was told that, with Roosevelt's hearty approval, the Administration would assume some of the costs of plant expansion. The plan called for the Reconstruction Finance Corporation (R.F.C.) to loan the money needed for such capital expenditures; it would be paid back as the goods were sold. Britain would pay only in proportion to what she actually purchased. Only standard American goods would be so financed. Purvis was pleased with this new policy, but it was actually put into practice in only a few cases, largely because of difficulties in agreeing on standard goods usable by both sides.[38]

The deteriorating military situation on the European continent, which stimulated increased Allied-American military planning, also aroused fears below the Rio Grande. The constant clamoring of the Latin American countries for arms and munitions, always loudest in Washington, took on a different tone. Instead of readying defenses against their neighbors, the South Americans were worried about a European threat to the Western Hemisphere. The one foreign policy that found Roosevelt and his bitterest enemies publicly united was the Monroe Doctrine. Any hint of a challenge to that sacred cow invariably brought on long speeches and longer promises, and this was no exception.

Military policy discounted the contribution the Latin American countries could make to their own defense, particularly since a build-up of their forces could be accomplished only at the expense of American rearmament, and American military planning called for the United States to defend the hemisphere. This did not help Congressional peace of mind, and on June 15 Congress approved an old resolution that had been lying around since it was introduced by Representative Sol Bloom of New York in July, 1939. Rechristened the Pittman resolution (Pittman was Chairman of the Senate Foreign Relations Committee), the bill specifically authorized the sale of surplus coast defense and anti-aircraft equipment to Latin American nations, as well as permitting them to build warships in United States naval shipyards. The bill did not permit sales to European countries, even though the Administration had already assumed the power. In fact, it administered a mild rebuff to the President by prohibiting the Latin American republics from transferring outside the hemisphere goods

---

[38]Memo from Cochran to Morgenthau, May 30, 1940, Morgenthau Diary, 267:324; memo by Morgenthau of conversation with Purvis, May 29, 1940, *ibid.*, 267:212. Data on the R.F.C. loan is in *ibid.*, June 13, 1940, 272:122-23, 140-43. Hall, *North American Supply*, pp. 167-68. See also below, pp. 102-4. The persistent problem of the standardization of arms is succinctly discussed in H. Duncan Hall and C. C. Wrigley, *Studies of Overseas Supply*, History of the Second World War: United Kingdom Civil Series, ed. Sir Keith Hancock (London: Her Majesty's Stationery Office and Longmans, Green and Co., 1956), pp. 91-107.

purchased under the act.[39] Again the variance between public and private policy was apparent, for near the end of June, Roosevelt told the military that only token aid would be available for Latin America since American preparedness and aid to countries actually fighting the Axis were far more important. As a result, only a few thousand rifles and some obsolete coastal artillery were transferred under the act's provisions.[40]

In spite of its emasculation, the Pittman Act was a significant psychological step toward Lend-Lease. In approving the bill Congress approved the basic principle of providing aid to others when it would aid the national defense of the United States. Indeed, the authors of the Lend-Lease Act later attempted to take advantage of this by originally drafting Lend-Lease as an amendment to the Pittman resolution. But the major barrier, money, was yet to be overcome. Welles recommended to Roosevelt that something be done to authorize at least modest credits for the Latin American republics, but nothing could be done at the time. There was, in fact, little sense in worrying about such credits since, until American production picked up, their needs were low on the priority list.[41]

As if Britain's dollar shortage and America's low production levels were not enough, another problem continually plagued the program of aid to Great Britain—what Arthur Purvis called "uncontrolled purchases." Although he and Morgenthau maintained a remarkably close relationship, they were not always able to obtain the same degree of co-operation from other departments within their own governments. Not until March, 1940, did the State Department finally decide to refer to the President's Liaison Committee, all representatives of foreign governments, diplomatic and otherwise, who had the job of purchasing war materials. Hull, still piqued at Morgenthau's role in the aid program, waited two months before instructing his department to pass only to Philip Young, one of Morgenthau's assistants, all information regarding the Anglo-French Purchasing Commission and its work. The Army, however, remained uncooperative, an attitude

[39]George Fennemore, "The Role of the Department of State in Connection with the Lend-Lease Program" (Washington, D.C.: Dept. of State, Division of Research and Publication, May, 1943), p. 18. Hereafter cited as Fennemore, "State Department and Lend-Lease." This manuscript is in the custody of the Historical Division of the Department of State. The text of the Pittman resolution is in *Documents on American Foreign Relations*, II, 173-75. Officially the resolution is Pub. Res. No. 83, 76th Cong.

[40]Leighton and Coakley, *Global Logistics*, p. 40. The entire subject is well treated in Stetson Conn and Byron Fairchild, *The Framework of Hemisphere Defense*, United States Army in World War II: The Western Hemisphere, ed. Kent Roberts Greenfeld (Washington: Office of the Chief of Military History, 1960).

[41]The Pittman Act was cited as a legal precedent for Lend-Lease in a mimeographed paper entitled "Evolution of the Lend-Lease Idea: President's Liaison Committee," FEA records, box 227, "Lend-Lease," files of the President's Liaison Committee, p. 9. Langer and Gleason, *The Challenge to Isolation*, II, 619. The drafting of Lend-Lease is discussed below, chap. V.

made worse by the Woodring-Johnson feud over the question of aid to the Allies. Morgenthau complained bitterly until finally, on May 24, Roosevelt sent a memo to Woodring and Johnson instructing them to clear all new orders for airplanes and airplane engines with Morgenthau until a new and more permanent organization was established. In uncharacteristically strong language Roosevelt warned them to carry out his instructions "in toto." Just what the President had in mind when he wrote of setting up the "final machinery" is not clear, but ultimately the Lend-Lease Administration did the job.[42]

The confused American chain of command had accentuated a similar situation that plagued Purvis. As head of the Anglo-French Purchasing Board he did not initially have the responsibility for buying machine tools and steel. As a result, both English and French buyers often bypassed both the Board and the Liaison Committee. This caused priorities to get fouled and often resulted in higher prices because of competition among the various Allied purchasers as well as with the American military—just what the Liaison Committee was designed to prevent. Although in mid-June Purvis did receive the authority to supervise the buying of machine tools, iron, and steel in the United States, the problem soon cropped up again during the summer over the purchase of aircraft and was not adequately worked out until the Lend-Lease Act became law.[43]

Desire to buy is of no avail when the goods are nonexistent, and that was just the position in which the British found themselves as of mid-June, 1940. Little wonder that Roosevelt did not appear overly concerned about Britain's predicted dollar shortage, for immediate British spending was severely restricted by limited American production. That was soon changed. The status of the large number of purchasing contracts the French had negotiated in the United States became a subject of increasing concern to government officials on both sides of the Atlantic as the French armies melted away before the German advance. With a German victory in metropolitan France virtually assured, this worry deepened as it became uncertain whether France would continue to fight on in North Africa.

From the beginning of the war, French purchasing policy had been far more expansive than that of Great Britain. The French knew all

[42]Hancock and Gowing, *British War Economy*, p. 195; memo by Joseph Green (Dept. of State, Division of Controls) of conversation with Collins (Chairman, Liaison Committee), March 18, 1940, State Dept., 841.24/263; memo by Charles Yost, May 17, 1940, *ibid.*, 841.24/263. On Morgenthau's recommendation, Young became the Treasury Department's representative and thus chairman of the President's Liaison Committee in July, 1940. See Morgenthau to Roosevelt, June 28, 1940, and Roosevelt to Morgenthau, July 1, 1940, Hopkins Papers, box 302, "Book III: Background of Lend-Lease." Blum, *From the Morgenthau Diaries,*, II, 142-43; memo from Roosevelt to Woodring and Johnson, May 24, 1940, *F.D.R.: His Personal Letters*, II, 1030.

[43]Morgenthau Diary, May 8, 1940, 260:268, 320; *ibid.*, May 15, 1940, 264:238; Hancock and Gowing, *British War Economy*, p. 195.

too well that there was no channel separating them from Germany, and to make long-range plans so as to get the most for their money would have done little to build up France's ability to withstand the expected invasion. France entered the war better prepared to make purchases in the United States. Not only had her planning been more extensive, but she had more gold and about the same amount of dollar resources. The greatest amount of French purchases had been made in the area Britain most desperately needed to build up—airplanes. In the period from January 1 to June 30, 1940, Britain and France ordered over 8,000 airplanes and 13,000 airplane engines. Of these, well over half were ordered by the French since it was not until March, 1940, that the two countries began to make joint purchases of aircraft. The size of the airplane contracts was well known to General Marshall, who told Roosevelt in May, 1940, that Allied airplane buying had increased American production capabilities by four times.[44] Morgenthau was more specific in March when he commented on French airplane engine contracts: "From the standpoint of national defense, the best thing that has happened to this country was when the French came in here and gave us money with which to build up these engine factories."[45]

Prompted by a letter from Monnet to Churchill, the idea of pooling French and British resources was under discussion early in June.[46] Obviously Britain faced an enormous dilemma. They needed every airplane they could beg, borrow, or buy, and if they did not somehow assume the French contracts should France surrender, the American military would do so. Equally important was the need to maintain the confidence of American industry in Britain's ability to survive, a belief that might well be shattered should the French contracts be allowed to lapse. The problem was money.

On June 14, 1940, the streets of Paris echoed to the sound of jackboots and German tanks, as grown men—veterans of the Marne and Verdun—wept unashamedly. With Paris, the very soul of France, taken by German troops, the British government knew that a French surrender was a matter of days, if not hours away. The next day, after receiving a rundown on the situation, Purvis asked for complete authority for "instant action," and within hours London granted his request. In a followup telegram, the British government made it clear something had to be done to guarantee that the French contracts would be assigned to Great Britain, and all day on Sunday, June 16, the French and English Purchasing Commissions held negotiations. Not until two in the afternoon, when the news of Prime Minister Paul

[44]Hancock and Gowing, *British War Economy*, pp. 181-82, 194, 190-91; Stettinius, *Lend-Lease*, p. 22; Blum, *From the Morgenthau Diaries*, II, 122.

[45]As quoted in Langer and Gleason, *The Challenge to Isolation*, I, 291.

[46]Kennedy to Hull, June 6, 1940, State Dept., 740.0011EW, 1939/3487 2/10. Hall, *North American Supply*, p. 147n.

Reynaud's resignation reached New York where the talks were going on, did the head of the French Air Commission, Colonel Jacquin, assume the authority to effect a transfer. On instructions from London, Purvis attempted to purchase only the items Britain needed, but the French insisted on all or nothing. An attempt to transfer $500 million of French gold to the British account was approved by the United States, but the French Ambassador balked at the proposal. The word that Marshal Philippe Pétain had asked for an armistice brought the approval of the French officials who handled non-aviation purchases, and by three in the morning on June 17, the contracts were ready; they were drawn up in haste to beat Pétain's expected order not to sell. With the full knowledge and approval of Secretary Morgenthau, Purvis and the French representative, Jean Bloch-Laine signed. As Purvis later told his friends, the decision to sign was the biggest of his life. Although he did not know just how much was involved, he did know the obligation he assumed in the name of His Majesty's Government was enormous. Not until September were the French books straightened out and the enormity of the sum fully disclosed. Purvis had committed Britain to pay in the neighborhood of 612 million dollars. In a few quick strokes of his pen he had doubled her dollar liabilities. A member of Churchill's Ministry, speaking in the House of Lords in July and with the assumption of the French contracts in mind, took note of Purvis' unusual position. "Never have wider powers to commit this country been delegated to any Mission," he observed, "and it is true also to say that no Mission has ever carried so grave a responsibility,"—a surprisingly strong statement in a nation that had long made a practice of giving its overseas representatives substantial authority to make decisions.[47]

Although there were a few loose ends left to be gathered,[48] the main event was over. In February, Purvis had told a reporter that Britain was primarily window-shopping in the American market, but those days were done. Never more important were "God, love and Anglo-American relations."

---

[47]Morgenthau Diary, June 18, 1940, 273:192-203. The story of the assumption of the French contracts is taken from Stettinius, *Lend-Lease*, pp. 29-30; and Hall, *North American Supply*, pp. 146-55. Some of the contracts which Purvis signed, plus a summary of the French contracts are reproduced in *ibid.*, pp. 498-504. The quotation is from Hall, *North American Supply*, p. 76.

[48]For example, on June 18, Purvis informed the man in charge of building up American production, William Knudsen, that Lord Beaverbrook had informed him Britain would assume 2,700 Rolls Royce airplane engines the French had contracted for with the Ford Motor Company. Purvis to Knudsen, June 18, 1940, Morgenthau Diary, 273:183.

CHAPTER III

OF GARDEN HOSES AND OTHER STORIES: SUMMER AND FALL 1940

It was a strange, almost surrealistic summer. It began with a wild suggestion by Senator Gerald Nye of North Dakota that Roosevelt resign and let the Vice-President, "Cactus Jack" Garner, take over since Roosevelt was carrying out internationalist policies after being elected as a non-interventionist if not an isolationist.[1] It closed with the Destroyers-for-Bases deal and the Reconstruction Finance Corporation loans for plant expansion, two frantic attempts by the Administration to stretch every conceivable executive power to fit the policy of aiding Britain without getting Congressional approval.

On the day after Paris was occupied by Hitler's troops, Secretary of the Interior Harold Ickes wrote in his diary: "I would support a resolution right now declaring war against both Germany and Italy. We could not send soldiers but we could send munitions and ships and airplanes and permit volunteers. We could provide food and credits, and, in the meantime, we would have a real purpose in preparing at the utmost speed."[2] To a great degree, this sentiment reflected the general American attitude. Although most opposed entering the war and would not have accepted even Ickes's curious suggestion of declaring war without fighting it, there is no doubt that they heartily supported increased aid to Britain. The public-opinion polls show the percentage favoring more economic assistance for the United Kingdom rose from below 20 per cent early in March, 1940, to just below 80 per cent by the time of the Franco-German armistice. At the same time, virtually no one—less than 6 per cent at any time during the

---

[1] Wayne S. Cole, *Senator Gerald P. Nye and American Foreign Relations* (Minneapolis, University of Minnesota Press, 1962), p. 173.

[2] Ickes, *The Lowering Clouds*, entry for June 15, 1940, p. 209.

period March–September, 1940–wanted a declaration of war against the Axis, and the number who would have liked to see credit extended to Britain remained below 50 per cent, although it rose sharply during the French crisis. The period from the invasion of the Low Countries to September, 1940–right after the Destroyer-Bases deal–was the only time that the portion of Americans who believed the Allies would win dropped below 50 per cent. As if these figures are not confusing enough, polls also showed that by June, 1940, 65 per cent of those asked expected the United States to be in the war before it was over.[3] Polls can be misleading, but one conclusion seems justified: Americans wanted to have their cake and eat it too. To put it bluntly, they hoped for a British victory but were unwilling to risk American lives to insure the result. Nor was this a case of acting like a Sunday football fan who cheers fiercely for one side but knows the final outcome will not really affect his life. As early as May, 1940, a sampling showed 65 per cent thought the destruction of Anglo-French naval power would mean a German war on the United States.[4] Roosevelt's awareness of the public's attitude was repeatedly demonstrated. In one speech on defense prepared early in July, a draft originally stating that the United States opposed war asserted in the final form that no American men would fight in European wars.[5] From the passage of "cash and carry" until the Pearl Harbor disaster, every step taken by the Administration which increased the level of American participation was viewed–and to a great degree, presented–as the last thing required to give the British the needed edge. The American public refused to see the logic in the caustic comment of Senator Burton K. Wheeler of Montana that "you can't put your shirt-tail into a clothes wringer and then pull it out suddenly while the wringer keeps turning."[6] This ostrich-like approach was strikingly evident in the very name of an Administration-sponsored group, the Committee to Defend America by Aiding the Allies, organized in May, 1940, to marshal public opinion. Even more significantly, its leader, William Allen White, was a life-long Republican from the heart of isolationist country, the Mid-West. The business community, previously wary of the European war and aid to Britain, also swung over behind the Administration, so much so that opponents of Roosevelt labelled William Allen White a "minion of Wall Street."[7]

[3]Forrest Davis and Ernest K. Lindley, *How War Came: An American White Paper: From the Fall of France to Pearl Harbor* (New York: Simon and Schuster, 1942), p. 52; Fleron, "The Isolationists and the Foreign Policy of FDR," pp. 224-29, graphs 1-4.

[4]Davis and Lindley, *How War Came*, p. 52.

[5]Harold D. Smith Papers (Franklin D. Roosevelt Library, Hyde Park, New York), July 9, 1940.

[6]As quoted in Goodhart, *Fifty Ships*, p. 66.

[7]Stromberg, *The Journal of Economic History*, XIII, 74.

Even with the polls showing support for increased aid to Britain, and letters from friends like newspaper publisher Frank Knox in Chicago saying the program of helping the English "now commands overwhelming support in the Middle West,"[8] Roosevelt moved cautiously. There was still an election to be fought and more than that, the debacle of the Pepper resolutions made it quite evident that Congress did not reflect the prevailing opinion of the public.

Still limited to improvements in style rather than content in the aid program, Roosevelt finally, on June 19, put some new, though not young, blood into the Departments of War and Navy. Both Knox and Stimson were Republicans, internationalists, and strong believers in rearming the United States and aiding Britain simultaneously, and each was well-known to the public. Colonel Frank Knox, who had turned down an earlier offer of the post of Secretary of the Navy, now accepted on the condition that another Republican be appointed simultaneously to the Cabinet. With the isolationist views of Secretary of War Woodring a constant embarrassment to the Administration, Roosevelt decided to replace him with Colonel Henry L. Stimson. Stimson's credentials were impressive. He had been Secretary of War during the Taft Administration and had served as Secretary of State under Herbert Hoover.[9]

Roosevelt's motives for choosing the two were, as always, complicated. Clearly he would gain greater support in the Cabinet for his foreign policy; in fact, Knox and Stimson advocated even more aid to Britain and more definite moves designed to put America on a war footing. In two letters to his wife, written while he awaited public announcement of his new position, Knox remarked that he was happy to see Roosevelt, in his Charlottesville speech, stop talking about measures "short of war," and instead speak merely of aid. He commented that "from now on we are in the war until Germany and her jackal partner Italy are well licked." Scoffing at the notion that the United States could keep out of the war, since that was Hitler's decision, he believed American entry was bound to come. "The sooner we declare war the sooner we will get ready."[10]

Like Knox, the new Secretary of War firmly believed American entry into the conflict was merely a matter of time. The night before

[8]Telegram of Knox to Roosevelt, June 7, 1940, Roosevelt Papers, PPF 4083, "Knox."

[9]The general background on the appointment of Knox and Stimson is in Langer and Gleason, *The Challenge to Isolation*, II, 509-11. Knox replaced Charles Edison as Secretary of the Navy. According to Langer and Gleason, Edison was a poor administrator. If so, he learned better habits quickly, for after being elected governor of New Jersey in 1940, he proved a vigorous and effective administrator. See Warren F. Stickle, "New Jersey Politics—1940: An Acid Test of the Roosevelt Coalition" (Master's thesis, Georgetown University, 1967), pp. 43-51, 78-82, 220-21.

[10]Knox to Mrs. Knox, June 11 and June 15, 1940, Knox Papers, box 3 (correspondence with Mrs. Knox).

he was made Secretary of War, Stimson, in a radio speech, publicly advocated full American support for England, including sending war goods in American ships convoyed by the United States Navy. He did not mention active participation in the war, but the thrust of the speech was that if aid did not succeed, America would have to fight. [11]

Obviously Roosevelt was also politically motivated in his appointment of Knox and Stimson. The political aspects may have been minor, as Langer and Gleason claim, but in an election year everything takes on exaggerated political significance. Certainly the President must have calculated the effect on the public of creating a "War Cabinet." In England, Churchill had done it in order to eliminate partisan party politics during the crisis, and obviously Roosevelt would not have been displeased if Americans should get the same idea. Even though the two were thrown out of the Republican Party for consorting with the enemy, the public heartily supported the President's action by an overwhelming margin. Even Republicans approved by a margin of 57 per cent to 43 per cent.[12] If the selections had little to do with politics, they certainly did not lose Roosevelt any votes.

For the remainder of the summer, Roosevelt operated the aid to Britain program within the limits set by two concurrent yet contradictory American desires: preparedness and the need—particularly compelling in an election year—to carry on life as usual, or as Harding put it, for "normalcy." An additional problem was the gnawing fear in America that England could not win, an idea Roosevelt did not share in the least. Purvis told one of Mackenzie King's subordinates late in June that there was greatly increased feeling in America that aid to Britain was a waste of money, and a representative of the British Treasury, Sir Frederick Phillips, who came over in mid-July for talks with Morgenthau, commented when he arrived that "95 per cent of the population expected the Germans to win," even though they favored a British victory.[13]

Generally, both sides were forced to ignore the crucial but not yet critical issue of money. Occasionally a question would be raised, such as when William Knudsen expressed doubt that the British had the cash to carry out the obligations they had assumed in the French contracts. Purvis testily replied that the British government had been able to maintain the position of keeping its word, but he went on to discuss the broader question of the United States providing capital for

---

[11]Henry L. Stimson and McGeorge Bundy, *On Active Service in Peace and War* (New York: Harper and Brothers, 1948), pp. 318-20. Langer and Gleason, *The Challenge to Isolation*, II, 511.

[12]Cantril, ed., *Public Opinion*, p. 82, item 14; Langer and Gleason, *The Challenge to Isolation*, II, 510-11.

[13]Pickersgill, *The Mackenzie King Record*, I (1939-44), 127. Phillips is quoted in Sayers, *Financial Policy*, p. 367.

plant expansion.[14] Yet even a solution to that particular drain on the United Kingdom's dollar resources would not solve the problem. To England's chagrin, a balky Congress combined with the normal political caution of an election year made truly comprehensive solutions out of the question.

Equally a problem was the lack of novel ideas. Almost all Americans, including the Administration, could agree that World War I had proven loans and credits to be a bad way to finance an ally,[15] but no one came up with any other alternative. In one sense, the events of the summer and fall of 1940 can be seen as a slow but steady series of steps toward the solution they were seeking.

The presidential campaign was already underway by the summer, but the nomination in late June of Wendell Willkie as the Republican candidate effectively eliminated the foreign policy issue from the early stages of the campaign. Morgenthau remarked to General "Pa" Watson, Roosevelt's secretary, that although the Republicans had chosen "a tough guy," the battle would be over domestic issues and the Administration could continue aiding Britain. He also noted in his diary that Willkie's nomination meant they had another four months of freedom of action in foreign affairs, and the issues would "be settled one way or the other" by that time. The irrepressible Harold Ickes immediately wanted to take advantage of the Republican platform and push for a change in the existing laws so as to permit full sales of war goods and full discretion for the Administration on such matters. Roosevelt—knowing the Congressional Republicans would not be bound by that platform—effectively killed the idea by referring it to Hull for a reply. As expected, Hull denounced Ickes's proposal as unneutral and likely to invite accusations that Roosevelt wanted to get the United States into the war. In addition, Hull noted that the National Defense Act of June 28 required certification by either the Chief of Naval Operations or the Army Chief of Staff that goods were not essential to the national defense before they could be sold. Since Congress had just passed such a law, it was doubtful they would change it a week later.[16]

Knowing there was no sense in awaiting a broad solution to either supply or finance, the British constantly pressured Morgenthau and his aides for specific items. Purvis and Jean Monnet left London after the fall of France with instructions to "talk big and at once!" Ironically,

[14]Morgenthau Diary, June 26, 1940, 276:31-58. The Purvis-Knudsen exchange is on pp. 31-32.

[15]Fleron, "The Isolationists and the Foreign Policy of FDR," pp. 224-29, graph 3.

[16]Telephone conversation between Morgenthau and Watson, June 28, 1940, Morgenthau Diary, 277:108; Blum, *From the Morgenthau Diaries*, II, 164; Ickes to Roosevelt, June 28, 1940, State Dept., 841.24/277; memo of Roosevelt to Hull, July 2, 1940, *ibid.*; Hull to Roosevelt, July 5, 1940, *ibid.*

although Morgenthau had been pushing the B.P.C. for a comprehensive list of needs, when the British submitted just such lists on June 27 and 29, the Secretary felt constrained to warn Purvis that it would be unrealistic to expect "any more help or any less help" until the election was over.[17] The size of the commitment Britain wanted was more than the American public was willing to make.

This reaction and the general American attitude was clearly on the mind of the British Foreign Office when it wrote an *aide-mémoire* delivered to Secretary of State Hull in early July. The memo concerned two major items—American production and money. The British warned from "bitter experience" that it was not possible to have a full supply of both guns and butter. They recommended that the United States set up the necessary priorities immediately. There followed a brief but cogent status report on British financial plans. After promising to pay cash for as long as possible, they bluntly told Hull that this could not be done indefinitely. The dollar shortage was especially troublesome with regard to long-term contracts. The memo also brought up Britain's growing lack of shipping and wishfully expressed the hope that American ships would be permitted to enter "combat areas." On the advice of Ambassador Kennedy, the memo stopped short of specifically asking for credits. No official reply was made to this communication, but about ten days later, Ambassador Lothian reported receiving informal assurances that there was no need "to worry too much" about dollars.[18]

Certainly renewed British worries about their dollar supply were justified. Not only had the new purchasing policy and the assumption of the French contracts resulted in an enormous actual as well as potential dollar drain, but by the summer of 1940, wartime pressures had forced the British Treasury to give up its plan to maintain sterling as a free currency. Increasingly strict controls were placed on currency exchange—a violation of long-standing British traditions—in order to obtain "hard" currency, that is, currency convertible to gold or dollars.[19]

It was the financial quandary that Morgenthau had in mind when he called Purvis on June 26 and asked him to have Sir Frederick Phillips sent over by the British for talks. British reaction to the July an-

[17]Hancock and Gowing, *British War Economy*, p. 196. Monnet was asked by Churchill to act as an adviser to the British Purchasing Commission after France surrendered. Morgenthau is quoted by Blum, *From the Morgenthau Diaries*, II, 163-64. See also Langer and Gleason, *The Challenge to Isolation*, II, 709.

[18]*Aide-mémoire* from British Embassy to the Dept. of State, July 3, 1940, *FR*, 1940, III, 42-46; Hall, *North American Supply*, p. 243. Hall quotes Lothian's assurer but does not name him. The American materials do not mention any such assurances.

[19]The entire currency exchange question is thoroughly discussed in Sayers, *Financial Policy*, pp. 226-51. See especially pp. 250-51. See also Butterworth (London) to the Treasury Dept., July 18, 1940, Morgenthau Diary, 284:32-35.

nouncement of the Phillips mission was generally hopeful, though cautious. Reports from London indicated that leading newspapers, such as the *Manchester Guardian*, firmly believed finances would have to be discussed but warned against any expectations of an early extension of credits from America. There also were complaints that the continued liquidation of assets in order to obtain dollars was inordinately wasteful.[20]

Once he learned Phillips was coming, Morgenthau had instructions sent to Kennedy in London to have the Ambassador suggest that Phillips bring an estimate of British purchasing needs for the next twelve months as well as the latest figures on British production of airplane frames and engines. On the same day he commented that he hoped to talk to the Englishman about all those "frozen assets" the British had. The Secretary's hopes for the meeting were high, and he noted that at least now he could get some accurate information. He told his staff to make sure the agenda included discussions of the extent of British-owned gold, dollar securities, and direct investments both in the United States and Latin America and cautioned them not to bring up the subject of loans since public opinion was staunchly opposed to such actions.[21]

The talks between Phillips and American officials lasted for four days, July 15 through 18, and centered around the problem of Britain's rapidly declining dollar balances. It was probably the statistics Phillips had provided and which Roosevelt disclosed to a few of the Congressional leaders that Senator James F. Byrnes characterized as "frightening."[22] They showed that Britain's adverse balance of payments with the United States to June, 1941, was $1,552,000,000. When added to a similar imbalance with other nations, including Canada, the total of British liabilities ran to $2,332,000,000. This was offset by estimated loans and credits of about $700 million, leaving a net drain on the British dollar exchange resources of $1,632,000,000. This figure, compared with the United Kingdom's gold and dollar reserves, left little doubt of the truth of Phillips' claim that Britain would require financial assistance within a year. Of the $1.4 billion of gold in the Exchange Equalization Fund, $600 million had to be maintained since the fund provided exchange services for the entire sterling bloc. To go any lower would prevent those nations from buying in dollar areas. The fund held about $108 million, but this was considered the minimum required for working capital. There were an estimated $700 million worth of dollar securities as yet unsold, but to

[20]Butterworth to the Treasury Dept., July 12, 1940, Morgenthau Diary, 282:177-78.

[21]*Ibid.*, June 28, 1940, 277:1-2, 169-71; July 15, 1940, 282:370, 384-85; Blum, *From the Morgenthau Diaries*, II, 169-70.

[22]James F. Byrnes, *All in One Lifetime* (New York: Harper and Brothers, 1958), p. 113.

realize cash from them was a long, slow process. Obviously Britain could not hope to meet her expected expenses, and forced sales of securities, confiscation of gold ornaments and art, and similar extreme measures would hardly dent the deficit. Use of gold and assets from those European nations then under Nazi domination would help, but there seemed no legal way to get their hands on the money.[23]

Morgenthau, who handled the bulk of the talks for the American government,[24] never challenged the basic conclusions that flowed logically from such statistics. The Secretary did not argue with Phillips' warning that by June, 1941, Britain would have to ask for "massive assistance." Instead, Morgenthau adopted a tack that he and the Roosevelt Administration followed until the Lend-Lease Act passed in March, 1941. He asked Phillips for a balance sheet showing Britain's financial relations with the rest of the world and advised that the United Kingdom sell such direct British investments in America as Shell Oil, American Viscose, Lever Brothers, Dunlop Tire, and Brown and Williamson Tobacco. Morgenthau noted that this would not only bring in badly needed dollars but would also convince the American public of Britain's good intentions. When Phillips questioned the wisdom of including in the balance sheet fixed foreign assets that could only be sold in the United States, such as Argentine railways, Morgenthau replied that he had a responsibility to American business which had been inquiring about the ability of Britain to meet her contracts. Phillips' complaint that forced sales of British-owned American investments would severely damage Britain's postwar economy brought the response from Morgenthau that it was no time to worry about such matters. The Secretary's interest in Britain's foreign investments was echoed by the President when Phillips visited the White House on July 17. Roosevelt showed particular interest in the sale of British assets in Latin America, and Morgenthau received such strong backing that he characterized Roosevelt's performance as "perfectly swell."[25]

The emphasis by the Roosevelt Administration on sales of British-owned foreign investments raises the question of American motives. Morgenthau's urgings that Britain sell her major holdings in the United States and his repeated references to British assets in Latin America all indicate a possible desire on the part of the Administration to take advantage of Britain's woes. The United Kingdom could ill afford to

[23]Hall, *North American Supply*, pp. 247-48.

[24]Cordell Hull was present for some of the talks, but not surprisingly, his main contribution was a discussion of British restrictions on free trade.

[25]Data on the Phillips mission is taken primarily from the Morgenthau Diary, July 15, 1940, 282:363-85, 508-18; July 16, 283:121-24; July 17, 283:205-8; July 18, 284:77-88, 160-61. Additional information and Phillips' comment are in Hall, *North American Supply*, pp. 246-49; Morgenthau's remark about Roosevelt is in Blum, *From the Morgenthau Diaries*, II, 170-71.

take a hard line on the question of preserving her economic empire at the risk of alienating the Americans. Nevertheless, such thoughts on the part of American officials appear to be largely wishful thinking rather than part of a conscious plan. Morgenthau's attitude throughout the talks indicates his acceptance of the ultimate need to assist Britain financially, and he told Purvis, on the last day of the meetings, not to worry about the over-all situation, for he would tell the Englishman when the problems got out of control. The persistent American interest in Britain's overseas holdings appears more indicative of a very real political need to convince the American public, including many government officials, that Britain was not trying to pull the United States into the war via American loans. The revisionist historians of World War I had done their work well. Americans, from President Roosevelt on down, found it hard to believe that the British Empire could not continue to come up with the cash it needed.

Morgenthau's comment to Purvis also demonstrates the failure of the British to convey the feeling of urgency they held about their finances. Even Phillips admitted that the real crisis was probably a year away, while his concern for Britain's postwar economic position aroused no sympathy inside the Administration. Typically, the American attitude was to fight the war now and worry about the peace later. Morgenthau's real feelings were revealed when, after the talks with Phillips were completed, he told his staff that Britain ought to assume the initiative in dispelling the defeatist attitude that was so prevalent in America.[26]

Phillips was invited to return in the fall, after the election, to talk again about the financial question, and with that the Administration was left to mull over the hard facts. With the British hanging on the ropes, this was no time to take the chance of ruining their morale as well as any American beliefs that Britain could survive, so no inkling of the impending money crisis was made public. In a press release on July 19, the Treasury Department limited its comment on the meetings with Phillips to the statement that the question of the balance of payments had been carefully examined. Interestingly, the British drafted a press release that mentioned that financial discussions in relation to the war effort had taken place. Otherwise, the British statement was more cryptic than the Treasury Department version. Morgenthau's preference prevailed, and the reporters received the American release—without any reference to the financial discussions.[27]

As would be expected, Phillips and Morgenthau had decided to keep close tabs on the balance of payments situation. The news was

[26]Morgenthau Diary, July 18, 1940, 284:160-61.

[27]Hall, *North American Supply*, p. 250. Morgenthau Diary, July 19, 1940, 284:163, contains the British draft. The official press release of the same date is in *ibid.*, 294:140.

not good. It became quickly apparent Purvis had been right and that British estimates of imports from the United States had been far too low. This was driven home when the statistics showed the total dollar and gold loss for July had been $210 million. In late August, the Chancellor of the Exchequer told the British government that the new estimate for spending in the United States by June, 1941, was $3.2 billion, almost double the figure given Roosevelt! Since the total gold and dollar drain for August was even higher, $228 million, it was clear the day of reckoning would arrive sooner than expected.[28]

In spite of the glum financial picture, within a few days after Phillips' departure the Administration took action that bore out the informal assurance to Lothian not to worry about money. The significance of air power had long been apparent to military men, and the German tactics had forced even the most skeptical to be believers. If Britain were to be able to defend herself, much less think about offense, she had to have airplanes, and lots of them. Now that the Churchill Ministry had opened the coffers, the only limiting factors were United States production and the requirements of the American air forces. With American factories unable to meet all the orders both parties wanted to place, the problem became one of priorities as well as increasing production.

In mid-July, William Knudsen attempted to obtain for the American military 8,000 airframes on which the British had an option. In essence this would have frozen British airplane purchasing to its existing levels. Morgenthau and Purvis decided to take up the gauntlet. Purvis pointed out that British orders had been tailored to fit American production, not British needs, and Morgenthau noted that any attempt to restrict British purchasing only brought the United States closer to being forced actively to enter the war. Privately, Morgenthau told Knudsen that Purvis was deeply depressed by the defeatist attitude around Washington, and at a meeting held on July 23, Morgenthau told Stimson, Knox, and the head of the Army Air Force, General Henry "Hap" Arnold, that they were violating the President's policy. In strong terms he warned that such actions were stupid and not in harmony with the Charlottesville speech. Stimson and Knox both protested that Morgenthau knew full well they supported the President's program, but they also had the responsibility of preparing America's defense.[29]

With American industry able to produce only 550 planes per month, and half of those trainers, Britain's share of 250 planes per month was pitifully small. Aircraft production in the United States

[28]Hall, *North American Supply*, pp. 250-51.

[29]Blum, *From the Morgenthau Diaries*, II, 171-75, contains Morgenthau's account of this meeting, while Purvis' side is presented in Hall, *North American Supply*, pp. 170-71.

was expanding, and discussions between Knudsen and Purvis the next morning moved in the direction of a future limit of about 700 planes per month for Britain, a figure low enough to send Purvis hurrying out of the meeting to seek Morgenthau's support. The Secretary of the Treasury had himself been worried about setting fixed limits, and he and Purvis agreed to propose that the United States set its sights on accepting British orders of an additional 3,000 planes per month as of January, 1941. Knudsen was initially shocked by the idea, but Stimson and Knox—who had joined the group along with Hull and "Hap" Arnold—were enthusiastic. Although Knudsen continued to assert that it would be the end of 1942 before such goals could be achieved, he went along with the basic approach of a drastic increase in production targets.[30]

During the quick strategy session Morgenthau and Purvis held between meetings on July 24, one of the Treasury Department aides commented: "Purvis, you fellows have got your teeth all set for a nice large sum" and that "it is going to cost like hell." Purvis calmly replied: "The war is costing like hell anyway and perhaps if we had let it cost a little more earlier . . . it would have been better. . . . Mr. Hitler has told us some things." As Stettinius pointed out in his study, Morgenthau (and Purvis) had shrewdly forced Knudsen and the American planners to rethink completely their production planning,[31] but the piper had to be paid.

At a press conference on July 25, Morgenthau announced the 3,000 per month airplane production scheme, and reporters asked if Britain could pay the cost that they estimated at seven billion dollars. Morgenthau evasively answered "they have plenty of money—plenty." Whether or not he intended it, his statement was interpreted by the British as implying eventual financial assistance from the United States, since they knew all too well that they could not hope to pay that kind of money. The costs of capital construction, which were to be assumed by Great Britain and which Knudsen estimated at $880 million, brought even closer the day of financial reckoning.[32] With such costs involved, and Phillips' cold figures staring them in the face, there can be little doubt that Roosevelt and Morgenthau did accept a large portion of the financial responsibility by permitting such a long-term commitment to be made.

A more flamboyant and thus better known piece of aid to Britain before the election of 1940 was the Destroyers-for-Bases deal, which was announced on September 3, 1940. The details of the arrangement

---

[30]Blum, *From the Morganthau Diaries*, II, 175-76; Hall, *North American Supply*, pp. 171-72; Stettinius, *Lend-Lease*, pp. 47-48.

[31]Morgenthau Diary, July 24, 1940, 286:116; Stettinius, *Lend-Lease*, p. 48.

[32]Hall, *North American Supply*, pp. 251, 172.

are not part of this story and have been well told in numerous other places.[33] There are, however, some actions and attitudes that pertain to the broader questions that eventually brought the Lend-Lease Act into being.

Churchill's first request for destroyers came in his initial message as Prime Minister to Roosevelt. He carefully asked for a loan of forty or fifty old destroyers, and that set the tone for the talks and communications thereafter. At no time, either before or after Roosevelt became receptive to the plan, did anyone seriously consider a cash payment for the ships. Not only would that have caused a financial crisis, but the President doubted that the American public would approve such a full commitment with only money in return. Shrewdly, Roosevelt appealed to the Yankee businessman and the desire to best the English, which lay just beneath the surface in every American. Getting the best of a swap had the excitement of the marketplace—a thrill that national marketing techniques had largely eliminated from the American scene. The lesson could not have been lost on Roosevelt, for it became an integral part of the publicity campaign when the Lend-Lease Act was under debate. There are no documents that directly connect the destroyer-bases deal and the Lend-Lease concept, but the seed was obviously planted. The word "lease" was actually used by Ambassador Bullitt when he cabled from Paris in mid-May recommending the United States provide twelve destroyers for France.[34]

Although the idea of Britain leasing some Caribbean bases to the United States had come up as early as September, 1939, it was Roosevelt who suggested leasing the bases in August, 1940, as part of the deal so as to avoid violating the provisions of the agreement recently reached at the Pan-American conference in Havana which prohibited transfers of territory within the hemisphere. Since it was an old idea, too much should not be made of it in connection with Lend-Lease, but the fact remains that it was fresh in the President's mind.

A recurring suggestion among many non-interventionists, and one long proposed by the *Chicago Tribune*, was an exchange of British colonies in the Western Hemisphere for the old World I debts. The British suspected Roosevelt of harboring similar intentions, but when

---

[33]The basic story is well covered in Langer and Gleason, *The Challenge to Isolation*, vol. II. Two monographs on the subject, Goodhart, *Fifty Ships*, and David W. Dellinger, "Destroyers for Bases: An End to the Illusion of Neutrality" (Master's thesis, Georgetown University, 1967), pull the story together into a neat package and add a different perspective and additional color. Unless otherwise cited, the material on the destroyer-bases deal is taken from these three sources. The best primary source on the deal is Churchill, *Their Finest Hour*, pp. 398-416. Although I frequently refer to the Lend-Lease debates during this discussion of the destroyer-bases deal, I have omitted further citations to avoid excessive footnoting. The references can be found below in Part II.

[34]Churchill, *Their Finest Hour*, p. 24; Bullitt to Hull, May 15, 1940, *FR*, 1940, I, 222-23.

Lothian sounded out the President on the proposal Roosevelt's response was emphatic. "See here Philip, you may as well get this straight once and for all: I'm not purchasing any headaches for the United States. We don't want your colonies."[35] The trade was brought up again during the Lend-Lease debate, and again Roosevelt firmly refused to consider it.

The negotiations for the destroyers also found a change of attitude taking place within the State Department. Cordell Hull, previously more concerned with the idealistic concepts of international law, adopted the same position he would repeat with force and conviction in his opening statements to the Senate and House committees considering the Lend-Lease Bill. He noted in his *Memoirs* that although international lawyers might argue that the deal violated the Hague Convention of 1907 by selling warships to belligerents, the neutrals, such as Belgium and Denmark, were witnesses to the fact that Hitler was no respecter of international law. Stimson may have been somewhat unfair when he noted in his diary that Hull's absence during the early stages of the talks in August was perhaps "not at all a disadvantage to the President."[36]

The signal lack of ideas within the Roosevelt Administration on how to handle the Anglo-American financial problem was reflected in the most influential of the private organizations that worked for the destroyer-bases deal. The Century Group, an informal interventionist organization within the White Committee, was a prime mover behind the destroyer-bases swap, but it never came up with anything more original than an extension of credit as a solution to the money question.[37]

Two other recurring items cropped up in connection with the deal. Consistent with his entire approach to the aid question, Morgenthau constantly pushed the British to make full disclosures of their naval losses. The Secretary was convinced that a complete accounting was the only way to get quick and effective support, and he maintained this position at the time of the Lend-Lease proposal. The other matter was small but persistent. There had been substantial confusion over the failure of the United States to include some rifles, planes, and ammunition that had been part of the exchange. The dispute was not settled until the passage of the Lend-Lease Act, but a temporary agreement as recorded by Ambassador Lothian gives an idea of the awkwardness of any attempt to make financial arrangements between the two countries. Britain tentatively agreed to pay for the items, but the United States promised to find a way either to offset or refund the

[35] As quoted in Davis and Lindley, *How War Came*, p. 86.

[36] Hull, *Memoirs*, I, 842; Stimson Diary, Aug. 19, 1940.

[37] Goodhart, *Fifty Ships*, p. 114.

money before British dollar resources ran out. An awkward and unusual solution—but also a clear hint of things to come.[38]

Although the title of a recent study of the destroyer-bases deal, *Fifty Ships That Saved the World*, is overly melodramatic and exaggerates the importance of this one event, it is true that the bargain was a milestone. British Cabinet discussions indicate that they looked at it as a major step on the path to America's active entry into the war. Certainly the American press and public leaders generally agreed—whether they were pro or con—that it spelled the end of traditional American neutrality. Certainly the Germans looked at it in that light, although in accordance with Hitler's desire to avoid giving America any excuse to enter the war, nothing official was said. Roosevelt was aware of the magnitude of the deal, and in August commented that "Congress is going to raise hell about this but even another day's delay may mean the end of civilization . . . . If Britain is to survive, we must act." Strong words, yet the next step—Lend-Lease—was delayed far more than a day. There was an election to be fought, a public to be convinced, and a Congress to be won, before the commitment of September could become the reality of effective aid in March. As Stettinius succinctly put it: "The issue of all-out aid . . . with less immediate and tangible benefit to the United States, was still to be thrashed out."[39]

As usual, it was Churchill who, though a participant, succeeded in providing instant historical perspective. In a speech to Parliament shortly before the destroyer-bases deal was consummated, he gathered the essence of the arrangement in a few striking sentences.

Undoubtedly this process means that these two great organizations of the English-speaking democracies, the British Empire and the United States, will have to be somewhat mixed up together in some of their affairs for mutual and general advantage. For my own part, looking out upon the future, I do not view the process with any misgivings. I could not stop it if I wished; no one can stop it.

---

[38]Hall, *North American Supply*, pp. 141, 144. The mixup over the extra items was, according to Hull, Stimson, and Morgenthau, an oversight. Hall, working from Purvis' and Lothian's reports, asserts the planes, guns, and ammunition were purposefully dropped out for fear of adverse public opinion. Hull, in a talk with Lothian and Roosevelt, claimed they were originally omitted by accident but feared that adding them later would cause speculation that similar add-ons would occur. Thus the United States decided not to redress the error. Memo of conversation between Roosevelt, Hull, and Lothian, Sept. 16, 1940, Hull Papers, correspondence, box 58. *Ibid.*, box 47, contains a draft of the destroyer-bases agreement written on British Embassy stationery and apparently sent to Hull around August 27. It did include the rifles, planes, and other items. There is nothing to show that Hull actually read it, but its timing and location in Hull's papers lends credence to the position that Hull purposefully left out the additional goods.

[39]Butler, *Grand Strategy*, II, 245; Langer and Gleason, *The Challenge to Isolation*, II, 774-75. Warren F. Kimball, "Dieckhoff and America: A German's View of German-American Relations, 1937-1941" (Master's thesis, Georgetown University, 1965), p. 30. Roosevelt's comment is from Tully, *F.D.R.: My Boss*, p. 244. Stettinius, *Lend-Lease*, p. 71.

Like the Mississippi, it just keeps rolling along. Let it roll. Let it roll on—full flood, inexorable, irresistible, benignant, to broader lands and better days.[40]

The barter principle of the destroyer-bases deal was soon applied again. Long and tortuous negotiations had been taking place between Morgenthau and Chiang Kai-shek's government. The Chinese wanted money, but the Administration was somewhat reluctant. The destroyer-bases swap with Britain brought a similar proposal from the Chinese government. This got the ball rolling, and eventually Roosevelt approved a loan via the Import-Export Bank, with repayment in the form of tungsten ore.[41] Thus the idea of repayment in kind, part of the basic Lend-Lease approach, was part of American policy by the end of the summer of 1940.

Late in June, when the financial mess had become apparent to all within the British government, the Minister for Aircraft Production, Lord Beaverbrook, had proposed trading British military secrets for cash or its equivalent. Although Beaverbrook later lost confidence in the United States, a proposal from Morgenthau in mid-June that the United Kingdom provide the American military with the blueprints and production rights for the highly reliable Rolls Royce-Merlin airplane engine met with his enthusiastic approval. The arrangement was highly informal and left the settlement of patent fees and such matters to "subsequent determination and adjustment between the two countries."[42] Stettinius caps his brief treatment of this arrangement with a story that is both amusing and typical of American inexperience. The blueprints were shipped from England by battleship. When the government official who was to pick them up arrived on board, the ship's captain asked how they were going to be transported. When the official pointed to his briefcase, the captain escorted him below decks and showed him the two tons of crates that contained the plans.[43]

The transfer of the Merlin engine plans and patents was only a first step in what became large-scale exchanges of scientific and technical data and set a precedent for the specific authorization of such trades in the Lend-Lease Act. A mission was sent from London to Washington in late September to arrange similar exchanges and achieved remarkable success even before Lend-Lease. Alfred Loomis, a member of the American group that worked with the British mission, told

---

[40]Churchill, *Their Finest Hour*, p. 409.

[41]William L. Langer and S. Everett Gleason, *The Undeclared War, 1940-1941* (New York: Harper and Bros., for the Council on Foreign Relations, 1953), p. 17.

[42]As quoted in Hall, *North American Supply*, p. 191. The other details are taken from Stettinius, *Lend-Lease*, pp. 48-49; and Young, *Churchill and Beaverbrook*, pp. 147-48.

[43]Stettinius, *Lend-Lease*, p. 49. Donald M. Nelson, *Arsenal of Democracy: The Story of American War Production* (New York: Harcourt, Brace and Co., 1948), p. 81, relates a slightly different version of the same story.

Stimson in early October, 1940, that the British had been most frank and that the United States was getting "infinitely more" than it could give to the English.[44]

Similar exchanges of military information on strategy and tactics, later authorized by the Lend-Lease Act, began in earnest in the summer of 1940. An American military mission composed of representatives from the Navy, Army, and Army Air Force arrived in London in August. Their primary job was to report to Roosevelt on Britain's ability to withstand a German attack. They were unanimously impressed by the English performance during the height of the "Battle of Britain," and the Army representatives told General Marshall that it looked as if Great Britain would hold out, although they still recommended that all available American production go to building up its own forces. The Navy delegate, Rear Admiral Robert L. Ghormley, the Assistant Chief of Naval Operations at the time, was greatly impressed by the frankness of the British, who exposed to him their weaknesses as well as their strengths. When Ghormley asked point-blank of the British Chief of Air Staff, Air Chief Marshal Sir Cyril Newall, if British planners were counting on steadily growing American aid, Newall coolly replied: "The economic and industrial co-operation of the United States were fundamental to our whole strategy."[45]

While Britain and the United States grew closer and closer, the British dollar problem grew larger and larger. During August the payment of gold and dollars to the United States steadily increased. This was a result of increased purchasing and the demands by American industry for larger advance payments—a reflection of their lack of confidence in Britain's ability to pay. This was doubly troublesome since an excessive drain on her gold and dollars would eliminate the convertibility of sterling and badly disrupt British supply lines within the Empire and to the neutrals. It was obviously a situation that would worsen, for not all the Ministries had yet been able to make the psychological adjustment to what seemed like reckless spending and fiscal irresponsibility. In spite of urging to the contrary from Purvis and others, once the French crisis had subsided, the Supply Ministry became more cautious in its purchasing policies, and as late as August

---

[44] Stimson Diary, Oct. 2, 1940. The Merlin engine deal is given a contemporary evaluation in FEA records, "Evolution of Lend-Lease," pp. 41-42a. The British Scientific and Technical Mission is briefly treated in Hall, *North American Supply*, pp. 190-91.

[45] As quoted in Matloff and Snell, *Strategic Planning*, p. 22. The material on the Ghormley mission is taken from *ibid.*, pp. 21-25; Hall, *North American Supply*, pp. 191-92; Samuel E. Morison, *The Battle of the Atlantic, September 1939-May 1943*, History of United States Naval Operations in World War II, vol. I (Boston: Little, Brown and Co., 1947), pp. 40-41, 50. The other two members of the mission were Major General D. C. Emmons, of the Army Air Force, and Major General George V. Strong, Assistant Chief of Staff of the Army and head of the War Plans Division.

22, the War Cabinet generally approved spending dollars only for vital needs and on short-term contracts.[46]

Surely the Exchequer had reason to be worried. Near the end of August that office estimated the British deficit for the next ten months at three billion, two hundred million pounds sterling—a staggering amount. At the same time, British optimism showed through. The Minister of Supply submitted to the War Cabinet a study of the supply situation which discounted the dollar problem in its calculations, on instructions from the Defense Committee.[47]

Although nothing public was said of the growing money crisis, the British made certain that the Administration was aware of it. Churchill's public speeches in August and September made no mention of finances, but in mid-September, Ambassador Lothian, during an evening conversation with Stimson, repeatedly mentioned that Britain had nearly exhausted her dollar resources, or would do so more quickly than most people thought. The prevailing British confidence that America would come across when the chips were down was exhibited by Lord Keynes in a speech given on September 23. He confidently predicted that the United Kingdom's capital resources would last until credit was extended by the United States. Like most Englishmen, Keynes too was a prisoner of the credit concept.[48]

The closing days of September found the Treasury Department and the British Purchasing Commission actively discussing the dollar deficit. The monthly financial statements that had been arranged during the Phillips mission were expanded earlier in the month, and the more complete data caused some concern. Morgenthau had meanwhile received word from Churchill, via Stimson and General Strong, that Britain's gold reserves were getting dangerously low, and after refiguring British financial resources, the Treasury Department estimated that they would need $900 million by February, 1941, but were capable of raising only $450 million, mainly through gold sales. Lothian told Morgenthau that the United States had all the money and all the munitions but that England could "hang on until April." Temporarily, Morgenthau appeared more concerned that word would leak out to the American public about the extent of Britain's money problems.[49] Widespread speculation about what aid America would have to provide under such circumstances had to be avoided until the election was over.

[46]Sayers, *Financial Policy*, p. 368; Hall, *North American Supply*, pp. 174-75.

[47]Butler, *Grand Strategy*, II, 345; Blum, *From the Morgenthau Diaries*, II, 198.

[48]Stimson Diary, Sept. 17, 1940; Johnson (London) to State Dept., Oct. 3, 1940, State Dept., 841.51/1629.

[49]Morgenthau Diary, Sept. 24, 1940, 308:25-28; Sept. 25, 1940, 308:187-209; Sept. 27, 1940, 309:167. Hall, *North American Supply*, pp. 252-53.

One seemingly rational solution came to light when Sir Andrew Agnew of the B.P.C. suggested to the President of Standard Oil of New Jersey that his company accept sterling instead of dollars as part payment on their sales to Britain. When the company complained to Morgenthau that they felt pressure being applied, the Secretary sternly warned Agnew that such actions would be interpreted as meaning England was out of money. Agnew replied that such was the case, and Morgenthau admitted he knew it. Morgenthau met with Purvis the same day and angrily related the story. Purvis, on the defensive, surmised that it was an attempt by the British Treasury to force the issue of money and characterized the squeeze play as "extravagant." Apparently agreeing, Morgenthau decided to demonstrate curtly the channels he demanded they use and told Purvis to tell Lothian that Great Britain was to send over a "liquidator" to take care of selling British-owned American properties. Agnew agreed to contact Standard Oil and drop the proposal so as to scotch any rumors of English insolvency. There was no sense in hindering Purvis' efforts to negotiate contracts before the Administration was in a position to act—that is, until after the election. Actually, politics was not the only barrier to such an arrangement. Cordell Hull was violently opposed to anything resembling a payments agreement whereby the United States would exchange dollars for sterling, and the idea never made the slightest headway within the Roosevelt Administration.[50]

Although the scheme was never presented to the general public, Hull probably reflected a widespread attitude. To exchange dollars for sterling would be the same as investing in Great Britain, and there was far too much pessimism about British chances to permit that. The Battle of Britain, which dates from August 13, 1940, the beginning of the German campaign to destroy the Royal Air Force, was not won until October 12, when Hitler postponed Operation SEA LION, the invasion of England. Until it became clear in America that the English would survive the blitz, there existed doubt about her chances within as well as outside the Administration. Ambassador Kennedy was outspoken in his belief that the British could not withstand the attack and predicted that even if they did, they would be so shot up that they would be unable to help the United States against the Axis.[51] Breckinridge Long, on the day the German air offensive began, wrote in his diary that he expected England to give in to Germany, although

[50]Morgenthau Diary, Sept. 26, 1940, 309:13-20, 102-07; Sayers, *Financial Policy*, p. 372.

[51]Kennedy to Hull, Sept. 27, 1940, *FR*, 1940, III, 48-49. Langer and Gleason, *The Undeclared War*, p. 56. Whalen, *The Founding Father*, pp. 314-18. Whalen claims the cable Kennedy sent to Hull on September 27, referred to above, was substantially edited before being printed in *FR*. According to Whalen, who based his conclusions on German materials, Kennedy predicted a British defeat, begged Roosevelt not to make any firm commitments, and predicted Britain would actively try to get America into the war. *Ibid.*, pp. 317-18.

he believed there would be a long struggle and victory was possible. This same pessimism about English chances was reflected in the proposal of former President Herbert Hoover and Republican Senator Robert Taft that the United States provide enough aid to Britain to enable her to negotiate a better peace with the Germans. Stimson commented on the problem of dealing with Congress under such circumstances when he appropriated Wilson's words in a letter to Justice Felix Frankfurter. He noted that Congress was "still allowing itself to be misrepresented and hamstrung by a 'little group of willful men' but one by one we are getting measures through." The formation of the America First Committee epitomized this gloomy outlook on the Battle of Britain. Organized in September, 1940, it consistently opposed the transfer of military goods to the United Kingdom because this interfered with the American preparedness effort. They did not oppose the sale of war goods but insisted that such sales be subordinated to America's military needs.[52]

The contortions inherent in any attempt to aid the British effectively and at the same time satisfy the demands of certain Administration officials that American military requirements were of greater importance were vividly demonstrated in the attempt to arrange capital financing via the Reconstruction Finance Corporation (R.F.C.). After persistent requests from Purvis for some sort of joint financing of plant expansion, Morgenthau told him on June 14 that the Administration had decided to permit the R.F.C. to advance the necessary money. The Allies would pay back the R.F.C. in proportion to the goods they actually purchased from such plants. A major stumbling block to the effective application of this scheme was that any such advances could be only for factories producing goods that could be used by the American military. Few items were common to the armaments of both nations, and the British were understandably reluctant to adopt American-type weapons.[53]

The Administration struggled with the idea continually during the summer of 1940. On July 8, Roosevelt indicated he was willing to utilize either of two methods: the government could build the plants and have the companies buy them back over a ten-year period, or the R.F.C. could lend the money and then be paid back from defense orders. Jesse Jones, the Secretary of Commerce and head of the R.F.C., had balked at the portion of the arrangements which was designed to cut down the size of the advance payment Britain had to

[52]Long, *War Diary*, entry for Aug. 13, 1940, pp. 122-23; Selig Adler, *The Isolationist Impulse: Its Twentieth Century Reaction* (New York: Collier Books, 1957), p. 262; Stimson to Frankfurter, Aug. 20, 1940, Henry L. Stimson Papers (Yale University, Sterling Memorial Library, New Haven, Connecticut); Wayne S. Cole, *America First: The Battle Against Intervention, 1940-1941* (Madison: University of Wisconsin Press, 1953), pp. 39-42.

[53]Hall, *North American Supply*, pp. 168-69.

make on plant expansion. Jones said the R.F.C. would advance money only in the same percentage as the supplies actually would go to the United States, and when Edward Foley, Morgenthau's legal adviser, told Jones it was legal for the R.F.C. to loan the money since the plants would benefit national defense, Jones replied that he did not care. Even if the Attorney General ruled it was permissible, he did not want to do it. Foley continued to gather legal arguments in favor of the arrangement, but Jones was adamant. A month later, in mid-August, the disagreement was still there. Jones complained that Morgenthau had delayed the entire operation by promising too much to the British, and he further noted that to build a plant that would serve primarily the British would violate international law. He flatly asserted he did not have the authority to lend the money if he knew some of the production would go to Great Britain.

Frustrated, the British tapped their reserves and began putting up the large amounts of cash necessary to get construction started, and Morgenthau returned to his original proposal of a few months previous—that the government build the plants and retain ownership. This notion, however, was dismissed by the National Defense Advisory Commission as socialistic. Tempers flared as Morgenthau privately characterized Jones's excuses as "perfectly stupid." Philip Young finally managed to get Jones cooled down and late in August reported to Morgenthau that he believed Jones, if he were left alone, would work out a solution. Young had a hunch that Jones wanted a larger role in Anglo-American financial planning and if given credit for the deal would eventually go along.

On September 10, it appeared things were running smoothly at last. The British had put down a payment on some tank engines, and the R.F.C. seemed ready to co-operate, but except for this one contract with the Packard Corporation, this pattern of financing was rarely used. On November 7, Purvis sent a memo to Morgenthau complaining that the authorities were reluctant to certify to the R.F.C. that further plant expansion was necessary for the national defense, and the program was again delayed. Purvis was finally forced to caution the London authorities that they had best not expect the United States to pay any capital costs.[54]   Thus, in spite of an old-fashioned college try by

[54]The details on this episode are found throughout the Morgenthau Diary for the summer and fall of 1940. The specifics mentioned in this summary are in Morgenthau Diary, July 8, 1940, 280:332-35; July 12, 1940, 282:546-52; July 15, 1940, 282:323-24; July 23, 1940, 285:191-205; July 24, 1940, 286:11, 174, 243ff.; Aug. 3, 1940, 288:247; Aug. 13, 1940, 292:113-14, 196-200, 207-12; Aug. 15, 1940, 294:6, 177-86; Aug. 22, 1940, 295:137-40; Aug. 28, 1940, 296:178-80, 181-85; Sept. 10, 1940, 304:258-59; Oct. 1, 1940, 317:275-77; Nov. 7, 1940, 330:3-11. A little additional information can be found in Stettinius, *Lend-Lease*, pp. 54-55; Hall, *North American Supply*, pp. 208-9; and FEA records, box 227, file of President's Liaison Committee, "Lend-Lease," mimeographed paper entitled "Evolution of the Lend-Lease Idea: President's Liaison Committee," pp. 7-8.

Morgenthau, petty jealousies, timidity, the lack of effective leadership by an election-conscious Roosevelt, and a general reluctance to circumvent so obviously the spirit of existing laws, all combined to insure that Britain's dollar reserve rapidly continued to disappear.

As inconclusive as were the events of the summer, one seed was planted which ultimately blossomed beyond anyone's expectations. On August 2, Harold Ickes wrote a personal letter to Roosevelt, primarily in support of the destroyer-bases deal, which he ended with a now familiar story. "It seems to me that we Americans are like the householder who refuses to lend or sell his fire extinguishers to help put out the fire in the house that is right next door although that house is all ablaze and the wind is blowing from that direction."[55] The analogy stuck in Roosevelt's mind, and a few days later in a talk with the recently returned Ambassador to France, William Bullitt, the President retold the story, with some small but significant changes. According to Bullitt's account:

> The President cocked his cigaret holder, stared at the ceiling, then scratched his head and said: "Bill, if my neighbor's house catches fire, and I know the fire will spread to my house unless it is put out, and I am watering the grass in my back yard, and I don't pass my garden hose over the fence to my neighbor, I am a fool. How do you think the country and the Congress would react if I should put aid to the British in the form of lending them my garden hose?"[56]

If Bullitt's recollection is accurate, then in the few days between receiving Ickes's letter and talking to Bullitt, the President dropped the word "sell" and instead spoke of "lending them my garden hose." Too much should not be made of that change in wording, especially since Bullitt's memory or notes might not be completely accurate. What is most significant is Roosevelt's reference to putting the question to Congress. Clearly, the President realized that subterfuge was no longer sufficient. If aid to Britain were to become truly effective, Congress and the President had to get together. In four months' time, the garden hose story would become public property, but first there was an election to be fought.

There was no hint of financial relief for Britain in either of the platforms of the two major parties in 1940. Each generally supported aid to Britain—although not specifically by name—but only to the degree that it was consistent with law. There were no promises of credits, loans, or major legislative chances that would ease the money crisis at hand, In fact, a reference to the World War I debts in the

[55]Ickes to Roosevelt, Aug. 2, 1940, Roosevelt Papers, PSF, Ickes.

[56]William C. Bullitt, "How We Won the War and Lost the Peace," *Life*, XXV (Aug. 20, 1948), 88.

Republican platform was a clear endorsement of the "cash and carry" concept.[57]

Never were Franklin Roosevelt's public and private actions more at variance than during the 1940 election campaign. The question of paying for aid to Britain was one of the biggest non-issues of the campaign. Willkie was personally in favor of aid to nations fighting Germany, but any attempt to propose more assistance than the Administration was giving would have destroyed the unity of the Republican Party. The old-liners and isolationists were already upset at the failure of Taft and Vandenberg to get the nomination. Willkie's position made it easy for Roosevelt. With the Republican nominee unable to advocate additional aid to Britain, the President was assured of the support of the internationalists and interventionists without having to promise bigger and better assistance programs. Thus he could—and did—take a vague position on aid which enabled him to avoid alienating those who wanted to go slow.[58]

Since both candidates strongly supported the preparedness program, it was no issue. In fact, Roosevelt hung an albatross around Willkie's neck in the form of the chant, "Martin, Barton, and Fish," coupled with a reference to the early Republican opposition to any significant buildup of the American military.[59]

Even though the European war was the most critical question of the day, the position of the two major candidates apparently effectively neutralized it as a meaningful issue.[60] The election temporarily put the public aspects of the aid to Britain program in cold storage. But out of the glare of publicity, the wheels still turned.

With Roosevelt thinking in terms of Congressional action as the solution to the over-all problem of supplying the British, an ancillary dispute took center stage. Ever since the R.F.C. loan principle had been worked out, the entire scheme had been held up by the inability of Britain and the United States to agree on common types of weapons. This Anglo-American disagreement coincided with a relatively gentle but persistent feud between Stimson and Morgenthau

[57]William R. Catton, Jr., "Origin and Establishment of Lend-Lease Policy: A Study in Symbolic Paralysis," *Etc.: A Review of General Semantics*, VII, no. 3 (Spring, 1950), 184.

[58]The 1940 election has not yet been adequately examined. There are some excellent studies of Roosevelt as President which deal with the national aspects of the election. One of the best is James MacGregor Burns, *Roosevelt: The Lion and the Fox* (New York: Harcourt, Brace and Co., Harvest book edition, 1966). Langer and Gleason, *The Undeclared War*, chap. VII, examine the national campaign and foreign policy. More work is needed at the state and local level to determine adequately the effect of foreign policy on the election. One good example of this type of study is Warren F. Stickle, "New Jersey Politics—1940."

[59]Burns, *Roosevelt*, pp. 448-49.

[60]Langer and Gleason, *The Undeclared War*, p. 212, conclude this on the basis of the broad, national evidence. Stickle, "New Jersey Politics—1940," pp. 106-28, demonstrates that this was true at the local level in New Jersey.

regarding the Treasury Secretary's role. Stimson had insisted, as the price of accepting a Cabinet post, that he have full authority to run the War Department, but Morgenthau's concern for overseeing the entire program of aid to Britain inevitably brought him into conflict with the preparedness efforts of the military.[61] American production continued to be far too low to satisfy the demands from both sides of the Atlantic, and there was constant vying for Roosevelt's support.

The informal structure through which American war supplies flowed to Great Britain had quickly developed dinosaur-like proportions after the fall of France, a process accentuated by Roosevelt's penchant for informal administrative arrangements. In the case of aid to the Allies, the President's Liaison Committee was a classic example, but it was not the only one. Theoretically, the Council of National Defense had the primary authority for co-ordinating the American defense effort—but it never met. Instead, in May, 1940, Roosevelt established the National Defense Advisory Commission (N.D.A.C.). This commission was constantly embroiled in jurisdictional arguments with the Departments of War, Navy, and the Treasury, and to make it worse, it had no chairman. As Stimson put it, the N.D.A.C's only chairman was "the President who has not the time to run it."[62]

The Secretary of War was a strong critic of Roosevelt's administrative techniques and spent a substantial amount of time trying to "regularize" the relationships between his department and the rest of the Executive branch. Upon arriving at the War Department and finding the Secretary of the Treasury in charge of British purchases, he termed the arrangement "a very singular situation," and on July 22 he noted that there was no co-ordination between War, Navy, and the British regarding a proposed purchase of aircraft engines.[63] Although some progress had been made by the fall, Stimson strongly supported the idea of centralizing the aid program. When the Lend-Lease Bill was proposed, he testified that one of its most valuable aspects was that it would enormously increase efficiency in the aid program and in American production as a whole.[64]

In spite of their own differences, Morgenthau and Stimson sympathized with each other over the lack of organization but agreed that it was doubtful Roosevelt would effectively eliminate it as it was not

---

[61] Blum, *From the Morgenthau Diaries*, II, 183-84.

[62] As quoted in Langer and Gleason, *The Undeclared War*, p. 181.

[63] Stimson Diary, Sept. 10, 1940; July 22, 1940. Stimson virtually ignores this problem in his memoirs, Stimson and Bundy, *On Active Service*, but his diary is full of complaints about such matters. For example see Stimson Diary, Sept. 24, 26, 1940.

[64] U.S., House of Representatives, Committee on Foreign Affairs, 77th Cong., 1st sess., *Hearing on H. R. 1776: A Bill Further to Promote the Defense of the United States, and for Other Purposes* (Washington: U.S. Government Printing Office, 1941), pp. 87-89. (Hereafter cited as HFAC, *Lend-Lease Hearings*.)

his nature to act that way. But the lack of co-ordination was not all the fault of the President. Britain was frequently guilty of purposely bypassing known channels, though sometimes the confused American setup baffled them and caused mistakes. At the time of the fall of France, there were nine different British purchasing missions operating in the United States. Purvis attempted to bring them all under his cognizance as Morgenthau demanded, but this took time. One of the official British histories mildly criticized Purvis, saying, "perhaps he did other things better." It would take a detailed examination of Purvis and the British Purchasing Commission adequately to evaluate the truth of that statement, but either way, Purvis had his troubles. Since he was not given truly adequate authority for the job until December, 1940, when he became chairman of the British Supply Council in North America, it is probably safer to assume that the talent was there, but not the tools.[65]

Not until July 10 could Morgenthau report that Purvis had supply plans for the entire British Empire for the first time, and it soon became clear that the information Purvis had was woefully incomplete. Just as troublesome as the information gap was the all too frequent bypassing of the British Purchasing Commission and the Purvis-Morgenthau channel. Lord Beaverbrook, Churchill's aircraft production czar, combined imperiousness with impatience and attempted to eliminate what he considered unnecessary delays. During the summer he was admonished by Ambassador Lothian that attempts to work with the State Department instead of with Purvis and Morgenthau would only damage the over-all purchasing program, but as late as October, 1940, the projected cost of new aircraft programs had to be requested specially by Purvis. This was not the only attempt by a British purchasing agency to avoid the B.P.C. In early August, Donald Nelson of the N.D.A.C. wrote to Philip Young in the Treasury Department that since July 1 he had been receiving complaints from businessmen about attempts by the British Ministry of Supplies to place orders without going through the B.P.C.[66] Other nations were also attempting to purchase goods in America, and they too added to the confusion by trying to bypass the President's Liaison Committee. Since most of these purchases were by governments-in-exile located in London, Britain attempted to regulate such buying. The Canadians began using the Morgenthau-Purvis channel early in August, but as late as December 28, 1940, the British government was forced to send a stern set of instructions to the governments of Belgium, Poland,

[65]Blum, *From the Morgenthau Diaries*, II, 186; Hancock and Gowing, *British War Economy*, pp. 229-30.

[66]Morgenthau Diary, July 10, 1940, 281:192; Hall, *North American Supply*, pp. 76-77, 252; FEA records, files of the President's Liaison Committee, Philip Young files, "Britain-British Purchasing Commission," box 40.

Turkey, the Netherlands, Norway, and Greece. They were told to co-ordinate all purchases in North America through the British government and to conserve dollars as much as possible.[67]

This confused and tangled administrative arrangement forced Purvis to make a plea to London for aid. The British government responded by sending Sir Walter Layton, Director-General of Programmes for the Ministry of Supply, to the United States in late September. Layton was empowered to inform the Americans of British supply planning and to make recommendations to the British government as to future action. He was specifically enjoined from making any financial arrangement without prior approval from the British Treasury, nor could he commit the War Office to any arrangement he might work out on priorities or use of American-type weapons. He could make "such current and urgent decisions as are necessary concerning negotiations which are at present in progress," but it was evident that he was coming to talk, not act.[68]

Layton arrived at a time when American attention, public and official, was primarily focused on the situation in East Asia. The Tripartite Pact, between Germany, Japan, and Italy, was signed with pomp and ceremony in Berlin on September 27, and since its obvious target was the United States, the pact and the American response dominated the news for the time being. Roosevelt and his Administration were probably quite pleased that the Layton mission did not receive an inordinate amount of publicity since campaign strategy dictated playing down evidence of close Anglo-American co-operation.[69]

Morgenthau was quite annoyed by the Layton mission and openly expressed his resentment on the grounds that it interfered with his relationship to Purvis. When Layton was stranded briefly in Lisbon while enroute, Morgenthau helped arrange further transportation only at Purvis' insistence, commenting all the while that he did not think Layton was worth the trouble. To make it worse, Layton was an old friend of Stimson's, and the Secretary of War was all too eager—in Morgenthau's view—to work with the new English representative. At

[67]H. D. Hodgkinson, "History of the Empire and Allied Requirements Division of the British Supply Council" (a manuscript used in the preparation of *North American Supply* and supplied through the courtesy of the author, H. D. Hall), p. 77, 134. This contains a reproduction of the message, which is British Foreign Office message No. 12491/79/49, dated Dec. 28, 1940. Pickersgill, *The Mackenzie King Record*, I (1939-44), 140-41.

[68]Hall, *North American Supply*, p. 184, discusses and quotes from Layton's instructions. Hall feels Layton had a relatively wide range of functions assigned, but his own evidence seems to belie that interpretation.

[69]J. Pierrepont Moffat, American Ambassador to Canada at the time, visited Washington on Oct. 6-10. In his gossipy diary he made no mention of any significant talk around the State Department about the Layton mission or British financial problems. Everyone appeared preoccupied with the Japanese situation. See J. P. Moffat, *The Moffat Papers*, ed. Nancy Hooker (Cambridge: Harvard University Press, 1956), pp. 330-36.

Morgenthau's insistence, Roosevelt instructed Layton to bring Purvis with him for all meetings, and a few days later Morgenthau happily noted that Layton had refused to discuss the detailed situation privately with Stimson because the President had told him to take up such matters with Purvis and Morgenthau. Nevertheless, Stimson's attitude continued to annoy Morgenthau. Late in October, the Treasury Secretary told Stimson that they should work with Purvis. When Stimson commented that Layton was Purvis' boss, Morgenthau vehemently denied it. Stimson then made the point that it was Roosevelt, not the British, who had put Purvis in charge and that they both should be present for all conferences. Morgenthau agreed but insisted that the channel to and through Purvis be kept in order.[70]

Layton's activities quickly brought Morgenthau to a boil. The night of September 25, Roosevelt and Layton had discussed a set of supply statistics which the Secretary of the Treasury had never seen. In addition, the British had attempted to work out the question of the rifles and other goods that had been either dropped or forgotten in the destroyer-bases deal by dealing directly with Roosevelt. The lack of complete information on British plans and production had annoyed Morgenthau all summer, but combined with his attitude toward Layton it infuriated him. He angrily dismissed Layton as a political hack who had been unloaded on America to get him out of the way. He bitterly complained to Purvis about being out in the dark and suggested the Englishman get on the telephone to Churchill or Beaverbrook and straighten things out. Both decided to check further into the matter, and after Purvis left, Morgenthau told his staff to check with the State Department about any cables from Kennedy or Churchill forwarding British requests for war materials. The Secretary wanted to eliminate what he called his "blind spot," from which he had suffered since early September.[71]

Morgenthau also took up the matter with the President, and the next morning he and Purvis expressed pleasure that Roosevelt had told

[70]Morgenthau Diary, Sept. 18, 1940, 306:267-68; Oct. 1, 1940, 317:123; Oct. 21, 1940, 324:62-66; Blum, *From the Morgenthau Diaries*, II, 182-83; Stimson Diary, Sept. 10, 1940.

[71]The details of the conferences of Sept. 26 are in Morgenthau Diary, Sept. 26, 1940, 309:3-4, 102-7; Sept. 26, 1940, 317:45-47. Additional material is in Blum, *From the Morgenthau Diaries*, II, 185-86. The message that Morgenthau had not seen is not available in the printed or manuscript sources. There is a message dated September 26 from Lothian to Hull, but it says nothing about British supply plans or the items left out of the destroyer-bases deal. See *FR*, 1940, III, 75-76. As Churchill admits in his memoirs, there were about 1,750 messages exchanged between him and Roosevelt, but only a mere fraction of these are available to scholars. Churchill, *Their Finest Hour*, p. 23. Although many of the cables from Churchill to Roosevelt went via established channels, including Purvis and Morgenthau when applicable, many were sent directly. Morgenthau must have been used to that before the fall of 1940, and one suspects that the real cause of his anger was Layton, to whom Morgenthau had developed a personal as well as an official antipathy. Hall, *North American Supply*, p. 79, discusses the routes of the Churchill-Roosevelt correspondence, and there are various examples in *FR* of messages that did and did not follow channels.

Layton that he should not go anywhere in his official capacity without Purvis. Morgenthau was also gleeful that Layton had been told, in no uncertain terms, to supply the Treasury Department with every bit of information he requested.[72]

Actually, Morgenthau may have been somewhat harsh in his belief that Layton was concealing information. One of the problems the British faced was a lack of complete statistical data on financial matters. This created a serious credibility gap in Washington, where officials were used to having such data at their fingertips. Not only was there a traditional British distrust of relying on statistics, but the fear of security leaks in America made them reluctant to part with what they had. Compounding these problems was a general reluctance to deal with anything except absolutely exact figures, while the Americans were constantly making predictions and long-term projections based on a certain degree of guesswork. To top off the awkward situation, the long tradition of confidence between the Bank of England and the customer made the Treasury very loath to give out what they considered privileged information. Americans, conveniently oblivious of their own sins, were certain that the only aim of British financiers was to perpetuate commercial imperialism, and thus they invariably looked for the worst. Consequently, the combination of American distrust and the leaving of British finances in the hands of what one historian calls "shrewd amateurs" created a touchy situation.[73]

The arguments between Layton and the War Department over common types of weapons were long and detailed, but the Englishman was fighting a losing battle from the start. If they could not work out some agreement with the Americans, it would take virtually all their remaining dollars to finance the construction of the facilities they required, obviously an unacceptable solution. The British hoped to equip fifty-five divisions for use in defense of the British Isles (called the British Army "A" Program), but the War Office insisted on British-type weapons. As a substitute, the United States proposed that it provide full equipment for ten divisions of the British Army and continue supplying these troops throughout the war (the "B" program). Actually, Purvis had brought up this notion in June, 1940, but it had never been taken seriously by the British government. Layton was cautious, but Churchill, eager to commit the United States to any sort of additional support for Britain, cabled him on October 28: "This is splendid. You should accept at once."[74] In actuality, largely

[72]Morgenthau Diary, Sept. 27, 1940, 309:164-70.

[73]This thesis concerning British financial attitudes is taken from Sayers, *Financial Policy*, pp. 379-81. See also above, p. 8.

[74]Hall, *North American Supply*, pp. 160-63, 183-85, 187-89; Morgenthau Diary, Oct. 29, 1940, 326:13-58. Typical examples of the Layton-War Department talks are in the Stimson Diary, Oct. 17, 22, 1940.

because of British lack of enthusiasm for the plan, its implementation was delayed, and with the passage of the Lend-Lease Act it became meaningless and was dropped. Instead, the British concentrated on their "A" program. The Secretary for War, Anthony Eden, typified the British reaction by claiming that the ten-division scheme would cripple their Army. In a letter to Churchill written on November 30, Eden accused the United States of sacrificing its stated policy of all aid to Britain in favor of "an almost entirely American policy." Although admitting this was not Purvis' fault, he recommended that the head of the B.P.C. be a Minister and have the full authority of the War Cabinet behind him.[75] If this was a veiled criticism of Purvis, it is one of the few that has come to light.

From the British viewpoint, one of the successes of the Layton mission was that it forced the United States to realign its sights in matters of production. In the face of the requests for war materials which Layton presented to Roosevelt and Morgenthau, it quickly became clear that the existing production plans in America could not hope to meet the British requests and American rearmament needs at the same time. On October 25, Purvis wired London that "the critical moment had arrived for action from the highest quarters," and he expressed his conviction that the Administration had been convinced that it could not maintain its peacetime economy and still meet British and American military orders.[76] Early that afternoon, Roosevelt decided to make a public commitment along those lines and told Morgenthau to have Purvis obtain a letter from Churchill. As Morgenthau put it, he wanted a statement from the Prime Minister "in Churchill's own language—he is a writer—that the President can use to the Boston Irish." The Secretary made it clear that the purpose of the President's speech was to announce the new British purchasing program, and he recommended that Purvis contact William Allen White's committee and get their assistance in polishing up any draft.[77]

Churchill responded quickly and on October 27 dispatched a message to Roosevelt, via Purvis and Morgenthau. Actually, the message was—at least for Churchill—relatively dull and uninspiring. It said little that had not been repeated time and again since May, and the thing Roosevelt apparently wanted most—ringing and impelling phrases—was absent. It was a pedestrian recounting of all the worldwide British

[75]Eden, *The Reckoning*, pp. 203-4. Stettinius, *Lend-Lease* pp. 51-52, states that Layton proposed the "B" program and that those divisions were to be stationed in the Middle East. He believes it was a distinct step toward Lend-Lease, but from the other evidence that seems highly questionable. Leighton and Coakley, *Global Logistics*, p. 38, also claim the "B" program was Layton's idea and give Hall, *North American Supply*, as their authority. Hall clearly states that the proposal was made by the Americans.

[76]As quoted in Hall, *North American Supply*, p. 210.

[77]Morgenthau Diary, Oct. 25, 1940, 325:45-52.

commitments and presented the usual plea for faster delivery of airplanes. The only aspect that could be considered even mildly new was the very complete admission that American supplies were necessary for British survival, an admission that must have pained the Prime Minister even though its truth had long been apparent. A memorandum was attached which listed the supplies that the Layton mission had worked out, and though the language was technical, the impact of that list was far greater than Churchill's rhetoric. Requests for such items as 10 destroyers per month as of April, 1941; 50 PBY planes; 20 million rounds of 50-caliber ammunition; 1,000 30-caliber machine guns; and an open-ended plea for merchant vessels were frightening when added to American military requirements and then compared to the production levels.[78]

Before passing on the message to the White House, Purvis attached a draft statement which refuted the accusation of the Republicans that the Administration had failed to live up to its promise of all aid short of war. Although Roosevelt told Morgenthau that he liked the Churchill-Purvis drafts, it is difficult to find evidence of this in his speech as it was ultimately delivered in Boston on October 30. He did announce the new British purchases—12,000 more planes and an unspecified amount of ordnance—and coupled it with a brief but clear warning that more plants would have to be constructed. But this was no frontal attack designed to sweep aside opposition and to prompt action as Purvis had hoped, nor was it the policy commitment of great magnitude that some historians have taken it to be. Nevertheless, brief and underplayed as it was, a promise had been made to increase aid to Britain substantially—and only a few days before the election. Those who point a finger at Roosevelt and flatly accuse him of consciously misleading the American public regarding aid to Britain have not carefully examined his Boston speech. At Boston the President provided an intentionally small but unmistakable glimpse of his belief that further aid to Britain required public and eventually Congressional approval. Without having worked out the details or even the broad concepts, the President had taken a step toward the Lend-Lease Act.[79]

[78]Churchill's message and the attached memo are in *FR*, 1940, III, 16-18.

[79]Langer and Gleason, *The Undeclared War*, p. 189, assert that "it is not easy to exaggerate the importance of President Roosevelt's statement at Boston," which seems to me to be an exaggeration. The Boston address is reprinted in Roosevelt, *Papers and Addresses* (1940), pp. 514-24. The material on the background to the speech is found in Hall, *North American Supply*, pp. 210-11; Blum, *From the Morgenthau Diaries*, II, 191-94; Langer and Gleason, *The Undeclared War*, pp. 187-90. Churchill makes no mention of it in his memoirs. The orders that were finally placed differed somewhat from what Roosevelt approved in principle. A good brief rundown of this is in Leighton and Coakley, *Global Logistics*, pp. 38-39. Historians have generally concentrated on Roosevelt's promise that "your boys are not going to be sent into any foreign wars," while ignoring other elements of the speech.

Although Layton eventually spent most of his time trying to unravel the tangled problem of ordnance types, financial questions continually arose. On October 2 he wrote Morgenthau and asked that the principle of the United States paying the initial capital expense for orders that were complementary to both armies, which Roosevelt had approved in July, be put into practise.[80] But it was easy to ask for help and hard to agree on common types for weapons.

The press attempted to dig up some information about the Layton mission but got nowhere. At a press conference on October 4, Roosevelt refused to comment on reports that the British were pressuring America for increased aid, including money, but he did deny that the United States was not living up to its promise of "all aid short of war."[81]

All the while, appalling statistics continued to come in. On October 10, the British Embassy informed Morgenthau that the new estimate of the adverse balance of payments for the sterling area was up from $1.6 billion to $3.5 billion,[82] and the next day the State Department received a similarly gloomy report from the financial section of its London Embassy. The memo analyzed the British financial position in some detail. It was highly complimentary about British efforts to organize their own internal finances and discussed the co-operation the Empire had provided. But the statistical tables that were attached indicated the seriousness of the British money crisis. Appendix VII to the report stated that Britain's cumulative import surplus over exports and re-exports was £618,000,000 by August, 1940—which jibed with the figures given to Morgenthau by the British Embassy. More forbidding was that this drain continued to rise from £40 to £60 million per month. The memorandum's conclusions betrayed the persistent belief among State Department officials that Britain was holding back some kind of financial reserve. While predicting the British would ask for credits as soon as the American elections were decided, the sale of Britain's gold, securities, and direct investments—particularly those in South America—received equal emphasis.[83]

In spite of the deepening financial crisis, the upcoming election restrained the British from publicly requesting credits. In a speech written by Lothian and delivered by Sir Walter Layton in Boston on October 17, there were no references to money, but privately, Lothian told Morgenthau that Sir Frederick Phillips would like to make another trip to America in order to "raise the red light signal in

[80]FEA records, files of the President's Liaison Committee, Philip Young files, "reports of Sir Walter Layton."

[81]Roosevelt Papers, PPF 1-P, vol. 16, p. 255, press conference of Oct. 4, 1940.

[82]Morgenthau Diary, Oct. 10, 1940, 322:77-78.

[83]U.S. Embassy in London to Hull, Oct. 11, 1940, State Dept., 841.51/1633.

connection with our finances."[84]   Although Roosevelt continued to express a desire to see Britain liquidate her Latin-American investments, and Morgenthau seemed primarily concerned with the slowness of British sales of direct investment held in the United States, there could be no doubt that Phillips was not coming to discuss those matters. Ten days earlier he had cabled Morgenthau that he was highly doubtful that such sales would provide any meaningful amount of dollars, and the Secretary admitted that the time had passed when Britain could make the most of such procedures. Extensive credits were on the Englishman's mind, and everyone knew it. Roosevelt and Morgenthau were ready to talk to Phillips but told him to wait until after the election. Morgenthau made his position clear in a meeting with his staff when he said that he "would never be part and parcel of lending them money again, and if we got to the place where they couldn't pay, I would recommend that we give it to them."[85]

On October 21, Morgenthau told his staff that for the next two weeks he would be preoccupied with the campaign and unable to handle details,[86] yet to the British, the major detail—money—had been subject for many months to a different kind of "red light signal"—a stoplight instead of a warning. With the election at hand, Lothian had judiciously chosen to return to England for brief talks. Forced to bide their time, the British impatiently awaited the outcome of what Churchill once called America's "quadrennial madness."

Although his majority was substantially reduced from its high-water mark in 1936, Roosevelt still achieved victory at the polls. American elections are not in the parliamentary tradition and cannot be interpreted as votes of confidence on any single issue, no matter how important it may be. Certainly the election of 1940 is no exception. Langer and Gleason aptly state: "In sum . . . the effect of the 1940 election on the general form and direction of American foreign policy was negative, almost to the point of anticlimax."[87]   Just why Roosevelt won can be argued, but the over-all effect of his victory is a little clearer. The German Chargé d'Affaires cabled his government from Washington that the President had conducted his campaign with "extreme caution" and in foreign affairs had left himself virtually

---

[84]Address to the Associated Industries of Massachusetts, Oct. 17, 1940, Philip H. Kerr, 11th Marquis of Lothian, *The American Speeches of Lord Lothian: July 1939 to December 1940* (London, New York, and Toronto: Oxford University Press, 1941), pp. 122 ff. Morgenthau Diary, Oct. 15, 1940, 321:325. Lothian's statement is also quoted in Blum, *From the Morgenthau Diaries*, II, 199; and Hall, *North American Supply*, p. 253, but the wording they quote is slightly though not significantly different from the entry in the Morgenthau Diary.

[85]Morgenthau Diary, Oct. 5, 1940, 322:76. Hall, *North American Supply*, pp. 253, 273-75. Morgenthau is quoted in Langer and Gleason, *The Undeclared War*, p. 188.

[86]Morgenthau Diary, Oct. 21, 1940, 327, pt. 2:15.

[87]Langer and Gleason, *The Undeclared War*, p. 212.

complete freedom of action. Certainly this does not correspond with the interpretation given Roosevelt's campaign promises by his critics, but it is significant that the Germans saw a difference between "campaign oratory" and meaningful commitments.[88]

[88]Thomsen to the Foreign Ministry, Nov. 6, 1940, *DGFP*, XI, no. 292, pp. 476-77. A typical critic, Frederic R. Sanborn, in *Design For War*, p. 168, flatly asserts that Roosevelt won in 1940 because he convinced the electorate he would keep America out of war.

PART TWO

THE CRISIS FACED AND SOLVED
NOVEMBER 1940–MARCH 1941

CHAPTER IV

"MONEY—ABOVE ALL, READY MONEY"

Money—above all, ready money. There was the hobble which cramped the medieval kings; and even now it counts somewhat."[1] Churchill wrote those words in 1939 about England's King Edward IV, but when he was rereading them in 1950, just prior to their publication in *A History of the English-Speaking Peoples,* he must have recalled late 1940. As he knew all too well, the nature of Britain's financial crisis in November, 1940, made those casual words uncomfortably close to prophecy.

From the outset of his ministry, Churchill and his representatives had warned Roosevelt that cash payments could not last, but the President had invariably put them off with vague promises and generalities. The Prime Minister, in attempting to anticipate England's money problem, had met with precious little success in getting America to plan ahead. There were many reasons for Roosevelt's reluctance to make the long-term commitment Churchill wanted: the major ones were public and Congressional opinion, the desire to avoid another war-debts problem, and the lack of finished goods available in America for Britain to purchase. Just as important was Roosevelt's style. During the Yalta conference in 1945, Lord Moran, Churchill's personal physician, recalled his initial impression of the President when they met shortly after the Pearl Harbor attack: "He doesn't like thinking things out, but waits for situations to develop and then adapts himself to them."[2] That was hardly a novel characterization of

---

[1]Winston S. Churchill, *A History of the English-Speaking Peoples,* 4 vols. (New York: Dodd, Mead and Co., 1956-58), vol. I, *The Birth of Britain,* p. 474.

[2]Lord Moran (Sir Charles Wilson), *Churchill: Taken From the Diaries of Lord Moran; The Struggle for Survival, 1940-1965* (Boston: Houghton Mifflin Co., 1966), p. 239.

Roosevelt's methodology, but never was it more apt than during the development of Great Britain's enormous dollar deficit in the first year of World War II. With Roosevelt safely re-elected, England anticipated speedy action that would provide the necessary supply of ready money. The British were to be disappointed–temporarily.

Two days after the election, at a meeting of the Administration officials most concerned with the aid to Britain program, procrastination again seemed the order of the day. There was no mention of Britain's financial problem, only references to the fact that Sir Frederick Phillips was coming in December to discuss the question. Phillips' new mission may well have brought on a certain amount of stalling within the American government, since it seemed a waste of effort to worry about the question of credit until the Englishman arrived with additional data. Morgenthau took the election to mean that increased aid to Britain was publicly supported and proposed sending some of the new B–24 "Liberator" bombers, commenting at the time that if the Cabinet did not like the idea he was willing to take it to Congress. Though he had no specific legislation in mind, he clearly believed the time had come for Congress to take some action.[3]

At a Cabinet meeting held on November 8, the discussion continued but remained restricted to gimmicks designed to evade existing restrictions rather than proposals that would provide any over-all solution. Roosevelt decided to put into practice a "rule of thumb" he had mentioned earlier to Morgenthau which would split American airplane production with Britain on a fifty-fifty basis. Later that day the President publicly announced his support for such an arrangement. Though a promising idea, the Justice Department told Stimson a few days later, that the law would not permit the Administration to put it into effect.[4]

When the question of money came up at the Cabinet meeting, Roosevelt seemed unconcerned. He readily admitted that loans or credits would have to be eventually arranged but stated that the $2.5 billion of credits and property that the British held in the United States would first have to be converted into dollars and spent. He gave no reason for this precondition, but it would seemingly indicate that the President had not yet freed himself from the concept of conventional financing and again raises the suspicion that Roosevelt hoped to force Britain to sell her American holdings. Yet in almost the same breath he brought up a novel solution which he had discussed with Morgenthau and Purvis over lunch the day before the Cabinet meeting.

---

[3]Morgenthau Diary, Nov. 7, 1940, 330:75; Langer and Gleason, *The Undeclared War*, pp. 215-16.

[4]Langer and Gleason, *The Undeclared War*, pp. 216-18. Hall, *North American Supply*, p. 211. Roosevelt, *Papers and Addresses* (1940), pp. 563-64.

Significantly, Roosevelt operated on the assumption that it would be about six months before British financial resources were exhausted. Purvis had outlined Britain's disturbing losses of merchant ships due to Germany's submarine attacks, and the President almost casually ruminated aloud about the possibility of building ships and then lending them to England. He brought up the notion at the Cabinet meeting and, according to Harold Ickes, added the proposal that they lease "any other property that was loanable, returnable, and insurable."[5] There is no record of any discussion of this suggestion, and the context of Ickes' report leads one to believe it was a casual remark. But it did not die there. The question of leasing ships surfaced from within the bureaucracy about three weeks later, and the more general leasing proposal Roosevelt brought up appears to be a logical extension of the "fire hose" story of August.

The isolationists attempted to anticipate the expected Administration push to increase aid to Britain and remove cash restrictions, when Senator Nye introduced a resolution calling for a Congressional investigation of all property, real and otherwise, in the United States owned by Great Britain and the British Empire. The clear implication was that Britain was a long way from actually needing financial aid—an argument that cropped up again during the Lend-Lease hearings. The bill was referred to the Foreign Relations Committee and never heard of again.[6] Before the bill could be dealt with by the committee, the session ended. When the Seventy-seventh Congress convened in January, Roosevelt took the initiative.

Publicly, the Administration ignored the growing money problem, but under the surface the pressures were building. In England, the Priorities Board had, on November 9, approved the purchasing of 12,000 additional airplanes, but at the same time the question in Churchill's mind was where was the money coming from.[7] The obvious answer was the United States, but the problem was when, and how? The Administration's attempt to play down the British dollar shortage did not hide its existence from the more well-informed public, and the Treasury Department received numerous suggestions on how to handle the situation. Virtually all proposed some sort of end run around the Johnson and Neutrality Acts, but by November

[5]Ickes, *The Lowering Clouds*, entry for Nov. 9, 1940, p. 367. Langer and Gleason, *The Undeclared War*, p. 217, mention the idea of leasing cargo ships but do not mention either Roosevelt's comment regarding British assets in America or the extending of the leasing concept to other items. Hall, *North American Supply*, pp. 256-57. Stettinius, *Lend-Lease*, pp. 62-63, states that Roosevelt had mentioned the leasing of American merchant ships to Britain during a meeting of the Defense Advisory Commission late in the summer of 1940.

[6]S. Res. 334, *CR*, 76th Cong., 3d sess., LXXXVI, pt. 12, Nov. 25, 1940, pp. 13718-19.

[7]Churchill, *Their Finest Hour*, pp. 554-58.

both Roosevelt and Morgenthau were convinced such a course of action was out of the question.[8]

The German government quickly grasped the propaganda potential in American reluctance to face the money crisis. On November 19, an official in the German Information Department recommended that future German propaganda in the United States stress, among other things, the idea that America was being deceived by England as to the real value of English holdings in Latin America and East Asia. As so often happened in the Foreign Ministry during Hitler's regime, the Washington Embassy succumbed somewhat to its own propaganda and actually reported that Bernard Baruch and Morgenthau were advising Roosevelt not to provide credits to Britain as the United States had in 1916 and 1917 but to make it pay until it was out of money. The author of the report, Chargé d'Affaires Hans Thomsen, ignored the effect of domestic political pressures and inferred that such advice was motivated by a desire to bankrupt the British.[9] Morgenthau consistently warned that financial aid to the English could pass Congress only when the country at large was convinced that there was no other choice, but never did he indicate any desire to use the wartime situation as a means of bettering America's economic position vis-à-vis Great Britain. There is no hard evidence to show that any major official in the American government supported such a position, although occasionally a little subconscious glee over Britain's discomfort crept in.[10]

Roosevelt outlined the reasons for his reluctance to act in a letter to King George VI. In discussing the destroyer-bases deal, the President noted that if he had submitted the proposal to the Legislative branch first, as the "legalists" had demanded, "it would still be in the tender care of the Committees' of the Congress!" Obviously Roosevelt hoped to avoid the problem of how to provide and pay for aid to Britain until he was sure of the end result. As Stimson pointed out one

---

[8]FEA records, President's Liaison Committee, files of Philip Young, folder titled "Britain-General and Misc., vol. I," box 39. This folder contains many proposals, some from bankers with an obvious self-interest, others from the general public. None contained anything resembling the Lend-Lease idea.

[9]Memo by an official of the Information Department, Nov. 19, 1940, *DGFP*, XI, no. 359, pp. 624-27. The basic ideas in this memo were probably outlined by the German Ambassador to the United States (*in absentia*), Hans H. Dieckhoff. Certainly they closely follow his line of reasoning. See Warren F. Kimball, "Dieckhoff and America: A German's View of German-American Relations, 1937-1941," *The Historian*, XXVII (Feb., 1965), 218-43. An example of such propaganda can be found in the *New York Times*, Nov. 27, 1940. Thomsen to the Foreign Ministry, Nov. 30, 1940, *DGFP*, XI, no. 427, pp. 751-52.

[10]One such example was a speech by W. L. Batt, a deputy commissioner for one of the N.D.A.C.'s divisions, in which he stated that British economic imperialism was dead and the days of her financial aristocracy were ended. N.D.A.C. press release, Dec. 4, 1940, Morgenthau Diary, 335:255.

evening to Grenville Clark, even a relatively small request by Britain for relief from having to pay cash for capital expansion of production facilities faced all sorts of legal obstacles and Congressional opposition.[11] A few days later, the Secretary began what ultimately became a successful attempt to obtain the support of the defeated Republican Presidential candidate, Wendell Willkie, for the preparedness program and eventually for Lend-Lease. He got in touch with one of Willkie's aides, George Roberts, who replied that Willkie was too exhausted to think straight at the time but suggested that Stimson and Willkie meet in the near future.[12] Although the specific program had not been devised, the campaign to obtain bipartisan support for aid to Britain was underway.

November also found the major United States military leaders solidly supporting increased aid to Britain. On November 12, Admiral Stark sent a memo to Secretary Knox which proposed four alternative grand strategies regarding Europe and Asia. The fourth of these, Plan "D" (DOG), was the one finally adopted by the military and the two military secretaries. Although Roosevelt never formally endorsed it, Cordell Hull claimed the President was in "general agreement" with it.[13]

Apparently, Plan DOG had begun in April, 1940, with discussions held at the Naval War College, but not until late October did it finally work its way to high-level staff planning. It was designed to spell out American policy in the event of war and envisaged a conflict in two theaters. It called for offensive action in Europe and defense against Japan—exactly what was eventually done. The adoption of Plan DOG by the military made certain policies almost inevitable. Joint planning with the British was an obvious corollary, but more important for the moment was that aid to Britain was, in terms of such planning, clearly in the best interests of the United States. Although General Marshall was slower to accept the idea, once he did so in late November he flatly stated that the Administration had to "resist proposals that do not have for their immediate goal the survival of the British Empire and the defeat of Germany." Since it assumed that Germany was a threat to the Western Hemisphere, aid to Britain was now a matter of American national security. The remarkably close relationship between the British and American navies is borne out by the fact that only ten days after Stark sent his memo to Knox, Churchill mentioned

[11]Roosevelt to King George VI, Nov. 22, 1940, Roosevelt Papers, PSF, "Great Britain, 1939-40"; Stimson Diary, Nov. 14, 1940.

[12]Roberts to Stimson, Nov. 19, 1940, Stimson Papers.

[13]As quoted in Matloff and Snell, *Strategic Planning*, p. 28. Stark's memo to Knox was sent on to Hull and is in Hull Papers, box 48.

it in a note to his naval chiefs and instructed them to do all they could to support Stark.[14]

On November 23, the British Ambassador, returning from his election vacation in London, provided the catalyst that forced the Roosevelt Administration publicly to face up to the question of the British dollar shortage. As he alighted from the plane at New York's LaGuardia Airport, Lothian held an impromptu press conference. Casually and without elaboration he flatly stated: "Well boys, Britain's broke; it's your money we want."[15] This took the dollar problem from the seldom-read analytical columns on the editorial pages to a headline on page 1. It could hardly have been a spur of the moment indiscretion since Lothian willingly repeated it for the newsreels and other reporters a few minutes later. The Ambassador refused to comment on how this was to be done and would not discuss the question of repeal of the Johnson and Neutrality Acts. All he would admit was that Britain had to have financial aid in 1941 and that Sir Frederick Phillips was coming over to discuss such problems. The urgency of his warning was mitigated only slightly when he told reporters in Washington, later that day, that Britain could pay cash only for six months to a year longer.[16]

The precise origins of Lothian's statement are not clear. His biographer, who was also an editor of a portion of the official British History of the Second World War and thus was privy to the British government documents, calls the Ambassador's remarks a "calculated indiscretion" and encloses the phrase in quotation marks, but he does not footnote it. Certainly it is absurd to assume that such a remark by the British Ambassador at that particular time could have slipped out accidentally. A person of his experience and position knew full well that such a frank admission would have broad repercussions, and it seems logical to suspect that just such publicity was his purpose. More important, Lothian had just returned from a month's stay in England, during which time he had consulted with Churchill. Also in England at the same time was Arthur Purvis, who, better than anyone else, understood the political problems that beset the Roosevelt Administration.

[14]As quoted in Leighton and Coakley, *Global Logistics*, p. 43. Plan DOG is discussed in detail in most of the sources for the period, although none of them give the story in its entirety. Among the most informative are Pogue, *Marshall*, pp. 122-27; Langer and Gleason, *The Undeclared War*, pp. 221-23; Matloff and Snell, *Strategic Planning*, pp. 25-28; Watson, *Chief of Staff*, pp. 118-21. For Churchill's note, see Churchill to First Lord and First Sea Lord (Gen. Ismay to see), Nov. 22, 1940, *Their Finest Hour*, pp. 890-91.

[15]As quoted in Wheeler-Bennett, *King George VI* p. 521. The London *Times*, Nov. 25, 1940, does not record Lothian's use of the phrase "Britain's broke" but quotes him as saying that England needed war goods "and perhaps a little financial help."

[16]The *New York Times* gave Lothian's statement a headline equal to those given Rumania's joining the Axis and Greek victories in Albania. On the same day the paper carried a column written by Howard Callender which briefly mentioned that it was certain British dollar reserves would soon be exhausted. *New York Times*, Nov. 24, 1940.

Churchill points out in his memoirs that he and Lothian fully discussed the entire question of American aid to Britain and the financial crisis, and they agreed the time had come to submit detailed lists of British requirements even if they were not met. In fact, it was this decision that finally resulted in the now famous Churchill letter to Roosevelt which was "finally dated" December 8, 1940.[17] Yet, in spite of the evident significance of Lothian's remarks to the press, Churchill made no mention whatsoever of them in his memoirs. In addition, although the Ambassador received a mild rebuke from the Chancellor of the Exchequer, Sir Kingsley Wood, for not checking with the Treasury first, no such reprimand from Churchill is recorded. Evidently the Prime Minister was impatient, for on December 2 he complained that American actions since the election had been disappointing, although he admitted it was possible Mr. Roosevelt was waiting for the election fever to cool down. Others have said Lothian was somewhat remorseful after speaking out, but that is strictly hearsay evidence. If he did have any misgivings, they were brought on by the misinterpretation that Britain was flat broke instead of merely short of dollars. When Morgenthau administered a dressing down to Lothian about a week after the Ambassador's remarks, the Englishman said he had spoken out on his own authority—but he could hardly have said anything else under the circumstances.[18] Negative evidence is, at best, inconclusive, but one suspects that the calculation behind the indiscretion may well have been made at the highest level.

Lothian's purposes in dropping his bombshell are far less clouded. In a letter to Morgenthau written two days after his arrival, Lothian told the Secretary he had made the statement because of the imminent arrival of Sir Frederick Phillips for further talks about financial matters. The Ambassador believed the "public initiative in asking for a discussion" should come from the British in an informal way. He reminded Morgenthau that just prior to his departure for England before the election, he had warned that the "red light had gone up about finance" and that when he arrived in Britain, plans were already being made to broach the subject. A few days later, Lothian informed his London superiors that Americans were "saturated with illusions that we have vast resources available that we

[17]Butler, *Lord Lothian*, p. 307; Churchill, *Their Finest Hour*, pp. 554-58; Butler, *Grand Strategy*, II, 418. There are no records available of any discussions between the Prime Minister and Purvis, but they obviously took place since in a message to Morgenthau delivered by Lothian, Churchill thanked the Secretary of the Treasury for all his help and said he had heard his work praised by Purvis and others. See letter from Lothian to Morgenthau, Nov. 25, 1940, Morgenthau Diary, 331:273.

[18]Butler, *Lord Lothian*, p. 307; Hancock and Gowing, *British War Economy*, p. 235; Hall, *North American Supply*, p. 258; *New York Times*, Nov. 25, 1940; Blum, *From the Morgenthau Diaries*, II, 199-200. When Lothian returned to Washington, he said to his staff, "Oh, yes, I know what I said, and I know that I shall get my head washed for it both in London and in Washington, but it is the truth none the less." Lord Casey, *Personal Experience, 1939-1946* (New York: David McKay Co., 1962), p. 43.

have not yet disclosed and that we ought to empty this vast hypothetical barrel before we ask for assistance." As two official British historians put it: "The United States Administration was fertile of suggestions to the British for stripping themselves bare." Even the Germans could see what Lothian was trying to accomplish. In report on a meeting between Lothian and President Roosevelt held on November 26, the German Embassy told Berlin that it had learned from a reliable source that the Englishman was "greatly depressed" because the question of credits had not been discussed.[19]

With the press chasing down every rumor and angle they could find, the general Administration policy quickly began to emerge. On Monday, November 25, the *New York Times* noted that Lothian's statement had come only twenty-four hours after Roosevelt had told reporters the United States was not considering any specific financial aid programs for Britain. The paper also reported that "informed sources" said financial aid would require changes in existing laws. The following day, Senator Barkley, after an hour and one-half meeting with Roosevelt and the other Congressional leaders, told the press that the question of credits for Britain would not come up in the current session of Congress—which was due to adjourn in December. That same day, Secretary of State Hull refused to comment on Lothian's remarks. When the reporters tried to pin him down as to which department would handle any negotiations for credits, Hull said he did not want to get into any interdepartmental controversy—though he must have ached for the chance to take a swipe at Morgenthau. Commenting on a British Press Association suggestion that Britain might trade war goods for some West Indian islands, Hull, who later supported such a swap, said he could not discuss that until it was fully talked out inside the Executive branch.[20]

Roosevelt played down the money question even more effectively at a press conference on November 26, the day after his conference with Lothian at the White House. When a reporter asked whether the British Ambassador had presented any specific requests for "additional help," Roosevelt wisecracked: "I am sorry, I shall have to disappoint quite a number of papers; nothing was mentioned in that regard at all, not one single thing—ships or sealing wax or anything else." The press corps laughed and did not bring up the question again

[19]Lothian to Morgenthau, Nov. 25, 1940, State Dept., 841.51/1691; Hancock and Gowing, *British War Economy*, p. 233. Lothian's evaluation is immediately followed by their own comment. Thomsen to the Foreign Ministry, Nov. 30, 1940, *DGFP*, XI, no. 427, 751-52.

[20]*New York Times*, Nov. 25, 1940; Nov. 26, 1940; memo of press conference, Nov. 25, 1940, Hull Papers, box 124. *New York Times*, Nov. 26, 1940. The British Press Association proposal is reported in *ibid.*, Nov. 25, 1940. The existence of a faction within the Administration which believed Britain should sell her Latin-American holdings before the United States should give financial aid is mentioned in *ibid.*, Nov. 27, 1940.

that day. Lothian echoed Roosevelt's remarks when he spoke to reporters about his talk with the President. Morgenthau was typically unsubtle. At a press conference on November 28, a reporter tried to bring up the "subject of loans or other financial aid to Britain," but Morgenthau bluntly stated he was not prepared to air his views at that time, and changed the topic. Yet the next day a Treasury Department press release lent credence to Lothian's warning. It summarized the dollar balances in the United States of foreign nations and noted that although most nations were building up such balances, Great Britain had withdrawn $320,924,000 between August 30, 1939 and September 4, 1940. In addition, the release called attention to the fact Britain had made heavy sales of gold in order to pay for purchases of war materials.[21]

Roosevelt apparently made use of his favorite tactic of leading with someone else's chin when, on November 26, the same day he denied knowledge of any specific proposals, the White Committee put out a press release that asked the President to take stronger measures to provide aid to England. It called for keeping open the sea lanes—a not so veiled reference to convoying—and a massive shipbuilding program, with the ships that were constructed either rented or leased to the British. Since Roosevelt is known to have used the White Committee for trial balloons, his earlier advocacy of the ship-leasing idea indicates the Committee's press release began in the White House.[22]

Although there was no great outcry of public support for the ship-leasing plan, Morgenthau brought it up with Frank Knox and Admiral Emory S. Land, head of the Maritime Commission. Land opposed it, claiming the United States could not support a large fleet of tramp steamers returned by Britain after the war. In addition, the British did not want the same type of ships the Maritime Commission wanted to build. Although Morgenthau continued to give it desultory support, all three men agreed that far broader measures were needed to solve Britain's over-all problems, and the plan was never pushed any further. Nevertheless, as John Morton Blum points out, it "suggested a useful direction of thought."[23]

Unperturbed as the Administration appeared on the surface, privately officials expressed both annoyance and disbelief at Lothian's

[21]Roosevelt, *Papers and Addresses* (1940), p. 581; *New York Times*, Nov. 26, 1940; Morgenthau Press Conferences, press conference of Nov. 28, 1940, vol. 16, p. 92; Press Releases of the Treasury Department, Henry Morgenthau, Jr., Papers (Franklin D. Roosevelt Library, Hyde Park, N. Y.), vol. 22, release dated Nov. 29, 1940.

[22]Langer and Gleason, *The Undeclared War*, p. 224; Johnson, *The Battle Against Isolation*, p. 171. Johnson's study of the Committee to Defend America (the White Committee) contains numerous examples of Roosevelt's use of it to send up ideas without personally sponsoring them.

[23]Blum, *From the Morgenthau Diaries*, II, 200-201; Langer and Gleason, *The Undeclared War*, p. 219.

revelation. Cordell Hull remained unconvinced that Britain was at the end of her financial rope—a belief he maintained throughout the period prior to the actual introduction of the Lend-Lease Bill. Roosevelt and Morgenthau were worried that Lothian's bluntness would alienate Congress. The "court-packing" bill in 1937 and the unseccessful attempt to revise the neutrality legislation in the summer of 1939 made the President reluctant to try any frontal assaults on Congress. Rather, as with the destroyer-bases deal, he apparently hoped that the public initiative for financial aid to Britain would come from Congress itself.[24]

Reliable public evidence of the Administration's annoyance came in an article in the *Washington Post* on November 26, which quoted a "high authority" as saying the Lothian request for assistance was "premature," a statement that brought on a British protest. The piece went on to mention the fact that Britain still owned some eight billion dollars worth of untapped investments in the Western Hemisphere—a figure suspiciously close to the President's nine billion dollar figure for the same assets. The article also noted that the Johnson Debt-Default Act did not forbid outright gifts or swaps—such as in the destroyer-bases deal.[25]

Morgenthau, in a letter to Hull, wrote that he thought Lothian had shown poor judgment but that he did not want to discuss it in writing with the Ambassador. Morgenthau was also worried about the effect the warning might have on British negotiations with American business, which would now be even more suspicious of Britain's ultimate ability to pay. As Morgenthau noted in his diary after a talk with the British Ambassador on December 2, "It is not difficult to understand why the impression had gotten around in Washington that things are going badly with England after one listens to Lothian." Although Lothian's announcement caused problems, Morgenthau was honest enough to admit, during a chat with the British Ambassador and Sir Frederick Phillips on December 4, that Lothian had forced him and Roosevelt to deal with the money question then and there. Nevertheless, the Secretary remained piqued at Lothian's failure to consult with him or Roosevelt prior to disclosing England's fiscal plight. When he talked to Canadian Prime Minister Mackenzie King on December 5,

---

[24]Hull's attitude is recorded in Morgenthau's Diaries; see Blum, *From the Morgenthau Diaries*, II, 199. As is typical in his memoirs, Hull ignores any sort of controversy and states that Lothian said nothing that he did not already know and understand. Hull, *Memoirs*, I, 871-73. Joseph Alsop maintains that Roosevelt consciously used that sort of strategy. As Alsop put it, Roosevelt never minded being called a "poltroon" for not taking action, so long as the complainers were pushing him in the direction he wanted to go. Alsop interview, May 24, 1967.

[25]Morgenthau Dairy, Nov. 26, 1940, 332:97-98. The British protest is mentioned in the index to volume 332, p. W. See also Hall, *North American Supply*, p. 258.

Morgenthau complained that Lothian's comments had upset the delicate situation and "did not help one damn bit!"[26]

Certainly Morgenthau did not ascribe to the belief that Britain had plenty of money left to spend. Roosevelt told Lothian that his remarks to the press were premature until Britain liquidated her nine billion dollars worth of investments in the Western Hemisphere, but Morgenthau quickly corrected that estimate when he forwarded a memo to the President containing the Treasury's calculation of British resources. The memo estimated the over-all world total of British and British Empire foreign assets at $9,490,000,000, which indicated that Roosevelt's estimate of her Western Hemisphere assets was badly inflated. The note went on to warn that much of the wealth of the Empire could not be liquidated and could serve only as collateral. The Treasury effectively refuted Roosevelt's ideas when it estimated the British dollar deficit between November 1 and June 30, 1941, at $2,105,000,000. The best guess was that this would leave Britain some seventy million dollars short even if she succeeded in liquidating all her existing dollar resources.[27]

British newspapers devoted substantial space to Lothian's statement. They generally registered surprise at the immediacy of the problem, but later editions took note of the fact that the Ambassador's warning came well in advance of the actual crisis. Most seemed to assume that some type of credits would have to be extended, although the *Financial News* did mention British-owned direct investments in the United States as a third source of dollars. The only real criticism was of Lothian's failure to differentiate adequately between Britain's dollar holdings and her over-all financial resources.[28] This confusion over British economic wealth and her lack of dollars cropped up regularly until after the Lend-Lease bill was signed into law.

[26]Morgenthau to Hull, Nov. 28, 1940, State Dept., 841.51/1691; memo by Cochran, Nov. 26, 1940, Morgenthau Diary, 331:295–96. Blum, *From the Morgenthau Diaries*, II, 200. Morgenthau was also referring to some of Lothian's other pessimistic comments, particularly regarding British shipping losses. Morgenthau's comment to Lothian and Phillips is from Hall, *North American Supply*, p. 258. He does not mention it in his diary. The phone conversation with King is in Morgenthau Diary, Dec. 5, 1940, 336:101.

[27]Blum, *From the Morgenthau Diaries*, II, 199. This is the only source that mentions such an exchange between the President and Lothian. It apparently refers to their conversation of November 25–the same one that both Roosevelt and Lothian denied flatly had concerned any discussion of financial questions. The statistics are in memo for the President from Morgenthau, (n.d.), State Dept., 841.51/1691. It is important to differentiate between the estimate of total resources–which is made in dollars–and the estimate of actual dollar resources, which is far lower. Many inside the government failed to make that distinction, including Secretary of State Hull.

[28]Johnson to Hull for the Treasury Dept., Nov. 26, 1940, State Dept., 841.5151/1739. This cable contains a summary, with quotations, of British press reaction to the Lothian press conference of Nov. 23. A copy of this cable can be found in Morgenthau Diary, 331:299-301. See also *New York Times*, Nov. 25, 1940.

From the election until early December, most discussions of the British dollar shortage took place in connection with the wrapup of the Layton mission. These talks centered largely around the "ten-division" or "B" program, which called for the United States to equip fully and supply ten British divisions. Although the British were decidedly unenthusiastic about the plan, they had no reasonable alternative. The negotiations were made more difficult by the obvious tension that existed between Layton and Morgenthau. Morgenthau complained to his staff about articles in the *New York Times* and the *Washington Evening Star* which attributed to Layton complaints about the American procurement program and a recommendation that there should be a single ministry of supply. Morgenthau could not help but take those remarks as a direct criticism of his own work, since he was the primary co-ordinator of such activities for the Roosevelt Administration. It is quite likely that Morgenthau's attitude was reflected by the White House when "Pa" Watson informed the British Embassy that Roosevelt would not be able to see Layton before he left for Britain. In fact, the memo of the request has a big "NO" pencilled in the margin.[29]

Probably the key reason for Morgenthau's dislike of Layton was what appears to have been a gnawing suspicion that he had permanently replaced Purvis, who had returned to England on November 16 for consultations. Early in December, during a telephone conversation with Prime Minister King of Canada, Morgenthau insisted that Purvis be sent back to the United States in place of Layton. The Secretary told King that Layton was "a perfectly nice fellow but a fussy old woman." He further commented that he really did not understand Layton's position, which appears to be a reference to Purvis' extended absence. Morgenthau asked King to tell Churchill that he could not work with Layton, which King did at once. A similar call from Morgenthau to Purvis in London brought a quick response. On December 6, King called Morgenthau to tell him that Churchill was recalling Layton immediately and sending Purvis back to Washington, where he would be under the authority of the Ambassador. Churchill had commented that Purvis' new position had taken "a good many personal adjustments." Morgenthau said he was not too happy about Purvis working for Lothian since the Ambassador's remarks to the press on November 23 had caused him no end of trouble, but he told King not to bother to pass that on to Churchill.[30]

[29]Morgenthau Diary, Nov. 6, 1940, 328:255-56; Roosevelt Papers, OF 48, "England, 1938-40."

[30]Memo of phone conversation between Morgenthau and King, Dec. 5, 1940, Morgenthau Diary, 336:41-44. Memo of phone conversation between Morgenthau and Purvis, Dec. 6, 1940, *ibid.*, pp. 176-80. Pickersgill, *The Mackenzie King Record*, I (1939-44), 183-84. King ignored Morgenthau's instructions and told Churchill of Lothian's unpopularity with the Secretary; see *ibid.*

Although the main barrier facing the "ten-division" plan was the inability of England and the United States to agree on common types for weapons and equipment, the requirement that Britain pay all or part of the plant expansion costs in advance and in cash posed an equally difficult problem. When Layton gave Morgenthau a memo that outlined British desires to order $2.1 billion of supplies, plus $700 million of capital investment and an advance payment of $500 million, Morgenthau immediately wrote a note to Roosevelt requesting to meet with him. Morgenthau warned that since the British could not pay for such orders, it would be unwise to let the matter remain unresolved. The Secretary told his staff that he would not tell William Knudsen, who was in charge of defense production, that Britain had the necessary dollars without some guidance from Roosevelt. Both Layton and Stimson adopted the same tack; that is, since the British orders were for American-type weapons, they complemented American defense and thus could be financed by the United States, but Morgenthau derisively rejected such a plan because of the legal barriers.

On December 1, Roosevelt held a meeting in the White House with Morgenthau, Philip Young, and Harry Dexter White. Morgenthau gave the President the British request and also a Treasury estimate of British financial resources. Roosevelt, upon looking over the latter paper, commented: "Well, they aren't bust—there's lots of money there."[31] The President went on to say that the plants should be built with United States funds so as to have them as a standby for American defense, but he agreed with Young that the British should pay a proportionate share of the construction costs as a surcharge. Morgenthau asked Roosevelt to write a note that he could show to Stimson, Knudsen, and Jesse Jones saying that American funds were to be used for plant expansion. The note simply read:

Secretary of War, Navy, Treasury, and Knudsen.
Planes, munitions, use U.S. RFC funds for plant
Capital on U.S. orders.

Before writing the memo Roosevelt remarked that the ships the British wanted could be financed on the "loan idea," but Morgenthau told him that Admiral Land did not like that plan. After the others left, Morgenthau stayed briefly with Roosevelt and when he emerged told Young and White that he had asked the President if he really wanted the British orders placed. Roosevelt had answered emphatically that he did. Thus, in spite of Morgenthau's warning to the President

[31]Memo of White House conference of Dec. 1, 1940, FEA records, President's Liaison Committee, files of Philip Young, 1940–July, 1941, box 13, file entitled "Reports of Sir Walter Layton."

that the British claimed they did not have the cash to pay for the orders, Roosevelt gave the green light to Great Britain to make commitments they could not meet. The die was cast.[32]

As important as Roosevelt's commitment was his obvious awareness of the need for a broad solution. When Morgenthau told Stimson of the President's decision, the Secretary of War said that Roosevelt believed that the time had come to decide just what the United States would do for England, for doing it this makeshift way was just like doing nothing.[33] The Administration was eager to obtain the up-to-date financial statistics that Sir Frederick Phillips was to bring on December 4, but the broad nature of the crisis was now well known to all and the initiative lay with the United States.

Stimson was likewise convinced that the time had come to turn to Congress. On December 2, he received from Arthur E. Palmer, one of his top young administrators, a memo that flatly warned that even the troublesome "B" program ("ten-division" plan) would require legislation. Palmer believed that the Secretaries of War and the Navy should be given the authority to effect a transfer of title to military property without having to obtain certification from the Chief of Naval Operations and/or the Army Chief of Staff that the goods were not needed for the national defense. He further suggested that the proceeds from such sales be credited to the pertinent appropriation. Without such legislation, the War Department believed interminable legal hassles would result. Without even considering the financial issues, Stimson found himself in an awkward legal position.[34]

Though his memoirs are far from reliable, Cordell Hull claims in them that during a series of meetings held in November and early December, he and his advisers also concluded that the legal barriers in the way of effective aid to Britain should be removed by Congressional action.[35] Thus, by December, 1941, the key members of the Administration, including the President, were all preparing to turn finally to the Legislative branch.

With the political pot beginning to boil furiously, Franklin Roosevelt left Washington on December 2, for a two-week voyage on one of the Navy's cruisers, the U.S.S. *Tuscaloosa.* Just why he left at

---

[32]The sources for the critical White House conference of Dec. 1st, and the events leading up to it are: *ibid.*; Morgenthau Diary, 331:281-82; 333:200-210.; 334:1-3, 100, 188-93; 332:206-17, 223-29; Blum *From the Morgenthau Diaries,* II, 201; Langer and Gleason, *The Undeclared War,* pp. 226-28; Hall, *North American Supply,* pp. 214, 259; Stimson Diary, Nov. 12, 1940; memo re: financing, Nov. 29, 1940, Stimson Papers. A copy of the note authorizing the use of R.F.C. funds is in Morgenthau Diary, Dec. 3, 1940, 335:100.

[33]Langer and Gleason, *The Undeclared War,* p. 228. Memo by Morgenthau of conversation with Knudsen, Dec. 2, 1940, Morgenthau Diary, 334:111-13.

[34]Memo to Stimson from Palmer, Dec. 2, 1940, Stimson Papers. Stimson and Bundy, *On Active Service,* pp. 359-60.

[35]Hull, *Memoirs,* I, 872-73.

that tense moment is not entirely clear. Certainly he was tired after the campaign and needed a vacation. He took only his two military aides, his personal physician, and personal adviser Harry Hopkins, and the stated purpose was to inspect some of the recently acquired base sites that had been negotiated in the destroyer-bases deal. Robert Sherwood wrote that those who knew "Roosevelt's vacation habits suspected that such inspections might be somewhat desultory and superficial and that the main business of each day would be fishing, basking in the sun and spoofing with cronies." Harold Ickes noted that the President had promised to work on a major foreign affairs address during the voyage and had taken with him two or three hundred bundles of correspondence, but he later told Ickes that he had not even opened them. It seems probable that Sherwood's analysis was accurate. Although the British were upset at what seemed to them to be a decidedly cavalier attitude, the President had consistently treated the dollar problem as a future rather than immediate one. His remark of December 1 to the effect that England was not yet out of money indicates that he did not really view the situation with alarm. He left his Cabinet with an ambiguously worded note and the admonition to Morgenthau to "use your imaginations" regarding Britain's financial problems.[36]

December 3, the day Roosevelt's ship pulled out to sea, found those Administration officials concerned with the aid to Britain program scurrying from one conference to another as they attempted to solve the dilemma. Not surprisingly, they concluded eventually that a Presidential decision was needed for any of the programs they could dream up. Although their deliberations apparently did not directly influence the process by which Roosevelt came up with the Lend-Lease concept, they are still of interest. It was these men who would draft the actual legislation and fight for it in the committees of Congress—and their overview of the situation shows through clearly during this two-week period. Equally significant was the obvious dependence of the Administration officials on their President for leadership.

Hull began the day's talks by calling Knox and Stimson to his office that morning for a discussion of the over-all situation. Hull was quite gloomy about the British position, and certainly all three men agreed that her position was critical. Of most concern to them was the inability of American industry to meet the number of orders that British and American military sources wished to place. There was little sense in worrying about increasing aid to Britain if the goods were not available. The three agreed that the country, particularly the business community, was far too complacent about the international situation and needed to be aroused if either the aid program or America's own

[36]Sherwood, *Roosevelt and Hopkins*, p. 222; Ickes, *The Lowering Clouds*, entry for Dec. 1, 1940, p. 376; entry for Dec. 21, 1940, p. 395. Morgenthau Diary, Dec. 3, 1940, 335:100.

defense needs were to be met in time. Later that day, the three Cabinet members met with members of the National Defense Advisory Commission and began planning their education program for the public and the business community.[37]

The first two conferences on that December day had both ignored the immediate problem—money. In fact, the Cabinet member most informed on that question, Henry Morgenthau, had attended neither of them. All the decisions of those talks were essentially meaningless until some solution were found for Britain's lack of dollars. Thus, the afternoon meeting which Secretary Morgenthau called for would have to provide the key to any further moves.

Morgenthau's agenda called for a determination of how the United States government could legally put into effect President Roosevelt's decision that Britain be permitted to place orders for the $2.1 billion worth of goods that Layton had requested. Interestingly, Morgenthau came directly from another meeting with British Air Commodore J. C. Slessor of the British Purchasing Commission at which he had warned the Englishman that Britain should emphasize good news, for Americans would be more likely to help in that case. He cautioned that the United States could not be scared into aiding Great Britain. The scars of Lothian's remarks a week earlier were apparent.[38]

A large group of key Administration personnel gathered in the office of the Secretary of the Treasury at three P.M. Navy Secretary Frank Knox attended, with his Assistant Secretary, James Forrestal—whom Morgenthau had specifically asked Knox to bring. Stimson represented the War Department, with Assistant Secretary Robert Patterson, Arthur Palmer, Assistant Secretary John J. McCloy, and General Marshall. For some unexplained reason Cordell Hull was not present, but State was well represented by Sumner Welles and Herbert Feis, Economic Adviser in the Department. Secretary of Commerce Jesse Jones attended in his capacity as head of the Reconstruction Finance Corporation, and William Knudsen represented the N.D.A.C. Morgenthau was supported by Phil Young, Harry Dexter White, Assistant Secretary Daniel Bell, and one of Morgenthau's long-term economic advisers, Jacob Viner.

The Secretary of the Treasury began the proceedings by filling in everyone on the gist of his White House meeting on December 1. He noted that he had asked to talk to the President because Lothian had publicly "put us on notice that they didn't have enough money."

[37]Langer and Gleason, *The Undeclared War*, pp. 228-29. Hull, *Memoirs*, I, 910, mentions such a conference, but as often is the case, his chronology is not clear. See also Stimson Diary, Dec. 3, 1940; and Stettinius, *Lend-Lease*, pp. 63-65.

[38]Memo of meeting between Morgenthau, Young, and Slessor, Dec. 3, 1940, Morgenthau Diary, 335:29-30.

Morgenthau was convinced that Roosevelt expected them to come up with a workable solution while he was on his two-week cruise.

Harry White followed with a discussion of the British report of their financial position—the same report that Roosevelt had seen on December 1. Britain claimed that the $600 million of gold and $300 million in dollar balances which were left were absolute minimums needed to conduct trade with other parts of the world and that a forced sale of their $850 million of dollar assets would depress the price disastrously. After presenting the British picture, White took strong exception to it. He flatly stated that Britain could sell $300 million of her gold and use $200 million of her dollar resources without harm and disagreed with the British estimates of their assets in other areas, complaining that they had not included British-held assets of German-occupied countries, particularly Allied gold reserves, nor various dollar assets of the Empire nations. He estimated Britain's available collateral at about nine billion dollars. If they posted such collateral, White asserted, they had ample assets to meet their long-range needs. As Robert Patterson pointed out, this implied changing the Johnson and Neutrality Acts to permit the lending of money, and obviously this was what White believed to be the best approach.[39]

Herbert Feis took issue with White as well as with Forrestal, who had shrugged off the claim that a forced sale of British overseas assets would be of little help. Feis believed White's estimate of British overseas assets was badly inflated, particularly those in South America, and stated that three billion dollars collateral was a more reasonable figure. Morgenthau broke off the argument by noting that Sir Frederick Phillips would arrive the next day with complete financial data. He also said that he expected Britain to use the French gold in Canada. He complained that they had been talking about it for two months but that Britain and Canada did not seem to understand that they were at war. The discussion then returned to the two estimates of Britain's money situation as they worked to get the complicated figures straight. No one answered when Frank Knox, unsophisticated and annoyed by details, rhetorically asked the key question point-blank: "We are going to pay for the war from now on, are we?" When Morgenthau asked whether the United States should permit England to place the orders, Knox again cut through the fog of finance to say, "Got to. No question about it."[40] Knudsen backed up Knox by

[39]In view of White's alleged connections with the Soviet Union, it should be noted that, in essence, his proposal would certainly have done great damage to Britain's postwar position and to Anglo-American relations. Even more serious would have been the effect of any British pressure on the Empire and Allied governments-in-exile for access to their assets. This proves nothing, nor does it disprove any of the allegations about White.

[40]Langer and Gleason, *The Undeclared War*, p. 229, misquote the Knox statement as recorded in the Morgenthau Diary by substituting the word "choice" for "question."

querying whether Britain would have to pay cash for the goods after they were made. Morgenthau begged that question by saying that all he wanted to do was meet the President's instructions to place the orders and then sell the goods.

The most reluctant lion was Jesse Jones. Obviously stunned by the enormity of placing over two billion dollars of orders in the name of the R.F.C. for subsequent sale to a nation that claimed to be broke, he asked Morgenthau if he thought the R.F.C. could place the orders and finance plant construction. When Morgenthau answered yes, Jones remarked, "Well, I will have to get a little lower down in the chair." [41] He then warned that it would be foolhardy not to consult Congress first lest the United States end up going to war to protect its investment. There was some truth in Knox's teasing remark that when Jones got through, he would own the British Empire. Morgenthau and Stimson agreed that Congress had to pass on the program, and by this stage of the discussion everyone seemed to be working on the assumption that Britain could scrape up the cash for the two billion dollar order. Stimson commented in his diary that the entire thing had been "a rather unpleasant process" and that he was shocked by the cost of the orders to the United States. After some persuasion, Morgenthau got Stimson to authorize Marshall to certify that the outlay of R.F.C. money would create facilities useful to the national defense. Patterson pointed out that the military could not buy the goods for Britain unless the British money was "in sight," and with that pessimistic remark the meeting adjourned, to meet a week later, Tuesday, December 10.[42]

For all the conferences, the close of the day found relatively little accomplished in terms of concrete decisions. A campaign had begun designed to bring on public and business awareness of the American production problem and its effect on national security, and the various members of the Administration had once again agreed that aid to Britain had to continue. But the key problem—the cash problem—was put off. As critical as the situation was, the American officials seemed generally agreed that the final decision could wait a little longer.

Throughout the deliberations runs the thread of a firm belief in British opulence. Even as late as 1942, a quasi-official history of the Roosevelt Administration's policies in 1940 and 1941 reflected that image. It flatly stated that all Britain needed was credit since she had

[41]Blum, *From the Morgenthau Diaries*, II, 202.

[42]The greatest portion of the treatment of the conference in Morgenthau's office on December 3, 1940, is taken from Morgenthau Diary, Dec. 3, 1940, 335:97-136. Unless otherwise footnoted, all quotations from the conference are taken from that source. Additional information is in Stimson Diary, Dec. 3, 1940; Blum, *From the Morgenthau Diaries*, II, 201-3. Langer and Gleason, *The Undeclared War*, pp. 229-30, give a briefer summary of the meeting using the same sources.

plenty of wealth and was short only of ready money. One aspect of the talks shows through quite clearly. No one was thinking of anything more inventive than loans or credit. In spite of Roosevelt's numerous hints about leasing or lending ships, and his obvious desire to avoid the old war debts problem of World War I, his subordinates were planning on recreating the same system, substituting only the federal government for private lending agencies. If the Lend-Lease concept came from this group, it certainly had never surfaced by the close of December 3. Cordell Hull aptly characterized the situation when he told reporters on December 4 that the financial discussions that were taking place within the Administration were "more sporadic than they are systematic." Morgenthau facilely rejected one proposal forwarded to him by Harold Ickes. The Interior Secretary had received a letter suggesting that the United States buy sterling from Britain, which would provide the necessary exchange funds, but Morgenthau merely noted that such action was prohibited by the Gold Reserve Act. The idea of changing the legislation never seems to have entered his mind, yet it was just that sort of action—called by one historian the "sterling overdraft"—which enabled Canada to provide substantial financial aid to Britain.[43]

The news of the meetings of December 3 soon leaked out, which, added to the announcement the next day that Sir Frederick Phillips had arrived to continue discussions begun in July, had reporters anticipating some type of big news. At press conferences on December 4 and 5, Hull was continually forced to deny any knowledge of a plan calling for extending credits to Britain based on a guarantee against future British gold production. When Jesse Jones told the press he considered the United Kingdom a good credit risk, speculation was rampant. Even the London papers picked it up, and one, the *Times*, accurately noted that whenever such meetings were held by Morgenthau some announcement about aid to Britain always followed.[44]

Morgenthau, in particular, and the Administration, in general, looked to the Phillips mission to solve one of their most troublesome problems, the lack of adequate statistical data about British financial needs and assets. On December 5, Stacy May, the Director of the Bureau of Research and Statistics in the Treasury Department, wrote to Phil Young requesting additional information on orders and payments by the B.P.C. and for as much advance data as possible. At the

[43]Davis and Lindley, *How War Came*, p. 113; memo of press conference, Dec. 4, 1940, Hull Papers, box 124; Morgenthau to Ickes, Dec. 5, 1940, Morgenthau Diary, 336:84; The "sterling overdraft" is fully discussed in Sayers, *Financial Policy*, pp. 324-37.

[44]Memo of press conference, Dec. 4, 1940, Hull Papers, box 124. Memo of press conference, Dec. 5, 1940, *ibid.*; Johnson (London) to Morgenthau, Dec. 5, 1940, Morgenthau Diary, 336:98; Treasury Dept. press release dated Dec. 4, 1940, Morgenthau Papers, vol. 22.

conference in his office on December 3, Morgenthau had told those present that financial decisions would have to await the new information which Phillips was to have, information which Purvis had said would be made available. The Americans did have access to certain elements of the picture. For example, regular and complete reports were submitted on the sales of British-owned dollar securities that had come under the various vesting orders, and the Federal Reserve Bank of New York sent periodic reports of dollar disbursements out of British Empire and French accounts that it held. But these were only a small part of the total British financial position. What Morgenthau wanted was a complete disclosure of the entire British economic status, with an accurate prediction of future requirements. Such a request was unparalleled in the history of alliances, and the British were understandably reluctant to meet it.

Joel Pinsent of the B.P.C. asked Merle Cochran if Congress would demand full disclosure of Britain's financial situation, considering that to give it to them publicly would also give it to the enemy. Cochran replied that it would be necessary and further warned that he had never heard of a secret session of Congress. Yet eventually, public disclosure of the statistics became the only course of action in the light of consistent suspicion, both in the United States and Canada, that Great Britain was not making the maximum financial effort. The fact that her dollar receipts were invariably, if "mysteriously," a little above the estimates—just enough to avoid defaulting—added to those suspicions.[45]

Phillips returned to the United States with instructions to obtain a "gift" of aircraft and munitions, or failing that, a loan that would be repaid after the war to the extent that British exports exceeded her imports in her trade with America. The British Treasury was also quite worried about the problem of selling British direct investments in the United States and had outlined for Phillips a group of three classifications into which such investment sales fell. Although some could be sold profitably, many could not bring a good price because they were either highly dependent upon the British parent company or in the case of insurance companies required maintenance of connections with the British parent for credit and prestige.[46]   Although a com-

---

[45]Memo by Cochran of conversation with Pinsent, Nov. 26, 1940, Morgenthau Diary, 331:295-96. There have been secret sessions of the U.S. Congress, but they have been very rare. Sayers, *Financial Policy*, pp. 386-87, contains a fascinating discussion of American suspicions regarding British finances. Stacy May's letter to Philip Young is dated Dec. 5, 1940, and is in FEA records, President's Liaison Committee, Philip Young files, "Britain-BPC," box 40. For Purvis' promise to Morgenthau, see above, p. 102. The reports on vesting order sales are found throughout the Morgenthau Diary, as are the reports from the New York Federal Reserve Bank.

[46]Hall, *North American Supply*, p. 256; Sayers, *Financial Policy*, p. 369.

plete set of Phillips' instructions are not available to historians, from the material that is open one gets the strong flavor of a British desire to maintain the offensive rather than supinely placing themselves in American hands.

The first meeting between Phillips and Morgenthau took place on Friday, December 6, and proved decidedly unproductive. Phillips talked primarily about the problems of forced sales of securities and direct investments, claiming they would not really help matters, while Morgenthau doggedly pushed for their sale regardless. When Phillips brought up his proposal of either a gift or a loan, Morgenthau bluntly told him that he believed Congress would find both suggestions unacceptable and re-emphasized the need to convince the American public that Britain was making the maximum sacrifices.[47]

During the weekend that followed the initial talks between Morgenthau and Phillips, Winston Churchill, uncharacteristically silent since before the American elections, took the initiative. When Ambassador Lothian had returned to England early in November, he had asked the Prime Minister to write a letter to President Roosevelt regarding finances, and on November 16 Churchill cabled the White House that he was putting together a long letter on the subject. Since it had to be reviewed by the British Chiefs of Staff, the Treasury, and the War Cabinet, it was not ready to be sent back to the United States when Lothian returned later in the month. On November 26 Churchill again telegraphed Roosevelt that he was "still struggling" with the letter, and not until December 7 was it finally ready to go.[48] The message was sent via the British Embassy and was received by the State Department on December 9. Lothian, in his covering letter to Hull, emphasized that Churchill wanted Roosevelt to see the message as soon as possible "and before he gets back to the bustle of Washington." By 2:30 that afternoon it was forwarded to the Navy for further

[47]Morgenthau Diary, Dec. 6, 1940, 336:147-73. Although Morgenthau did not specifically mention it, the whole issue of World War I war debts and the bad taste they had left was most certainly also on his mind. In a ludicrous example of Parkinson's laws in action, the Treasury Department continued to send out notices of payment due on those American loans. By December 15, 1940, the interest had reached about $1,122 million while the principle was $239 million. As late as June 9, 1941, Morgenthau wrote to Hull that he saw no need to change this routine procedure. The basic correspondence on the war loans is in United States, Treasury Dept., Bureau of Accounts, record group 39, Great Britain, box 113, folder entitled "G.B., Loan by the U.S.; notices of payments due" (National Archives, Washington, D. C.).

[48]Churchill, *Their Finest Hour*, p. 558. The message itself is reproduced in *ibid.*, pp. 558-67 and *FR*, 1940, III, 18-26. Churchill states that it was finally dated December 8, but the State Department dated it December 7. This was probably caused by dating it according to local time, since if Churchill sent it early in the morning of December 8, the translation of GMT to EST would have put the date back to December 7. There are a few minor differences between the two copies of the message which usually consist of substituting a synonym for a single word. Whether this was due to the decoding process or some editing by Churchill when he wrote his memoirs is not certain.

delivery by airplane to the President at sea and was due in his hands by late that afternoon.[49]

The greater portion of the message was concerned with the strategic picture, particularly the problem of merchant shipping losses. It summarized British plans for aircraft production and outlined the desperate need for destroyers, merchant ships, and aircraft—needs that only American production could meet. In each case Churchill carefully avoided any mention of money, saying only that "some means" should be found to provide merchant ships, the destroyers should be given, lent, or supplied, and that 2,000 planes ought to be ordered "on joint account." Not until the final paragraphs of the letter did Churchill come to grips with the most pressing logistical problem— dollars. He basically reiterated what Lothian had already made clear, that increased purchasing merely brought closer the day when Britain could no longer pay cash, and he noted that the total of orders placed, orders under negotiation, and plant expansion costs, already came to more than the total of exchange resources available. Although he promised that Great Britain would make every "proper sacrifice," he quickly went on to define what he meant by "proper." He flatly stated it would be against principle to squeeze England dry and hinted that it would have a disastrous effect on British morale. He correctly warned that the postwar American economy would benefit from an economically stable Britain. Without proposing any sort of a solution, he put his Empire at the mercy of the United States:

> Moreover, I do not believe that the Government and people of the United States would find it in accordance with the principles which guide them to confine the help which they have so generously promised only to such munitions of war and commodities as could be immediately paid for. You may be certain that we shall prove ourselves ready to suffer and sacrifice to the utmost for the Cause, and that we glory in being its champions. The rest we leave with confidence to you and to your people, being sure that ways and means will be found which future generations on both sides of the Atlantic will approve and admire.[50]

When Winston Churchill wrote "the rest we leave with confidence to you," he was writing the epitaph to the British Empire as he knew it. For in this case, "the rest" was what really counted.

On Monday, December 9, Morgenthau put his staff to work on some additional figures he had received from the British. He and White agreed that although the British had done a "very workmanlike job," there were still too many gaps. The Treasury wanted to know what Britain would need up to September 1, 1941, and how they proposed to pay for it. It is not clear just when Morgen-

---

[49]Lothian to Hull, Dec. 9, 1940, Hull Papers, box 48. The time schedule for the letter's transmittal to the President is in a handwritten note in the corner of Lothian's letter.

[50]Churchill, *Their Finest Hour*, pp. 566-67.

thau received a copy of Churchill's message to Roosevelt, but if he had seen it before his talk with Phillips that night, Morgenthau gave no indication of it. Morgenthau began by putting heavy pressure on the Englishman. He passed on General Marshall's complaint that Britain seemed to ask for only a little at a time, apparently for fear of scaring off the Administration. Morgenthau also demanded again that Britain take steps to sell its overseas assets, particularly its railroad holdings in Argentina—one of Roosevelt's pet peeves. The Treasury Secretary vociferously demanded full disclosure of the entire British financial picture, including sterling assets, although Phillips kept insisting that since sterling assets were not convertible into dollars there was no need to provide that data. After one particularly heated exchange, Morgenthau finally exploded. He flatly told Phillips that Britain would just have to trust the United States. He harshly warned that the real problem was convincing the American public and Congress that Britain was not trying to pull a fast one and suggested that the attitude he wanted to develop was one where Americans said to themselves, "Well, we can't ask the British to do as much as this. This is too much to ask of them." In essence what Morgenthau asked was for Great Britain to gamble by offering all her financial assets and trust that America would not cash in its chips. Throughout the evening's talks, Morgenthau continually tried to create the impression that all he wanted was an I.O.U., and they could work out the details later. But Phillips refused. Morgenthau attempted to create a new "mental attitude" by asking Britain to do what Beaverbrook had done with the Rolls-Royce engine, that is to send it over now and worry about charges later, but Phillips would not budge. It was a long, frustrating meeting, and as Morgenthau left he remarked that they had been closeted long enough to really give the reporters something to write about.[51]

The following day, Morgenthau met with Hull and somehow came away with the impression that the Secretary of State was the Cabinet's strongest advocate of aid to Britain. As Morgenthau put it, "He is red hot." Even though it did not take long for Morgenthau to return to his old opinion of Hull as a conservative, the impression lasted long enough to provide him with a hearty morale boost in time for the scheduled meeting of Administration leaders in his office that afternoon. The same group that had met on the afternoon of December 3 again convened in Morgenthau's office, with a few extra assistants tacked on. Morgenthau had been shown a copy of Churchill's letter by Hull, probably during their talk earlier that day, and he had been most impressed. He told the meeting that if Phillips did not become just as

[51]Morgenthau Diary, Dec. 9, 1940, 337:43-52, 108-64. Blum, *From the Morgenthau Diaries*, II, 304, contains a briefer summary of the conference.

open and frank as the Prime Minister, Hull should ask Churchill to send over someone else who would co-operate. Jesse Jones picked up where he had left off the week before by saying the R.F.C. could not build plants for the British or have any dealings with them except on a cash basis until Congress approved it, and Stimson agreed. Morgenthau's main concern was whether the orders Britain wished to place would benefit the United States defense effort even if Britain fell. Since the orders would be for American-type goods, General Marshall gave an unqualified affirmative, and Stimson backed him, saying any delay would hurt both countries. Stimson noted in his diary that the figures were "discouraging." Britain wanted five billion dollars worth of orders and capital expenses covered, and her exchange assets were far short of that mark. Harry White insisted that Britain was not revealing all her dollar resources, but Stimson considered him overly suspicious and lacking proof. Morgenthau proposed that they ask Congress to let Britain place the orders with the guarantee that the United States would either take for itself or give to Britain what they could not pay for, but Jones objected that it was too soon to start talking to Congress about giving things away. Although Morgenthau wished to face the entire problem right then, and harshly berated Lothian for having forced their hand before they had a chance to work it out slowly and thoughtfully, the others went along with Jones. Jones then worked out a formula that would permit the R.F.C. to provide enough money to get construction of plant facilities started while Congress was working on the measure. After deciding to send a proposal directly to Roosevelt without first consulting with the British, they worked out a three-point cable. First, it stated that the Army could make good use of the facilities should Britain default. Then it proposed Jones's scheme that the R.F.C. advance $100 million and Britain come up with a $200 million down payment plus $50 million for capital expenses, which would get the program started. The telegram closed by saying that this would tide them over until Congress could take up the financial crisis when it convened in January. Morgenthau passed on the essentials of the plan to Phillips and the B.P.C. that evening, making it crystal clear that this was strictly a stop-gap measure until Congress could take action.[52]

---

[52]The main source for the account of the conference is Morgenthau Diary, Dec. 10, 1940, 338:35-91, 107-14. Stimson Diary, Dec. 10, 1940, contains a few brief remarks. Blum, *From the Morgenthau Diaries*, II, 206-7; and Langer and Gleason, *The Undeclared War*, pp. 233-35, depend upon the same sources. Langer and Gleason incorrectly state that the meeting was called because of Churchill's letter, *ibid.*, p. 233. Actually the meeting had been scheduled when they adjourned a similar conclave on December 3. Langer and Gleason also cite the article by Morgenthau in *Collier's*, CXX, 16ff., but that piece says nothing about this conference. Secretary Hull obviously was kept informed, for on December 11 he cabled the President that an answer to Churchill's letter was being submitted for his approval. Hull to Roosevelt, Dec. 11, 1940, Hull Papers, box 48.

Roosevelt was less than enthusiastic about the proposal. Harry Hopkins, the only close adviser with him on the *Tuscaloosa,* supported an outright gift, but the President believed that was too sweeping and also would hardly sit well with British pride. When Morgenthau sent a message on December 13 asking for an answer to the plan, Roosevelt replied the next day, as he disembarked at Charleston, South Carolina, with instructions to hold off any action until he returned and could discuss the issue in detail.[53]

On December 11, Lord Lothian again applied the spurs—though more gently this time—to the American government. In a speech before the American Farm Bureau Federation in Baltimore, read for him by Nevile Butler, the First Secretary of the British Embassy, Lothian attempted to prove to the United States that the survival of Britain was essential to their own self-defense. He had considered it his most important speech and had worked on it ever since the end of November. His major emphasis was on demonstrating the Axis powers' desire for world domination. Lothian then asserted that only Great Britain and the British Empire stood between the aggressors and success. He strongly denied that wartime measures would turn England into a Fascist state—a favorite claim of the isolationists—and promised that with American military and financial aid, Britain would be victorious. He warned that speed was essential but claimed that timely aid would do the trick. It was the perfect response to what Morgenthau had complainingly termed "this blue fog here in Washington, that Britain is licked."[54]

Tragically, Lothian died on the very night his speech was delivered for him. Churchill, in a telegram to Roosevelt two days later, called Lothian "our greatest Ambassador to the United States." Although eulogists are universally prone to exaggerate, in this case he may well have made an accurate assessment. His ashes were deposited with honors in Arlington National Cemetery and remained there until December, 1945, when an American warship brought them to their final resting place in Scotland.[55]

The rapid-fire chain of events which had taken place since his arrival finally convinced Sir Frederick Phillips that British interests would be best served by being fully candid with Morgenthau and the American

[53]Davis and Lindley, *How War Came,* p. 115; Morgenthau to Roosevelt, Dec. 13, 1940, Morgenthau Diary, 339:389. Blum, *From the Morgenthau Diaries,* II, 207.

[54]Lothian's speech is reprinted in *The American Speeches of Lord Lothian,* pp. 132-44. A more readily available source that contains an extensive excerpt is *Documents on American Foreign Relations,* III, 370–79. Morgenthau's comment is in Morgenthau Diary, Dec. 11, 1940, 338:252.

[55]Butler, *Lord Lothian,* p. 318. Lothian died of what was later diagnosed as uraemia. He was a devout Christian Scientist and died without consulting a medical doctor, a fact which brought on some decidedly uncharitable comments in both Washington and London. A convincing case is made for Lothian's success as Ambassador by Butler, *ibid.,* pp. 312-21.

government. A Treasury Department aide attached to the London Embassy succinctly summed up the situation: "The British government is well aware that it is not in a position to resist quid pro quo demands from the United States. . . . Though in some cases reluctantly . . . the fact remains that they will in the last analysis stand and deliver."[56] Surely Phillips would have smiled, if wanly, at the use of the traditional highwayman's phrase. On December 12 he gave the Treasury Department a list of Canadian assets and met with Administration officials the next day to work out plans for increasing the pace of securities sales in the United States. He agreed when Morgenthau explained that the best means of obtaining dollars from America was to create the impression that England was being pushed as hard as possible to pay cash, and Morgenthau remarked to his staff that he had learned more in a fifteen-minute car ride that day with Phillips than he had since his arrival. The Englishman warned that French Canadian opinion made it highly unlikely that the French gold on deposit there could be used by Britain, but he promised to try again. He agreed with Morgenthau that a loan would violate the spirit of the Johnson Debt-Default Act but realistically pointed out that that did not solve Britain's dollar problem.[57]

For the next few days the Administration, and particularly the Treasury Department, busied itself getting ready to discuss the financial question once the President returned to Washington. Morgenthau continued to be unhappy with British methods of selling their American securities and finally told Phillips that he, Forrestal, and others would tell Britain how to handle those sales. The British representative in charge of such sales admitted he had never been told to sell the securities quickly and surmised that he would soon receive new instructions. Morgenthau told Phillips that any American commitment would have to await the President's return but confessed that he favored an outright gift.[58]

Morgenthau expected Roosevelt to request data on British and Canadian assets as well as a progress report on British sales of their securities. Although the United Kingdom representatives had suggested borrowing on their assets in America rather than liquidating them, Morgenthau stuck to his guns and demanded from Phillips a nightly report of securities sales. By December 17, the statistics were ready for the President. The Treasury Department concluded that Britain would have an estimated deficit of $5.44 billion fall due on

[56]Butterworth to Morgenthau, Dec. 13, 1940, Morgenthau Diary, 339:399-401.

[57]Morgenthau Diary, Dec. 12, 1940, 339:208. Blum, *From the Morgenthau Diaries*, II, 208.

[58]Morgenthau Diary, Dec. 13, 1940, 339:337-57. Blum, *From the Morgenthau Diaries*, II, 208.

September 5, 1941. Morgenthau noted that Roosevelt was not familiar with the Layton proposal of December 2 which called for a program costing $2.7 billion, which was in addition to $1.2 billion worth of other orders. There were also some three billion dollars of new orders that Britain hoped to place. Thus three programs were involved: the Layton plan; the one that had been under negotiation previously; and the new one that Morgenthau designated the "unborn child." Altogether, with the United States assuming $1.3 billion under the terms of Jesse Jones's arrangement, the British needed $5.4 billion. The Treasury Department's Division of Monetary Research pulled together a listing of British assets as of December 10, 1940 based on British figures that showed an estimated total dollar deficit of $8.5 billion, plus a current monthly dollar deficit to be met.[59] Every statistic was a cry for help.

In addition to a full dossier of information, the first team was reassembled for Roosevelt's return. Arthur Purvis returned from England on December 16. As Churchill promised, he possessed substantial new authority. He had been given a prestigious appointment to His Majesty's Privy Council and had also been designated head of the newly created British Supply Council in North America, which was to co-ordinate all British purchasing in that continent.[60]

In a press conference on December 16, Morgenthau made it quite evident that a major policy decision was around the corner. A reporter noted that Mrs. Roosevelt favored aid to Britain in the form of a gift rather than a loan, but the Secretary refused comment. Morgenthau had stated, on December 12, that Britain had not asked for a loan, and one correspondent wondered if that were the case as of four o'clock on the 16th. The Secretary facetiously replied "my clock stopped." Morgenthau then talked off the record, in spite of warnings from the press that it would leak out within two days, and said he preferred the phrase "financial assistance" instead of "loan." Congress would have to be consulted, and rumors about trading some British islands for cash were wrong, for the government was interested only in their "liquid" or "quick assets."[61]

Intentionally or not, the President had managed to create an atmosphere of high drama surrounding his return to the capital. Churchill, wise in the ways of American politics, had asked for help but had

[59]Morgenthau Diary, Dec. 16, 1940, 340:5-35, 56-79. The list of British assets and the estimated deficit is in FEA records, President's Liaison Committee, files of Philip Young, 1940-July, 1941, box 10, folder titled "British Empire Foreign Exchange Assets and Requirements."

[60]Hall, *North American Supply*, p. 260. Morgenthau Diary, Dec. 16, 1940, 340:149-51.

[61]Morgenthau Press Conferences, conference of Dec. 12 and 16, 1940, vol. 16, pp. 185-86, 191-200. A copy of the transcript of this conference was sent to the President and is filed in the Roosevelt Papers, OF 48, England, 1938-40.

carefully refrained from suggesting any specific methods. The Cabinet had wrestled with the money problem, but could only suggest a solution. From Whitehall to Washington men eagerly awaited the decision that could be made only by Franklin Roosevelt.

CHAPTER V

THE "SHOOT THE WORKS" BILL:
LEND-LEASE, INCEPTION TO PROPOSAL

While the British chafed at the bit, and official Washington churned about in search of some solution to England's dollar crisis, Franklin Roosevelt relaxed in the warm Caribbean sun—at least until Churchill's letter arrived like a thundercloud on December 9. The only information about Roosevelt's immediate reaction to that letter comes from Harry Hopkins, who was with the President aboard the *Tuscaloosa*. In his memoirs, Churchill recalled that Hopkins told him that Roosevelt read and reread the letter and for about two days seemed unsure of what to do. In 1944, Churchill told Lord Moran that Roosevelt had sat with the letter all day after its arrival and then saw no one at all on the next day. Then the following day he came up with the Lend-Lease idea. Sherwood, basing his description on talks with Hopkins, states that Roosevelt was profoundly affected by the message and gives the entire credit for the idea to the President. Only Davis and Lindley, in their "approved" history of the period, indicate that Roosevelt and Hopkins discussed the letter at any length, and even they give full credit for the lending and leasing idea to Roosevelt.[1]

Although there is no concrete evidence that Hopkins tried to play down his influence at this time, it seems implausible to accept his story fully. Known events, both before and after the *Tuscaloosa* cruise, show very clearly the close relationship between Hopkins and the President, and there is no good reason to believe that the same rapport did not exist in December, 1940. Historians have often quoted Hopkins' self-effacing comment that he was "only the office boy" in

---

[1]Churchill, *Their Finest Hour*, p. 567. Lord Moran, *Moran Diaries*, p. 202. Sherwood, *Roosevelt and Hopkins*, p. 224. Davis and Lindley, *How War Came*, p. 115. See also chap. IV.

the White House, but they fail to mention that Hopkins also advised an acquaintance not to waste time with the boys with the big titles but rather to "make friends with their office boys. They're the real Big Shots." Hopkins admits that Roosevelt told him of the concept two days after the receipt of Churchill's letter, but apparently the President made no attempt to fill in his Cabinet on his thinking, in spite of Morgenthau's obvious impatience.[2]

Roosevelt returned to Washington on Sunday evening, December 16, and the following day met with Secretary Morgenthau over lunch at the White House.[3] He appeared well rested and in excellent humor when, after some small talk, he asked Morgenthau if Britain had asked for a loan while he was gone. Morgenthau explained what had transpired, including Phillips' reluctance to co-operate, and commented in his notes on the conference that Roosevelt had been "a tiny bit displeased" over his actions. It is not clear just what this refers to, but it is probably a reflection of Roosevelt's general dislike of the Cabinet proposal of December 10 and Morgenthau's admission to Phillips that he personally preferred a gift of money rather than a loan. After hearing the Secretary out, Roosevelt laid out the ideas he had developed during his sea voyage. He bluntly stated that he believed "the thing to do is to get away from the dollar sign" and the idea of loans, and he suggested instead that the United States increase its production and then give Britain what she needed with the proviso that she return the goods after the war in kind, properly repaired, with any depreciation also paid in kind. Morgenthau enthusiastically embraced the proposal, although he could not refrain from commenting that "if I followed my own heart, I would say, let's give it to them." He acknowledged, however, that it would be better to appear to be driving a hard bargain. In a moment of impulsive overoptimism, Morgenthau surmised that Congress might say Roosevelt was too hard

---

[2]Interestingly, both of these quotes are on the same page in Sherwood, *Roosevelt and Hopkins*, p. 202. One biographer of Eleanor Roosevelt believes that Roosevelt passed on the outline of the Lend-Lease scheme to his executive clerk, Rudolph Foster, and cites the following cable sent to Mrs. Roosevelt on Dec. 12: "See you Monday. Rudolph will tell you confidential plans just made." It seems somewhat ridiculous to assume that the President would tell his clerk and wife about Lend-Lease, but not his Cabinet. It seems far more logical to assume that the confidential plans the President referred to were related to his itinerary—probably his decision to stop off in Warm Springs, Georgia, over the 14th and 15th. See Joseph P. Lash, *Eleanor Roosevelt: A Friend's Memoir* (Garden City: Doubleday & Co., 1964), pp. 205-6.

[3]Blum, *From the Morgenthau Diaries*, II, 208, infers that Morgenthau and Roosevelt lunched privately, which seems likely since the Secretary brought up his problems with Phillips. Langer and Gleason, *The Undeclared War*, p. 238, state that some British guests (unnamed) were present and cite Morgenthau's Diary. I could not find the document they cited. Blum relied on Morgenthau's papers for his account of the luncheon, but that cannot be verified since those papers are not open to scholars. It does seem more probable that the President would prefer to discuss the matter privately first.

in demanding the return of each and every item, or its equivalent, after the war.[4]

That same afternoon, Roosevelt faced an expectant group of reporters and publicly laid his idea on the table. In a casual, offhanded, yet carefully planned opening statement, he first denied there was any real news and then proceeded to make a liar of himself. After admitting that there might be one item worth bringing up, he came to the point. Scoffing at "a great deal of nonsense" put out recently by those who could think of finances only in "traditional terms," he then primed his audience by commenting that never had any major war been lost because of lack of money. Ingenuously interposing that he had not prepared these comments and was just providing some background for the reporters, he then presented the basic Administration rationale for continuing and increasing aid to England. Claiming to speak "selfishly, from the American point of view," he flatly stated that British defense orders had been and were "a tremendous asset to American defense." Though he never admitted that Britain had asked for financial aid, he spoke of "encouraging" additional British purchases and characterized as "banal" the suggestions that the Johnson and Neutrality Acts be repealed so as to permit loans. Misleadingly, he asserted that his Administration had been working on a solution to the problem for three or four weeks and more truthfully confessed that nothing specific had been decided upon. Then came the key phrases. Calling it only one of many possible methods, the President proposed that the United States take over British orders and then "lease or sell" what we thought Britain needed, all based on the basic policy that defending Great Britain was in the best interests of American national security. In an understandable moment of braggadocio he labelled his idea of getting "rid of the silly, foolish old dollar sign," as "something brand new in the thoughts of practically everybody in this room." He followed with a retelling of the same firehose analogy that had been on his mind since Harold Ickes had passed it on to him in the summer. The main difference between this version and the way Roosevelt told it to William Bullitt in July was the addition of the idea that should the hose get damaged in the fire, the borrower would later replace it. Specifically, he suggested that munitions could be lent on that basis and if damaged or used, then they would be replaced. Roosevelt summed up the concept saying the idea was "leaving out the dollar mark in the form of a dollar debt and substituting for it a gentleman's obligation to repay in kind."

[4]Blum, *From the Morgenthau Diaries*, II, 208-9. Morgenthau, *Collier's*, CXX, 72. On December 19, 1940, Prime Minister King of Canada received a note from Morgenthau in which the Treasury Secretary expressed the opinion that all future American aid to Britain should be in the form of an outright gift. Morgenthau admitted, however, that such a proposal had better wait until Great Britain was at "the bottom of the assets." Pickersgill, *The Mackenzie King Record*, I (1939-44), 185.

Ignoring his request not to ask detailed legal questions, the press pulled some additional information out of Roosevelt by asking which nation would retain legal title. The President, apparently thinking on his feet, immediately cut off the possibility of having his program founder on any legalistic shoals by sharply retorting that it did not make any difference. We would get the goods back, so it was a moot point. It was like the man who signs a mortgage and thinks he owns a house. Legally he does not, but it is redeemable. As to who would have legal title to goods transferred to Britain, Roosevelt commented, "I don't know, and I don't care."

One correspondent asked if this took the United States closer to war since American goods were involved. Roosevelt rejected the idea, noting that nations do not go to war for legalistic reasons—a clear reference to Germany and the fear that such American actions might give her an excuse to declare war on the United States. When another reporter asked if naval craft would be included, the President quickly denied it, knowing that to talk about giving away the fleet would mean sure defeat of the legislation. Roosevelt claimed that there would be no need to amend or repeal the Neutrality Act and apparently considered providing American merchant vessels to Britain under the subterfuge of flying foreign colors with non-American crews. He readily admitted that the plan would have to be approved by Congress but predicted it would not be submitted until around January 3, since it had to be ironed out in both Washington and London. Some damage was done to Morgenthau's policy of convincing the public that Britain had paid all she possibly could when the President remarked, in reference to payments for things already ordered, that Britain had "plenty of exchange," but with that small exception the press conference was a masterful exhibition of Roosevelt as politician.

The newsmen could get nothing more, since Roosevelt himself had not gone much further in his thinking. As general as his comments were, one thing was evident. For the first time since the election the public, through its elected representatives, would have a chance to pass on a basic aspect of Roosevelt's foreign policy. In fact, this time the issue would be relatively clear-cut, not clouded by a multitude of domestic considerations. Granted the deck was stacked in Roosevelt's favor. As President he had an enormous publicity advantage as well as a working majority in both houses of Congress. More important, his was a positive program, whereas the opposition ultimately managed to unite on only one issue—their common dislike of Roosevelt's over-all domestic and foreign policy. Still and all, the President was finally turning to the Congress. It was the last real chance the non-interventionists would have.[5]

Some of the origins of the December 17 press conference are very clear. The history of the fire-hose analogy has already been recounted. It was no spur-of-the-moment parallel, for Edward Foley, one of Morgenthau's assistants, recalled hearing the story before Roosevelt met the press.[6]

The word "lease" had been bouncing around Washington ever since the destroyer-bases deal, and Roosevelt himself had toyed with the idea in connection with merchant ships. In addition, during World War I, when he was Assistant Secretary of the Navy, Roosevelt had discovered that although the government could not sell guns in order to arm merchantmen, they could be leased under an old law. Woodrow Wilson never made use of the suggestion, but it may well have come to mind in 1940 when Roosevelt was searching for ways to avoid some of the problems that arose from that earlier war. Edward Stettinius wrote that the idea came out of a discovery in the Treasury Department of an old statute which permitted the Secretary of War to lease Army property for up to five years when it would be in the public interest, provided the goods were not required for public use.[7]

One historian of Anglo-American affairs tells of an early example of Lend-Lease which occurred during the quasi-war between France and the United States. Though the parallel is somewhat strained, it serves to illustrate that Lend-Lease as a completely new idea is nonsense. The plan was novel only in relation to the time, circumstances, and most of all the scale. Certainly there is not the slightest evidence to show that this historical incident was ever known to the President.[8] Lend-Lease evolved out of a series of events between September, 1939, and December, 1940, but adding the final link in the chain took both imagination and political savvy. Subsidies to allies in time of war are as old as war itself, but no other such subsidy took place under the

[5]The quotations and description of Roosevelt's press conference of December 17 are taken from Roosevelt, *Papers and Addresses* (1940), pp. 604-15.

[6]Foley interview, Nov. 3, 1966.

[7]Burns, *Roosevelt: The Lion and the Fox*, p. 63; Stettinius, *Lend-Lease*, p. 63. The statute Roosevelt found was probably The Act of Aug. 29, 1916, 39 Stat. 556, at 559. Stettinius referred to a similar act, The Act of July 28, 1892, 27 Stat. 321. See memo by Ernest R. Feidler, Nov. 2, 1966, "Regarding the Lend-Lease Act of 1941," Stephen J. Spingarn Papers (Harry S. Truman Library, Independence, Mo.).

[8]In 1798, Secretary of State Timothy Pickering asked the British government if they would sell or lend or give back some 24-lb guns that had been captured when the British took Charleston during the Revolution. Britain agreed, provided they could have them back upon request, and sent along powder and shot to boot. Later, George III returned the document the United States had signed and told the Americans they could keep the guns. See Catton, *Etc.*, VII, 186-87; and John B. Brebner, *North Atlantic Triangle; The Interplay of Canada, the United States and Great Britain* (New Haven: Yale University Press, 1945), pp. 72-73.

peculiar political conditions in which Franklin Roosevelt had to operate.

That the Lend-Lease concept was the President's own invention, there seems no doubt. James F. Byrnes recalled that Roosevelt repeatedly claimed it was his own idea, although he too referred to the probable influence of the leasing law dug up by the Treasury lawyers. In spite of an overwhelming desire to prove it had been inspired by Churchill, even as vitriolic a Roosevelt critic as Charles Beard was forced to settle for the milder position that some sort of decision had been prompted by the Churchill letter of December 7. In a memorial tribute to Roosevelt made by Churchill in 1945, the Prime Minister flatly stated that the President was the one who devised the Lend-Lease program. Certainly the British were not thinking of anything but traditional forms of financing when Sir Frederick Phillips departed for the United States in early December, for he was instructed to ask for a loan if he could not arrange a gift of supplies. In fact, the British representatives in Washington were surprised by Roosevelt's proposal. It was hard for non-Americans to realize that for political reasons, Roosevelt believed he had to devise a give-away program that did not look like one. Early in December, Oliver Lyttelton, the President of the British Board of Trade, suggested that American goods might be obtained with the promise they would be returned in kind beginning in five years or so, but there is absolutely nothing in the records to indicate that this idea ever left London. Samuel Rosenman, one of Roosevelt's speechwriters, claimed that Lord Keynes best described the plan when he labelled it one of Roosevelt's "brain waves," and similarly, Morgenthau christened it one of Roosevelt's "brilliant flashes."[9]

Roosevelt's chief advisers were generally in favor of the novel proposal. In his luncheon talk with the President on December 17, Morgenthau had indicated his personal preference for an outright gift but expressed his admiration for the political palatability of the idea. Stimson cautiously commented in his diary that "it's a clever scheme and may be useful," noting at the same time that it was a subterfuge

[9]Byrnes, *All in One Lifetime*, p. 115. Charles A. Beard, *President Roosevelt and the Coming of the War, 1941: A Study in Appearances and Realities* (New Haven: Yale University Press, 1948), pp. 29-30. Beard refers to the Churchill speech of 1945 on p. 295n. He notes that the *New York Times* reported Churchill as saying "we devised" Lend-Lease, but he admits that that was probably an error. The British surprise as well as Phillips' instructions are from Hall, *North American Supply*, p. 256; and Hall interview, Sept. 28, 1966. Lyttelton's idea is in Sayers, *Financial Policy*, pp. 372-73. Keynes's comment is quoted in Samuel I. Rosenman, *Working With Roosevelt* (New York: Harper and Brothers, 1952), pp. 256-57. Morgenthau, *Collier's*, CXX, 74. As is so often the case, Hull's memoirs badly confuse the chronology of these events. He claims that the Lend-Lease idea was discussed in Washington with Phillips during Roosevelt's cruise on the *Tuscaloosa* and that the nature of the legislation was discussed before December 17. That is in total disagreement with every other source and further demonstrates the unreliability of those memoirs; see Hull, *Memoirs*, I, 872-73.

which would get through Congress far more quickly than a direct attack on the Johnson Act. He did appear unconvinced that Roosevelt's over-all strategy, which entailed a long-term campaign to educate public opinion, would be fast enough in view of the dangers involved, and he wondered if it might not be best to go ahead and try to get the Neutrality Act repealed. At a long Cabinet meeting on December 19, Stimson implicitly challenged Roosevelt's entire approach when he told what he called his "leaky bathtub" story. Specifically referring to the heavy losses of British shipping to submarine attacks, he told the President "it was a pretty high price to put so much new water into the bathtub instead of plugging the leaks." Characteristically impatient with Roosevelt's attempt to obtain some sort of consensus before taking any radical steps, Stimson clearly believed it was silly to send over huge quantities of goods unless we made sure they got there—that is, unless the United States convoyed the merchant vessels. Hull claimed he had long felt loans were a bad method of aiding Britain and opposed any attempt to repeal the Neutrality and Johnson Acts because of the conflict it would cause with Congress. Whether or not he really liked the Lend-Lease plan is not clear, though to the very end he remained convinced that Britain had untapped assets. Apparently Hull was on the road to accepting what Knox and Stimsom had realized long before—that war was very nearly upon the United States. A day or so after Roosevelt's announcement of the Lend-Lease idea, Hull remarked to Breckinridge Long that, depending upon Hitler's actions, America could be in the war within ten days or six months. Long, who was closely akin to Joseph Kennedy in his views of the situation, was more inclined to believe that America's belligerency would depend on the amount and type of aid given to Great Britain. Either way, both men found their thoughts running in the direction of war as a result of the President's newly announced program. [10]

Publicly, Administration officials naturally supported the plan, but they could not provide any details about it since there were none. Even the syndicated columnists, who usually managed to dig out some sort of information about such matters, remained in the dark during those final two weeks in December. The reason was simple. Not until after his Fireside Chat of December 29, did Roosevelt instruct his subordinates to work on the Lend-Lease proposal.

Although substantiating research is not available, it appears that the American public greeted Roosevelt's proposal with favor. The polls clearly indicated that over-all public opinion supported aid to Britain, but there were no samplings of the reaction to the December 17 press

[10]Stimson Diary, Dec. 18, 1940; Dec. 19, 1940; Stimson and Bundy, *On Active Service*, p. 367; Hull, *Memoirs*, I, 872-73; Long, *War Diary*, entry for Dec. 19, 1940, p. 163.

conference. Nevertheless, by December, 1940, over 60 per cent of those questioned favored aid to Britain even at the risk of war, and about 70 per cent favored revising the Neutrality Act in order better to aid the English.[11]

The American Chargé d'Affaires in London, Herschel Johnson, summarized British editorial opinion in a cable to Hull on December 19. The idea was universally praised. The London *Times* called it the "first gleam of economic sanity in a world bedevilled by finance." The *Financial Press* and the *Financial Times* both discussed the foreign exchange implications and concluded that Roosevelt's plan avoided the old exchange difficulties. The *Financial News* put its finger on a nerve when it noted that although the American leaders still supported gold as an international currency, "further considerable additions to a redundant gold stock serves merely to ensure that ultimately the United States will suffer the fate of Midas." British cartoonists best captured the over-all British feeling when they filled the papers with drawings of Roosevelt pictured as Santa Claus.[12]

In Russia and Germany, where the press could be counted on to reflect official thinking, the reaction to the Lend-Lease concept was quite nonchalant. In Moscow, *Tass* merely published a reasonably accurate summary of the press conference, while the German papers commented that American production, not promises, was what counted. Obviously, the Germans hoped to cast doubts on American industrial capabilities. Only the Japanese seemed worried. Foreign Minister Matsuoka expressed the fear that such aid might include building up British naval forces in the Pacific.[13]

The analysis of the Roosevelt proposal made by the German Chargé d'Affaires in Washington, Hans Thomsen, was an amalgam of understanding and statements obviously designed to please his Nazi superiors. The Chargé accurately labelled the plan as a long-range one

[11]Fleron, "The Isolationists and the Foreign Policy of FDR," pp. 224-29, graphs 2 and 5. The drop-off of those supporting revision of the Neutrality Act, which occurred in January, 1941, was because people preferred the Lend-Lease Act to any such revision. The entire question of public opinion during this period is in need of detailed examination, particularly in the area of interest groups and their influence.

One suggestion of how to handle the financial problem which Roosevelt received is both amusing and indicative of the general naïveté of the American public in matters of national finance. A small businessman in Baltimore suggested that instead of lending money or leasing war materials, the whole thing be run like the March of Dimes. If every man, woman, and child who was able contributed one dollar, the government "could raise a fabulous sum for Britain's war chest." The maximum of $132 million this could have provided was, of course, a mere drop in the bucket. This and similar letters are in Roosevelt Papers, OF 4193-Misc., box 4.

[12]Johnson to Hull, Dec. 19, 1940, State Dept., 841.24/376. All the quotations are Johnson quoting the British papers. A copy was sent to Morgenthau and is available in the Morgenthau Diary, Dec. 19, 1940, 341:202-5.

[13]Steinhardt (Russia) to Hull, Dec. 19, 1940, State Dept., 841.24/377; Morris (Germany) to Hull, Dec. 19, 1940, *ibid.*, 841.24/383; Morris to Hull, Dec. 20, 1940, *ibid.*, 841.24/386.

based on the assumption that as long as Britain did not fall within the next few months, she would survive, and American aid would ultimately make possible a British victory. Unlike his predecessor, Ambassador Dieckhoff, he did not predict quick American entry into the war but rather implied that Roosevelt hoped to have the Lend-Lease arrangement slowly create a huge investment in Britain which the United States, as in World War I, would then be willing to fight to save. Thomsen also repeated his earlier allegation that the Jewish financial leaders hoped to bleed England dry so as to shift control of world finance to New York City as well as to avoid losing assets in case of a Vichy-type arrangement between Germany and Great Britain. He surmised that Roosevelt desired to "remain master of all developments in his own country" and suggested that Lend-Lease was designed to increase the President's political power.[14]

For about two weeks following his historic press conference on December 17, Roosevelt busied himself with a variety of matters, from reorganizing the N.D.A.C. to discussions on the China problem, but Lend-Lease seemed to lie dormant. About a week after the announcement, Roosevelt decided to make a major foreign policy address and got his speechwriting staff to work after giving them a general indication of what he wanted to say. To set the stage for the speech he arranged for the White Committee, ironically no longer really run by White, to send him a telegram staunchly supporting the Lend-Lease concept and asking the President to present the issues to the people. The telegram was signed by a number of prominent citizens, ranging from James Conant to William O. Douglas, but the only significant responses were even longer lists of names—twenty-four pages of them—from the America First Committee criticizing Roosevelt's plan. Verne Marshall's isolationist group, the No Foreign War Committee, sent a similar listing that contained about 3,500 signers, with the promise of a longer list to come by mail.[15]

[14]Thomsen to the Foreign Ministry, Dec. 19, 1940, *DGFP*, XI, no. 534, pp. 905-6. The Chargé's claim that Lend-Lease was largely designed to increase Roosevelt's political control was repeatedly brought up by the isolationists during the hearings on the bill. This is not to say, or even intimate, that those men were sympathetic to Hitler. It was just a logical and possibly justified argument. Dieckhoff's predictions are summarized in Kimball, *The Historian*, XXVII, 218-43.

[15]The Conant round-robin, as the White Committee telegram was called, is described briefly in Langer and Gleason, *The Undeclared War*, pp. 246-47. The opposition responses are in the Roosevelt Papers, OF 4193-Misc., box 4. White was not asked to sign the round-robin because of his heated feud with the Century Group. When he protested, his name was added to the list. See Johnson, *The Battle Against Isolation*, pp. 189-90. Sherwood, *Roosevelt and Hopkins*, p. 226, deals with the drafting of the speech. Neither the White Committee nor its interventionist segment, the Century Group, played a significant role in the development of the Lend-Lease concept or the writing of the legislation. In addition to the references listed above, see Mark Chadwin, *The Hawks of World War II* (Chapel Hill: University of North Carolina Press, 1968), which is an excellent study of the interventionists, especially the Century Group.

The British, understandably anxious, tried ever so gently to find out just what Roosevelt had in mind but had no success. Always the master dramatist, Roosevelt did nothing to elaborate on the Lend-Lease scheme, either privately or publicly, until after his Fireside Chat on December 29. As striking and effective as his "fire-hose" press conference had been, Roosevelt realized that public opinion could be molded far more speedily and reliably by the wider and more personal contact of his radio program. Roosevelt rejected State Department revisions of the draft he sent there, retaining such strong phrases as "we must integrate" American defense requirements with the war needs of Britain and the other Allies, in place of State's more insipid wording, "we must take care of" those war needs. Roosevelt had decided to make a full and frank commitment to aid England logistically, and Hull's innate caution had no effect.[16]

The basic strategy of the entire Lend-Lease campaign shone through in the very first paragraph of the talk. "This is not a fireside chat on war," said the President, but rather a discussion of how to keep out of the conflict. For the first half of the address, Roosevelt concentrated on creating a sense of crisis. Roosevelt compared the world situation to that which existed in March, 1933 when he became President and concluded America now faced the greatest danger in its history. Dwelling on the danger inherent in any German victory over the British fleet, he warned that ignoring the facts could not change them. To those who advocated a policy of negotiation he thundered that "a nation can have peace with the Nazis only at the price of total surrender." After reiterating that American security and the chances of staying out of the war were in large part dependent upon British survival, he denied that his policies were aimed at involving the United States in that war. Warning that present industrial efforts were not great enough, he described what role America should play. "We must be the great arsenal of democracy." The inference was very clear. The United States was to provide the wherewithal by which Britain would fight the Axis, and without specifically mentioning it, Lend-Lease was to be the legal means for carrying out this broad policy. Roosevelt placed no limit of any kind on the material aid to be given, and totally committed the United States to providing full aid to Britain. The combination of the "fire-hose" press conference on December 17 and the "arsenal of democracy" chat twelve days later, left absolutely no doubt in anyone's mind about how far Roosevelt would go in order to save Great Britain. Although he eschewed the need for America to

---

[16]Fleron, "The Isolationists and the Foreign Policy of FDR," asserts that Roosevelt's use of the "fireside chat" was highly selective and most successful. See pp. 190-91; Rosenman, *Working With Roosevelt*, pp. 261-62; The best summary of the background of the speech is in Langer and Gleason, *The Undeclared War*, pp. 214-15, 244-46.

enter the war as a belligerent, he did not equivocate about his complete commitment to the survival of Britain.[17]

Roosevelt was surprised by the speed with which widespread public support for the talk developed. Steve Early, his secretary, told him that letters and telegrams on it were running 100:1 in favor, and the Gallup poll found that, among those who heard or read the speech, 61 per cent agreed with the President's position whereas only 24 per cent were opposed. Equally significant was that 59 per cent of those polled had listened to it, while another 16 per cent had read it in the newspaper—the highest number of readers and listeners of any of his speeches for which there are polls.[18]

A few observers put their finger on the logical culmination of Roosevelt's commitment. As Henry Stimson noted in his diary, "We cannot permanently be in the position of toolmakers for other nations which fight," though he also admitted that the subject of American intervention could not yet be broached. J. Pierrepont Moffat, the American Minister in Canada, reported a general undertone of criticism about the stated purpose of American policy, that was, to keep the United States out of the war, while isolationists in the United States began their cry that if it is America's war, then let us call a spade a spade and fight our own fight. But in general, the British and the American press, as well as the British government, had nothing but high praise for the speech.[19]

The "arsenal" talk brought an immediate response from the America First Committee. The chairman, General Robert Wood, voiced concern that Roosevelt had rejected implicitly any thought of a negotiated peace and asserted the President was thus personally responsible to a large degree for the continuation of the war. But as Hans Thomsen pointed out in a dispatch to the *Wilhelmstrasse*, Roosevelt made few concrete proposals and left very little for the isolationists to attack. Thomsen did comment that he believed the speech was primarily designed to give moral support to Britain, to build up sentiment in favor of increasing the rearmament program, and to develop internal war hysteria by condemning the Axis as immoral.[20]

[17]The text of the speech is in Roosevelt, *Papers and Addresses* (1940), pp. 633-50. All quotations are from that source. The origin of the "arsenal of democracy" phrase, and the reluctance to use it because of the knowledge of the intended German invasion of the Soviet Union, is discussed in Sherwood, *Roosevelt and Hopkins*, pp. 226-28; and Rosenman, *Working With Roosevelt*, pp. 260-61.

[18]Langer and Gleason, *The Undeclared War*, p. 249. Cantril, *Public Opinion*, p. 588, item 4. Public reaction to the address is graphically displayed in Fleron, "The Isolationists and the Foreign Policy of FDR," pp. 224-29, graph 5.

[19]Stimson, Diary, Dec. 29, 1940. Moffat to Hull, Dec. 31, 1940, State Dept., 740.0011EW, 1939/7348. Langer and Gleason, *The Undeclared War*, pp. 249-51.

[20]Thomsen to the Foreign Ministry, Dec. 31, 1940. *DGFP*, XI, no. 585, pp. 989-90; Cole, *America First*, p. 43.

Nevertheless, historian Robert Osgood may well have made a valid point when he called the "arsenal of democracy" speech the most extreme commitment ever proposed by an American President. More important, Roosevelt realistically related American ideals with her national interests when he condemned Nazi aggression while identifying British survival with American national security.[21]

In a press conference on December 31, Roosevelt finally gave a brief but meaningful indication of what sort of legislation he hoped to get. When a reporter asked if there was anything at all concerning the Lend-Lease plan that Roosevelt could pass on, the President replied that the press already knew the general outline. Then he casually mentioned that such a plan would have to be couched in "fairly general language," since details might hamper its operation. He admitted that it could include more than just guns but airily dismissed as "silly" the notion of trading British-owned islands for such goods. Casual as those remarks seemed to be, they showed the direction of his thought.[22]

Roosevelt's attempt to garner public support for his aid to Britain program was helped all along by the overwhelming American sympathy for two other nations fighting the Axis powers. From the beginning of their involvement in the war, China and Greece had found the American public on their side. Americans had historically backed China and clung to the notion of some sort of special relationship between themselves and the Chinese, while the automatic American sympathy for the hopelessly outclassed underdog, especially if he proves courageous, guaranteed the Greeks popular backing. By December, 1940, both countries were in desperate financial straits. China, not subject to the strictures of the Johnson Debt-Default Act, ultimately received a loan, but the Greeks were less fortunate. Although the Lend-Lease Act came too late to aid them effectively (that even immediate aid would have helped is unlikely), they did contribute to the passage of the act. One of the members of the B.P.C. recalled, after the war, that a long list of Greek requirements submitted to the American government in late December, 1940, probably helped stimulate the development of the Lend-Lease Act. Certainly the vast store of public sympathy for those two nations made the Lend-Lease Act more popular with many Americans.[23]

[21]Robert E. Osgood, *Ideals and Self-Interest in America's Foreign Relations* (Chicago: University of Chicago Press, Phoenix ed., 1964), p. 417.

[22]Press conference of Dec. 31, 1940, Roosevelt Papers, PPF 1-P, vol. 16, pp. 393-94. *New York Herald-Tribune*, Jan. 1, 1941.

[23]Hodgkinson, "History of the Empire and Allied Requirements Division of the British Supply Council," p. 73. The problem of aid to Greece is briefly presented in Langer and Gleason, *The Undeclared War*, pp. 116-18.

With the campaign for public backing well underway, Roosevelt finally got down to cases regarding his Lend-Lease idea. On Monday, the day after his "arsenal of democracy" talk, the President met with Morgenthau and Purvis to discuss British needs and American plans. When Purvis had gone to England he had posed three basic questions: how much did Britain need, how much could she produce, and how much would she have to get from the United States? The first two were answered in the sixteenth paragraph of Churchill's letter of December 7, but the Ministry of Supply refused to give any figures as to the value of goods Britain would have to obtain from America because it believed such data would be misleading. Knowing full well that he would be asked to provide just such a statistic, Purvis took remarkably full advantage of both his new authority and the traditional British policy of giving substantial freedom of action to men in the field. He and his staff worked out an estimate on their own and came up with a staggeringly high figure—fifteen billion dollars, far more than any amount previously mentioned to the American government. When, at the conference of December 30, Purvis finally worked up to the point of giving the "balance sheet" to Roosevelt,[24] the President took it calmly and then told Morgenthau to be ready to have the Treasury Department write the necessary legislation when it got the "green light." Roosevelt went on to explain, in general terms, what sort of a bill he hoped to get. He wanted full and unhampered authority to order what he, the President, deemed necessary and to send it where he thought it would do the most good. Morgenthau personally doubted that Congress would go along with such a broad grant of power but thought it worth trying. On New Year's morning he told Secretary Hull, "I'm going to try my damnedest to think of some way to keep the thing moving."[25]

In writing about the genesis of the Lend-Lease idea, historians have insisted upon emphasizing its novelty rather than its evolution. The standard textbooks in American diplomatic history refer to Roosevelt

[24]The balance sheet technique had been developed by Jean Monnet early in 1940. It was a highly simplified means of presenting Allied requirements to American officials in a way that produced maximum understanding and shock, while avoiding the confusion of comprehensive statistics. The sheet was divided into three columns: the estimate of requirements, the estimate of production, and the deficit that had to be filled by the United States. At the time, the British government was convinced that the technique was an essential factor in obtaining the amount of money finally appropriated in March, 1941, to put Lend-Lease into operation. See Hancock and Gowing, *British War Economy*, pp. 193n., 232; and Hall, *North American Supply*, p. 264.

[25]Hall, *North American Supply*, p. 264. Morgenthau, *Collier's*, CXX, 72, 74. Morgenthau's comment to Hull is in Morgenthau Diary, Jan. 1, 1941, 343:191. Blum, *From the Morgenthau Diaries*, II, 210-11. Blum gives the same quote but his wording does not correspond precisely to that of the Morgenthau Diary. In addition, Blum claims that the call was made at the stroke of midnight, ushering in the New Year, but the memo of the call in the Morgenthau Diary notes the time as 9:30 A.M.

hitting "upon the novel idea" and finding an "unprecedented" solution, phrases that are unintentionally misleading.[26] The Lend-Lease Act was the culmination of months of thought and the heavy pressure of events. Roosevelt's penchant for procrastination, which resulted from both personal inclination and political necessity, should not obscure the fact that Lend-Lease was developed rather than invented. Although credit for an ingenious practical solution to Britain's money problem must be given to the American government, unlike Minerva the idea did not spring full-grown from the head of a single person.

The amount of detail concerning the drafting of the Lend-Lease Act which is available to researchers is frightening. Primarily through the Morgenthau Diary, it is possible to trace the development of the legislation almost hour by hour. Although there is nothing truly surprising in that process, a description of it provides what is probably the most exhaustive case study that can be put together of that particular governmental activity.

On Thursday, January 2, the "green light" flashed from the White House, and Morgenthau convened a noon meeting with Purvis and their staffs, including Edward Foley and Oscar Cox, the Treasury's two top lawyers. Morgenthau, with an occasional comment from Purvis, proceeded to outline what Roosevelt had indicated he wanted on December 30. The essence of the plan was a broad and general grant of authority. The President, said Morgenthau, clearly wanted blanket permission as to how much and to whom to distribute war goods. The Secretary had the impression that Roosevelt wanted it written so that the United States could lend the materials and then have the law very vague on how they were to be repaid. It was to be, as one of Morgenthau's subordinates put it later, a "shoot the works" bill.[27]

Morgenthau told Purvis that Britain should place its trust in the President. He was sure that America would aid the British in the reconstruction period and that the words repayment "in kind" would be interpreted in the loosest manner. Significantly, he stated that Roosevelt's only concern was "to make sure that you win" and not to worry about what happened after that. It is an indication of Morgenthau's attitude that he used the words "you win." In private conversation it is likely that someone who expected to enter the war in the near future would have unconsciously used the plural "we."

---

[26] For examples of this approach, see Richard Leopold, *The Growth of American Foreign Policy* (New York: Alfred A. Knopf, 1962), pp. 569-70; Julius W. Pratt, *A History of United States Foreign Policy*, 2nd ed. (Englewood Cliffs, N.J.: Prentice-Hall, 1965), p. 392; Samuel F. Bemis, *A Diplomatic History of the United States*, 5th ed. (New York: Holt, Rinehart and Winston, 1965), p. 861; Alexander DeConde, *A History of American Foreign Policy* (New York: Charles Scribner's Sons, 1963), p. 592.

[27] Memo from Stephen Spingarn to Larry Bernard, Jan 6, 1941, United States, Treasury Dept., Office of the General Counsel, legislative section files, "Lend-Lease Bill (77th Congress)." Hereafter cited as Treasury Dept. files, "Lend-Lease Bill."

Interestingly, Morgenthau used the same phraseology in a conversation with Sir Frederick Phillips later that month.[28]

When Morgenthau asked Foley and Cox to have a rough draft ready by 10:30 the next morning, Foley asked about the possibility of designing the new legislation as an amendment to the Pittman Act of June, 1940. The Secretary quickly interrupted that Roosevelt wanted no "monkey business" about loans through the RFC and the like, and Purvis noted that the President was afraid the Neutrality Act would have to be amended before loans could be made to belligerents. Morgenthau never directly answered Foley's query, but quoted Roosevelt as saying he wanted the whole thing "right out in the open."[29]

Late that afternoon, Foley assigned the initial drafting job to Stephen Spingarn and Ernest Feidler, two young Treasury Department lawyers. Possibly at Foley's suggestion, they obtained a copy of the Pittman Act in hopes of finding some useful language. It was a happy thought, for the legislation, which dealt with military assistance to Latin America, was easily adapted to meet the requirements Foley and Cox had outlined. Within a few hours the draft was ready. Foley and Cox did some more work on it plus an additional memorandum concerning interim financing. Ten minutes before the stroke of midnight the draft was ready.[30] The next morning Morgenthau looked it over briefly and then called in the British representatives, led by Purvis and Phillips. After a brief discussion of the memo on interim finance, they went over the proposed resolution, section by section.

The first paragraph authorized the President "to sell, transfer, exchange, lease, lend, or otherwise dispose of" defense articles to countries whose defense he considered "related" to that of the United States. Repayment terms were left completely to the President and could be either "direct or indirect consideration." Purvis suggested that if a nation had nothing left but its fighting ability, that could be

[28]Morgenthau Diary, Jan. 2, 1941, 344:72; Jan. 10, 1941, 346:333.

[29]The drafting of the Lend-Lease Act is also treated in Langer and Gleason, *The Undeclared War*, pp. 254-58; and in Blum, *From the Morgenthau Diaries*, II, 211-17. I have not made use of them unless they added something beyond what my research uncovered. A transcript of the January 2 conference is in the Morgenthau Diary, Jan. 2, 1941, 344:67-83. There is also a very handy summary and "Time Schedule" of the drafting of the Lend-Lease Act in *ibid.*, 344:149-170. They will be cited as Morgenthau Diary, "Summary" and Morgenthau Diary, "Time Schedule" plus the page number.

[30]Memo by Stephen J. Spingarn, Oct. 29, 1966, entitled "Who Wrote the Lend-Lease Act of 1941?," Spingarn Papers: memo by Ernest R. Feidler, Nov. 2, 1966, "Regarding the Lend-Lease Act of 1941," *ibid.*; memo from Spingarn and Feidler to author, July 10, 1968, "Regarding Drafting of Lend-Lease Act," a copy of which is available in the Franklin D. Roosevelt Library; Arthur Krock in the *New York Times*, Jan. 22, 1943; Morgenthau Diary, "Summary," p. 149. Blum, *From the Morgenthau Diaries*, II, 213, mistakenly states that the draft was written as an amendment to the Neutrality Act. The Diary of Oscar Cox in the Oscar Cox Papers (Franklin D. Roosevelt Library, Hyde Park, N.Y.), Jan. 2, 1941, p. 3, states: "I prepared the first draft of the proposed legislation," but that does not preclude the spadework having been done by Spingarn and Feidler. Additional data was provided during an interview with Spingarn and Feidler on Sept. 5, 1968, in Washington, D.C.

considered payment by the President. When Harry White protested that such an interpretation seemed broader than Morgenthau wanted to go, the Secretary rebuffed him, saying he preferred that the legislation be "as broad as the world, and then let somebody else tighten it up." He followed by expressing fear that Congress would do just that. Although the bill specifically mentioned Britain, Greece, China, and the American republics, the phrase "or any other country" effectively removed any restrictions on the President's freedom of action. The only limit placed on the grant of power was that the national defense of the United States had to be served, and no transactions could violate international law as interpreted by the State Department. Foley had recalled a proposal made by Stimson before he joined the Administration to the effect that those fighting Germany be allowed to use American repair facilities, and he included such an authorization in the first section. When Harry White commented that it seemed redundant to limit the President by the requirement of serving American defense and then to say the President was the one to determine when national defense was served, Ed Foley admitted, "It is window dressing."

Section two permitted passing on information needed for the use of any goods transferred, while section three forbade the resale of any Lend-Lease items to a third party. Succeeding paragraphs put administrative control of the act into the Treasury Department and authorized an appropriation.[31] Although Daniel W. Bell, who had been Director of the Budget before joining Morgenthau's staff, protested, the resolution set up a two-year revolving fund that would have permitted monies realized from repayment of Lend-Lease goods to be spent again under the provisions of section one, providing they were used by the end of the following fiscal year. Patent rights and payments were to be the responsibility of the Secretaries of the Navy and War, and those officials were also authorized to purchase outside the United States for further transfer any defense items not produced inside the country.

After the entire act had been read, Morgenthau complimented Foley and Cox for having completely caught the spirit of his instructions and told them the next revision was due on Monday, January 6. When Morgenthau told his staff to go over it word by word with the British, White expressed some misgivings about unfavorable public opinion should word leak out that it was a joint project, but although the others agreed, they decided to work together anyway.[32]

[31]One of the strange customs that arose in the American political system was the separation of authorizations and appropriations. Foreigners have rarely understood that it takes both before a penny of public funds can be spent—and each bill can turn out to be a separate struggle in Congress.

[32]The transcript of the meeting of Jan. 3 is in Morgenthau Diary, Jan. 3, 1941, 344:237-57. The draft resolution is in *ibid.*, pp. 156-60. See also Cox Diary, Jan. 3, 1941.

For an hour the group went over the details, and Purvis was delegated the task of drawing up a memo summarizing why the proposed joint resolution should be quickly passed into law. The first key change was suggested by Ben Cohen, the long-time personal adviser to the President then with the Interior Department.[33] Knowing full well that Roosevelt wanted no part of legalistic hassles, he recommended eliminating the section prohibiting any transactions in violation of international law. Cohen also suggested broadening the section permitting the use of American repair facilities to make it very clear that it included vessels actually owned by Britain.   Both ideas were adopted.

That evening, in accordance with arrangements made by Morgenthau the night before, Foley, Cox, and Cohen went over the draft with Supreme Court Justice Felix Frankfurter. Frankfurter's role in foreign policy during this period is very difficult to determine. Certainly there is no question that Roosevelt had a very high respect for the Justice's opinion, although Sherwood claims Roosevelt consulted him only occasionally. Stimson, in his memoirs, admits to checking with Frankfurter regularly, but he refrained from further comments because Frankfurter was still on the bench when the book was written. The Justice had a wide circle of friends. He had been in regular contact with Ambassador Lothian and had quickly become a friend of Frank Knox's after the latter joined the Roosevelt Cabinet. J. P. Moffat, home from Canada in March, 1941, never one to resist picking up gossip, commented in his diary that people in the State Department referred to Frankfurter as the "power behind the throne" and "the lawyer for the British case." Certainly it is evident that his suggestions regarding the draft of the Lend-Lease proposal were carefully listened to and generally followed.[35]

---

[33]Blum, *From the Morgenthau Diaries*, II, 213, erroneously states that Cohen was with the Department of State. As noted on the Morgenthau Diary, "Time Schedule," p. 164, one of the meetings that day was held in Cohen's office at the Interior Department. There is no record of Purvis ever having submitted his assignment.

[34]Morgenthau Diary, "Summary," pp. 149-50.

[35]Morgenthau Diary, Jan. 2, 1941, 344:91. Sherwood, *Roosevelt and Hopkins*, p. 230. Stimson and Bundy, *On Active Service*, p. 334. Butler, *Lord Lothian*, p. 316. Letters from Knox to Frankfurter, dated Oct. 7, 1940, and Nov. 19, 1940, and letters from Frankfurter to Knox dated Oct., 1940, and Nov., 1940, all in the Knox Papers, box 1. Moffat, *The Moffat Papers*, pp. 350, 354.

According to archivists I have spoken to, Frankfurter took steps to insure that manuscript materials concerning his political activities during the late thirties and forties were removed from public view. From the dearth of meaningful materials relating to Frankfurter's influence inside the Roosevelt Administration, particularly after his appointment to the Supreme Court, I am inclined to accept that statement. Frankfurter materials that were recently deposited in the Library of Congress contain nothing on his relations with Roosevelt during this period. The recently published *Roosevelt and Frankfurter: Their Correspondence, 1928-1945*, ed. Max Freedman (Boston: Little, Brown and Co., 1968), contains nothing of value regarding Frankfurter and Lend-Lease.

Frankfurter's comments were perceptive and largely aimed at accomplishing two goals: emphasizing the bill as a defense measure in order to increase its political acceptability and broadening the authority given the President. To the first end he suggested that they adopt the title, "Joint Resolution to Promote the Defense of the United States," and further proposed that a preamble be inserted which stated the necessity and purpose of the bill "in quotable language." In order to enhance the freedom of action granted the President, he opposed any listing of countries that would be eligible and also objected to the long list of specific things that could be accomplished under the terms of the resolution. As the hour-long meeting ended, Ben Cohen suggested the first section state that the legislation be called "an Act to aid nations whose defense is related to the defense of the United States," but as it turned out, Frankfurter's proposed title stuck. Cox and Foley returned from Justice Frankfurter's chambers at the Supreme Court to the Treasury Department and spent the next hour incorporating the various revisions suggested during the day's talks.[36]

The following morning, Saturday the fourth of January, Morgenthau called from his farm in Dutchess County, New York—only a few miles from Roosevelt's Hyde Park residence—and left a message for Foley instructing him to contact immediately the Legislative Counsel of the House, Middleton Beaman. As Morgenthau told Foley, Roosevelt had told him at a Cabinet meeting on Friday that he wanted the " 'aid to Britain' bill to have the 'look' of originating in [the] House."[37] House Speaker Sam Rayburn convinced Roosevelt to have the bill drafted by Beaman and the Legislative Drafting Service in order to make such an expansive grant of power to the Executive a little more digestible to Congress.

Before checking with Rayburn and Beaman, the two Treasury lawyers went to the office of Secretary Stimson. Stimson and John McCloy went over the bill briefly, and Stimson commented that he

---

[36]Morgenthau Diary, "Time Schedule," p. 164; Morgenthau Diary, "Summary," p. 150. Blum, *From the Morgenthau Diaries*, II, 213, states that Frankfurter's changes were designed to strengthen the constitutionality of the bill. That may well have been true, but there is nothing in the sources he cites to indicate that such was the Justice's thinking. Constitutionality was not the problem—the hard job was to obtain the broadest possible support.

[37]Morgenthau to Foley, Jan. 3, 1941, copy in Morgenthau Diary, 344:391. See also Morgenthau Diary, "Time Schedule," p. 164, and Morgenthau Diary, "Summary," p. 150. Both of these, written about a month after the events—Feb. 14, 1941, to be exact—say Morgenthau told Foley to see Speaker of the House, Sam Rayburn. Blum, *From the Morgenthau Diaries*, II, 213, incorrectly gives Beaman's title as Parliamentarian, an entirely different job.

[38]Interviews with D. B. Hardeman, former research assistant to the Speaker of the House of Representatives, the Hon. Sam Rayburn (Washington, D.C., various occasions in the fall of 1966 and the spring of 1967). Morgenthau Diary, Jan. 6, 1941, 345:89-92; Cox Diary, Jan. 6, 1941.

believed it sufficiently broad to accomplish what was needed.[39] Pressed for time, Foley and Cox stayed only about a half-hour and then left to meet Rayburn and Beaman in the Speaker's Office. As they left, Stimson offered McCloy's services anytime they wanted to go over the resolution in detail. Rayburn quickly assigned Beaman and his staff to assist Cox and Foley, and they spent the rest of the afternoon in Beaman's office going over the draft. Early that evening copies of the redraft were sent to Justice Frankfurter, Cohen, and McCloy. At seven P.M. that same day, Charles Ballantyne of the B.P.C. met with Cox in the Treasury to pass on some questions about the bill posed by Sir Frederick Phillips. He wondered if the language would be broad enough to include existing orders, thus alleviating the problem of interim finance, and if it would enable the military services to transfer goods and weapons they actually had right then. Cox replied that the first question depended at present on the size of the appropriation and reassured Phillips that the proposed bill did cover existing stocks. That evening, Oscar Cox received a call at home from John O'Brien, a young Irishman who was on Beaman's staff. O'Brien offered his services to help work on the bill the next day—a Sunday—and, as Edward Foley later recalled, got very wrapped up in the task and proved of great assistance.[40]

Sunday was no day of rest, for Morgenthau had left word that he wanted a draft ready to show the President by 9:30 Monday morning. Cox and Foley began again at 11:15 A.M. and were joined shortly by John O'Brien. Felix Frankfurter was contacted and proposed only minor changes in wording, and around noontime, Morgenthau—always the worrier—called from New York to get a progress report. He was told that there was work left to be done, and the redrafting process continued into the night. McCloy, Larry Bernard of the Treasury Department, Cohen, and others helped out, but the primary load was shouldered by Foley, Cox, and O'Brien. On Morgenthau's instructions, Foley showed the bill to Dean Acheson—soon to be Assistant Secretary of State—whose only remark was that he wished he could come up with brilliant suggestions, but he had none. Foley also brought a copy of the proposed legislation over to Frank Knox's office. The Secretary of the Navy had no criticisms, and, at Morgenthau's suggestion, Foley next called Cordell Hull at home after missing him at the State Department. Hull said he would be unable to do much with the draft because of a death in the family and suggested they have Green

---

[39]Langer and Gleason, *The Undeclared War*, p. 256, state that the War Department had drawn up its own draft of a proposed bill—largely the work of McCloy—and cite Watson, *Chief of Staff*, p. 323. Although that is the page where Watson discusses the drafting of the Lend-Lease Act, in no place does he refer to any original War Department draft, nor have I found any evidence that one existed.

[40]Morgenthau Diary, "Summary," pp. 150-51, and Morgenthau Diary, "Time Schedule," p. 165. Foley interview, Nov. 3, 1966. Stimson Diary, Jan. 4, 1941.

Hackworth, one of the State Department lawyers, look it over. Hackworth did so later in the evening and commented merely that he liked it and hoped it would pass. Although Morgenthau called at 8:15 that night to tell them that Roosevelt would not be able to look at the draft until Tuesday morning, Foley and Cox stayed in the Treasury until shortly before midnight preparing a memo summarizing the resolution. Actually, for all the frantic efforts and the drudgery of constant redrafting, there were no positive, substantive changes from the original draft prepared by Spingarn and Feidler and revised by Foley and Cox on January 2. The bill had been broadened somewhat, and the language had been considerably tightened so as to avoid later problems of interpretation, but essentially it remained as it had begun—the broad concept in the form of an amendment to the Pittman Act.[41]

By that time, the public knew the wheels were turning in the direction of aid for Britain. On January 3, in his Annual Budget Message, Roosevelt had warned of aid programs that would require appropriations not called for in that budget, and three days later, in his State of the Union Address, he laid down his plans. He asked Congress for the authority and the money to supply those at war with aggressors, all the while emphasizing that those nations needed money and supplies, but not men. A loan that would have to be paid back in dollars was rejected in favor of some sort of repayment in kind.[42] But disclosure of the details was still a few days away.

Monday morning found Foley and Cox still making minor revisions in the draft, and that afternoon O'Brien and McCloy both called with suggestions, but by this time all the changes were strictly minor ones and primarily concerned with language. Roosevelt changed his schedule, possibly at Morgenthau's prompting, and shortly after he had delivered his State of the Union Address he met with Morgenthau and Foley at the White House where they went over the entire proposal. Roosevelt began by asking what they thought of the idea of setting up a corporation, in the same manner as the R.F.C., which would handle the whole program of aid, but when Foley pointed out that such a course of action would necessitate repealing the Johnson and Neutrality Acts, the President quickly dropped it. There is nothing in the documents to indicate precisely what suggestions were made by Roosevelt, but he did instruct Morgenthau to get the draft initialed by those Cabinet members who were interested in the plan.[43]

[41]Morgenthau Diary, "Summary," pp. 151-52, and Morgenthau Diary, "Time Schedule," pp. 165-67. A copy of the summary memorandum and the draft resolution can be found in Treasury Dept. files, "Lend-Lease Bill."

[42]Roosevelt, *Papers and Addresses* (1940), pp. 652, 668-69.

[43]A copy of the actual memo and draft shown to President Roosevelt on January 6 is in Morgenthau Diary, 345: 171-81. The conferences on January 6 are recounted in Morgenthau Diary, "Summary," p. 152, and Morgenthau Diary, "Time Schedule," p. 167.

By eleven o'clock on Tuesday morning, Foley, Cox, and O'Brien had incorporated the necessary changes and were ready to begin gathering initials. Morgenthau and Foley ran the draft over to Cordell Hull. He called in Hackworth, and they went over the resolution in detail. Always the politician, Hull preferred to make it a separate bill instead of an amendment to the Pittman Act and thus steer it away from the Senate Foreign Relations Committee, which he felt Vice-President Garner had permitted to become packed with isolationists. Hull also objected to naming any specific countries. Since he knew of the German plans to invade Russia, it is possible he envisaged extending aid to the Soviet Union and did not want to face any restrictions should the desire arise.[44] Hull's objection to introducing the scheme as an amendment had been echoed the day before by Stimson for the same reason. In fact, the Secretary of War talked to Roosevelt about it that afternoon and noted in his diary that the President seemed to agree. Whether or not Roosevelt mentioned it to Morgenthau and Foley on Monday afternoon is not known, but when Hull made the same suggestion on Tuesday morning, Morgenthau agreed to it.[45]

After going over some of the changes in wording with Beaman, O'Brien, and an Army representative, Colonel Edward Greenbaum, Foley showed the latest revision to Hull, who, at 3:25 P.M., initialed the bill. After getting Morgenthau's approval, Foley took it over to the Navy Department, Knox asked to be shown which provisions would deal with ships and then, without comment, initialed the draft at 4:20 P.M. That left only Stimson, who readily gave his approval at 4:29 P.M. once he was shown the changes. Eager to get the bill started, Morgenthau and Foley rushed to the White House, arriving at five minutes after five. The President, "in a grand humor," grinned as he cracked, "This is really a fast piece of work for Washington and I'm not one to be outdone." With that, at 5:15 P.M., he broadly stroked an "OK, FDR" on the draft.[46]

It had been a truly remarkable *tour de force*, particularly by Foley and Cox, who had worked continuously on the bill from January 2 until Roosevelt initialed it on January 7. As so often was the case in the New Deal, it was written hastily and under the enormous pressure of an impending crisis. Unlike such ill-fated laws as the National Industrial Recovery Act, the lawyers and drafting experts who worked under such pressure in 1941 managed to write a bill that could be accepted—by both Congress and the courts.

[44]Langer and Gleason, *The Undeclared War*, p. 257, speculate that such was Hull's motive.

[45]Stimson Diary, Jan. 6, 1941. Morgenthau Diary, "Summary," pp. 152-53, and Morgenthau Diary, "Time Schedule," pp. 167-68.

[46]Morgenthau Diary, "Summary," pp. 154-55, and Morgenthau Diary, "Time Schedule," pp. 168-70. Stimson Diary, Jan. 7, 1941. Stettinius, *Lend-Lease*, pp. 68-69. The draft is in the Roosevelt Papers, OF, Lend-Lease Agreement, 1940-43, box 1-2.

During the Lend-Lease hearings and among some historians in later years the accusation has often been made that the Lend-Lease Act was written by the people in the Treasury Department without obtaining the proper advice and guidance from the other Executive departments who also were entrusted with defending the national interest.[47] Although the question of Administration reluctance to describe the process candidly is easily explained—though not justified—as a means of avoiding a political hassle with Congress, it seems clear from the evidence that those Cabinet members concerned had ample opportunity to make their views known. Granted, Hull was greatly piqued at Roosevelt's choosing the Treasury to take charge of the drafting, but his subordinates helped create the myth by exaggerating his lack of influence. One State Department official, James Dunn, told J. P. Moffat that Hull had been consulted only four hours before the bill was introduced, which was sheer nonsense. More important, Hull had no complaints about the bill as it stood on January 7. Nevertheless, Morgenthau's statement before the Senate Foreign Relations Committee that the bill "was a product of many brains" was mildly misleading.[48] Many brains had a chance to look it over, but its effective genealogy was clear: Franklin Roosevelt, as interpreted by Henry Morgenthau, Jr., as interpreted and put into legal language by Edward Foley and Oscar Cox and their staff.

That family tree may put Roosevelt a little too far removed from the actual drafting process. Although there is no mention at any of the drafting sessions of any suggestions about language or provisions from Roosevelt, there is the distinct possibility that the President made his views known through the person of Ben Cohen. At a Group Meeting of Morgenthau's staff held at 9:30 P.M. on January 6, the Secretary asked Foley if Roosevelt had taken the aid to Britain bill in their form, and Foley replied that as far as Ben knew, the President had approved.[49] It is safe to assume that the Ben mentioned was Benjamin Cohen, since he was continually involved in the drafting of the bill and is the only participant with that name. Surely it would have been no novelty for Cohen to have acted as a go-between for Roosevelt.

Just how secret the drafting process really remained is open to question. At a press conference on January 9, Morgenthau was asked about the progress of the bill and referred the reporters to Middleton

---

[47]For this theme as it was presented during the hearings on the bill, see below, chap. VI. Beard, *President Roosevelt and the Coming of the War*, pp. 24-30, is highly critical of the drafting process and the secrecy that surrounded it.

[48]Moffat, *The Moffat Papers*, pp. 349-50; Hull, *Memoirs*, I, 873-74; SFRC, *Hearings*, p. 36. According to Langer and Gleason, *The Undeclared War*, p. 275n. near the end of January Morgenthau claimed the bill had been written "*in toto*" in the Treasury Department. Unhappily, that portion of the Morgenthau Diary which they cite is not open to scholars at present, and the context of the statement cannot be determined. Certainly that boast, without any qualifications, does not jibe with all of the other materials in the Morgenthau Diary.

[49]Morgenthau Diary, Jan. 6, 1941, 345:51.

Beaman and the Congressional drafting commission. The press retorted that Congress kept telling them that Ed Foley was writing the bill.[50]

With the bill written, the question of legislative strategy came to the fore. The suggestion by Stimson and Hull that the bill be written as a new piece of legislation rather than tacking it on to the Pittman Resolution was inspired by their desire to keep the bill out of the hands of the isolationist-dominated Senate Foreign Relations Committee. Morgenthau and Stimson surmised that Speaker Rayburn preferred the bill to go to the Foreign Affairs and Foreign Relations Committees. Stimson wanted to send it to the Senate Finance Committee, which was well under the thumb of Senator Pat Harrison of Mississippi, a steadfast supporter of aid to Britain. His greatest worry was that the bill would be "turned into a Roman Holiday to be discussed all winter by the Committee." Roosevelt echoed Stimson's sentiments concerning Harrison when he initialed the draft on January 7, but did not oppose Foley's suggestion that the two majority leaders, Representative John McCormack of Massachusetts and Senator Alben Barkley of Kentucky, introduce the bill. Since Administration-sponsored bills are usually introduced by the pertinent committee chairmen, Roosevelt had apparently not made a decision on committee referral. The President's only stricture was that the bill be introduced simultaneously in each House.[51]

Once the basic structure of the legislation had been agreed upon, Rayburn advised Foley that they had better decide which committees the bill was to go to before it came to him, and Foley told him of the meeting Hull had set up to decide the issue. At that get together, Lewis Deschler, the House Parliamentarian and the one who would have to rule on where the bill would be referred, informed Hull, Morgenthau, and the House leaders that unless the bill were rephrased he would send it to the Foreign Affairs Committee. The only opposition to this came from Majority Leader McCormack, who wanted it sent to the Ways and Means Committee as a method of avoiding Sol Bloom. Bloom had badly botched the floor fight to repeal the Neutrality Act in the summer of 1939, and the fact that he was a Jew would provide the opposition grounds to challenge his objectivity.[52]

[50]Morgenthau Press Conferences, conference of Jan. 9, 1941, vol. 17, pp. 13-14.

[51]Morgenthau Diary, Jan. 6, 1941, 345:89-92; Stimson Diary, Jan. 6, 1941; Morgenthau Diary, "Time Schedule," p. 170; Cox Diary, Jan. 6, 1941.

[52]Morgenthau Diary, Jan. 8, 1941, 346:1. Telephone interview with Lewis Deschler, Parliamentarian of the United States House of Representatives, 1928-present (Washington, D.C., Oct. 26, 1966). Morgenthau Diary, "Summary," p. 153. Blum, *From the Morgenthau Diaries*, II, 215, erroneously states that Rayburn was not at this conference.

Lewis Deschler claims that McCormack denies that it was his suggestion to bypass Bloom. Deschler recalls suggesting the idea to Sam Rayburn and assumes he brought it up at the strategy conferences. This does not correspond with the evidence in the Morgenthau Diary which was recorded at the time rather than Deschler's memory of an event which occurred twenty-five years earlier. Deschler interview, Aug. 1, 1967.

No response to McCormack's idea is recorded, but the conferees did not appear worried about the bill going to the Foreign Affairs Committee since Rayburn had four vacancies that he could fill with supporters of the bill. As it turned out, Rayburn's four appointees all proved loyal if taciturn proponents of the Lend-Lease Act.[53]

Following the meeting with the House leadership, Morgenthau sent a memorandum to "Pa" Watson, to be passed on to the President. He discussed the morning's talks and wrote that they planned to introduce the bill on Friday, January 10. The question of which committee it would be sent to was still up in the air but would be decided that afternoon by Barkley and Rayburn. The Speaker was quite insistent that the appropriate committee chairmen be invited to the White House for the strategy meeting scheduled the next afternoon, January 9, and Morgenthau recommended that Hull be added to the list of those attending that meeting. Secretary Hull wrote a memo that day to Morgenthau, telling him of a visit from Congressman James Wadsworth of New York, and suggested that Roosevelt would be wise to invite a member of the minority who strongly supported Lend-Lease. Morgenthau passed on the suggestion that evening to "Pa" Watson, but apparently Roosevelt did not agree, for neither Wadsworth nor any other Republican was asked to attend the January 9 meeting.[54]

Morgenthau's concern for insuring that Hull remained in the mainstream of planning for the Lend-Lease Bill may have been stimulated by Hull's complaint that he had not had enough time to go over the draft. Though he did not pass on Hull's complaints in his message to Roosevelt, in an earlier phone conversation with Frank Knox, Morgenthau said that Hull had requested they delay introduction of the bill until Monday, January 13, because he wanted time to read it. Knox and Morgenthau agreed that Hull was not opposed to the measure but was under considerable pressure from his subordinates to go against the bill. Knox facetiously suggested organizing "a hanging bee over there some day," and Morgenthau retorted that "we won't leave many people over there." Knox laughed and said that was all right. Since Hull had had ample opportunity to go over the proposed legislation, it appears that Morgenthau and Knox were correct in their analysis of the real problem in the State Department. Certainly some of Hull's closest associates, like Breckinridge Long, believed that giving aid to Britain was pouring good money after bad and that all would be lost in the expected British surrender to Germany. Hull definitely did not embrace the Lend-Lease Bill with the same fervor found among Morgenthau, Stimson, and Knox, and at one conference of State De-

[53]The four Democrats appointed were: Noble Gregory (Ky.), Thad Wasielewski (Wisc.), Robert Sikes (Fla.), and Jacob Davis (Ohio).

[54]Morgenthau Diary, Jan. 8, 1941, 346:5-7, 24, 39.

partment officials he expressed the fear that some of Roosevelt's previous supporters would react unfavorably to the President's support for a bankrupt and defeated nation.[55] This sentiment, added to his indignation at the role played by Morgenthau and the Treasury Department in drafting the bill, accounts for his decided reluctance later in the month to provide really effective support before Congress for the Lend-Lease Act.

One of Hull's pet ideas, which cropped up during the drafting of the bill and again during the Congressional debate, was the fixation that Britain had substantial collateral which she might post. Hull was never very clear about just how this collateral was to be used while still avoiding the dollar sign, but the very idea caused no end of problems for Morgenthau and Purvis. Part of Hull's position was based on the misconception that Britain had total assets of $18 billion. With that kind of wealth, he saw no reason why Britain could not put up two or three billion dollars of collateral as a sign of good faith. During the last few days before the Lend-Lease proposal was to be introduced, Herbert Feis, the Economic Adviser in the State Department, confessed to Morgenthau that he had been unable to disabuse Hull of such beliefs, and Morgenthau decided to send over Sir Frederick Phillips in an attempt to convince the Secretary of State. Even the President briefly flirted with the collateral idea and casually mentioned the concept at the Cabinet meeting of January 9. Morgenthau must have asked Roosevelt for some help, for in a letter to Hull written up at Hyde Park, the President reversed himself, stating that the $18 billion figure was far too high, and estimated the usable British assets at about eight or nine billion dollars. He also made it clear to Hull that he considered foreign assets in places like India and the Far East of very doubtful value to the United States in the long run and scoffed at the notion of acquiring Caribbean islands as payment in view of the administrative headaches they would cause. Pacific islands he dismissed as too much of a strategic liability. Roosevelt admitted he would favor requiring Britain to put up security if it were necessary to get the Lend-Lease Bill through but doubted the British had very much of value to offer.[56]

Vice-President Garner, Frank Knox, and Jesse Jones all supported Hull, and the idea soon was taken up by the Republicans. Phillips' visit to Hull made no impression on the Secretary, who complained that he could not get any specific facts or figures out of the Englishman.

[55]Memo of phone conversation between Morgenthau and Knox, *ibid.*, Jan. 8, 1941, 346:15-17; Long, *War Diaries*, entry for Jan. 10, 1941, p. 170.

[56]Morgenthau Diary, Jan. 9, 1941, 346:412; Jan. 10, 1941, 346:413, 337-41, 344-46, 318. Blum, *From the Morgenthau Diaries*, II, 217-18, summarizes the collateral dispute and is also the only source of information on the Cabinet meeting of Jan. 9. Roosevelt's letter to Hull, dated Jan. 11, 1941, is in *F.D.R.: His Personal Letters*, II, 1103-5.

Ironically, in his memorandum of the conference, it was Hull who complained that "I made no impression whatever." Fortunately for Britain, Phillips was more successful with Knox, who finally admitted that he had previously been unaware of the distinction between assets and dollar reserves. Hull remained obdurate in spite of Roosevelt's letter and as late as January 14, the day before the hearings on the Lend-Lease Bill began in the House, continued to argue for collateral.[57]

For all of his reluctance regarding collateral, Hull strongly favored aiding Britain, and like the rest of the Cabinet he was greatly concerned about legislative strategy in the Senate. The isolationists had a strong grip on the Senate Foreign Relations Committee, and Stimson, Hull, and Morgenthau all firmly opposed letting the bill get into their clutches. Once again the Democrats had some seats to fill, but even so, pushing the bill through the Foreign Relations Committee would be an ordeal. The meeting to discuss Senate strategy was held in Secretary Hull's office at four o'clock on January 8, and Morgenthau, Foley, Senator Barkley, Senator Harrison, and the Senate Parliamentarian agreed that they would "kick" the bill into the Military Affairs Committees of the House and Senate, provided Sam Rayburn approved. In a phone conversation with John McCloy following the meeting at the State Department, Foley mentioned that Representative Wadsworth, a Republican internationalist, had told him that it would be unwise to let the bill go to Bloom's committee and thought the House Military Affairs Committee would be the ideal solution.[58]

In the series of meeting held on January 8, the Congressional leadership had its opportunity to make its mark on the proposed bill. None of the changes they suggested were substantive, although Rayburn, McCormack, and Lewis Deschler all agreed that Frankfurter's title for the act was "too pointed" and recommended adding a phrase so that it read "To promote the defense of the United States, and for other purposes."[59] That idea was adopted and stuck.

The final strategy meeting before the bill was introduced took place in the White House late in the afternoon on Thursday, January 9.

---

[57]Langer and Gleason, *The Undeclared War*, p. 261, mention Garner and Knox's attitude; and Blum, *From the Morgenthau Diaries*, p. 218, discusses Jones's support for the collateral idea. Senator Wiley (R.-Wisc.) publicly supported the idea; see Turner Catledge in the *New York Times*, Jan. 10, 1941. Hull's memo of his talk with Phillips is in *FR*, 1941, III, 4-5. Phillips' talk with Knox is reported in the Stimson Diary, Jan. 13, 1941, and Knox's comment in *ibid.*, Jan. 14, 1941. Hull's last-minute try is mentioned in Blum, *From the Morgenthau Diaries*, II, 220.

[58]Morgenthau Diary, Jan. 8, 1941, 346:1, 3, 4. Langer and Gleason, *The Undeclared War*, p. 257, understandably confused some of the conferences held that day. They state the decision pertained only to the House Military Affairs Committee and that Sam Rayburn was present at that afternoon conference.

[59]Morgenthau Diary, Jan. 8, 1941, 346:1-4.

Jesse Jones, as Director of the R.F.C., and William Knudsen, the head of the new Office of Production Management, were added to the expected Executive branch attendees—Morgenthau, Hull, Knox, Stimson, and Foley. Speaker Rayburn, House Majority Leader McCormack, and Senate Majority Leader Barkley led the Congressional delegation, and since Sol Bloom, Chairman of the House Foreign Affairs Committee, was the only House committee chairman present, it appears that Roosevelt and Rayburn had decided to send the bill to that committee, at least in the House.[60] Bloom was seconded by Luther Johnson of Texas, the number two man on the Foreign Affairs Committee. Pat Harrison, Chairman of the Senate Finance Committee, and Senator Walter George, who had just replaced the late Key Pittman as Chairman of the Foreign Relations Committee, were both present, so apparently at the start of the conference the referral decision in the Senate was not firm. Tom Connally, who was soon to succeed George as chairman of that committee and who vigorously supported the program of aiding Britain, also sat in on the conference.

The President began by reading each section of the proposed legislation.[61] Although he claimed that Britain had ample funds to cover existing contracts, new orders were being held up until the bill could be passed. After a few comments on the interim financing plan, the talk turned to the Lend-Lease Bill itself. There was very little comment on the actual provisions of the bill. Luther Johnson queried whether it might be well to set a limit on the amount of aid which could be made available, but Roosevelt quickly responded, "Emphatically, no." The President said he had no idea what the costs would be and gave the same answer to Bloom when he asked about the amount of the first appropriation. Roosevelt apparently expected Congress to limit the total authorization—and mentioned the figure five or six billion dollars.[62] When Foley admitted to Senator Connally that the battleship *Texas* could legally be transferred under this bill, the Senator proposed limiting the legislation to new materials.

---

[60]Rayburn and Roosevelt regularly contacted each other by phone. Since both men consciously avoided making any written notations about such calls, historians have their problems reconstructing what happened between the two. As an indication of how frequently the two exchanged views, it is worth noting that Foley told Morgenthau that on the evening of Jan. 5, Roosevelt and "Sam" had talked together two or three times. See *ibid.*, Jan. 6, 1941, 345:51. Like Roosevelt, Rayburn firmly opposed any public disclosures of the more private aspects of political life. When Harold Ickes published his highly opinionated and gossipy memoirs, Rayburn expressed both annoyance and disgust. Hardeman interview, various times, 1966-67.

[61]A copy of that draft is available in Treasury Dept., "Lend-Lease Bill." It is dated Jan. 9, 1941, 11:15 A.M.

[62]This was in spite of Purvis' attempt to convince Roosevelt that something in the neighborhood of fifteen billion dollars would be required. On January 5, Purvis had given Roosevelt additional information to show how he had arrived at that figure, but apparently the President remained unconvinced. See Hull, *North American Supply*, p. 265.

Roosevelt quickly beat down that idea. He made it clear that he had no intention of giving away any battleships and the like but feared that any restrictions on his authority in that area might prevent the transfer of just the item that a country needed at the time.

Most of the conference was taken up with the question of legislative tactics. Rayburn broached the subject first when he announced that he and his staff had decided that, as written, House rules would require that the bill be referred to the Foreign Affairs Committee. Their fear was that if normal channels were avoided, Congress would resent it and delay the bill. Senator Barkley stated that although he had originally favored sending it to the Military Affairs Committee, considering Rayburn's decision he believed it should go to the corresponding Senate committee. Senator George then raised the problem of the large number of isolationists on his committee. He noted that even if the two vacancies were filled by supporters of the bill, it would barely pass. Roosevelt had already given some thought to that problem and had earlier asked Connally what the chances were of getting James Byrnes of South Carolina and Carter Glass of Virginia assigned to fill those two seats. Though no decision on that question was made at the January 9 conference, Byrnes and Glass were appointed, and Byrnes played a major role in shepherding the Lend-Lease Act through the Senate.[63]

Walter George, in what was quite obviously a pre-planned maneuver, then suggested that each majority leader introduce the bill in his house. Barkley at first demurred, saying that traditionally that was done by the proper committee chairman, but after some discussion with Senator George, he agreed. George gave as his reason the hope of eliminating controversy on the floor as to where to refer the bill—though it is hard to see how such a move would accomplish that goal. Bloom, realizing he was about to be squeezed out of the limelight he loved so dearly, vigorously protested the action as most unusual, but Sam Rayburn, without any attempt to be tactful, said it was not at all uncommon and threatened to send the bill to another committee by merely changing a few words. Quieting somewhat, the Speaker pointed out that delay could be avoided if McCormack introduced it in the House, and Roosevelt, picking up his cue, chimed in that since the bill was so very important he believed it best for it to be handled by the majority leaders, though with the full co-operation of the committee chairman. Outgunned and outmaneuvered, Bloom said no more.

Just before the meeting adjourned, Rayburn again suggested that Roosevelt invite some of the Republicans on the Foreign Affairs Com-

---

[63]Connally and Byrnes comment on the problem of filling the vacant seats on the Foreign Relations Committee in Connally, *My Name is Tom Connally*, pp. 241-42; and James F. Byrnes, *Speaking Frankly* (New York: Harper and Brothers, 1947), pp. 11-12.

mittee to the White House, and Barkley added that Senators Warren Austin (R.–Vt.) and Wallace White (R.–Me.) should also be called in. Roosevelt was unenthusiastic. He said he would see one or two Republican House members, but he refused to see Ham Fish and laughingly noted that Hull would not let him see George Tinkham.[64] The President then commented that he had no doubt that White would vote for the bill, but if the leadership would get together on it, he would talk to a few Republicans from each house. Rayburn, sensing his reluctance, suggested the Republicans talk to Hull instead of bothering Roosevelt, and the matter was dropped. After assigning the Treasury the job of drafting a press release for Barkley and Mc-Cormack to use when they introduced the bill, the meeting broke up.[65]

As much as the leaders in Washington publicly talked about the Lend-Lease plan as a means of keeping England in the war, they knew full well that meaningful aid under that program was a year or more away. Of immediate importance were the orders Britain had already placed—orders she said she could not pay for. From the time of Lothian's press conference in late November, 1940, until well past America's active entry into the conflict, the Churchill Ministry assiduously worked at convincing the Roosevelt Administration that their economy could not handle the cash payments due on goods ordered during the period from early December, 1940, until the actual passage of the Lend-Lease Act on March 11, 1941. This was the troublesome and exasperating question of interim finance. Not until the late spring of 1942 did the British dollar balances pick up sufficiently to remove the issue from the urgent list.[66]

The interim finance problem had little direct effect on the nature of the Lend-Lease Act and was a byproduct of Roosevelt's habitual procrastination. The question is most illuminating as an example of that persistent American fear of being conned by the wily English. Although in relation to the over-all Lend-Lease costs by the end of the war, the amount involved in the interim finance problem was relatively small; in terms of British finance in the early months of 1941, it

[64]Hamilton Fish was an isolationist and Roosevelt-baiter who, ironically, represented Roosevelt's home district in New York's Hudson Valley. Tinkham was from Massachusetts and was a constant thorn in Hull's side. The exchange between the two at the outset of the committee hearings almost descends to slapstick. See HFAC, *Hearings*, pp. 17-31. See also chap. VI.

[65]The main source on the conference of January 9 is Morgenthau Diary, Jan. 9, 1941, 346:222-25. A little additional information is found in the following sources, but most of it merely corroborates the Morgenthau Diary: Stettinius, *Lend-Lease*, p. 69; Turner Catledge in the *New York Times*, Jan. 10, 1941; Morgenthau, *Collier's*, CXX, 72; Stimson Diary, Jan. 9, 1941.

[66]Sayers, *Financial Policy*, p. 397. Pages 383-97 of the study just cited contain the most complete treatment of the problem, although there is substantial additional data on the American position in the Morgenthau Diary.

was truly a critical matter. It was that sense of crisis that brought together—but failed to unite—the Lend-Lease and interim finance questions. One of the most persistent complaints heard during the Congressional hearings on the Lend-Lease Bill was that the legislation was not really necessary because Britain was nowhere near being as financially strapped as she made out to be. It was during the fight over interim financing that Great Britain fired the first guns in her battle to convince Americans and the Roosevelt Administration that she had told the truth.

Basically the British position boiled down to a request that the Lend-Lease Act be written so that the United States would assume the costs of the "old commitments" made before it was passed. Those "old commitments" were divided into two groups; those actually negotiated before December 17 and those the British wished to place during the gestation period of the Lend-Lease Act, with the latter group being the most difficult and also the most important. These new orders would cost $5.3 billion, and there was some confusion as to just what costs the United States would assume.[67]

Since the British admittedly could not pay for any new orders, the American government, and particularly Morgenthau, was reluctant to permit the placing of any new orders. With only a few exceptions, Britain was not allowed to place any new orders after December 19, and after January 16, 1941, all new orders had to be countersigned by Morgenthau and Phillips. In early February, Morgenthau limited new British orders to $35 million per week—an allowance that remained in effect until the Lend-Lease Bill became law. Some money was found in the War Department's budget which could be switched over to pay for a start on the "B" program ("ten-division" program), but the amounts involved were relatively small.[68]

Some new orders were placed under the provisions of the R.F.C. scheme that Roosevelt had approved earlier. The R.F.C. was to take care of initial plant expansion and down-payment costs, but it took until January 22 for Morgenthau to work out the details. The delay was largely a result of opposition from those who were convinced that Britain was holding out. Morgenthau's comment about the persistent belief that Britain still retained hidden dollar assets was a despairing, "It just drives me nuts." Even then the plan covered only part of what the British considered absolute requirements and was limited to American-type goods. Roosevelt feared that to do more might appear

---

[67]FEA records, President's Liaison Committee, files of Philip Young, 1940-July 1941, box 13, file entitled "correspondence re: Sir Frederick Phillips," copy of letter from the British Embassy dated Dec. 19, 1940; Hall, *North American Supply*, pp. 260-61.

[68]Hall, *North American Supply*, pp. 260-63, 270-71; Morgenthau Diary, Jan. 2, 1941, 344:78; Stimson Diary, Jan. 18-20, 22, 1941; Blum, *From the Morgenthau Diaries*, II, 223-24.

to be an attempt to circumvent Congress, thus hurting the Lend-Lease Bill's chances.[69]

The American government's major efforts in the area of interim financing centered on pressuring Britain to utilize all her available dollar resources. Roosevelt enthusiastically endorsed a proposal of Sir Frederick Phillips that quantities of gold be transferred in American ships from the Empire, primarily South Africa, to the United States. Churchill and the British Treasury were disturbed and shocked by the proposal, but Roosevelt insisted and the British complied.[70]

Even more beguiling was the £285 million of French gold held in trust in Canada and in Bank of Canada accounts in New York City. Morgenthau, always willing to demand that Britain ignore legal restrictions while he carefully tried to carry out the "spirit" of such legislation as the Johnson Act, strongly recommended that Britain make use of the French gold. Canadian Prime Minister Mackenzie King adamantly opposed any such move. Ever since the fall of France, the Ottawa government had been apprehensive of French Quebec's loyalty, and spending the French gold reserve might be the spark that would enflame the ever-smoldering French nationalism of that province. King resisted all the American pressures, and nothing came of the plan.[71] To pay for the permitted ration of orders and the "old commitments," Britain had to rely on additional sales of South African gold, purchases of sterling by Canada, and a loan of $300 million in gold from the Belgian government-in-exile in early March.

Thus, on the morning of January 10, 1941, Great Britain found herself in a proud yet humiliating position, unique in her history. On the one hand she was fiercely proud of her resistance under appalling odds, but on the other, she found herself forced to come to the United States, hat in hand, for the material goods she needed to

[69]Blum, *From the Morgenthau Diaries*, II, 223-24; Hall, *North American Supply*, pp. 270-71; Stimson Diary, Jan. 22, 1941.

[70]Memo by Cochran to Young, Dec. 19, 1940, Morgenthau Diary, 341:190-94; Dec. 23, 1940, 342:49A-49E; Jan. 3, 1941, 344:237-38, 262; Sayers, *Financial Policy*, pp. 384-85; Hall, *North American Supply*, p. 262; Churchill to Roosevelt, Jan. 2, 1941, *FR*, 1941, III, 1-2; Churchill, *Their Finest Hour*, pp. 573-74. There are some curious differences between the material in *FR*, Churchill's memoirs, and the Morgenthau Diary. None of it changes the basic story of the gold transfer but does raise the suspicion that Churchill may not have been above editing his memoirs.

[71]Morgenthau Diary, Dec. 19, 1940, 341:190-94; Dec. 23, 1940, 324:49A-49E; Sayers, *Financial Policy*, pp. 335-36; Pickersgill, *The Mackenzie King Record*, I (1939-44), 187.

[72]Hall, *North American Supply*, p. 272. The Canadians were most generous in their financial support of England and permitted her to pay for goods without exchanging sterling for dollars, which was, in effect, a loan without interest. They also bought sterling during the interim period, which gave Britain the dollars she desperately needed, since Canadian dollars could readily be exchanged for American dollars. Sayers, *Financial Policy*, pp. 321-39, 370-71, deals with Canadian financial aid to Britain during the war and the loan from Belgium.

continue the fight. Allies were nothing new to British policy-makers—they had long been adept at using them to suit British goals and interests. But this alliance was being forged on American terms, not British ones. Now Britain suffered all the uncertainty of the pleader, while America prepared to pass judgment. H. Duncan Hall, who was attached to the British Embassy in Washington at the time, captured the tense emotion: "For the first time in its history the United Kingdom waited anxiously on the passage of an American law, knowing that its destiny might hang on the outcome. London waited with an imperfect knowledge of American legislative processes and little understanding of American public opinion."[73] The effects of the Great War, long hidden from public view, had wrought a permanent change in the Britain of Castlereagh, Kipling, and Churchill. The king was dead—long live the king!

[73]Hall, *North American Supply*, p. 259.

CHAPTER VI

"GOD SAVE AMERICA FROM A KING NAMED GEORGE"
—OR FRANKLIN: THE CONGRESSIONAL DEBATE

House Majority Leader John McCormack was somewhat uneasy. He was personally willing, even eager, to do all he could to insure the speedy passage of the President's Lend-Lease Bill for the anti-Christian aspects of naziism had long ago convinced him that Germany threatened those things in life he held most dear.[1] But the professional Irishmen who dominated his south Boston constituency were likely to become irate over any aid-to-Britain legislation, and having it tagged the "McCormack Bill" would put him at the receiving end of their anger. Yet if he introduced it in the House—as planned—that is just what would, in all likelihood, happen. Long-standing political tradition, both inside and outside Congress, caused bills to be tagged with the names of their sponsors or co-sponsors, unless the reporters attached something more colorful. Massachusetts' Twelfth Congressional District was safely Democratic, but no smart politician—and John McCormack was certainly that—gives some unknown future opponent any sort of ammunition if he can avoid it.

Lewis Deschler, Parliamentarian of the House of Representatives, was aware of McCormack's discomfiture. For no real reason that he could ever recall, it occurred to Deschler that numbering the bill, H.R. 1776, could solve Mr. McCormack's problem. Certainly it would be an easy thing to arrange since they had reached the 1700's in bill numbers for that session anyway, and no reporter could ask for any-

[1]Divine, *The Illusion of Neutrality*, p. 328.

151

thing more ironically fitting than to assign the number 1776 to a bill designed to aid England.[2]

Deschler suggested the number to Speaker Rayburn, who casually gave his approval, and instructions were sent to H. Newton Megill, Assistant Enrolling Clerk, to assign 1776 to the bill when McCormack introduced it on the floor, and as simply as that a famous number was attached to an almost as famous bill. Following the enrolling of the bill, Deschler told McCormack what he had done and why. The Majority Leader was most appreciative. Not only would it end any mention of the "McCormack Bill" and thus solve his own private dilemma, but the implicit appeal to patriotism would aid in building public support for the bill itself.

We have a great desire to attribute such fortuitous actions to careful planning, or at least to our national heroes, and are most reluctant to admit that minor officials could have come up with what hindsight shows to have been a clever maneuver. Publicly, the Clerk of the House insisted the number was a mere coincidence, but no one believed him. Robert Sherwood cautiously admitted he was not certain but wrote that the number sounded like a "Rooseveltian conception," and others have taken a similar line. In reality it sprang from political necessity. An ineffective floor leader who also happened to be a Jew, an Irishman who preferred to avoid being known as a friend of the English, and an imaginative minor bureaucrat, all combined to stamp a number permanently in the history books—for the second time.[4]

In spite of this shrewd move, McCormack remained somewhat uncomfortable for about ten days—at which time he returned briefly to Boston. While there, an argumentative female constituent vigorously attacked him for having introduced and supported a bill designed to aid the English spalpeens. McCormack's reply was the classic example

[2]Mr. Deschler, who is still the Parliamentarian of the House at this writing, surmised that he thought of that number because he happened to notice it was about due on the calendar. Deschler interview, Oct. 26, 1966. His memory was probably correct, for the last bill introduced in the House before it convened on January 10, 1941, was H.R. 1764. See *CR*, 77th Cong., 1st sess., LXXXVII, pt. 1, Jan. 8, 1941, p. 80.

[3]Deschler interviews, Oct. 26, 1966, Aug. 1, 1967. Telephone interview with H. Newton Megill, Assistant Enrolling Clerk of the U.S. House of Representatives in 1941 (Washington, D.C., June 29, 1966). Interview with Speaker of the House, John W. McCormack, Majority Leader in 1941 (Washington, D.C., March 18, 1967). Hardeman interview, Aug. 26, 1966. In my interview with him, Speaker McCormack readily admitted that, at the time, he had been quite happy to let the bill be known as H.R. 1776 and let his name fade into the background. In *Roosevelt and Frankfurter: Their Correspondence*, p. 582, editor Max Freedman erroneously credits Frankfurter with suggesting the number 1776 for the bill.

[4]The Clerk's claim of coincidence is reported in the *New York Times*, Jan. 11, 1941. On the assigning of the number 1776, see Sherwood, *Roosevelt and Hopkins*, p. 228; Langer and Gleason, *The Undeclared War*, p. 258, where they sarcastically state the bill was "happily designated" 1776; Blum, *From the Morgenthau Diaries*, II, 217, who calls the number "symbolic": and two contemporary historians who blandly call it "reminiscently numbered," Davis and Lindley, *How War Came*, p. 184. All imply that it was a planned stratagem.

of a politician thinking on his feet—yet it also reflected, in a small way, what may well have been his own deep-felt conviction. He calmly answered: ":Madam, do you realize that the Vatican is surrounded on all sides by totalitarianism? Madam, this is not a bill to save the English, this is a bill to save Catholicism."[5]

Shortly after noon on Friday, the tenth of January, 1941, McCormack introduced on the floor of the House of Representatives "a bill further to promote the defense of the United States and for other purposes." In accordance with plans, Alben Barkley introduced the same piece of legislation at almost the same time on the floor of the Senate. A press release, prepared in the Treasury Department and issued in the name of Barkley and McCormack, outlined the basic nature and purposes of the bill.[6]

The press release laid down the guidelines for the Administration's defense of the bill. Although no attempt was made to hide the extensive grant of power given the President, the emphasis was placed on other items. It noted that only American-type goods would be ordered under this act and further explained that Congress would still maintain control since a separate appropriation was required. In an attempt to anticipate an opposition argument, the release stated that the bill in no way authorized sending American merchant ships into the war zones. Nevertheless, in spite of the attempt to speak of other things, the repeated use of such phrases as "the President is empowered" or its equivalent made it clear that this gave Mr. Roosevelt all he had requested.[7]

On January 9, the day before the bill was scheduled for introduction, Roosevelt began his push to gain public support for the legislation. He passed on the word to the interventionist Century Group that he wanted outside aid on the Lend-Lease proposal since he feared party lines would be drawn which would delay the bill's passage.[8] The President himself started the public campaign in a low key during his

[5]I must confess to having repeated a story for which I have only hearsay evidence. D. B. Hardeman interview, Aug. 26, 1966. During my interview with Speaker McCormack I repeated the story to him and asked him if it were true. He propped his long legs up on his desk, grinned broadly, took a long puff from his cigar, and told me he was not going to answer my question. Then he pointedly commented that all sorts of things leaked out from Capitol Hill. Taken within the context of the interview, I consider that comment as verification. True or not, the story bears repeating, and I suspect that even if Speaker McCormack did not say it, he wished he had. McCormack interview, March 18, 1967. Lewis Deschler recalls hearing the story but could not vouch for its authenticity. Deschler interview, Aug. 1, 1967.

[6]CR, 77th Cong., 1st sess., LXXXVII, pt. 1, Jan. 10, 1941, pp. 87, 101. The press release and the bill were printed in the CR at Barkley's request; see ibid., pp. 87-88. Blum, From the Morgenthau Diaries, II, 217, mentions the Treasury's authorship of the press release, as does the Morgenthau Diary, Jan. 10, 1941, 346:354.

[7]The bill as it was finally passed is in the appendix. The amendments are discussed in chap. VII.

[8]Chadwin, The Hawks of World War II, p. 152.

press conference on January 10. He denied that the bill effectively repealed the Neutrality and Johnson Acts and claimed that the phrase "not withstanding the provisions of any other law" was a standard legal phrase. As with the Barkley-McCormack press release, he too emphasized that Congress would still have to pass an appropriation and specifically asked the press to publicize that. For the record, Roosevelt disavowed any power grab, saying "nobody wants—Lord knows I don't want—the power that is apparently given in this bill" but went on to warn that situations could well arise which would necessitate immediate response and "if the policy of the Nation is to help the democracies survive, you have to have methods of speed that are legalized." In spite of a dozen different peripheral issues that were raised, the major question that opponents and proponents of the bill discussed was that very one—Presidential power.[9]

The opposition was quick to attack the bill from all angles. The most famous remark—thanks to Roosevelt's reaction to it—was made by Senator Burton K. Wheeler of Montana, one of the isolationist Democrats whose greatest joy in life seemed to be to plague Roosevelt. During a radio debate on the Mutual Broadcasting System program, "American Forum of the Air," Wheeler labelled the bill "the New Deal's triple A foreign policy; it will plow under every fourth American boy." Although the *New York Times* made little mention of the crack in its report of the debate, Roosevelt himself brought up the subject at his press conference on January 14, after one reporter asked about the "blank-check" label some had attached to the bill. Heatedly, and telling the press they could quote him, the President said he regarded the comment (he did not know who had said it, or so he claimed) "as the most untruthful, as the most dastardly, unpatriotic thing . . . that has been said in public life in my generation."[10]

Samuel Rosenman, one of Roosevelt's speechwriters and friends, noted eleven years later that it was difficult to really remember "the force and volume" of the isolationists. He recalled that although men like Wheeler constituted a small minority, they were "quite vocal and efficient." Vocal they were. Representative Hamilton Fish called Lend-Lease a Fascist bill and echoed Wheeler by claiming it was a

[9]Roosevelt Papers, PPF 1-P, vol. 17, press conference of Jan. 10, 1941, pp. 64-65, 68-72; *New York Times*, Jan. 11, 1941. The President insisted on calling it the "aid to democracies" bill long after the newspapers and government officials had settled on either H.R. 1776 or the Lend-Lease Bill. See Rosenman, *Working with Roosevelt*, p. 272.

[10]Wheeler's talk was reprinted in the *CR*, 77th Cong., 1st sess., LXXXVII, pt. 10 (app.), pp. A178-79. For Roosevelt's press conference, see Roosevelt, *Papers and Addresses* (1940), pp. 711-12. The day after Roosevelt's attack, Wheeler told the press he supposed that the President had lost his temper. Years later, in his memoirs, the Senator recalled that when he wrote his speech he had given the phrase little thought, but—repenting somewhat— commented that the words had sounded "somewhat harsh" when he spoke them. *New York Times*, Jan. 13, 15, 1941. Burton K. Wheeler with Paul F. Healy, *Yankee From the West* (Garden City: Doubleday and Co., 1962), p. 27.

declaration of war. Senator Hiram Johnson of California said he declined "to change the whole form of my government on the specious plea of assisting one belligerent," while Robert Taft of Ohio asserted only a "rubber-stamp" Congress would pass such a bill. The accusation that the bill constituted an act of war—a position that most directly challenged the President—was also made by Senators Gerald Nye, Bennett Clark, Robert LaFollette, Jr., and C. Wayland Brooks. Clark, an isolationist and anti-Roosevelt Democrat from Missouri, had called the original suggestion on December 17 "the King's royal tax for the support of the British Empire" and had continued in this vein after the bill was introduced by commenting that the number should correspond to the date of the French and Indian War since America was then a British colony. The most influential and responsible of the isolationist organizations, the America First Committee, found it impossible to believe that Hitler could defeat Britain and ludicrous to assume that Germany could threaten the United States under any circumstances. Since these were the only valid reasons for such an extensive grant of power to the President, the Committee opposed the bill as a power grab by Roosevelt.[11]

German papers published stories about the imminent financial collapse of Britain and futile British hopes of being bailed out by the Americans, while the Italians—playing the unaccustomed role of defenders of the democratic rule of law—labelled the proposal as both antidemocratic and unconstitutional, although they glumly admitted it would easily pass. Privately, the German Foreign Ministry advised that the only practical policy was to work at widening the gap between the isolationists and the interventionists and suggested that the German propagandists stick to a strict reporting of the facts, leaving American readers to draw their own conclusions. Shortly thereafterward, the German government, ignoring the Foreign Ministry's suggestion, stepped up its anti-American propaganda, reasoning that it could do little harm now that Lend-Lease had been introduced in Congress.[12]

[11]Rosenman, *Working With Roosevelt*, p. 192; *New York Times*, Dec. 24, 1940, and Jan. 11, 15, 1941; Cole, *America First*, pp. 37-39, 43-45.

[12]Regular reports on Axis reactions were made to the State Department by various persons: See State Dept., Morris to Hull, Jan. 11, 1941, 841.24/406; Kirk to Hull, Jan. 11, 1941, 841.24/407; Phillips to Hull, Jan. 11, 1941, 841.24/408. The German Foreign Ministry's recommendation was probably the work of Ambassador Dieckhoff; see memo by Weizsäcker, Jan. 16, 1941, *DGFP*, XI, no. 666, p. 1117. The German government's change in propaganda tactics is mentioned in Saul Friedländer, *Prelude to Downfall: Hitler and the United States, 1939-1941*, trans. Aline B. Werth and Alexander Werth (New York: Alfred A. Knopf, 1967), p. 168n. It should be noted that the Chargé in Washington had earlier reported that the German Embassy had excellent connections with the America First Committee and another isolationist group, the No Foreign War Committee. He had recommended their work be ignored by the German propagandists to avoid their being tagged as pro-German. Money was funnelled into these groups by the German Embassy, although most of the leadership and the overwhelming majority of the members were unaware of the source of these funds. Thomsen to the Foreign Ministry, Dec. 25, 1940, *DGFP*, XI, no. 563, pp. 949-50.

Generally, the response was quite favorable. In addition to support from the expected areas—the *New York Times,* the *Christian Science Monitor,* members of the Administration, the White Committee, and such—the legislation received an enormous boost when Wendell Willkie, the defeated Republican candidate in the 1940 presidential election, came out strongly in favor of the bill. Greatly concerned by the highly partisan "frontal assault" made on the Lend-Lease Bill by such leading Republicans as Herbert Hoover, Alfred Landon, Thomas Dewey, Robert Taft, and Arthur Vandenberg, Willkie felt it his duty to speak out in favor of the bill. He denounced those who would oppose the legislation merely because the Roosevelt Administration had proposed it and asserted that "if the Republican party . . . makes a blind opposition to this bill and allows itself to be presented to the American people as the isolationist party, it will never again gain control of the American government." Willkie's commitment was largely achieved through the efforts of another Republican whose foreign policy ideas ran along the same lines—Secretary of War Stimson. Stimson had gotten in touch with Willkie two weeks after the Presidential election and from that time on took pains to keep the Republican leader as fully informed as was reasonably possible. There is no evidence to indicate whether Roosevelt was aware of Stimson's actions, but the ease with which Stimson arranged a meeting between Willkie and Roosevelt just before Willkie's visit to England in mid-January is suggestive.[13]

With the hearings in the House Foreign Affairs Committee scheduled to begin on January 15, the Administration forces had only a few days in which to organize their strategy. Morgenthau, afraid he would be accused of a lack of objectivity because he was Jewish, instructed Ed Foley to suggest that Hull lead off for the Administration at the hearings. Rayburn and Bloom agreed with that choice, and Foley suggested it to Hull, giving as a reason the fact that it seemed fitting for the Secretary of State to be the first witness before his counterpart committee. Hull's reaction was that of a petulant little boy. He complained that he had not been informed of all the financial aspects of the bill and was not clear on the technical sections either. Morgenthau countered that a State Department representative had been present at all the important conferences, but Hull remained obstinate. He warned that he would testify only regarding international affairs and would refer all technical questions to the Treasury. He again raised the ques-

[13]*New York Times,* Jan. 11, 1941; *Christian Science Monitor,* Jan. 13, 1941; Johnson, *The Battle Against Isolation,* p. 207; Ellsworth Barnard, *Wendell Willkie: Fighter for Freedom* (Marquette: Northern Michigan University Press, 1966), pp. 275-76. The quotations are from this study. *New York Times,* Jan. 19, 1941. For Stimson's contacts with Willkie, see Stimson Papers, George Roberts to Stimson, Nov. 19, 1940; Stimson Diary, Jan. 11, 13, 17, 1941; Langer and Gleason, *The Undeclared War,* pp. 273-74.

tion of collateral and told Morgenthau that the talk with Sir Frederick Phillips had not been "worth a pewter nickel." After talking with Hull, the Treasury Secretary called Knox and Stimson to enlist their aid in persuading the Secretary of State to put forth more than just a minimum effort. Knox indicated he sympathized with Hull regarding the collateral question, and Morgenthau replied that that was why he wanted to talk to the two of them together. Stimson, after obliquely commenting that an alliance was the proper step, agreed that Hull was wrong and said he would attend the conference with Hull and Knox scheduled for the next day.[14]

At that meeting Hull continued his opposition to Morgenthau's proposals. Although he reluctantly accepted the job of testifying first, the word in the State Department was that the Secretary was consulted only when the bill "struck snags." More significant was his strong opposition to Morgenthau's plan to divulge, in open session, the full state of British finances. The question had first come up at a meeting between Hull and Morgenthau on January 10. Morgenthau had tentatively volunteered to go up on the Hill and disclose the complete British money situation, but Hull had demurred, fearing such a public confession would cause a collapse of British morale. Morgenthau agreed then to talk it over first with the President and Hull before going any further.[15]

Hull's position was somewhat contradictory, for although he staunchly advocated forcing Britain to put down two or three billion dollars in collateral, at the same time he advised against publicizing the United Kingdom's financial status because the picture would be frighteningly bleak. The illogic of holding those two ideas simultaneously never seems to have bothered Hull, for he steadfastly continued to maintain them.

As Treasury Department officials had warned earlier, Morgenthau asked Joel Pinsent of the British Embassy to obtain permission from his superiors for the Secretary to open up to Congress the secret financial statistics that had been made available to the Treasury Department. Morgenthau argued that he had to be in a position to show that it was absolutely necessary for Roosevelt to act as he did in proposing the Lend-Lease Act. He promised not to disclose data on Empire finances unless he were asked but believed he should be ready for any and all questions. With Hull a reluctant and unenthusiastic witness, Morgenthau obviously anticipated rough treatment from the

[14]Morgenthau Diary, Jan. 13, 1941, 347:7-15, 30-31. Information on Morgenthau's reluctance to lead off at the hearings because he was Jewish is from the Foley interview, Nov. 3, 1966. Vice-President Garner also supported the collateral idea.

[15]Morgenthau Diary, Jan. 10, 1941, 346:337-41. See also Rosenman, *Working With Roosevelt*, p. 271; Blum, *From the Morgenthau Diaries*, II, 218-19; Moffat, *The Moffat Papers*, p. 350.

Foreign Affairs Committee. The Chancellor of the Exchequer agreed that England had no choice but to trust the Americans.[16]

Annoyed by Hull's reluctance, Morgenthau spoke that same day to Roosevelt who was taking a weekend rest at Hyde Park. The President promised that Hull would definitely testify, but Roosevelt was hesitant about changing the approach at that stage. He pointed out to Morgenthau that the Treasury had carried the ball up to that point, and the unasked question was "Why change?" Hull, in his memoirs, claimed the President asked him to lead the fight in Congress because he had more influence than Morgenthau with the isolationists and the waverers, but Hull's performance—and the fact that Roosevelt wrote at least part of Hull's opening statement—indicates he led the fight only in the sense of being the first to testify. The burden of carrying out the Administration's aid to Britain program remained where it had been since 1939—in the Treasury Department.[17]

The final strategy meeting before the hearings started was held on January 14. Hull continued to oppose full disclosure of Britain's financial position, but Morgenthau—hoping to place aid to England "on an idealistic plane"—believed Mrs. Roosevelt summed it up when she commented; "Henry, unless you tell these people everything, we are no different than J. P. Morgan was during the last war." Hull also returned to his collateral notion, but both Stimson and Morgenthau firmly rejected it. Stimson eschewed the role of pawnbroker, while Morgenthau warned that the "Birmingham crowd"—the appeasers in England—might cry that America was trying to take advantage of the war in order to bleed Britain dry and thus might agitate for ending the war. Although Knox, Stimson, Hull, and Morgenthau all agreed that ordinary business methods of loans and security would demoralize the British and probably have an untoward effect on her postwar position, Hull warned that care had to be taken to avoid giving the impression that Britain was bankrupt and not worth aiding. He told Morgenthau that throwing open the British books would only further convince Congress of the truth of Joseph Kennedy's cry that England was "busted." Hull again firmly insisted he would testify concerning only two basic themes: the dangerous world situation and the necessity of getting the weapons to England as quickly as possible. They all agreed that financial matters that arose at the hearings would be referred to Morgenthau, while Stimson would confine himself to the managerial and production

---

[16]*From the Morgenthau Diaries*, II, 219-20; Hall, *North American Supply*, pp. 268-69. Unhappily, Hall and the other official British historians do not comment on the reaction in London to the Secretary's request. One suspects it was less blasé than they make it seem.

[17]Morgenthau, *Collier's*, CXX, 74-75; Morgenthau Diary, Jan. 15, 1941, 348:32; Hull, *Memoirs*, II, 923.

aspects. That evening, Morgenthau, by telephone, told Roosevelt of their plans, and the President gave his approval.[18]

Morgenthau and Roosevelt were fully aware of the possibility of Hull's gloomy prediction coming true, and they were attempting to prevent it in other ways. If the public and Congress could be convinced of Britain's good faith, then they would tend to believe the steady stream of promises emanating from 10 Downing Street, guaranteeing an all-out, to-the-bitter-end fight by Britain. As further proof of British candor, over and above the disclosure of her finances which was planned, Morgenthau exerted heavy pressure on London to begin liquidating British-owned direct investments located in America. As the negotiations progressed it became clear that the Administration was primarily interested in some type of flamboyant, grand gesture, which would demonstrate that Britain was willing to make every possible sacrifice, but the nagging suspicion persisted among the British that the Americans were trying to milk the Empire dry.

Like the interim question, the sale of such direct investments was a problem that continued well past the passage of the Lend-Lease Act. The idea had come up earlier, but with the "aid to democracies" bill before Congress, Morgenthau believed the time had arrived for action. Obviously, the great British fear and complaint was their inability to obtain a fair price for such investments. As early as December, 1940, the Treasury received reports of attempts by American buyers to take advantage of even the small sales which were then being made.[19] Unhappy with the efforts made by Britain in this area, Morgenthau asked for and got a special agent from London, Sir Edward Peacock, the personal financial adviser to the Crown, to come over and organize the sale of direct investments. It was too late to accomplish anything in time to impress the House Foreign Affairs Committee, though Morgenthau, annoyed by the persistent British stalling on this matter, commented that he had been trying to get some action out of the British since July, 1940, before forced sales would cause the price to drop. Finally convinced that too many members of the Roosevelt Administration suspected Britain of holding out some of its dollar assets, Phillips and Purvis obtained permission from the Churchill government to sell direct investments and to put the money toward the "old commitments." Purvis was told to let Morgenthau know that negotiations were to begin immediately on the sale of $100 million

[18]The conference of January 14 is reported in the Stimson Diary, Jan. 14, 1941; and Blum, *From the Morgenthau Diaries*, II, 220. No mention was made in the notes on the conference of Knox's assignment, but all apparently assumed he would testify—as he did—on the general military threat that a British defeat would pose to America. Roosevelt's approval of the strategy is in *ibid.*, p. 221. Stimson's pawnbroker remark is from Morgenthau, *Collier's*, CXX, 74, though, as with the entire article, the chronology is somewhat vague. Mrs. Roosevelt's remark is from the Morgenthau Diary, Jan. 15, 1941, 348:18.

[19]Morgenthau Dairy, Dec. 21, 1940, 342:2-3.

worth of the investments, and at Morgenthau's request Purvis authorized him to make the news public at the Foreign Affairs Committee hearing. In what was apparently an attempt to prevent any drastic cut in the market price of the direct investments, Morgenthau mentioned no specific investments at the Foreign Affairs Committee hearing but admitted that such negotiations were being held since the news had already leaked out to the press.[20] The matter rested there until the Administration attacked it with renewed vigor shortly before the Senate hearings were scheduled to commence.

Determining the tactics and strategy adopted by each faction during a Congressional hearing is a most difficult job. Congressmen are notoriously reluctant to talk or even write about cloakroom strategy, even after they and the participants have left Capitol Hill. Most of the analysis must depend on *a posteriori* reasoning. Occasional bits and pieces can be gleaned from the Morgenthau Diary,[21] interviews, and some of the other primary sources, particularly the newspapers, but these do not tell the whole story.

The Administration forces on the House Foreign Affairs Committee should theoretically have been led and organized by the Chairman, Sol Bloom. But that was not the case. Although much of the routine administrative control could not be removed from the Chairman's hands, it is very evident from the hearings that the key man for the pro-Lend-Lease forces was Representative Luther Johnson of Texas. Bloom was unpopular with both Republicans and Democrats on the committee and many considered him pompous, arrogant, and an inveterate publicity hound. It was said that some of the Democrats on the committee once approached the Republican minority and asked if they would support a move to give the chairmanship to someone else. The Republicans said they would, provided the someone else was a Republican, and the suggestion was quickly dropped. True or not, the story is indicative of an unhappy committee.[22] That Bloom was chair-

---

[20.]The Peacock mission is discussed in Blum, *From the Morgenthau Diaries*, II, 236; and Hall, *North American Supply*, p. 274. The decision of the British government to proceed with the sales is reported in *ibid.*, pp. 274-75. See also, Stimson Diary, Jan. 14, 1941; Morgenthau Diary, Jan. 9, 1941, 346:156, and Jan. 10, 1941, 346:315. Morgenthau admitted the news leak at his press conferences of Jan. 13, 1941; Morgenthau Papers, press conferences, vol. 17, pp. 44-53. The only mention of the question of direct investments made by Morgenthau at the House hearings is in HFAC, *Hearings*, p. 62. The official British estimate of their direct investments in America was $900 million. This was quite close to the estimate made by the Federal Reserve as of Aug. 31, 1939, which was $1,185,000,000. See *ibid.*, p. 81.

[21.]The Morgenthau Diary is presently available only up to January 20, 1941. The period from then until January 20, 1945, will be opened in 1970. Thus, from this point on, the most valuable primary source for this study is no longer available. Blum's excellent summary, *From the Morgenthau Diaries*, II, helps fill the gap, but not completely. The Diary volumes in the closed years have been used by some privileged historians besides Blum, but of those only Langer and Gleason, in *The Undeclared War*, have written anything germane to this study.

[22]Interview with Senator Karl Mundt (R.–SD), member of the House Foreign Affairs Committee in 1941 (Washington, D. C., April 29, 1967). Bloom was replaced by Luther Johnson as floor leader during the debate over the attempt to revise the Neutrality Act in

man of the committee was not the result of the seniority system alone. The Democratic leadership was happy to see him in that job rather than some other, since the Foreign Affairs Committee had historically been a minor one. Not until World War II and particularly the Lend-Lease Bill did that committee come into its own.[23]

On January 15, the House Foreign Affairs Committee began the hearings on H.R. 1776, the Lend-Lease Bill. Boyd Crawford, a member of the committee staff, later recalled that he had never seen any hearing draw as large an audience before or since. It was held in the Ways and Means Committee room in the Longworth Building and was packed almost every day with some five hundred people. The crush was great enough to require forty special police on duty to handle the crowd. On days when controversial and popular figures like Charles Lindbergh and Joseph Kennedy testified, seating was by reservation in much of the gallery, and long lines of hopefuls waited to get into the chamber. On such days attending the hearings became somewhat of a social obligation, and the society writer for the *Washington Post* dutifully reported such items as the attendance of Mrs. Sol Bloom, Mrs. Robert Taft, and Alice Roosevelt Longworth.[24]

Public attention throughout the country focused on the hearings. They continually rated front-page coverage in the daily papers in the major cities, and even the small-town papers, dependent largely on the wire services for such news, apparently kept the story on the front page, though it often lacked in-depth coverage. In a very real sense, the Lend-Lease hearings were another of those so-called Great Debates over foreign policy which have periodically occurred in America during the twentieth century.[25]

June, 1939. See Divine, *The Illusion of Neutrality*, p. 269. Though hardly an unbiased source, Breckinridge Long characterized Blum as "arrogant and terribly ambitious for publicity." Long, *War Diary*, entry for June 20, 1940, p.110.

[23]Mundt interview, April 29, 1967. Interview with the Hon. Frances P. Bolton, member of the House Foreign Affairs Committee from 1941 to the present (Washington, D. C., March 16, 1967). Mrs. Bolton told the amusing story that when she first entered Congress in 1941 and was appointed to the Foreign Affairs Committee, she asked the Republican leadership why they had put her on it. The reply was that she was one of the few willing to serve who had a home large enough for entertaining. Social obligations were apparently considered more important than any other of the committee's "duties."

[24]Telephone interview with Boyd Crawford, Staff Administrator of the House Foreign Affairs Committee, Clerk of that committee in 1941 (Washington, D. C., Oct. 31, 1966). Mr. Crawford's recollection corresponds to the descriptions of the hearings carried in the *New York Times*, Jan. 16-30, 1941. One example of the society column coverage is under the byline of Hope R. Miller, *Washington Post*, Jan. 26, 1941.

[25]The *Chicago Tribune*, the *New York Times*, the *Washington Post*, and the *New York Herald-Tribune* all consistently placed the lead story on the hearings on their front page. My tentative conclusion regarding the attitude of small-town papers is largely based on an interesting study of the Lend-Lease debate as covered by the *Ann Arbor (Michigan) News*. See Phillip M. Barber, "The Lend-Lease Act and Public Opinion" (Honors thesis, University of Michigan, 1965), app. entitled "A Report . . . or How to Read Eighty-Eight Newspapers Without Drawing a Breath." Mr. Barber was kind enough to give me that appendix. The nature, short- and long-term effect, and general public reaction to this Great Debate cry out to be studied.

As was the established custom with Congressional hearings of any importance, a plethora of witnesses, pro and con, qualified and fraudulent, informative and polemical, were paraded before the committee. The Administration witnesses, Morgenthau, Hull, Stimson, Knox, and Knudsen, were all of importance in that they presented the Administration arguments for the bill. Many of the others who testified were called as being men of knowledge and experience in matters of foreign policy. William Bullitt, Joseph Kennedy, Norman Thomas, and even Charles Lindbergh, were all leading experts and spokesmen for certain important points of view. Other witnesses were called either for their antiquarian value, such as Amos Pinchot, the old Progressive and titular head of the American Defense Society, or because they exercised substantial influence over a large number of potential voters, such as William Green of the American Federation of Labor or Gerald L. K. Smith, the quasi-Fascist leader of the Committee of One Million.

Committee Chairman Bloom was flooded by requests for the privilege of testifying as well as suggestions as to whom the committee should ask to appear. Most submitted their request in businesslike and rational terms. The Committee to Defend America by Aiding the Allies wrote that it had hoped the bill would pass rapidly, obviating the need for them to state their position, but since the Foreign Affairs Committee had decided to hear a large number of witnesses, they too would like enough time to present a brief statement. Philosopher-historian Will Durant offered his testimony as a "nonpartisan" student of history. Requests from those opposed to the bill tended, not surprisingly, to be couched in excited and emotional tones. They invariably gave the bill an insulting or critical label, and reference was usually made to the need to save America from the same sort of mistake she had made in World War I.[26] Occasionally a request took a belligerent tone, such as the letter and telegram from Gerald Smith demanding that he have an opportunity to speak—or rather lecture—to the committee. Smith, an avowed anti-Semite and admirer of Hitler,

[26]These requests are in the files of the U.S., House of Representatives, 77th Congress, Committee on Foreign Affairs, "file on H.R. 1776" (Congressional Records Section, National Archives, Washington, D. C.) Permission to use these records is routinely granted by the Clerk of the House upon application via a member of the House of Representatives. These records are hereafter referred to as HFAC, "file on H.R. 1776." Copies of some of these requests are available in a small collection of Sol Bloom's papers owned by the Sol Bloom Elementary School, PS #84, in New York City, New York. I am indebted to the principal of that school, Mr. Milton Forrest, for permitting me to see and copy many of these documents, and to Mr. Boyd Crawford of the House Foreign Affairs Committee for leading me to that collection. The bulk of the Sol Bloom papers, deposited in the New York Public Library, provided no useful information on the Lend-Lease hearings or on Bloom as Chairman of the Foreign Affairs Committee. Such collections as that in Sol Bloom Elementary School are very common for committee chairmen who held office before the passage of the Executive Reorganization Act of 1949. Since then, committee correspondence has been classified as committee property instead of the personal property of the chairman and thus has been kept in the committee files.

slurringly addressed the Chairman as "Solomon Bloom" and threateningly warned that if he were denied the chance to speak, he would be "forced" to report to his two million followers (he was chairman of the Committee of One Million) that their appeals had been ignored. He claimed to have a petition opposing the bill which had two million signatures and suggested that Bloom contact House Minority Leader Joe Martin or Senator Vandenberg, both of whom would vouch for his group's "stability and integrity." In the same tone he cautioned that any mid-western congressman could attest to their strength.[27]

Smith's concern was probably a result of press reports of a heated exchange between Bloom and the senior Republican on the committee, Hamilton Fish. In accordance with Administration strategy, Bloom wanted each side to have its day in court[28] and indicated to Fish that as the leading Republican he could unofficially contact persons he wished to have testify. Fish, instead of following the usual formalities of submitting a list and having the official invitations go out in the name of the chairman, attempted to act as a sort of minority chairman and issued invitations himself. Whether he misunderstood Bloom's intentions or was attempting to put the Democrats at a disadvantage is not clear, but Bloom's reaction was swift and very plain. In a shouting match heard by reporters and spectators, Bloom loudly ruled that witnesses would be invited only by the committee, and he further protested Fish's asking people to speak on "the President's dictator bill." Fish stomped out of the committee room yelling, "You never were the committee and you never will be," and for a short time the minority members of the committee met in another room. Fish finally sent an emissary to Bloom and capitulated for the day, but the dispute surfaced again a few days later. On January 24, the committee met in executive session and again Bloom complained about Fish calling witnesses without going through the chairman. General Marshall had written Fish, with a copy of the letter sent to Bloom, stating he preferred not to come as a minority witness as Fish had requested since he would be testifying in his capacity as a member of the Administration. Admiral Stark and Army Air Force Chief of Staff General George Brett agreed. Bloom told Fish that the military leaders had been told to ignore Fish's request. Marshall had also asked to be heard in executive session, and after reconvening in open session, the committee voted for executive session when the military chiefs testified. Fish and some of the others protested that the public had a right to hear these men—obviously

[27]Telegram from Gerald L. K. Smith to Bloom, Jan. 18, 1941, HFAC, "file on H.R. 1776." Letter from Smith to Bloom, Jan. 20, 1941 (Sol Bloom Elementary School collection).

[28]Bloom later wrote that he had insisted all the arguments be aired. Sol Bloom, *The Autobiography of Sol Bloom* (New York: G. P. Putnam's Sons, 1948), p. 241.

hoping they would state that Germany was no threat to America—but in a party-line vote, the committee overruled them.[29]

The opposition to Lend-Lease immediately found themselves at a severe disadvantage. The classic problem was recognized at the time by *New York Times* reporter Turner Catledge, when he noted that in matters of military affairs and national security, the Administration maintains a virtual monopoly on meaningful and useful information.[30] Able to publish only what will help their case, while supressing or at least delaying public knowledge of those facts that seem to go against them, government officials have the benefit of what some would call the "power of positive thinking," or at least action.

Catledge also pointed out that the conservative coalition, in existence since Roosevelt's abortive attempt to "pack" the Supreme Court, did not function in the area of foreign policy. As many historians and pollsters have pointed out, the South supported the aid to Britain program with greater enthusiasm than any other section of the country. The day before the Lend-Lease Bill was introduced, the American Institute of Public Opinion published a poll that showed that of those asked, 91 per cent in the South supported changing the Johnson Act so as to permit loans to Britain. The next highest figure was 60 per cent in the Northeast, while the other areas all showed figures below 50 per cent. Ever since the fall of France, the South had consistently led all the other sections in supporting the Administration's foreign policy, and its domestic quarrels with Roosevelt had little effect on that stance. In the final votes on the Lend-Lease Bill, only two Southerners voted against the act.[31]

[29]The quotations from the argument between Fish and Bloom are as quoted in the *New York Times*, Jan. 17, 1941. The other data on the dispute are from *ibid.*, Jan. 15, 1941; Crawford interview, Oct. 31, 1966; U. S., House of Representatives, Committee on Foreign Affairs, "Minutes, Committee on Foreign Affairs, 1940-1946" (Committee files, Rayburn Building, Washington, D. C.), Jan. 24, 1941, pp. 70-72. (Hereafter cited as HFAC, "Minutes.") I am indebted to the Chairman of the House Foreign Affairs Committee, Dr. Thomas Morgan of Pennsylvania, and the staff Administrator, Mr. Boyd Crawford, for giving me access to the "Minutes" and other materials in the committee files which pertained to Lend-Lease. See also *New York Herald-Tribune*, Jan. 25, 1941. Bloom's dislike for Fish was of an earlier vintage. Not only did Bloom despise him for his Roosevelt-baiting, but he had also been forced to deal with Fish's obstructionist tactics before in committee matters. The story is told on Capitol Hill about the time one of the Democratic leaders—later a Speaker of the House—got so annoyed at Fish that he bluntly labelled him a "shit-ass." Sol Bloom, who thoroughly abhorred profanity and refused even to listen to an off-color joke, applauded.

[30]*New York Times*, Jan. 19, 1941.

[31]*Ibid.*; the AIPO poll is from Alfred O. Hero, Jr., *The Southerner and World Affairs* (Baton Rouge: Louisiana State University Press, 1965), pp. 97, 101. See also Wayne S. Cole, "America First and the South, 1940-1941," *Journal of Southern History*, XXII (Feb., 1956), 36-47; and Alexander DeConde, "The South and Isolationism," *ibid.*, XXIV (Aug., 1958), 332-46, both of whom come to the same general conclusions as Hero. The two Southerners were Representative Hugh Peterson of Georgia and Senator Robert Reynolds of North Carolina. Representative B. C. Reece of Tennessee also voted against the bill, but he was hardly a typical Southerner in that he was from a traditionally Republican district in that border state. The same was true of Ross Rizley of Oklahoma and John Robsion of Kentucky.

The Administration campaign during the Congressional hearings revolved around two seemingly contradictory approaches. The leadership was generally agreed that mass public support could be gained only by a full debate, even though it was clear from the outset that they had the votes to push the bill through anytime they chose. Even the *Times* of London flatly stated shortly before the hearings commenced that passage of the bill was assured, and late in January, Roosevelt wrote Harry Hopkins that the Lend-Lease Bill should pass somewhere between February 20 and March 1.[32] The question was not would it pass but could it be the means of achieving a consensus.

At the same time that the Administration was trying to achieve a long-term strategic goal, it was forced by tactical considerations to keep the actual subject matter of the debate as narrow as possible. One foreign observer, Jan Ciechanowski, the Ambassador from the Polish government-in-exile, recognized the problem that Roosevelt faced when he noted that the opponents of Lend-Lease were trying to maneuver the Administration into a general, open statement of policy—what the French call *mouvements de mauvaise humeur*. Roosevelt was apparently convinced that one step at a time was sufficient—and Lend-Lease was the pending step. Interventionists like Grenville Clark complained that the President was misleading the American public by implying that being an "arsenal of democracy" would be enough. But true to form, Roosevelt preferred to move with great caution and only when he was virtually sure of getting the response he wanted.[33] The President had proved consistently reluctant to discuss long-range policy in any but the vaguest and broadest terms even with his Cabinet and advisers. The idea of public dialogue with his opponents was simply unthinkable. Nor is that as undemocratic a position as it may seem. A "loyal opposition" is an ideal rarely if ever found in American history, and, as with most political debates, the truth in foreign policy usually lies somewhere between the two extremes.

A quick glance at the newspapers of the day clearly indicates which witnesses commanded the most official and public attention. Secretaries Hull, Morgenthau, Stimson, and Knox, and to a lesser degree William Knudsen, presented the Administration position, while the opposition case was put forth by former Ambassador Kennedy, Charles Lindbergh, Norman Thomas, and General Robert Wood of the America First Committee. Additionally, those opposed to the bill forcefully expressed themselves through the various members of the Foreign Affairs and Foreign Relations Committees. Senators Robert

[32]London *Times*, Jan. 13, 1941, p. 5. Roosevelt to Hopkins, Hopkins Papers, box 301, "Book III: Hopkins in London (A)," n.d.

[33]Jan Ciechanowski, *Defeat in Victory*, pp. 16-17; Clark to Stimson, Jan. 10, 1941, Stimson Papers.

LaFollette, Jr., Gerald Nye, and Arthur Vandenberg, and Representatives Hamilton Fish, George Tinkham, John Vorys, and Karl Mundt—all Republicans (save LaFollette, who was a Progressive)—carried the burden for the anti-Lend-Lease coalition.

The nature of the debate was essentially the same in both houses of Congress.[34] In the positive sense, the Administration concentrated on one major issue—national security. Its other arguments either stemmed from that basic position or were merely responses to opposition attacks.

The major elements of the Administration's strategy for the hearings became evident at the very start. As planned, Secretary of State Hull led off with a lengthy survey of the historical and diplomatic background to the world crisis, with a strong emphasis on the aggressive and calculated nature of German and Japanese actions. Although the opposition made no attempt during the hearings to defend the actions of either Germany or Japan, Hull's strong statements established from the start just who the villains were. After briefly citing the Tripartite Pact as proof of Axis complicity, he attempted to undermine the basic foundation of the isolationist's position. Noting that many believed Nazi Germany posed no threat to the United States, he argued that without British seapower, the Atlantic Ocean offered little security for the Western Hemisphere. Hull warned that the Germans were attempting to subvert American nations—a reference to Nazi fifth-column efforts in Latin America—and presented British survival as an element of hemisphere defense. His only mention of the bill itself was a brief reference to the need for speed in enacting a bill that would best enable America to provide for its own defense. Fittingly, it was Hull who read into the record a statement that justified the act in terms of international law. He asserted that Germany and Italy were international law-breakers who had violated their legal obligations. Bluntly he noted that international law and neutrality had provided precious little protection for Belgium, Holland, Norway, and Denmark, leaving only the law of self-protection as the practical course for the United States to adopt. Known as a staunch defender of the rule of law in international relations, Hull's statement was calculated to take the wind from the sails of those who maintained America had a legal obligation to remain truly neutral.

The basic approach of the Administration was clear. The Axis powers were defined as "outlaw" nations, acting in concert. British seapower served as an essential element of the defense of America and the Western Hemisphere, particularly in view of Nazi infiltration of Latin America. Thus, legally justified in terms of self-defense, the

---

[34]The legislative history of the bill, that is, committee action, amendments, and the like, were different in each house. That is discussed below in Chap. VII.

Lend-Lease Bill should be passed as quickly as possible.[35]   Secretary
Stimson succinctly summarized the Administration's public position
during his testimony before the Senate Foreign Relations Committee:

We are really seeking to purchase her aid in our defense. We are buying–not
lending. We are buying our own security while we prepare . . . . We are buying
the protection which is accorded us by the continuance of the British sea power
in the North Atlantic while our own main fleet is busy protecting us in the Pacific
. . . . In our own interest–and purely in our own interest–it is good national
policy to preserve today a hard-fighting Britain, a Britain which has not been
ground down by hard bargains sapping its resources. [36]

The proof that British and American security were linked rested
mainly with the argument that Britain's survival was militarily necessary for American defense against Hitler. This of course necessitated
proving that Germany posed an active threat to the United States. No
one seriously disputed the idea that Germany had been aggressive
throughout the 1930's, but the opposition refused to admit that
Hitler's victories in Europe made it necessary for America to wage
economic warfare against Germany. The bill's supporters, particularly
Hull, Knox, and Stimson, continually harped on the theme that
British seapower made the Atlantic Ocean a barrier to invasion, and
Senator Tom Connally, elaborating on that approach, commented that
without command of the sea it would become an express highway for
attack on the Western Hemisphere.[37]   Fittingly, Secretary of the Navy
Frank Knox presented the major arguments along this line. In his
statements to both Congressional committees as well as in numerous
public speeches he emphasized the historical importance of British
seapower in making the Monroe Doctrine meaningful, and he warned
that in spite of the development of a strong American Navy, it could
not defend two oceans simultaneously. In almost every speech that
Knox made during the first three months of 1941 he gave American
estimates of the comparative combat strength of the Axis and American navies, should the British fleet be destroyed.[38]   The statistics were
not encouraging. As of January 1, 1941, the Axis powers were supe-
rior in every phase of combat naval strength: 20 to 15 in battleships,
75 to 37 in cruisers, 271 to 159 in destroyers, and 284 to 105 in
submarines.[39]   The initial opposition answer to that argument claimed

[35]HFAC, *Hearings*, pp. 2-10.

[36]SFRC, *Hearings*, p. 87.

[37]*Ibid.*, p. 242.

[38]The opposition never seriously challenged the Administration assumption that Britain
would not surrender her fleet to Germany.

[39]HFAC, *Hearings*, p. 159. The estimate combined the German, Italian, and Japanese
navies. Copies of many of the speeches Knox made during this period, all of which followed
this same approach, can be found in the Knox Papers, box 4, "speech file."

that such scare tactics were invalid since any German attack on America would have to come over 3,000 miles of ocean, which would pose enormous logistical problems. They went on to point out that the Japanese Navy was hardly in a position to combine with the Germans in an attack on the United States, and then, in a typical "one American can lick any ten Indians" approach, claimed that American ships were better equipped and better manned anyway. Harold Ickes colorfully summed up this approach when he noted in his diary that they seemed to think like little boys—that the United States could take on the whole world singlehandedly.[40]

The demand of the opposition that the supporters of the bill demonstrate just where Germany posed any real threat to American security was answered by heading "South of the Border." The refrain began slowly. Hull briefly alluded to German infiltration of Latin America and warned that control of the seas was a prerequisite to controlling such subversion. Stimson presented the problem as one of keeping the war out of America rather than America out of war, but it was Frank Knox who most emphatically warned that Germany's threat to the United States was via Latin America. He bluntly predicted that should we "lose the power to control even a part of those seas, inevitably the wars of Europe and Asia will be transferred to the Americas." In his secret testimony before the Senate committee, Hull was even more explicit. Each of the bill's supporters on the Senate Foreign Relations Committee, in a seemingly planned maneuver, brought up the subject of German penetration of Latin America, and Hull invariably seized the opening to warn that if Hitler gained control of the Atlantic, then within a few months he would have puppet governments and military bases established in South America. The spectre of Nazi infiltration was not limited to the military and political sphere. Occasional references were also made by pro-Lend-Lease forces to the need of Latin America to maintain its trade with Europe. Both Hull and Knox warned that should Hitler dominate England, then the South American nations would be forced to trade with Germany. In short, the Administration openly presented Germany as a meaningful threat to that most sacred and unchallengeable of traditional American foreign policies, the Monroe Doctrine.[41]

Though historians today question the extent of the Nazi penetration in Latin America, the American government was apparently honestly fearful of a German attack from that direction. Army Air Corps intelligence had incorrectly assessed Axis air strength as 4,100

[40]SFRC, *Hearings*, pp. 231-33; Ickes, *The Lowering Clouds*, pp. 421-22.

[41]HFAC, *Hearings*, pp. 6, 101, 158; "Transcript of Executive Testimony before the Senate Committee on Foreign Relations, Jan. 26, 1941, on H.R. 1776," Cordell Hull Papers, pp. 21, 58, 100, 135-38. Hereafter cited as Hull, "Executive Testimony." SFRC, *Hearings*, p. 182.

planes, over and above their European requirements, capable of making the relatively short flight (1,600 nautical miles) from Africa to Natal, Brazil. Thus the military planners believed Germany had the capability of attacking Latin America. General Marshall, as early as October, 1940, asserted that as long as the British fleet remained intact, the Western Hemisphere was in little danger, but should that fleet be eliminated, "the situation would become radically changed."[42] The opposition to Lend-Lease was generally forced to concede the major part of this argument since it had to rely on the honesty of Administration witnesses who claimed to have classified knowledge of such Nazi infiltration. Men like Robert Wood, acting chairman of the America First Committee, settled merely for the position that they did not believe Germany would ever find it in her national interest to attack the United States, largely because of the distance involved, and ignored the problem of subversion in South America. The opposition made a brief, feeble attempt to show that the Lend-Lease Bill would violate the Declaration of Panama, a Pan-American agreement prohibiting, among other things, the outfitting of belligerent ships in the neutral Western Hemisphere countries, but that line of reasoning quickly petered out when Hull flatly asserted that the entire general American policy regarding defense of the Western Hemisphere had met with a largely favorable reaction in Latin America, though the Secretary was forced to admit that the United States government had not consulted with those countries about such a unilateral change in their agreements. German propagandists made some tentative moves in the same direction, but nothing came of it because of the general support for the bill in Latin America.[43]

Two additional approaches were used by the Administration to buttress its claim that British and American security were inextricably intertwined. The aggressive nature of German foreign policy was stressed, and the image of being surrounded by totalitarian powers was regularly invoked. Senator Tom Connally put it plainly when he rhetorically asked Hull: "Is there any possibility of our mollifying Mr. Hitler by pussy-footing a little more than we are or by avoiding a policy of violation of neutrality?" He answered his own question in the negative, and Hull, of course, agreed. During the same meeting of

---

[42]James L. Cate and E. Kathleen Williams, "The Air Corps Prepares for War, 1939-1941," *Plans and Early Operations*, ed. Wesley F. Craven and James L. Cate, The Army Air Forces in World War II, vol. I (Chicago: University of Chicago Press for the United States Air Force, Office of Air Force History, 1948), p. 120. Marshall is quoted in Stetson Conn and Byron Fairchild, *The Framework of Hemisphere Defense*, p. 417. This volume contains the most comprehensive summary of Latin American-American defense plans and problems.

[43]SFRC, *Hearings*, p. 343; HFAC, *Hearings*, p. 36. Some of the Latin American republics, such as Costa Rica, went so far as to pass resolutions favoring the passage of the Lend-Lease Bill. See State Dept., 740.0011 EW, 1939/9048. German reaction is reported in Morris (Berlin) to Hull, Feb. 3, 1941, *ibid.*, 740.0011 EW, 1939/8092.

the Senate committee, Connally gave Hull the opportunity to discuss the Tripartite Pact, and the Secretary of State labelled it as being aimed at the United States, though he was honest enough to admit it was not the closest sort of co-operation. Still, it was an essential part of the Administration's "we need the British Navy" argument, for the American Navy was tied down in the Pacific by the Japanese. Senator Claude Pepper of Florida, an ardent interventionist, declared that America did not at present have the power to withstand a totalitarian challenge from both oceans, and Knox and other Administration witnesses stressed the fact that building the necessary two-ocean navy would take at least four to five years.[44] Apparently the testimony of the three major military witnesses, Generals Marshall and Brett and Admiral Stark, bore out the Administration case, for nothing to the contrary was ever leaked to the press from those executive sessions. One of the historians who worked on the United States Army's official history of World War II commented that "the period of 1939-41 is not fully understandable unless one is aware of the part which a military witness played at that time in the decisions of a friendly and trusting Congress."[45] That position is borne out by the dispute that arose between Fish and Chairman Bloom over whether the military men should testify as opposition witnesses and in open session. Clearly, Fish and the opposition placed great stock in the honesty of the military leaders and believed their honesty would result in testimony unfavorable to the Administration position.

Traditional American concern with international law, plus a strong desire publicly to brand Axis actions as illegal as well as dangerous, made the proponents of Lend-Lease eager to find some sort of legal grounds for such an obvious violation of neutrality. From the very outset of the campaign, the opposition had hit at the Lend-Lease Bill as an act of belligerency. Senator Burton Wheeler, in the same speech in which he spoke of the "New Deal's triple A foreign policy," claimed that "never before has the Congress of the United States been asked by any President to violate international law." The Administration position was put into its briefest form by Democratic Senator James Murray who, unlike his fellow Montanan, Burt Wheeler, supported the bill. During Hull's executive session testimony before the Foreign Relations Committee, Murray asked simply if there had been a breakdown of international law, thus justifying the application of the doctrine of self-defense. Hull, of course, answered that such was the case.[46] Secretary Stimson went beyond a mere reference to self-defense and managed to dig up a statement by the International Law

---

[44]Hull, "Executive Testimony," pp. 50-60; SFRC, *Hearings*, pp. 246-48, 235.

[45]Watson, *Chief of Staff*, p. 8.

[46]*CR*, 77th Cong., 1st sess., LXXXVII, pt. 10 (app.), pp. A178-79; Hull, "Executive Testimony," pp. 101-2.

Association which not only branded the Axis as law-breakers but also justified such legislation as the Lend-Lease Act. The key provision of the International Law Association's interpretation of the Kellogg-Briand Peace Pact made that very clear:

> In the event of a violation of the pact by a resort to armed force or war by one signatory state against another, the other states may, without thereby committing a breach of the pact or of any rule of international law do all or any of the following things .... Decline to observe toward the State violating the pact the duties prescribed by international law, apart from the pact, for a neutral in relation to a belligerent.[47]

For many who sincerely were worried about the international legality of the Lend-Lease Bill, Stimson's answer quieted their fears. Those who were primarily concerned with defeating the bill consistently labelled it a violation of international law but did not further pursue the question with any Administration witnesses.

The opposition attack on the Lend-Lease Bill during the Congressional hearings centered around two major themes: the powers granted the President made him a virtual dictator and the bill would, and probably was designed to, get America into the war. The bill's supporters countered the first of these in a variety of ways. They carefully avoided any detailed discussion of the provisions of the proposed legislation, letting the language of the bill speak for itself. They characterized the world situation as one of extreme and unprecedented danger which required broad executive powers, at the same time referring to similar actions by previous Presidents, and they pleaded with the nation and Congress to put its trust in the man they had elected. Their defense against the claim that Lend-Lease was a "war bill" was the same as that which the Administration had followed with every measure passed since the revision of the Neutrality legislation in November, 1939.

Led by Hamilton Fish, the opposition in the House Foreign Affairs Committee concentrated heavily on the dictator charge. Fish began his questioning of Cordell Hull by saying he assumed the Secretary realized that the Lend-Lease Bill "vests the control of power in the hands of one man and takes away the constitutional power from the Congress." Hull replied by suggesting that Fish talk to the author of the bill, Henry Morgenthau, since he was there only to discuss the international situation. Opposition witnesses such as Hanford MacNider, ex-commander of the American Legion, asserted that "this legislation under the guise of aid to democracy abroad, destroys our

[47]"Report of the Thirty-eighth Conference of the International Law Association, Budapest, Hungary, Sept. 6-10, 1934," *American Journal of International Law*, XXXIII, no. 4, p. 825, as quoted in HFAC, *Hearings*, p. 104. At the request of the Clerk of the Senate Foreign Relations Committee, Oscar Cox forwarded two copies of the International Law Association report to that committee. See U.S., Senate, 77th Congress, 1st sess., "file on H.R. 1776 (S. 275)" (Congressional Records Section, National Archives, Washington, D. C.).

democratic processes at home," and Representative Bartel Jonkman (R.-Mich.) introduced a statement by the world-renowned international lawyer, John Bassett Moore, which followed the same line:

There can be no doubt that under the guise of certain phraseology the pending bill assumes to transfer the warmaking power from the Congress in its constitutional capacity to the Executive. This is evident upon its face .... It is evident that the tide of totalitarianism in government which has swept over many other lands has not only reached our shores, but has gone far to destroy constitutional barriers which, once broken down, are not likely to be restored.[48]

Writing some twenty years after the Lend-Lease debate, Joseph W. Martin, Jr., of Massachusetts, then House Minority Leader, repeated his original assertion that the Lend-Lease Bill was designed to perpetuate the dominance of the Democratic Party. Although Martin voted for the bill's final passage, he did so out of a desire to promote national unity, though at the time he believed that it upset the proper balance between the legislative and executive branches and threatened the two-party system.[49]

Such attacks on President Roosevelt were nothing new, and were clearly designed to appeal to those opponents of the bill whose main objections were *ad hominen*. As he wrote to Stimson after the Secretary had testified before the Senate Foreign Relations Committee: "It was indeed timely that you reminded the Committee members that the national interest would not be served by fettering a power which has existed untrammeled for one hundred and fifty years."[50]

At one point, obviously annoyed by the implication that the Lend-Lease Bill was designed to trick Congress into giving him power that could be used with reckless abandon, Roosevelt resorted to ridicule to sabotage the opposition's arguments. During his press conference held on January 17, a reporter asked why the President objected to some sort of limitation on his power to transfer elements of the United States Navy under the provisions of the bill, and Roosevelt facetiously replied, "I suppose they better put in standing on my head, too, and a

[48]HFAC, *Hearings*, pp. 14, 351, 366. MacNider spoke for himself not the American Legion, which supported the bill. See Roscoe Baker, *The American Legion and American Foreign Policy* (New York: Bookman Associates, 1954), pp. 145-46.

[49]Joseph W. Martin, Jr., *Joe Martin, My First Fifty Years in Politics*, as told to Robert J. Donovan (New York: McGraw-Hill Book Company, 1960), pp. 90, 92, 95.

[50]Roosevelt to Stimson, Feb. 4, 1941, Stimson Papers. Roosevelt was fully aware of the accusations that abounded concerning his desire to be a militaristic dictator. In an amusing letter to Mackenzie King, the President suggested that the Prime Minister design a white naval uniform to be worn on formal occasions in lieu of the uncomfortable formal attire government leaders had to wear. He mused that he might even try his hand at that for himself, since he was Commander in Chief, but feared that was one precedent he dared not break. It was fortunate that such idle thoughts did not become public, for the vehemence of Roosevelt's opponents brings to mind what happened to President John Adams in a similar situation. Adams had idly wondered whether the President ought to be addressed as "your Majesty" and was forever branded a monarchist. For Roosevelt's letter, see Roosevelt to King, Jan. 18, 1939, Roosevelt Papers, PSF, Gt. Britain, King and Queen, 1938-40.

lot of other things." Not surprisingly, the phrase received substantial attention in the press, and the general reaction was exactly what the President had aimed at, for the papers generally considered the accusation an insult to Roosevelt's integrity. Roosevelt was also taken with the remark and repeated it frequently. A few weeks later, when asked what would be the first thing he would do after the Lend-Lease Bill became law, the President laughingly answered: "Go out in the middle of Pennsylvania Avenue and stand on my head; because that is not yet prohibited!"[51]

Secretary Stimson, faced with similar questions during the hearings, responded with an appeal to simple common sense. When Representative Hamilton Fish incorrectly told Stimson that Morgenthau had first denied and then admitted that the Lend-Lease Bill gave the President the power to give away the entire Navy, Stimson stated that he had not come to discuss "fantastic interpretations" of the bill. When Senator LaFollette suggested that the bill permitted Roosevelt to buy the entire British war production and then lend it back to them, Stimson sarcastically answered that such an idea had "never entered my less-intelligent head" and added that he could not imagine any court allowing such an interpretation to stand.[52]

Outside the Congress others picked up the same refrain and let their Congressmen know about it. The Rev. Charles Coughlin, the Roman Catholic priest who spearheaded much of the virulent anti-Roosevelt activity in the country, pictured the bill as a plot designed to destroy private property and business. His magazine, *Social Justice*, stated that the legislation was not aimed at aiding England but was "concerned, however, with scuttling the last vestige of democracy in the world— American democracy." Speaker of the House Sam Rayburn was warned by a Baptist minister in Texas that dictatorship was the purpose of such a bill, and Representative Frances Bolton (R.-Ohio), who opposed the bill, exchanged numerous letters with constituents in which they commiserated with each other about the "unlimited authority" that the bill would give the President. Similar letters were read into the record of the committee hearings.[53]

[51]Press conferences of Jan. 17 and Feb. 4, 1941, Roosevelt Papers, PPF 1-P, vol. 17, pp. 82-84, 105. See the *New York Times*, Jan. 18, 1941, for a good example of the press reaction.

[52]HFAC, *Hearings*, p. 93; SFRC, *Hearings*, p. 114.

[53]*Social Justice*, Feb. 3, 1941, as quoted in Charles J. Tull, *Father Coughlin and the New Deal* (Syracuse: Syracuse University Press, 1965), pp. 227-28. Rayburn wrote few letters and saved copies of even less. His papers at the Sam Rayburn Library in Bonham, Texas, are sparse and virtually non-existent for this period. His research assistant, D. B. Hardeman, has a small collection of Rayburn papers for this period, and I am indebted to him for permitting me to use them. The letter mentioned was dated Jan. 27, 1941, and there are others of a similar vein. Mrs. Bolton, a member of Congress until 1968, was kind enough to permit me to examine her constituent correspondence file on H.R. 1776. The letters referred to above were all dated between January and March, 1941. SFRC, *Hearings*, pp. 259-61, contains additional letters. Letter dated Feb. 1, 1941, Rayburn Papers (Hardeman Collection).

Rayburn's reply to his disgruntled constituent typified one Administration approach to these attacks. The Speaker noted that the powers granted to the President under Lend-Lease were little compared to those he already had as Commander in Chief of the armed forces and further commented that Roosevelt had never betrayed his trust. In a speech delivered on February 9, Rayburn publicly took the same position.

There has been a great deal of talk about the extraordinary powers which the Lease-Lend Bill confers on the President. The powers are extraordinary because the emergency which they are designed to meet is extraordinary. As the President has said, "The Nation's hands must not be tied when the Nation's life is in danger."

Not surprisingly, the opponents of Lend-Lease were unwilling to place any trust whatsoever in Franklin Roosevelt, in spite of the pleas of men like Rayburn. Their personal hostility to the President showed through time and again in such exchanges as this one between Morgenthau and Congressman George Tinkham. After Tinkham said that the proposed bill contained no guarantee that American interests would be protected, the following exchange ensued:

Mr. Morgenthau: "I am speaking for myself and am more than willing to leave it to the President of the United States to make the best bargain possible."

Mr. Tinkham: "I am very sorry to say that I have not the same confidence in the President that you have."

Mr. Morgenthau: "That possibly, if you do not mind my saying, is why you are in the minority."

Mr. Tinkham: "In the majority do you count all the British as well as some of the Americans?"[54]

The references made by the bill's proponents to historical examples of broad assumptions of power by the President usually came in casual and brief comments. For example, Hull told the Senate Foreign Relations Committee that the existing situation was as grave as the one Lincoln faced at the outbreak of the Civil War and would have to be handled just as authoritatively.[55] Although no witness ever gave an organized presentation tracing the historical justifications for exercising such powers, the Treasury Department prepared a list of such precedents and forwarded it to Chairman Sol Bloom of the House

---

[54]Letter dated Feb. 1, 1941, Rayburn Papers, (Hardeman Collection); typecopy of speech made by the Hon. Sam Rayburn, Speaker of the U.S. House of Representatives, Feb. 9, 1941, entitled "Defend America Now," supplied through the courtesy of the Sam Rayburn Library, Bonham, Texas; the exchange between Morgenthau and Tinkham is in HFAC, *Hearings*, p. 65.

[55]Hull, "Executive Testimony," pp. 134-35.

Foreign Affairs Committee. The memorandum emphasized that there was insufficient understanding of the powers the President possessed as Commander in Chief of the armed forces. It cited the opinion of Supreme Court Justice George Sutherland in the *Curtiss-Wright* case as the legal authority for granting the President a broad degree of discretion in conducting foreign affairs and followed with a long list of occasions when various Presidents had done just that. Historians might not have been impressed with the references, but the members of Congress were rarely historians. Jefferson's purchasing of the Louisiana Territory, Lincoln's blockade proclamation, Monroe's enunciation of the Monroe Doctrine, and Wilson's policy in Mexico were all cited. Each case was accompanied by quotations from the opposition of the day, all predicting a dictatorship and other horrible consequences stemming from the President's unconstitutional assumption of power.[56] The reference to the *Curtiss-Wright* case, which also cropped up in some of the public testimony, was repeated in the report made by the majority of the Foreign Affairs Committee when it forwarded the bill to the floor of the House. Mr. Justice Sutherland's decision was a strong point in the defense of the Lend-Lease Bill, for its language was clear and unequivocal. Sutherland summed up the essence of his position when he wrote:

It is quite apparent that if, in the maintenance of our international relations, embarrassment—perhaps serious embarrassment—is to be avoided and success for our aims achieved, congressional legislation, which is to be made effective through the negotiation and inquiry within the international field, must often accord to the President a degree of discretion and freedom from statuatory restriction which would not be admissible were domestic affairs alone involved.[57]

The key part of the Administration's handling of the dictator charge was to avoid the issue. Not only did the witnesses stay away from any point-by-point refutation of the accusation, but even the reports of the majority on the two Congressional committees that dealt with the bill failed to come to grips with it. The House Foreign

[56]Memo entitled "The President's Powers under H.R. 1776 and some Prior Instances of Presidential Power," HFAC, "file on H.R. 1776." The document is not dated, but the forwarding letter indicates it was written sometime in January, 1941. A similar document titled "re: Charge that H. R. 1776 vests broader authority in the President than had ever before been vested in that officer" is in Treasury Dept. files, "Lend-Lease Bill." The document is not dated.

[57]*United States* v. *Curtiss-Wright Export Corp*, 299 U.S. 304, as quoted in U.S., House of Representatives, Committee on Foreign Affairs, 77th Cong., 1st sess., *To Promote the Defense of the United States*, Report no. 18 (to accompany H.R. 1776), 2 pts. (Washington: printed at the order of the House of Representatives, 1941), pt. 1, p. 6. Part 1 of this report, which was the report of the majority, will hereafter be cited as *House Majority Report on H.R. 1776*. Part 2 will be cited as *House Minority Report on H.R. 1776*. Secretary of War Stimson referred to the *Curtiss-Wright* case during his testimony before the Foreign Relations Committee. SFRC, *Hearings*, pp. 90-91.

Affairs Committee touched on the problem only briefly in the Majority Report by stating that the bill was "wholly consistent with our Constitution."[58] The Senate Majority Report merely claimed that "our national defense is provided ... with a wholly desirable and constitutional adaptability to rapidly changing and unpredictable world conditions." In addition, the Senate report strongly referred to the various limitations on Presidential power which the bill contained, particularly the clauses requiring consultation with the military chiefs before transferring any defense articles not specifically made for transfer under the Lend-Lease Act.[59]

The Republicans, and those few Democrats who also opposed the bill, remained unconvinced. The House Minority Report used the strongest language, stating that the "power requested is too much to give any man at a time when the country is at peace." The report went on to assert that the "bill gives the President unlimited, unprecedented, and unpredictable powers" and warned that "we cannot repeal war; we cannot repeal bankruptcy; and we cannot repeal dictatorship." The Senate minority was only slightly less harsh. In the conclusion of the report it dismissed the claim of the Administration that the bill was designed either to aid Britain or defend America and instead claimed that a realistic reading showed that the legislation would grant the President dictatorial powers to take the country into war.[60]

One minor aspect of the broad charge that the bill created an executive dictatorship was the accusation that the "revolving fund" established by the legislation violated the constitutional provision against appropriating funds for the military beyond a two-year period. The revolving fund permitted any money paid to the United States under the Lend-Lease Act to be used until June 30, 1946, to buy defense articles. Stimson, in his testimony before the Senate Foreign Relations Committee, submitted a list of eleven previous laws that had created similar funds, and the Senate Majority Report on the bill stated that the constitution was concerned with the maintenance of a large standing army, not the purchase of defense articles.[61]

The opposition's denunciation of the bill as a measure that would get America into the war showed up at the outset of the debate and

[58] *House Majority Report on H.R. 1776*, p. 6.

[59] U.S., Senate, Committee on Foreign Relations, 77th Cong., 1st sess., *Promoting the Defense of the United States*, Report no. 45, Calendar no. 51 (to accompany H.R. 1776), 2 pts. (Washington: printed at the order of the Senate, 1941), pp. 2-3. Part 1 will be cited as *Senate Majority Report on H. R. 1776*, and part 2 will be cited as *Senate Minority Report on H. R. 1776*.

[60] *House Minority Report on H.R. 1776*, pp. 13-14; *Senate Minority Report on H.R. 1776*, p. 6.

[61] Stimson was challenged by Senator Robert LaFollette, Jr., of Wisconsin on this point. SFRC, *Hearings*, pp. 109-11. *Senate Majority Report on H.R. 1776*, p. 7.

became the keystone of their attack in the Senate.[62] The basic Administration argument on this question was neatly synthesized by an exchange between Cordell Hull and Senator Theodore Green of Rhode Island during Hull's executive testimony before the Senate Foreign Relations Committee. Green asked if it would be fair to say the Administration position was "that the passage of this bill is less likely to lead to war than its non-passage." After some hemming and hawing, Hull replied: "That has been our position all the while." The opening statements of all the Administration witnesses placed little if any emphasis on Lend-Lease as a means of avoiding war, instead concentrating on presenting British survival as necessary to American defense, but the repeated attacks of the opposition forced the bill's supporters to defend the act as a measure designed to keep America out of war. Stimson, probably the most interventionist of all Roosevelt's Cabinet members, parried the war question by claiming that Hitler, not Lend-Lease, would get the United States into the war.[63]

Justice Felix Frankfurter's ingenuously worded title for the bill, "An Act Further to Promote the Defense of the United States," indicated at the outset just what approach the Administration would adopt. Its argument entailed more than just saying that the security of Great Britain was essential to the national defense of the United States. The main point was the assertion that the Lend-Lease Act was the last hope of enabling Britain and her Allies to win without the aid of American manpower. When Senator Claude Pepper asked Hull if the bill were not designed to stop Hitler without sending over American boys, that is, if it were not the cheapest means of defending the country, Hull agreed, and commented that we hoped to avoid having to make a decision on sending troops to Europe. Of the eighteen pro-Lend-Lease congressmen quoted by Charles Beard in his study of this part of the debate, only five failed to warn their listeners specifically that the Lend-Lease Bill was no guarantee that America would be able to keep out of the war, though each did emphasize that it was probably the nation's last chance of avoiding active participation in the conflict.[64]

Norman Thomas, the leader of the Socialist Party of America, presented the opposition's points most clearly in his testimony before the

[62]It should be noted at the start of any examination of this aspect of the debate that Charles A. Beard in his study *President Roosevelt and the Coming of the War*, pp. 44-68, has extracted from the *Congressional Record* statements by forty Representatives and Senators on the question of the Lend-Lease Bill as a "war bill." The quotations are accurate and not taken out of context and represent an excellent presentation of both sides of this argument.

[63]Hull, "Executive Testimony," pp. 125-26. Stimson's approach was planned before he testified. See memo from McCloy to Stimson, "for cross examination," dated Jan. 29-30, 1941, Stimson Papers. McCloy's memo posed the expected questions, and in this case the answer appears in the margin in Stimson's handwriting.

[64]Hull, "Executive Testimony," pp. 106-10; Beard, *President Roosevelt and the Coming of the War*, pp. 44-55.

House Foreign Affairs Committee. He surmised that President Roosevelt could have only one of two purposes in proposing such legislation: either to take an enormous gamble that the limited war the bill guaranteed would not spread or to take the country into war gradually, knowing the public would not stand for an outright declaration of war.[65]

Senator Robert A. Taft of Ohio hit at the most vulnerable part of the Administration position during an exchange with Senator Alben Barkley on the floor of the Senate. Shortly after Barkley, the Majority Leader, had made an impassioned speech defending the Lend-Lease Bill, Taft obtained the floor and proceeded to compliment Barkley on the force of his arguments. In fact, Taft sarcastically noted, "every argument he made might have been just as forceful on a resolution to declare war on Germany," and the Ohio Republican wondered why Barkley, if he believed what he had just said, did not ask for just such a war declaration. Barkley weakly replied that a declaration of war was not necessary in order to achieve the purpose of the Lend-Lease Act, and he also surmised that a declaration of war against Germany would probably not be as effective as the legislation being considered. Taft quickly realized Barkley's dilemma and proceeded to take advantage of it. He asked the Majority Leader if he thought an American declaration of war would be of no help to England. Barkley could not admit that, for to do so would be a virtual confession that American preparedness was so poor that the nation would not dare lend or lease military goods. He vaguely answered that he would cross that bridge when necessary and, in spite of further goading by Taft, would say nothing more. Again the pro-Lend-Lease forces had made it clear that they would not be drawn into any meaningful discussions of the long-term implications of the proposed legislation. Although Senator Taft's questioning was the most insistent on this point, the idea appeared repeatedly inside and outside Congress, and the Administration's answer was always basically the same. Congressman Hamilton Fish asked Stimson: "Is it not rather cowardly of us, if England is fighting our battle, not to go into the war?" The Secretary replied, "I am not going to pursue this line of argument. We are not concerned with it in this bill." Hull testified that a declaration of war would defeat the whole purpose of the Lend-Lease Bill, which was to delay our entry until we were prepared to withstand any attack—not meaning that America should then unilaterally declare war, but "then we can look anybody in the face."[66]

[65]HFAC, *Hearings*, p. 320.

[66]*CR*, 77th Cong., 1st sess., LXXXVII, pt. 1, Feb. 17, 1941, pp. 1039-40; HFAC, *Hearings*, p. 102; Hull, "Executive Testimony," p. 23. Taft's papers are deposited in the Library of Congress but are closed to scholars.

The Administration forces won an amusing verbal victory on this question during the testimony of one of the minor opposition witnesses, Hanford MacNider. MacNider had claimed the Lend-Lease Bill was tantamount to a declaration of war, and Congressman Pete Jarman of Alabama noted that Congress alone had the power to declare war. Jarman then went on to point out that if the bill surely meant war and was still passed by the Congress, then Congress had effectively exercised its Constitutional function.[67]

As the opposition attack on the bill as a "war measure" mounted, the Administration took a diplomatic step to back up the image of Lend-Lease as the last hope of keeping America out of war. Presidential Adviser Harry Hopkins, in Great Britain on a fact-finding mission for Roosevelt, assisted Churchill in writing a speech, much of which was clearly aimed at warding off American fears that the Lend-Lease Act was a prelude to sending their troops overseas. The Prime Minister delivered the address over the radio on February 9, 1941, and after speaking optimistically of British military actions in North Africa, closed with a promise:

Here is the answer I will give President Roosevelt: Put your confidence in us. Give us your faith and your blessing, and, under Providence, all will be well.

We shall not fail or falter; and we shall not weaken or tire. Neither the sudden shock of battle, nor the long-drawn trials of vigilance and exertion will wear us down. Give us the tools, and we will finish the job.[68]

The feeling of frustration experienced by the opposition because of the Administration's tactic of keeping the discussion as narrow as possible was emotionally expressed by the aging Senator Hiram Johnson of California. The old Progressive, during his questioning of Treasury Secretary Morgenthau, made a brief but vigorous speech in which he claimed that the only issue at stake was whether or not Hitler was the threat some people made him out to be. He complimented Virginia's Senator Carter Glass for being the only one honest enough to openly support a declaration of war, and he pleaded:

Do not get off on a tangent, like we are going to do with the bill here, that some of us believe will make a dictatorship in this country and that others believe begins a totalitarian government in this country. Let us not monkey with the subject and let us not dally with it, but let us go to bat at once as to whether we want war or whether we do not want war.[69]

His statement was unsophisticated and overly simplistic, but it contained a certain rugged honesty about it. He fully recognized that

[67]HFAC, *Hearings*, pp. 361-62.

[68]Churchill, *Blood, Sweat, and Tears*, pp. 453-62. Sherwood, *Roosevelt and Hopkins*, pp. 260-62.

[69]SFRC, *Hearings*, p. 73.

Congress no longer accepted the premises that had resulted in the passage of the famous piece of isolationist legislation which bore his name, but he wanted to go down fighting.

Clearly the most successful tactic was the deliberate refusal of the Administration leaders to co-operate with opposition attempts to turn the Lend-Lease hearings into a broad debate on over-all foreign policy. One of the more obvious examples of this strategy was the question of convoying. The issue had come up upon numerous occasions during White House meetings, usually at the prompting of Henry Stimson. The Secretary of War asked the same question that the opponents of Lend-Lease later posed: How would the war materials Britain needed be delivered in the face of an increasingly effective German submarine blockade? In spite of such pleadings, Roosevelt had steadfastly refused to make any public or private decision on the matter. At his press conference of January 21, the President flatly denied that he had ever considered providing escorts for British convoys, yet the very next day he privately admitted to Stimson that he had been thinking about the possibility of convoying and a diplomatic break with the Axis. That same evening Stimson gave Roosevelt a "sombre paper" that summarized the over-all situation in the light of the Lend-Lease Bill. The memorandum, which had been read and approved by Knox, Marshall, and Stark, assumed that Germany planned to invade England during the summer of 1941 but belittled the amount of aid which Lend-Lease could actually provide before that time. The paper emphasized that initially the bill would act primarily as an important morale boost for the British and warned that the utmost speed in getting it passed and implemented was necessary if the aid were to become effective by 1942. It ended with a strong recommendation that American warships convoy supplies to Britain. Stimson wrote in his diary that night that "it was altogether a very interesting, indeed almost thrilling evening. So I came back very well satisfied with what had happened." Considering Stimson's ardent support for convoying, only a favorable decision by Roosevelt on that matter could have left the normally pessimistic Secretary of War so enthused.[70]

Even without Roosevelt's decision on convoying, if there were one, the two military secretaries, Stimson and Knox, faced a personal dilemma during their testimony before the Congressional committees. Both were quite convinced that convoying was necessary if Lend-Lease was to be effective, yet to admit that fact might well defeat the Lend-Lease Act itself. Their solution involved a classic case of misdi-

[70]Stimson Diary, Jan. 22, 1941; Henry L. Stimson, "Resume of Situation Relative to Bill 1776," dated Jan. 22, 1941, in U.S., Congress, Joint Committee on the Investigation of the Pearl Harbor attack, *Hearings*, 39 pts. (Washington: U.S. Government Printing Office, 1946), XX, 4275-80; Langer and Gleason, *The Undeclared War*, pp. 272-73; the *New York Times*, Jan. 22, 1941, contains Roosevelt's press conference remarks.

rection. When Senator Robert LaFollette asked Stimson if he interpreted the Lend-Lease Bill as giving the President the authority to convoy the goods transferred under the act, Stimson replied that he did not think so, but he went on to point out that the question did not matter since "as Commander-in-Chief I think he already had that power." Although the leadership ultimately accepted an amendment that stated that nothing in the bill could be considered authorization for convoying, the Administration never retreated from the position that the President had the Constitutional power to order such escorting without the approval of Congress. The Majority Report of the House Foreign Affairs Committee stated that the amendment was included only to avoid any doubt on the issue and noted that even without the amendment it believed that the bill did not in any way enlarge the authority of the Navy to convoy shipping. The opponents of Lend-Lease carried this argument to the very end of the debate. They seized upon the statements of the Administration that the President already had the power to authorize convoying and accused the bill's supporters of amending the bill merely for the purpose of confusing the issue. As Senator Guy Gillette of Iowa claimed on the floor of the Senate: "The American people ... know that the use of vessels as convoys either for British or American ships would inevitably result in a state of war." Secretary Knox admitted as much during his testimony at the Congressional hearings, but the Administration still managed to avoid any discussion of the real question—would it order the convoying of the ships bringing Lend-Lease goods to Britain? [71]

Ironically, one of the Administration's key witnesses, Cordell Hull, provided the opposition with a troublesome means of attacking the attempt to limit carefully the range of discussion. After Hull finished his opening statement on the first day of hearings in the House Foreign Affairs Committee, Congressman Luther Johnson innocuously inquired whether Hull believed the proposed bill was "absolutely necessary for the defense of the United States?" Hull could not bring himself to give such a blanket approval and opaquely commented that he had "been very unwilling to be driven" to that conclusion. He further qualified his position by flatly stating that the Lend-Lease Bill had been prepared in the Treasury Department and that Morgenthau would discuss the actual provisions of the legislation. George Tinkham, the isolationist Republican from Massachusetts, seized upon Hull's apparent admission of ignorance about the provisions of the bill and feigned shock that the "premier" of the Cabinet had not been consulted on such a critical measure. Hull tried to parry the attack by

[71]*House Majority Report on H.R. 1776*, p. 9; *CR*, 77th Cong., 1st sess., LXXXVII, pt. 2, Feb. 21, 1941, p. 1241; SFRC, *Hearings*, pp. 96, 210; HFAC, *Hearings*, p. 185.

claiming he had been consulted on the foreign policy aspects of the legislation, but the damage was done.[72]

By indirectly violating the Administration's strategy, Hull put Morgenthau in a very uncomfortable position.[73] Not only did the Administration wish to avoid any discussion of the long-term implications of the bill, but Morgenthau himself was suspect in the eyes of many Congressmen as being overly sympathetic to the British, as well as being anti-German because he was a Jew. Worst of all, to pin authorship on one member of the government would defeat at the start any hope of fragmenting the opposition assault by means of restricting each Administration witness to his narrow area of official competence. In addition, the Treasury Department was worried that the Congress might find out that the British had actually helped to draft the bill, and all agreed that public knowledge of that fact would hurt its chances.[74]

When Morgenthau appeared before the Foreign Affairs Committee he attempted to anticipate the problem by stating that he assumed the committee was primarily interested in information on the state of British finances, but that did little good. Hamilton Fish straightforwardly asked Morgenthau if he had authored the bill, and the Secretary proceeded to give a description of the drafting process which was somewhat misleading. Although he left out only the names of Purvis and Phillips when he listed those who had been consulted, the over-all impression was that the original draft had been the work of the legislative drafting commission of the House. When Fish asked if the Treasury had initiated the bill, Morgenthau gave the technical truth by denying it. The bill had actually been initiated by the President, but in the more honest sense of the word the Treasury had certainly been the initiator. Under further questioning by Fish, Morgenthau implied that the bill had originated with President Roosevelt and Speaker Sam Rayburn.[75]

The same problem arose again during the Senate hearings. During executive testimony Hull had again described the Treasury Department as the principal author of the bill and had admitted he had not studied it for language or non-diplomatic matters. Morgenthau attempted to forestall any questions by stating he had come to testify only on financial matters, but Senators Robert LaFollette and Hiram

[72]HFAC, *Hearings*, pp. 8, 19.

[73]The anger in the Treasury Department over Hull's actions must have been quite intense, for Edward Foley, then the General Counsel in that department, when he was interviewed twenty-five years later, still recalled vividly that Hull had gone against policy and instructions. Foley interview, Nov. 3, 1966.

[74]Harry White brought this up when Morgenthau instructed him to work with Purvis and Phillips during the initial drafting stages. Morgenthau Diary, Jan. 3, 1941, 344:256-57.

[75]HFAC, *Hearings*, pp. 51, 57-58.

Johnson were not to be put off so easily. Morgenthau finally characterized the legislation as "a product of many brains" but stated he supported it in its entirety.[76]

Although the Administration was less than frank in its handling of this question, it was hardly of the essence. Senator Barkley hit at the heart of the question when he told the Foreign Relations Committee: "I wish merely to state that regardless of who wrote the bill, whether it was written by a taxicab driver or the Attorney General of the United States, the language speaks for itself. It is plain enough for anybody to understand, it seems to me, regardless of who had anything to do with the writing of the bill."[77] The opposition continually claimed during this argument that its only purpose was to find out who it could question about the specific provisions in the bill, yet anytime a specific question about the meaning of a section of the proposed legislation came up, they received a straight, if strictly limited answer from one or another of the government's witnesses. Representative Karl Mundt could complain that the Lend-Lease Bill had been secretly written and "placed before us, like a baby in a basket on our doorstep,"[78] but the fact remained that the Administration publicly supported it.

The examples of the Administration's indirection and evasion in answering broad and speculative questions are innumerable. Many times the questions were loaded, such as when Representative Frances Bolton asked Hull if he thought the present crisis justified giving the President virtual totalitarian powers. Hull replied by merely expressing the hope that nothing would delay the passage of the bill. When a frustrated George Tinkham accused Hull of being evasive, the Secretary replied that he appreciated the compliment. Stimson summed up the over-all approach of the Administration witnesses when he wrote in his diary that he had been able to prevent Senator LaFollette from "going into the irrelevant matters of my own opinions."[79]

The most meaningful refutation of the attacks made on Great Britain's motives and honesty came through the testimony of Treasury Secretary Morgenthau. The statistics that he presented were enormously persuasive, and the fact that Britain had authorized their release was far more convincing of British candor than any verbal

[76]Hull, "Executive Testimony," pp. 73-78, 158. SFRC, *Hearings*, pp. 33-36. Charles Beard, *Roosevelt and the Coming of the War*, pp. 24-30, discusses the authorship question and strongly implies that the Administration's purpose was to hide the true purpose of the bill, which he claims was to get the United States into the war.

[77]SFRC, *Hearings*, p. 58. Senator Guy Gillette facetiously commented that although Barkley had accepted the role of foster-father of the bill, there had apparently been some promiscuity on the maternal side. Barkley retorted that even so, it was still legitimate. *Ibid.*, p. 60.

[78]*CR*, 77th Cong., 1st. sess., LXXXVII, pt. 1, Feb. 5, 1941, p. 611.

[79]HFAC, *Hearings*, pp. 46-47; Stimson Diary, Jan. 29, 1941.

argument. The only possible way to attack that presentation was either to prove that Britain had given the American government false figures or to call Henry Morgenthau a liar when he stated that those statistics corresponded with Treasury Department estimates. They found it impossible to do the former and were unwilling to resort to the latter. Morgenthau's consistent honesty with the Congress, such as exhibited in his refusal to violate the spirit of the Johnson Debt-Default Act, had won for him a grudging respect even among the isolationists. It was within the rules to accuse Franklin Roosevelt of virtually anything, but the Cabinet was usually treated with courtesy and trust.[80] The figures Morgenthau submitted were extensive, but boiled down to their essentials, they showed that Britain would run up a dollar deficit, over and above estimated dollar receipts, of $1,464,000,000 by January 1, 1942. His questioners attempted to prove that the British Empire, particularly Canada, was not contributing its fair share, but Morgenthau easily fielded those questions. When he finished it was clear that even if the opposition's complaints about the Empire's dollar balances were correct, those dollars were not sufficient to meet the deficit anyway. Morgenthau anticipated one of the opposition's potential arguments when he introduced a table comparing the tax burden of Americans and the British. In every case they were substantially higher on the British side of the ledger. For a married couple with two children, earning ten thousand dollars per year, the English paid $3,451 in income taxes while their American counterparts paid only $440. British corporation taxes were at a rate of 42½ per cent compared to the American corporate tax rate of 24 per cent. Most impressive of all to the layman was the fact that the British paid a tax on alcoholic beverages which was over five times that paid in the United States.[81]

Morgenthau's response to honest questions regarding the British financial situation was invariably straightforward and informative. Senator Arthur Vandenberg made a lengthy effort to get the Secretary to admit that Britain had substantial assets available to her that she had not made use of, but Morgenthau had a reasonable answer for each question. Senator Nye also attempted to undermine the figures that the British had submitted, but Morgenthau invariably defended those statistics and was able to explain some minor differences between them and some official American estimates of British assets. Since the opposition later adopted the plan of loaning money to Britain as a tactical maneuver, it is difficult to assess the success of

[80] The principal exception to this rule of courtesy was Representative George Tinkham of Massachusetts, who was repeatedly rude and insulting during the hearings, particularly toward Cordell Hull; see HFAC, *Hearings*, pp. 17-31.

[81] SFRC, *Hearings*, pp. 14-15. Hall, *North American Supply*, pp. 224-42, contains a comprehensive discussion of Canada's extensive financial aid to Britain.

Morgenthau's testimony, but it is probable that the opposition's failure to make any meaningful dents in that testimony contributed to their decision to attempt to modify instead of defeat the Lend-Lease Bill. At any rate, the minority reports of both committees supported the concept of aiding Britain by some means other than the Lend-Lease Act. [82]

In spite of Henry Morgenthau's highly effective testimony regarding the sorry state of British finances, a large and vocal minority remained convinced that Great Britain had fooled the American government and was about to take the United States for a free ride, just as they supposedly had in World War I. Obviously, the old shadow of unpaid war debts hung over the entire debate, yet ironically, those who proposed a loan to England instead of the Lend-Lease "giveaway" were the very ones who had been most concerned over the World War I war debts. As other historians have pointed out, Anglophobia had long been the mainstay of a portion of isolationist sentiment in America, and this was no exception. [83]

This sentiment manifested itself in various forms. Senator Robert Taft, in a speech before the New York State Bar Association, claimed that the bill would "make Uncle Sam the best and biggest Santa Claus the world has ever seen." Representative Frances Bolton wrote one of her constituents that the United States was being asked to do more for Britain than her Dominions were doing. Senators Burton Wheeler and Gerald Nye announced they would introduce a resolution calling on the President to determine the war aims and secret treaties of the belligerents, and Senator D. W. Clark of Idaho asserted that England was not fighting for democracy but for "gold, trade, commerce and the maintenance of their ruling classes." With the exception of refuting factual error, the Administration merely accentuated the positive aspects of its proposal and ignored the anti-British attacks that regularly occurred. [84]

The opposition eventually supported an amendment to the Lend-Lease Bill calling for a loan of two billion dollars to Great Britain, but

[82]Morgenthau's testimony is in HFAC, *Hearings*, pp. 51-83, and SFRC, *Hearings*, pp. 9-76, 80-83. The British financial statistics that Morgenthau made available to the committees are printed in each hearing. Vandenberg's questioning is in *ibid.*, pp. 16-27, and Nye's is in *ibid.*, pp. 39-52. No mention of unused British assets is made in either of the two minority reports. The *Senate Minority Report on H.R. 1776* endorsed aid to Britain in a negative fashion by merely saying Lend-Lease was unnecessary since the United States was already aiding Britain to the utmost of its ability; see p. 6. The *House Minority Report on H.R. 1776* began with the statement that "we are for all aid to Britain short of war." See p. 13.

[83]Two good examples are Adler, *The Isolationist Impulse*; and Alexander DeConde, "On Twentieth Century Isolationism," *Isolation and Security*, ed. A. DeConde (Durham: Duke University Press, 1957), pp. 3-32.

[84]*New York Journal-American*, Jan. 26, 1941; Bolton Papers, "constituent correspondence file on H.R. 1776," letter dated Feb. 24, 1941. *New York Times*, Jan. 27, 1941; *New York Herald-Tribune*, Feb. 25, 1941, quotes Sen. Clark.

such a move hardly demonstrates any real desire on the part of the isolationists to aid England.[85] Many of the amendment's supporters had earlier made statements so critical of Great Britain that it was apparent that, forced to choose the lesser of two evils, they supported a loan only in hopes of defeating the Lend-Lease Bill. Senator Bennett Clark of Missouri, during his questioning of Undersecretary of the Treasury Daniel Bell, attempted to point out that it would be foolish to pass a bill that had no financial limits, particularly in view of Britain's failure to pay her World War I debts. Yet he had no qualms about supporting a move to give Britain a loan.[86]

The intense distrust of British motives and methods, born of the experience of World War I and older strains of Anglophobia rooted in the Populist Revolt, showed through in the testimony time after time. Former Wisconsin Governor Philip F. LaFollette, the brother of Senator Robert LaFollette, stated bluntly that the purpose of the Lend-Lease Act was "to guarantee to Britain an overwhelming victory, regardless of the consequences of war for the people of the United States." Senator Nye read some passages from the journals and letters of a British politician during World War I which showed the British leaders to have been highly materialistic and primarily concerned with power politics rather than ideals. He asked the witness then testifying, Henry Morgenthau, whether he thought current British leadership had a higher purpose. Morgenthau refused to comment, but Nye's inference was unmistakable. Yet Nye and LaFollette both supported the loan amendment.[87]

The Lend-Lease debate brought to the surface all the old shibboleths about Europe and Great Britain: imperialism was a bad as fascism; European power politics were un-American; trickery was to be expected of the corrupt British bankers and munitions-makers; Britain had been the enemy since 1776; and so on. Representative Martin Sweeney, a professional Irishman from Cleveland, Ohio, summed it all up when, shortly after the Lend-Lease Act passed, he sarcastically proposed a new battle hymn sung to the tune of "God Bless America."

---

[85] Manfred Jonas, "Pro-Axis Sentiment and American Isolationism," *The Historian*, XXIX, no. 2 (Feb., 1967), 236, all too casually makes that assumption. He admits that the motives of some of those supporting the amendment are suspect but still concludes that anti-British attitudes were not a key aspect of isolationism. The hearings and floor debates over the Lend-Lease Bill do not bear him out.

[86] SFRC, *Hearings*, pp. 76-80. On Jan. 23, 1941, the *New York Times* commented that it appeared the Republicans had changed their strategy of trying to defeat the Lend-Lease Bill and instead were trying to substitute loans or grants for the broad extension of Presidential powers.

[87] SFRC, *Hearings*, pp. 50-52, 263.

God save America from British rule:
Stand beside her and guide her
From the schemers who would make of her a fool.
From Lexington to Yorktown,
From blood-stained Valley Forge,
God save America
From a king named George.[88]

Although the pro-Lend-Lease forces made no serious attempt to cut off debate, one of their constant themes was the need for speed in passing the bill. The Administration and certain members of the military were thoroughly convinced that the real crisis in Europe would come within sixty to ninety days.[89] Although Stimson and others publicly and privately admitted that Lend-Lease's main contribution during 1941 would be to British morale rather than war materials, all emphasized that morale was as critical a factor as any other. Henry Morgenthau even went so far as to assert that if the Lend-Lease Bill did not pass, "there is nothing for Great Britain to do but stop fighting."[90]

Those members of the opposition who conceded that aid to Britain was necessary also usually admitted that speed was essential. Although heated arguments arose whenever the committee chairman attempted to speed up the debate, most Congressmen accepted the idea that if aid were to help the British, it had to arrive quickly. Representative Hamilton Fish, in a letter to the *New York Times,* presented the one significant attack on the Administration's request for speed. He cited Stimson and Knox as his authority for saying aid to Britain under Lend-Lease would not reach Britain until 1942 and then concluded that the only way the United States could provide meaningful assistance during the so-called sixty- to ninety-day crisis was to give away part of the Navy. Since Roosevelt had said he would not do that, the only possible purpose of such a sweeping grant of powers was the acquisition of power itself.[91]

The last major Administration argument in favor of the Lend-Lease Bill was the assertion that it would assist in organizing the defense industry in the United States. This argument was primarily advanced

[88]Strout, *The American Image of the Old World*, discusses the Lend-Lease Bill and the isolationist's attitude toward Europe on pp. 213-17. The poem is from *CR*, 77th Cong., 1st sess., LXXXVII, pt. 12, June 19, 1941, p. A2941, as quoted in *ibid.*, p. 217.

[89]Stimson and Knox referred to this sixty- to ninety-day crisis numerous times. For example see HFAC, *Hearings*, p. 151; SFRC, *Hearings*, p. 201.

[90]SFRC, *Hearings*, pp. 92-93; Stimson, "Resume of Situation Relative to Bill 1776," in *Pearl Harbor Attack*, XX, 4275-80. Morgenthau's comment is quoted in Stettinius, *Lend-Lease*, p. 77.

[91]Letter from Hamilton Fish to the editor, *New York Times*, Jan. 31, 1941. See HFAC, *Hearings*, pp. 116-18, for an example of attempts to speed up the debate.

by Secretary of War Stimson. Before both the Senate and House committees, Stimson gave the same pitch: the Lend-Lease Bill would eliminate the chaos that had characterized the manufacture of war goods in the United States for the preceding two years. This would be done in three ways. First, virtually all ordering would be done by the United States government, regardless of the ultimate destination. Second, such unified ordering would result in the standardization of weapons among the Allies, which would increase over-all efficiency. Third, the distribution of goods under the Lend-Lease plan would be done by those persons primarily interested in the security of the United States.[92]

The opposition attempted to create a dispute on this issue in February, when Senator Burton Wheeler released to the press some statistics regarding American air strength which had probably been presented in executive session testimony by Generals Marshall and Brett. Stimson's subordinates said the figures were accurate but advised against getting into any open argument with Wheeler. In an earlier radio speech, Wheeler had claimed that five-sixths of America's aircraft output was going to Great Britain. The Senator's violation of executive testimony security prompted Roosevelt to comment that Wheeler's disclosures must have been most interesting and satisfactory to Hitler. With that exception, the Administration generally refused to answer Wheeler's attacks, and the issue died out.[93]

The main challenge by the opposition to the argument that the Lend-Lease Bill would aid the American preparedness program came in the form of an attack on the President's potential power to transfer elements of the United States Navy under the bill's provisions. Roosevelt had originally treated such ideas as ridiculous, but the Administration's persistent refusal to accept an amendment to that effect convinced many that it might not be so ridiculous after all. This fear was accentuated by the testimony of Wendell Willkie before the Senate Foreign Relations Committee in which he suggested that the British should be given five to ten destroyers per month. That particular piece of testimony had repercussions within the Administration, for Secretary of the Navy Frank Knox had previously stated to the same committee that he opposed any further transfers of American naval

[92]HFAC, *Hearings*, pp. 87-89. SFRC, *Hearings*, pp. 85-86. A memo entitled "Possible Questions Which May Arise from Hoover's Letter of January 15, 1951 [sic], prepared by John McCloy and Arthur Palmer, annotated by Henry L. Stimson, dated Jan. 16, 1941, Stimson Papers, lists some examples ranging from barriers to the exchange of airplanes to the law that limited the transfer of dental sets to one per person.

[93]Transcript of press conference of Feb. 6, 1941, Stimson Papers. Memo from R. A. Lovett to Stimson, Feb. 11, 1941, *ibid. New York Times*, Feb. 5, 1941. Beard, *Roosevelt and the Coming of the War*, pp. 20-21. Langer and Gleason, *The Undeclared War*, p. 277n. It is quite possible that Wheeler obtained the statistics from some of the more disgruntled officers in the Army Air Corps.

vessels. There is some evidence that Willkie made his suggestion on the basis of talks with President Roosevelt, though the day after Willkie testified, Knox and Roosevelt met at the White House and when the Secretary of the Navy emerged he stated he still held his original views.[94] Although the opposition did not succeed in attaching to the bill an amendment prohibiting such transfers, a substantial number of Congressmen voted for such an amendment while still ardently supporting the Lend-Lease Bill itself.

The opposition made one other attempt to attack the proposed grant of powers which the leadership completely ignored in the public debate. Led by Representative George Tinkham and Senator Robert Reynolds, they proposed amendments to the Lend-Lease Bill which would have listed those nations that could receive such aid. In each case the purpose of the amendment was to prevent any Lend-Lease from going to the Soviet Union. Fears were expressed by some that the removal of the "moral embargo" on trade with the Soviet Union, which had occurred during the Lend-Lease hearings, was a first step toward appeasing "homicidal, communistic" Russia. Although many of those who supported such a campaign were honestly distrustful of the Soviets, it appears that in this case the overwhelming majority of those who supported it did so primarily in hopes of defeating or at least somehow limiting the powers granted the President in the Lend-Lease Bill.[95]

The Administration, which knew of German plans to invade Russia and thus suspected that the day might come when aiding Russia would be in the national interest, refused to discuss the issue in terms of aiding any specific nation except Great Britain and contented itself with the evasive and misleading comment that no one knew where Hitler would attack next, therefore the utmost flexibility was required in the Lend-Lease Act. This tactic was apparently most successful, for in July, 1941, *Fortune* magazine stated that during the Lend-Lease debates the influence of the Russian question had been negligible.[96]

One offshoot of the isolationist approach was presented during the Lend-Lease hearings by Charles A. Lindbergh. Made famous by his solo flight across the Atlantic Ocean in 1927, Lindbergh had remained in the public eye because of his expertise in aviation and the tragedy

[94]SFRC, *Hearings*, pp. 873, 210-11; Langer and Gleason, *The Undeclared War*, p. 280; Barnard, *Wendell Willkie*, p. 289.

[95]Rep. G. Tinkham in the *CR*, 77th Cong., 1st sess., LXXXVII, pt. 1, Jan. 29, 1941, p. 383. Raymond H. Dawson, *The Decision to Aid Russia, 1941; Foreign Policy and Domestic Politics* (Chapel Hill: The University of North Carolina Press, 1959), p. 40, presents a persuasive case for this point of view. He found that only five of those who supported the amendments proposed by Tinkham and Reynolds actually were true supporters of the Lend-Lease Bill.

[96]Dawson, *The Decision to Aid Russia*, pp. 31-32, 41.

of the kidnapping-murder of his child. His visits to Germany in the late 1930's which had received great publicity from both German and American sources, left with him the strong impression that Hitler's Germany was destined to conquer Europe. During his testimony before the House Foreign Affairs Committee one member asked Lindbergh which side he hoped would win, and Lindbergh answered "neither." To Lindbergh the question was meaningless since he believed that there was no way to prevent a German victory.[97] Lindbergh's primary argument was that America should concentrate on building her air power so as to insure that no other nation would dare attack her, although in his opening statements before each committee he claimed that geography provided both Europe and the Western Hemisphere with natural and impregnable defenses. In his words: "Personally, I do not believe it is possible for either America or Europe to invade the other successfully by air, or even by a combination of air, land, and sea, unless an internal collapse precedes invasion." He consistently denied that he hoped for a German victory in Europe, but he flatly stated that Germany would remain the dominant power in Europe and that America had to co-operate with any nation that controlled Europe. It is impossible to tell whether he advocated such a policy out of a desire to work with the Germans, whom he greatly admired, or out of a belief that the United States had no choice, but either way the result was the same.[98]

Although the crowds that attended Lindbergh's testimony were the largest and most vocal of the hearings, his appeals for a negotiated peace did not strike a responsive chord with either Congress or the public. Generally the Administration answered his arguments indirectly. Its indictment of Germany as an aggressive threat to the United States and its claim that England could win with American aid both struck at the core of Lindbergh's case. Lend-Lease supporters in the House were content to let Lindbergh disappear from the spotlight as soon as possible. He underwent a lengthy interrogation in the Foreign Relations Committee from Senators Barkley and Connally, but both of them seemed primarily interested in getting Lindbergh to state his views as clearly and unequivocally as possible. Only Senator Claude Pepper actually attempted directly to attack Lindbergh's testimony. Pepper hit hard at Hitler's failure to live up to his bargain at Munich and questioned the wisdom of trying to negotiate with such a man. He repeatedly got Lindbergh to oppose flatly any sort of aid to Britain and in doing so managed to isolate Lindbergh from the major-

---

[97]*New York Times*, Jan. 24, 1941. The report noted that Lindbergh's answer was drowned out by boos and catcalls from his supporters, who considered the question unfair and loaded.

[98]HFAC, *Hearings*, pp. 373, 385.

ity of the general public as well as to line him up against the opposition tactic that some kind of aid to Britain was necessary.[99]

Lindbergh was not the only witness whose approach differed from the usual tack taken by the bill's opponents. Although ex-Ambassador to Great Britain[100]   Joseph P. Kennedy was called as an opposition witness, it is difficult to tell from his testimony whether he hurt or helped the passage of the Lend-Lease Bill. Kennedy was obviously torn between a sincere dislike of the powers granted the executive under the bill and his faith in Roosevelt's patriotism and honesty, which he publicly defended during the hearings. Like Lindbergh, Kennedy was pessimistic about Britain's chances for survival, but he believed that democracy could still be saved if America stayed out of war. He hated Hitler and all naziism stood for, which made selling out England unthinkable, yet he believed it was too late to aid Britain effectively and feared that the Lend-Lease Bill could be misused in a dictatorial fashion. The final result was an extremely confused and often self-contradictory presentation during the Congressional hearings. Kennedy refused either to condemn or support the Lend-Lease Bill but instead repeatedly stated that Britain had to be aided as quickly and efficiently as possible. Yet during the same testimony he expressed the fear that America might be drawn into a war for which she was not prepared. He admitted he was opposed to some portions of the bill which gave extensive powers to the executive but regularly praised Franklin Roosevelt's ability, honesty, and motives. He flatly refused to suggest any amendments or endorse those proposed by the opposition. Roosevelt had expected Kennedy to launch a vigorous public campaign against the Lend-Lease Bill, but the ex-Ambassador's inability to develop a comprehensive and coherent anti-Lend-Lease platform eliminated that problem.[101]

The effect on public opinion of the debates over the Lend-Lease Bill, and vice versa, is worth a complete study all its own, although some obvious comments can be made. Between January 22 and March 7, 1941, eighteen polls were taken on the question of approval or disapproval, and every one found at least 50 per cent favoring the passage of the bill. Usually the percentage was 55 per cent or higher. The final poll, on March 7, recorded those in favor at 61 per cent with only 23 per cent firmly opposed, which indicates the success of the

[99]SFRC, *Hearings*, pp. 512-42; *New York Times*, Jan. 24, 1941.

[100]Kennedy had handed in his resignation, in accordance with protocol, on the day after Roosevelt was re-elected but made it clear that he meant it. His resignation was announced early in December, 1940. See Whalen, *The Founding Father*, p. 331.

[101]*New York Times*, Jan. 22, 1941; HFAC, *Hearings*, pp. 221-315. The contradictions become particularly evident at the close of his testimony on pp. 312-15. See also Whalen, *The Founding Father*, pp. 345-46. Kennedy's proposed campaign is mentioned in a memo from Adolf Berle to Roosevelt, Jan. 14, 1941, Roosevelt Papers, PSF, State Dept., 1941.

Administration's tactics. Apparently on instructions from Roosevelt, the White House office staff compiled almost daily memorandums summarizing the totals of pros and cons in correspondence received on the bill. Although the letters, telegrams, and cards that were opposed generally exceeded those favoring the bill by about two to one, such a ratio actually indicated general support for the legislation since politicians agree that the negative side of an issue is the one that engenders constituent response. This was particularly true since Lend-Lease appeared certain to pass Congress. The Treasury Department forwarded a summary of editorial opinion to the President which concluded that a majority of newspapers approved of the bill and most of those who opposed were quite temperate. It claimed that public opinion had favored the bill from the start and that there had been a sharp swing in support of the bill after the House and Senate hearings began. [102]

The two pressure groups most influential in foreign affairs, the America First Committee and the Committee to Defend America by Aiding the Allies, both carried out extensive campaigns to put forth their views. America First concentrated on convincing the public that a strong United States had nothing to fear from Germany and adopted the Lindbergh position that intervention would only prolong the war in Europe. As Wayne Cole points out in his study of the group, its efforts appear to have been wasted. In the East-Central part of the country, where America First was strongest, support for the Lend-Lease Bill increased from 39 per cent in mid-February to 50 per cent by March 1, 1941.[103]

The Committee to Defend America (the White Committee) spent large amounts of money and energy in an attempt to explain and justify the bill. Basically, it adopted the same positions as the Administration did in the Congressional debates. It is impossible to determine the effect of their work, but it is worth noting that in Chicago, where America First was powerful, the Committee to Defend America was most active. That unit mailed over 100,000 letters and handed out 30,000 handbills at industrial plants.[104] As mentioned above, in the East-Central part of the United States, centered around Chicago, support for the Lend-Lease Bill steadily increased.

[102]Cantrill, *Public Opinion*, pp. 409-10. The summaries of White House mail are in Roosevelt Papers, OF 4193-Misc., box 4; "Summary of Editorial Opinion," was compiled by Alan Barth and forwarded to Roosevelt by Morgenthau on Feb. 10, 1941, *ibid.*, OF 4193, Lend-Lease Agreement, 1940-43, box 1-2.

[103]Cole, *America First*, pp. 49-50. Senator D. Worth Clark of Idaho inserted into the *Congressional Record* a document prepared by the America First Committee entitled "A Factual Analysis of H.R. 1776." The basic conclusion of the Committee was that the bill gave the President dictatorial powers over both foreign affairs and the domestic economy. See *CR*, 77th Cong., 1st sess., LXXXVII, pt. 10, pp. A900-02.

[104]Johnson, *The Battle Against Isolation*, pp. 207-9.

Evidence on the attitude of the other pressure groups regarding the Lend-Lease Bill is sparse. The business community seems generally to have supported the legislation, while the Communist Party opposed the bill both openly and through its front organizations.[105] Various other organizations, such as the No Foreign War Committee, the German-American National Alliance, the Peace Mobilization Committee, and the German-American Bund, all opposed the bill violently, but their influence is suspect—though it has not been adequately studied. These and similar groups received direct as well as indirect support from the German government via its diplomatic representatives.[106]

The battle over the Lend-Lease Act can generally be characterized as a partisan one, although party lines were crossed, particularly in the Senate. The fact that Wendell Willkie testified for the bill did not eliminate it as a partisan issue. Willkie was read out of his party by many of the Republican leaders, and as a defeated candidate he commanded very little loyalty within the party anyway. Historians commonly lump the opposition to Lend-Lease under the term isolationism, but that is hardly an adequate description. Certainly the major elements of traditional isolationism were present in some arguments. The opposition continually spoke in terms of the Monroe Doctrine and the impregnability of the Western Hemisphere. Anglophobia, usually expressed in terms of distrust and grudging admiration, continually cropped up, while overshadowing every argument was the passionate desire to stay out of war. Though this was all the stock-in-trade of isolationism, others used the same rhetoric without the same goal. Pacifists, who believed in international co-operation in a world without war, condemned Lend-Lease as designed to get America into war, yet they did not believe in isolating America from Europe. Many others, typified by Charles Lindbergh, believed that aiding Britain would not stop a German victory and would instead prevent the United States from building up her defenses. The major opposition argument that Lend-Lease added to Roosevelt's dictatorial assumption of power was connected to isolationism only by virtue of a common enemy, not by any philosophical kinship. It provided the main common denominator for such diverse people as Senator Nye, a classic agrarian isolationist, and the respected international lawyer, John Bassett Moore.

Those opposed to the bill used two main tactical approaches. First and foremost, they claimed that the Lend-Lease Act would involve the

---

[105]Stromberg, *The Journal of Economic History*, XIII, 73. The Communist line is epitomized by the American Youth Congress; see Lash, *Eleanor Roosevelt*, p. 231.

[106]Thomsen to the Foreign Ministry, Feb. 9, 1941, *DGFP*, XII, no. 34, pp. 60-62. I have found no evidence of British financial support for pressure groups such as occurred prior to American entry into World War I.

United States in the war. The arguments given for avoiding such involvement differed but agreed that entry into the European War would not be in America's long-term interests. The second major opposition argument was in the form of a criticism of the dictatorial powers the bill bestowed upon the President. Although much of this argument was *ad hominem* and the product of those who opposed any proposal made by Franklin Roosevelt regardless of its merit, many were sincerely concerned about the entire momentum of the New Deal and believed the Lend-Lease Bill epitomized the expansion of executive power which they opposed. A third opposition argument revolved around the possibility of applying Lend-Lease to the Soviet Union, but the Administration forces carefully avoided biting at that hook, and its over-all effect proved negligible.

The Roosevelt Administration was not thoroughly honest and candid in its presentation of the Lend-Lease Bill. That raises a question which is yet to be answered: Does the democratic system, as Americans know it, require total disclosure by the party in power of all the pros and cons—including predictions of possible results—or is that the job of the opposition? Certainly all of the predictable, probable, and possible consequences of the Lend-Lease Act were presented in a most forceful fashion to the public by the opposition, and that same public chose to reject those arguments. Granted, the Administration had the enormous advantage of a base of power and the initiative, but that advantage was accentuated by the failure of the opposition to develop any sort of reasonable alternative to Lend-Lease. Most Americans worked from the basic assumption that they wanted to aid England without incurring another troublesome war debts problem, so the suggestion that the United States loan the British money fell on deaf ears. Wary of getting into war and worried about the accusations of a dictatorship, the public and its representatives, after weeks of intensive debate, gave their support to their President.

CHAPTER VII

"FROM SOMETHING LIKE DISASTER":
THE PASSAGE OF THE LEND-LEASE ACT

The Lend-Lease Bill did not sail through Congress unscathed. Even though Roosevelt had the votes at the very outset to pass the legislation, to obtain the unanimity he wanted would mean accepting some amending of the bill on Capitol Hill.[1] Morgenthau had expected as much, for when he gave the initial instructions for the drafting of the bill he said to write it as broadly as possible "and let somebody else tighten it up."[2] Some Congressmen proposed to do just that. Many of the amendments that were proposed were honest attempts by supporters of the bill to clarify the wording or to enlist the votes of less enthusiastic representatives and senators. Such changes posed no problem for the Administration, and they were readily agreed to. More troublesome were the rash of amendments proposed by those whose aim was to change the essential nature of the bill. This became a particular problem once the opposition became aware that it could not muster enough votes to defeat the bill. Some of these amendments were actually substitutes, whereas other attempts to emasculate the legislation were far more subtle.

---

[1]This is clear from the discussions recorded in the Morgenthau Diary. See also memo from Roosevelt for Code Room, Jan. 16, 1941, Roosevelt Papers, PSF, II Department Files, State Dept., 1940-41, 1943-44, box 28. Langer and Gleason, *The Undeclared War*, pp. 272-73, state that it was obvious to the Administration that if it was to get the bill passed by March 1, it would have to accept amendments. That is misleading. It was not speed that motivated Roosevelt to accept amendments, but the desire to obtain the maximum number of votes. In fact, if Sam Rayburn's estimate was correct, the bill could not pass without certain amendments. See below, p. 197.

[2]Morgenthau Diary, Jan. 3, 1941, 344:245.

As originally proposed on the floor of Congress, the Lend-Lease Bill contained nine sections.[3] The first section merely named the bill and assigned a short title. Section two defined the terms "defense article" and "defense information" as they were used in the act. Both definitions closed with a catch-all statement that permitted virtually anything to fall under one of those two categories should the President wish it. Section three was the heart of the proposed legislation. It opened with a phrase that eliminated any possible conflict with the Neutrality or Johnson Debt-Default Acts, or any other legislation, by clearly indicating that this act took precedence. It then authorized the President to manufacture or otherwise procure defense articles for any country "whose defense the President deems vital to the defense of the United States." He was also given permission to "sell, transfer, exchange, lease, lend, or otherwise dispose of" any defense article to such a government. Also included were the powers to repair the defense equipment of those countries and to transfer defense information to them. The terms for such transfers of goods and information were left completely to the discretion of the President. Section four forbade recipients of Lend-Lease to transfer such goods or information to another country without the President's permission. Section five required the respective Cabinet heads to report any transfers to a single executive agency, and section six was a routine authorization for an appropriation. A subparagraph of the sixth section established a revolving fund for any monies that came back to the United States in what was later called reverse lend-lease. The seventh section protected American patent holders and guaranteed their royalties, and section eight authorized the President to buy war materials in any country eligible for aid under section three. Section nine was a general clause authorizing the President to establish regulations needed to carry out the bill and permitting him to delegate his authority.

As with any major bill, a large number of changes were proposed by Congress. Almost as soon as the Lend-Lease Bill was introduced, sentiment grew for putting some kind of time limit on the powers the President could exercise. Wendell Willkie publicly endorsed such a move, though Cordell Hull refused to discuss such ideas and, as he did during his testimony before the Congressional committees, referred the reporters to the Treasury Department. Speaker Sam Rayburn announced on January 13 that he would not oppose such a time limit and from that point on the only option left to Congress was to recommend a specific duration.[4]

[3] See Roosevelt Papers, OF, Lend-Lease Agreement, 1940-43, box 1-2 for a copy of the actual proposal that Roosevelt and his Cabinet initiated on January 7. There were no substantive changes made between that time and its introduction in Congress, although the title was modified to read "A bill further to promote the defense of the United States and for other purposes."

[4] Memo of press conference on Jan. 13, 1941, Hull Papers, box 124; *New York Times*, Jan. 14, 1941.

Some suggestions were sent directly to the two chairmen whose committees would handle the bill. One Congressman suggested to Sol Bloom that his committee consider a section that would delay the effective date of the act for thirty days after the President had certified to the Speaker of the House and the President of the Senate that a peace which would maintain American security could not be achieved by intercession or negotiation with the belligerents. Another Congressman proposed that regular reports on the operation of the act be sent to the Comptroller General instead of an executive agency, since that official was responsible to Congress. He also suggested giving the President the authority to assume custody of British assets in the Western Hemisphere should Germany be victorious. Nothing came of these and a multitude of other proposals, private and public. [5]

Roosevelt did not have a closed mind on the question of amendments, for on January 17 he sent Hull a memo asking for the Secretary's comments on a group of amendments which had been suggested to Roosevelt by an old political acquaintance. Hull answered the same day and endorsed two of the suggested changes. One limited Lend-Lease to those nations actively engaged in defending themselves against aggression, and the other set an expiration date for the act of December 31, 1942. Hull also recommended that Roosevelt announce a policy of making public every thirty days all data on Lend-Lease transfers. [6]

Within a week after the hearings on the bill had begun, Speaker Sam Rayburn concluded that amendments would be necessary. Rayburn was more pessimistic than the President about the bill's chances and flatly asserted that without amendments it would not pass the House of Representatives. The primary thrust of the changes Rayburn wanted was in the direction of protecting Congressional prerogatives. The Speaker's concern was much more than just a desire to see the Lend-Lease Bill become law, although there is no doubt that he was a staunch supporter of the measure. His regard for the rights and duties of Congress, and particularly the House of Representatives, was a consistent part of his political makeup. He had exhibited such sentiments earlier when, at his insistence that the precedents of the House be followed, the decision was made to send the bill to the Foreign Affairs Committee. [7]

[5] Martin Kennedy to Chairman, House Foreign Affairs Committee, Jan. 16, 1941, HFAC, "File on H.R. 1776;" Charles S. Dewey to Bloom, Jan. 13, 1941, *ibid.* Additional suggestions are in this file.

[6] Memoranda, Roosevelt to Hull and Hull to Roosevelt, Jan. 17, 1941, Hull Papers, box 48.

[7] Rayburn's research assistant pictures the Speaker as a fervent defender of House prerogatives and traditions. Hardeman interviews, various times, 1966-67. The same sort of picture is drawn by a biographer, C. Dwight Dorough, *Mr. Sam* (New York: Random House, 1962).

Rayburn contacted Morgenthau, whose office was co-ordinating the legislative tactics, and called for a conference of the leadership to discuss the whole question of amendments. Hull, for reasons that are not clear, refused to attend such a strategy conference unless President Roosevelt instructed him to be present. Worried, Morgenthau called the President on January 25 and explained the situation. Roosevelt must have given Hull the necessary instructions, for on the following day Hull held the meeting Rayburn had wanted. All the Democratic Congressional leaders attended, as well as Hull, Morgenthau, and Edward Foley.[8] Rayburn took the initiative and stated that in addition to an amendment putting a time limit on the extensive powers granted the President, the Administration would have to accept one calling for regular and frequent reports to Congress on the operation of the bill. Rayburn also surmised that it might be necessary to make some sort of concession to those Congressmen who feared the bill might be used to provide aid to the Soviet Union, and he wondered if some farm votes might not be garnered by a clause calling for cash payments for food and other raw materials transferred under the act. Sol Bloom, with the experience behind him of eight days of hearings on the bill, suggested an amendment forbidding American warships to convoy belligerent shipping.

After some discussion, the group decided to recommend four amendments to the President. They accepted the idea of a time restriction on the President's powers but made it clear this did not apply any time limit on agreements made before the President's authority under the bill expired. They proposed requiring reports to Congress on the operation of the act every ninety days, although the President should not be obliged to reveal anything prejudicial to the public interest. Hull and Morgenthau apparently explained to the Congressmen that Roosevelt, as Commander in Chief, had the authority to order the Navy to escort belligerent convoys, but in an obvious attempt to give impression that Roosevelt intended no such action they proposed an amendment that stated that nothing in the Lend-Lease Act gave the President any additional authority along those lines. Finally, as a concession to those who feared the bill might be used to give away the Navy or some other essential national defense equipment already owned by the military, the conferees suggested an amendment that would require the President to consult the Army Chief of Staff or the

---

[8]The attendees were Speaker of the House Sam Rayburn, House Majority Leader John McCormack, Foreign Affairs Committee Chairman Sol Bloom and the number two Democrat on the committee, Luther Johnson, Senate Foreign Relations Committee Chairman Walter George, plus representatives of the State and Treasury Departments. Rayburn's fears and the steps leading to the meeting of January 26 are described in *ibid.*, pp. 308-9; Langer and Gleason, *The Undeclared War*, p. 273; Blum, *From the Morgenthau Dairies*, II, 224.

Chief of Naval Operations before transferring such goods. By telephone, Roosevelt gave his assent to such changes.[9]

Rayburn again recommended to Roosevelt that he hold a bipartisan
conference in the White House to discuss the bill. Although Stimson
had been working hard to court the votes of Republican Senators like
Warren Austin and Wallace White,[10] Rayburn believed a gesture by
Roosevelt was needed to make such efforts truly effective. Roosevelt
agreed, and on the evening of January 26 the meeting was held. In
attendance was the Democratic leadership plus two Republicans,
House Minority Leader Joe Martin and Senator Charles McNary of
Oregon, who had been his party's Vice-Presidential candidate in 1940.

Roosevelt followed the over-all strategy by downplaying his own
influence and telling the Congressmen that he would be "perfectly
willing to accept any amendments by Congress that were desirable."
Senator Walter George gave his support to three amendments: the
time limit, the one on convoying, and the requirement for periodic
reports to Congress, and subsequently the *New York Times* quoted
Sol Bloom as stating that the Administration would accept those same
three changes plus one calling for the two service chiefs to certify any
transfer of existing military equipment.[11] Since most newspaper
editors realized that the President had the votes to pass the bill anyway, his acceptance of amendments was generally greeted as a sign of
his reasonableness and generosity. Clearly it was a shrewd political
stroke as well, for as Henry Morgenthau commented later in February,
it indicated bipartisan support for the bill as amended. Actually House
Minority Leader Joe Martin voted against the Lend-Lease Act the first
time it passed the House, but his presence at the White House meeting
gave a different public impression.

At the same time, the opposition forces were attempting to drum
up public support for a series of amendments that, in the eyes of the
Administration, would have crippled the bill. Late in January, the *New
York Times* summarized the minority position as demanding seven
amendments. They rejected any notion of placing their trust in the
President, and in spite of his facetious remarks about there being
nothing in the bill to prevent him from standing on his head, they
demanded that transfers of American naval vessels be prohibited.
Minor as it may seem, this particular fear seems to have been respon-

[9]Blum, *From the Morgenthau Diaries*, II, 224-25. Langer and Gleason, *The Undeclared
War*, p. 273. Stimson complained that the consultation requirement would turn the military
chiefs into "yes men" but did not push the issue. See Stimson Papers, notes pertaining to the
proposed amendments before the House Foreign Affairs Committee, n.d., in Stimson's handwriting.

[10]Stimson Diary, Jan. 25, 1941.

[11]*New York Times*, Jan. 28, 29, 1941; Langer and Gleason, *The Undeclared War*, p. 273.
Consultation with the service chiefs was what Bloom meant, not certification by them.

sible for a fairly significant amount of sincere opposition to the bill. Although the minority approved of the idea of limiting the time during which the President could exercise this authority, they wanted more than that. Such further limitations on the powers granted the President called for a spending restriction of two billion dollars, a prohibition against convoying, elimination of the section permitting the use of American facilities for repairing belligerent ships and other equipment, and an amendment requiring Britain to post some kind of security until her own funds were completely exhausted.[12]

In addition to the list of opposition proposals given by the *New York Times*, substantial sentiment had developed for some sort of amendment that would prevent the Soviet Union from becoming a recipient of Lend-Lease aid. Although the proponents of such an amendment were generally more concerned with attacking the Lend-Lease Act than with the problem of Russia, it was, nevertheless, one of the stronger points in the isolationists' campaign. As early as January 13, Representative Kenneth Simpson of New York had proposed limiting Lend-Lease to Great Britain and Ireland and requiring the President to come to Congress in order to extend the act's provisions to any other nations. As time went on the bill's opponents became more direct, and finally George Tinkham of Massachusetts introduced an amendment specifically excluding the Soviet Union from the bill. Generally, the Administration's complaint about any amendment calling for Congressional approval of the specific countries to be aided was that any delay could be critically damaging because of the nature of modern warfare and that any specific exclusion of the Soviet Union was labelled unwise because it might encourage Japanese-Russian cooperation in the Far East. The strongest reason behind the Administration's opposition to any attempt to exclude the Soviet Union from Lend-Lease, its foreknowledge of German plans to invade Russia in 1941, could not be disclosed.[13]

The first battle over amendments culminated in the House Foreign Affairs Committee in a series of votes during executive sessions held

[12]*New York Times*, Jan. 29, 1941.

[13]Dawson, *The Decision to Aid Russia*, pp. 22-41, considers the isolationist position in detail. For proposed amendments, see *New York Times*, Jan. 14, 1941. *CR*, 77th Cong. 1st sess., LXXXVII, pt. 1, Feb. 7, 1941, p. 761. A memorandum on this problem prepared in the Treasury Department outlined the basic Administration approach. See undated memo, "Objection to Amendment . . . . ," Treasury Dept. files, "The Lend-Lease Bill." An example of the portion of the argument concerning Far Eastern strategy is in *CR*, 77th Cong., 1st sess., LXXXVII, pt. 1, Feb. 7, 1941, p. 763. It is difficult to find any clear evidence of Administration thoughts regarding aid to Russia prior to the passage of the Lend-Lease Act. Raymond Dawson, *The Decision to Aid Russia*, pp. 23-25, examines the available evidence and concludes that although some thought was given to the probability of eventually applying Lend-Lease to Russia, Roosevelt thought in far more general terms and wanted the broadest possible discretion. This corresponds to the evidence I have uncovered.

on January 29 and 30.[14] Generally speaking, the votes were along party lines, although party discipline was occasionally breached, particularly by Foster Stearns of New Hampshire, a Republican who ultimately voted with the Democrats for a favorable report.

The amendments that were sponsored by the Adminstration received approval with little trouble. Consultation with the service chiefs prior to the transfer of any goods not produced under the provisions of the Lend-Lease Act was approved by a vote of 20-5, and a time limit on the bill of July 1, 1943, was approved by 20-2, after two shorter time spans were rejected. Karl Mundt offered an amendment prohibiting convoying by American warships, but it was defeated 16-9, and instead the Administration's wording of "no additional powers" along those lines was adopted. The last of the Administration-approved amendments, one calling for reports to Congress every ninety days, was adopted by a voice vote. Three similar amendments, one specifying only the British Empire as eligible, one specifically excluding Russia, and an all-purpose one suggested by Hamilton Fish which prohibited aid to "aggressor states," were all rejected. The Tinkham amendment calling for the specific exclusion of Russia was rejected on a strict party-line vote, 14-10. An attempt to forbid the transfer of United States naval vessels was turned down by a vote of 14-11, with Democrat James Shanley of Connecticut joining the Republicans, and a prohibition against the use of American ports, except as provided for under international law, received only the votes of the Republicans. Karl Mundt offered a substitute calling for a two billion dollar loan to be repaid in goods, information, territory, and raw materials, but it lost by 15-9, with Stearns voting with the majority.

The next day, January 30, the committee again met to vote on other proposed changes and the bill itself. The figure two billion dollars seemed to hold some fascination for the Republicans, for they introduced three amendments that would have either substituted a two-billion-dollar loan or at least limited the appropriation to that sum. Each was rejected without any defections on the Democratic side. A relatively new idea, which later cropped up in more serious form in the Senate, was a proposal by Hamilton Fish which would have attached a clause stating that nothing in the act authorized the President to send American military forces outside the Western Hemisphere. Bloom ruled the amendment out of order, and his ruling was

[14]There were fifteen Democrats and ten Republicans on the Foreign Affairs Committee. The Democrats were Sol Bloom (N.Y.), Luther Johnson (Tex.), John Kee (W. Va.), James Richards (S.C.), James Shanley (Conn.), Joseph Pfeifer (N.Y.), Pete Jarman (Ala.), Laurence Arnold (Ill.), W. O. Burgin (N.C.), Wirt Courtney (Tenn.), Herman Eberharter (Penn.), Noble Gregory (Ky.), Thad Wasielewski (Wisc.), Robert Sikes (Fla.), and Jacob Davis (Ohio).

The Republicans were Hamilton Fish (N.Y.), Charles Eaton (N.J.), George Tinkham (Mass.), Edith Rogers (Mass.), Robert Chiperfield (Ill.), John Vorys (Ohio), Foster Stearns (N.H.), Karl Mundt (S.D.), Bartel Jonkman (Mich.), and Frances Bolton (Ohio).

sustained by a strict party vote of 15-10. Luther Johnson then moved for the adoption of a favorable report on the bill as amended, and his motion carried by 17-8. In addition to the expected fifteen Democratic votes plus Republican Foster Stearns, Edith Rogers of Massachusetts surprised everyone by voting for a favorable report. Since she later voted against the bill in the House, her reason for approving the bill in committee is difficult to understand, although she stated on the floor of the House that she had voted for the majority report in order to get it onto the House floor where she hoped it could be freely discussed. At the close of the session, Karl Mundt and Hamilton Fish both complimented Bloom for conducting what they considered fair and impartial hearings, though Fish commented that questioning Lindbergh about the Iron Cross he had received had been improper. The minority report submitted by the Republican members of the committee supported aid to England but asserted that the Lend-Lease Bill was too dangerous a way to go about it. It warned that passage of the bill could result in a complete change in both the domestic and foreign affairs of the United States. It was signed by eight of the ten Republicans on the committee, including Edith Rogers who had voted for a favorable report. Stearns signed the majority report, and the tenth Republican, George Tinkham, refused to sign either because he opposed all aid to Britain.[15]

The Administration's tactics were eminently successful in the Foreign Affairs Committee. Party discipline held firm and one Republican was converted. The only amendments adopted had been approved by Roosevelt and the Congressional leadership beforehand, and none of the opposition attempts to change the bill approached success. It was an impressive victory.

Karl Mundt, a member of the House Foreign Affairs Committee in 1941, stated twenty-five years later that a two-billion-dollar loan would have been approved by the committee and the House in a secret ballot but that Roosevelt exerted very heavy pressure on the Democrats to vote down such a proposal. Factual evidence to support such a claim is difficult to find, but it is certain that the Administration kept close tabs on the bill during its journey through Congress. Oscar Cox of the Treasury Department worked hand in glove with Sol Bloom, bombarding the Congressman with memorandums refuting the various opposition attacks on the bill. In addition, the *Majority Report on H.R. 1776* was written entirely in the Treasury, primarily by Cox and Stephen Spingarn. Though one suspects that the President and his lieutenants made some phone calls at the critical moments to insure a

---

[15]The voting and the comments by Fish and Mundt are in HFAC, "Minutes," Jan. 29-30, 1941, pp. 77-94. Roger's statement is in *CR*, 77th Cong., 1st sess., LXXXVII, pt. 1, Feb. 6, 1941, p. 713. *House Minority Report on H.R. 1776*, p. 15; Langer and Gleason, *The Undeclared War*, pp. 274-75.

favorable vote on certain amendments, in absence of hard evidence that can only be a guess and nothing more.[16]

Public attention was focused on the House of Representatives where the floor debate started after the bill was reported out of committee on January 30, even though the Senate Foreign Relations Committee had begun hearings on the bill on January 27. The isolationists made still further attempts to emasculate the legislation, but the Administration had spiked the opposition's guns quite effectively when it put through its package of four amendments. In an attempt to eliminate one major fear that still troubled many of the Lend-Lease Bill's supporters, the House leadership surprised everyone by supporting an amendment offered by Republican John Taber of New York which called for a limitation on the authority of the President to transfer goods already produced or purchased by other than Lend-Lease funds. In effect, the amendment would have limited transfers of existing stocks of war materials to $500 million. Sol Bloom immediately gained the floor and offered a substitute that set the limit a little higher by calling for restricting such expenditures to ten per cent of the total defense appropriation for fiscal year 1941. There is nothing to show that the House leadership consulted the White House before offering this amendment, although past performances indicate that in all likelihood Sam Rayburn contacted the President by phone before indicating his approval. Certainly the move had been planned ahead by the House leaders, for Rayburn had, at his fingertips, the figures needed to translate the 10 per cent into dollars. It came to roughly $1.2 to $1.3 billion. The following day, Minority Leader John McCormack proposed changing the wording of that amendment from 10 per cent of the 1941 fiscal year defense appropriation to a specific total of one billion three hundred million dollars' worth of existing military goods procured by appropriations other than a Lend-Lease appropriation.[17] This "billion three" amendment, as it was called, effectively ended the Anglo-American debate over the question of the United States assuming the so-called old commitments, that is, the items ordered by Britain through the American government before the passage of the Lend-Lease Act. Since those materials would not come out of any Lend-Lease appropriation, the maximum value the United States could fund was $1.3 billion.

---

[16]Mundt interview, April 29, 1967. There are numerous examples of Cox's aid to Bloom in the Morgenthau Diary, the House Foreign Affairs Committee files, and the Cox Papers. For example, see memo from Cox to Bloom, Feb. 4, 1941, HFAC, "File on H.R. 1776." The authorship of the majority report is from the Cox Diary, Jan. 29, 1941.

[17]CR, 77th Cong., 1st sess., LXXXVII, pt. 1, Feb. 7-8, 1941, pp. 780-81, 787-91; New York Times, Feb. 8, 1941. Joseph Alsop and Robert Kintner claimed in their syndicated column that Rayburn and the House leaders accepted amendments without checking with the President and generally made little effort to keep the bill intact. One has to suspect that the story may have been planted in an attempt to picture the Administration as a staunch respecter of Congressional prerogatives. See the New York Herald-Tribune, Feb. 12, 1941.

The Administration was saddled with one amendment largely as a result of a shrewd political move by Congressman Everett McKinley Dirksen. Waiting until sixty-seven Administration Democrats were out to lunch, he proposed an amendment that permitted Congress, by concurrent resolution, to terminate the powers granted by the bill. The Administration was unable to muster the votes to defeat the amendment, and it passed 148-141. The constitutionality of such a clause was immediately questioned, for such a repealer did not require the President's signature as would have been the case in a regular bill of repeal, but the leadership decided not to fight it and no attempt was made to eliminate Dirksen's amendment.[18]

The House leadership itself put through an amendment designed to head off a similar but more crippling change. On February 7, Sol Bloom proposed a clause stating that nothing in the act authorized the entry of American vessels into a combat zone in violation of the Neutrality Act of 1939. Since the President had the authority to modify that portion of the Neutrality Act anyway, the amendment was essentially just what Karl Mundt called it: "Charming language again but utterly meaningless." It was designed to head off an amendment proposed by Republican John Vorys which would, in essence, have amended the Neutrality Act by requiring Congress to approve any modifications of the combat zone provisions. Again, there is no evidence of any contact between the White House and the House leadership prior to the time Bloom offered the amendment.[19]

Tempers flared as the House moved into the final day of deliberations on the bill. After Hamilton Fish offered an amendment to strike out the enacting clause of the bill, John McCormack referred to him as the man "leading the Republican Party in the policy of opportunism."[20] The Republicans protested that such words violated House rules, but Speaker Rayburn rejected their objection. The debate continued along highly disorganized patterns for a while, as the opposition introduced a rash of amendments. Most were repetitions of the ones rejected earlier by the Foreign Affairs Committee, but during the debate and the votes on each, the members became increasingly impatient and critical of each other.

The one truly significant amendment left unresolved on the final day had previously been bandied about in the press but was not officially proposed until February 8. Its sponsor was Republican Congressman James Wadsworth of New York. Wadsworth had supported

[18]*New York Times*, Feb. 7, 8, 1941; *CR*, 77th Cong., 1st sess., LXXXVII, pt. 1, Feb. 6, 1941, p. 735.

[19]*Ibid.*, Feb. 7, 1941, pp. 753-61. The amendment passed by unanimous consent. Mundt's remarks are in *ibid.*, Feb. 8, 1941, p. 800.

[20]*Ibid.*, p. 796.

the Lend-Lease Bill from the very beginning, and his amendment was, according to his own statement, designed to elicit the maximum possible support for the bill without significantly limiting the powers President Roosevelt believed he needed. It simply called for a limit on the total cost of the Lend-Lease Act to the government of seven billion dollars. The opposition, which supported every limiting change proposed, regardless of its effectiveness, spoke for the proposal as a means by which Congress would retain power over the purse strings, while the leadership briefly but strongly spoke against it. The Administration's basic argument was that it usurped the functions of the Appropriations Committee and obviated the necessity of an appropriation bill. Luther Johnson, John McCormack, and Sam Rayburn all argued against Wadsworth's amendment, and it was easily defeated 38-122. Interest in the amendment had been fanned by press reports that there had been an attempt by the leaders of both parties to pass the Lend-Lease Bill by the highest margin possible in order to warn Hitler and speculation that such a bipartisan move depended upon the passage of the Wadsworth amendment. True or not, the Administration refused to permit the bill to be so severely limited, particularly before it had a chance to present its case for an appropriation.[21]

From the plethora of amendments rejected during the last two days of debate in the House, three are of interest. First, there is the irony of the Republican leadership suggesting that the bill be amended to prevent President Roosevelt from suspending any of the New Deal labor laws. This sad and unsuccessful little attempt to enlist support from organized labor and gain at least a small moral victory was led by many of the same men who had so bitterly opposed virtually every one of those same New Deal labor laws. Second, there was the indomitable and consistent courage of Representative Jeannette Rankin of Montana, a dedicated pacifist who had opposed the declaration of war against Germany in 1917, who opposed the Lend-Lease Bill as a warlike act, and who would ultimately become the only member of Congress to oppose a declaration of war against Japan after the Pearl Harbor attack. In deadly earnest, she proposed an amendment stating that nothing in the Lend-Lease Act could be construed to permit the President to order, lease, lend, or transfer any members of the armed forces outside the Western Hemisphere. Finally, a moment of comic relief. Vito Marcantonio, a member of the Communist-oriented American Labor Party, with tongue firmly planted in cheek, offered the following as section ten of the bill:

It is the declared policy of the United States that the original Thirteen Colonies are not obsolete or surplus. Any opinion of the Attorney General to the contrary

[21]*Ibid.*, pp. 806-09. *New York Times*, Feb. 8-9, 1941.

notwithstanding, nothing in this act shall be construed to authorize or to permit the President of the United States to lease, lend, or transfer the original Thirteen Colonies to King George of England.[22]

On February 8, 1941, nine days after the Lend-Lease Bill had been sent to the floor of the House by the Foreign Affairs Committee, it was passed by a vote of 260-165. In spite of Republican protestations to the contrary, the vote indicates that the bill was clearly a partisan measure. Only 24 Republicans, out of a total of 159 who voted, cast their ballot for the Lend-Lease Act. An even smaller percentage of Democrats, 25 out of 261, defected from the Administration position and voted against the bill. Since the Republicans controlled the majority of the Congressional seats in the Middle West,[23] that section not surprisingly led the vote against the bill with 92 against, out of a total vote of 124. Of those nay votes 79 were Republicans. Only one Southern Democrat, Hugh Peterson of Georgia, went against the bill, with every other Southern Representative—68 Democrats in all— voting with the Administration. The Border states and the Southwest, predominately Democratic, followed strict party lines except for one Missouri Democrat, Joseph Shannon of Kansas City, who opposed the legislation. This meant a total for the two sections of 65 aye votes and only 8 against the bill. From a percentage standpoint, Democratic defections were highest in the Far West where 8 out of 24 Democrats voted against the bill, but it is difficult to draw meaningful conclusions from such a small sampling. Those Republican votes garnered by the Administration were primarily from the Northeast. Out of 56 Northeastern Republicans 20, or 37.7 per cent, voted for the bill. Although the cause and effect relationship is not certain, it would seem that the President's attempt to court the Eastern Republicans paid off. At the same time, only 6 Democrats from that section opposed the act. It was an impressive victory for the President and his policy of aid to Britain. The number of Representatives voting, 425 plus 6 members paired out of a total of 435, was truly remarkable. Of

[22]New York Times, Feb. 8, 1941; CR, 77th Cong., 1st sess., LXXXVII, pt. 1, Feb. 8, 1941, p. 813; interview with Mrs. Rankin, Feb. 23, 1968 (Watkinsville, Georgia).

[23]I have arbitrarily divided the country into the following sections for the purpose of analyzing the Lend-Lease vote in both the House and the Senate.

Northeast:	New England, New York, New Jersey, Pennsylvania.
Border:	Maryland, Delaware, Tennessee, Kentucky, West Virginia, Missouri.
Middle West:	Michigan, Ohio, Illinois, Indiana, Wisconsin, Minnesota, Iowa, Kansas, Nebraska, North Dakota, South Dakota.
South:	Virginia, North Carolina, South Carolina, Georgia, Florida, Alabama, Mississippi, Louisiana, Arkansas.
Southwest:	Texas, Oklahoma, New Mexico, Arizona.
Far West:	California, Oregon, Washington, Colorado, Idaho, Montana, Nevada, Utah, Wyoming.

the 4 members who did not vote or announce as paired, one was Speaker Sam Rayburn, who voted only to make or break a tie, and the other 3 had died or were on their deathbeds at the time.[24] The House membership clearly considered this a time to stand up and be counted.

TABLE 1: HOUSE VOTE ON THE LEND-LEASE BILL[a]

	Northeast	Border	Middle West	South	Southwest	Far West	Total
total							
pro	77	36	32	68	29	18	260
con	43	7	92	1	1	21	165[b]
						total vote	425
Dems.							
pro	57	36	30	68	29	16	236
con	6	1	9	1	0	8	25
Reps.							
pro	20	0	2	0	0	2	24
con	36	6	79	0	1	13	135

[a]Breakdown of the vote on H.R. 1776 in the House of Representatives by section and party. The vote is taken from *CR*, 77th Cong., 1st sess., LXXXVII, pt. 1, Feb. 8, 1941. p. 815. The party affiliation is from the *Congressional Directory*, 77th Cong., 1st sess., 1st ed., corrected to Dec. 19, 1940. (Washington: U.S. Government Printing Office, 1941), pp. 147-54.

[b]Five votes from splinter parties were cast against the bill: three Progressives, one Farmer-Labor, and one American Labor Party.

Although the Chairman of the Senate Foreign Relations Committee, Walter George of Georgia, had hoped to hold off the Senate hearings on the Lend-Lease Bill until the House voted on the legislation, the House Committee hearings took so long that he changed his mind and on January 27 the Foreign Relations Committee began to hear testimony.[25] Senator George had been on President Roosevelt's

[24]The three were Walter Bankhead of Alabama, Sam Massingale of Oklahoma, and Kenneth Simpson of New York. All three died before mid-April, 1941. The vote is broken down by sections in Table 1. Leroy N. Rieselbach, "The Demography of the Congressional Vote on Foreign Aid, 1939-1958," *American Political Science Review*, LVIII, no. 3 (Sept., 1964), 577-88, includes a statistical analysis of the House vote on Lend-Lease which backs up my conclusions.

[25]There were sixteen Democrats, six Republicans, and one member of the Progressive Party on the Foreign Relations Committee. The Democrats were Walter George (Ga.), Pat Harrison (Miss.), Robert Wagner (N.Y.), Tom Connally (Tex.), Elbert Thomas (Utah), Frederick Van Nuys (Ind.), James Murray (Mont.), Claude Pepper (Fla.), Theodore Green (R.I.), Alben Barkley (Ky.), Robert Reynolds (N.C.), Joseph Guffey (Penna.), Guy Gillette (Iowa), Bennett Clark (Mo.), Carter Glass (Va.), and James Byrnes (S.C.).

The Republicans were Hiram Johnson (Calif.), Arthur Capper (Kans.), Arthur Vandenberg (Mich.), Wallace White (Me.), Henrik Shipstead (Minn.), and Gerald Nye (N.D.). Robert LaFollette, Jr., of Wisconsin was the Progressive.

"purge" list for the 1938 election because of his opposition to the Administration's reorganization plan for the Supreme Court, and his enthusiastic support for the Lend-Lease Bill was critically important to the Administration. Fortunately for Roosevelt, Senator George considered aid to Britain more important than intra-party squabbles and staunchly backed the Lend-Lease proposal. As in the House of Representatives, where the Lend-Lease Bill was the first major legislation put through by the team of Speaker Sam Rayburn and Majority Leader John McCormack, as well as being the first piece of major legislation considered by the House Foreign Affairs Committee in many years, so too in the Senate it was a first. Walter George had succeeded the late Key Pittman as Chairman of the powerful Senate Foreign Relations Committee, and this was his first piece of major legislation in that job.

Just as in the House Foreign Affairs Committee, it was evident from the start that the Lend-Lease Bill had the necessary votes in the Senate Foreign Relations Committee. Harold Hinton in the *New York Times*, on January 12, reported that Senator George believed the bill could be forced through but that the Administration would not use pressure since it wanted to create maximum national unity on the issue. An Associated Press poll of the Foreign Relations Committee on the same day listed eight in favor, four opposed, four undecided, and five unavailable. Of those not reached for comment, two, Senator Claude Pepper and Senator Robert Wagner, were known to favor the legislation, which gave it a minimum majority of thirteen out of twenty-one votes. In addition, the Administration had two vacancies to fill on the committee, and one of the appointees was expected to be Senator James Byrnes of South Carolina, another proponent of the bill. In the same article, Senator George was said to favor two amendments: a time limit on the powers granted the President and certification by the service chiefs before transferring any war materials already held by the military. By February 1, Senator George could predict to Vice-President Henry Wallace that the Lend-Lease Bill would be reported out of committee on February 12, which proved to be only one day off.[26]

The Senate Foreign Relations Committee dropped its own version of the bill once H.R. 1776 was passed by the House and instead worked with the House bill. This effectively eliminated any widescale amending by the Senate committee. The opposition proposed seven amendments and made their views public in an open letter from Senator Robert Taft to Senator George. In general they paralleled the proposals of the House Republicans and called for specific language

[26]*New York Times*, Jan. 12, 1941; memorandum from E. M. Watson to Roosevelt, Feb. 1, 1941, concerning telephone call from Vice-President Wallace, Roosevelt Papers, OF 4193, "Lend-Lease Agreement, 1940-43," box 1-2.

forbidding convoying, the use of American ports as bases for British ships, any transfer of United States naval vessels or equipment, and entry of American merchant ships into war zones. Three new amending proposals called for elimination of the provision permitting the purchase of arms in foreign countries, elimination of the revolving fund, and specific approval from Congress for any foreign aid funds. In a memorandum apparently circulated among the members of the Foreign Relations Committee, Taft, who was not a member of that committee, defended his views. The limits on convoying, use of American ports, and the sending of merchant ships into war zones were all designed to keep the power to make war in the hands of Congress, since each of those acts was in essence an act of war. His concern for the Navy grew out of the knowledge that the naval forces could not be built up as rapidly as those of the Army and Army Air Force, and the amendment regarding specific Congressional approval of funds for any foreign aid eliminated what Taft considered a blanket power to transfer goods without any appropriation. He also noted that his part of the proposed bill would even let the President aid the Soviet Union. He claimed that the revolving fund violated the Constitutional prohibition against any military appropriation covering more than two years, and he defended the amendment limiting Lend-Lease to American goods by noting that he saw no need to finance the British war effort except with American exports. Taft also publicly supported the idea of a loan as a substitute for the Lend-Lease Act and introduced such an amendment on the Senate floor on January 23. This amendment, along with others submitted by various Senators, was referred to the Foreign Relations Committee.[27]

On February 12 and 13, all the Taft amendments were defeated by the Foreign Relations Committee, as was a proposed amendment by Senator Arthur Vandenberg which would have required certification by the service chiefs before transferring any existing military goods instead of the consultation clause inserted by the House committee. The closest the opposition came was a vote of 13-10 on the Vandenberg amendment. The appointment of Senator James Byrnes and Senator Carter Glass to the committee provided the necessary margin, but the vote was uncomfortably close and foreshadowed a stiff battle on the Senate floor. The other amendments that had been passed on to the committee, all of which suggested changes similar to those beaten in the House, were likewise defeated by wide margins in the Foreign Relations Committee.[28]

[27]*New York Times*, Feb. 10, 1941; unsigned, undated memorandum,Senate, "file on H.R. 1776 (S. 275)." From the nature of this memo it seems apparent it was prepared for or by Senator Taft.

[28]Senate, "file on H.R. 1776 (S. 275)" contains a list of the committee votes in executive session but does not give any names. Also see *New York Times*, Feb. 13, 1941.

One ambiguous addition made by the Foreign Relations Committee to the bill as passed by the House was the so-called Connally amendment to the Dirksen amendment. Instead of permitting Congress, by concurrent resolution, to terminate the powers conferred on the President for any reason it chose, the new wording stated that such a resolution had to declare that those powers were no longer necessary to promote the national defense. In other words, Congress could abrogate the authority granted by the bill only if the emergency were over. If Congress were merely dissatisfied with the President's conduct, termination of the powers granted would require a normal repealer, which would be subject to a Presidential veto.[29]

The Foreign Relations Committee also approved an amendment supported by Senator James Byrnes. As originally passed, it required all activities under section three—the section that gave the President his powers to provide aid—to have either an appropriation or contract approved by Congress. Byrnes agreed with Senator Robert Taft's argument that, as passed by the House, the Lend-Lease Bill permitted the President to transfer goods purchased out of Army and Navy appropriations. The "billion three" amendment limited such action for goods already owned by the military, but there was no restriction on the President's power to do so in the future. Since Congress would have no choice but to pass another appropriation for the military in order to preserve the national defense, Byrnes and Taft believed Congress could maintain its legitimate power of the purse only if Lend-Lease transfers were limited to those items funded by a Lend-Lease appropriation. The Administration did not fight the change in the Foreign Relations Committee and the amendment was adopted unanimously, but it later became the cause of a major behind-the-scenes struggle during the floor debate.[30]

One change, proposed by Senator Allen Ellender of Louisiana, called for a clause stating that nothing in the Lend-Lease Act authorized the use of United States armed forces outside the United States or its territories. In this form it was easily defeated by a com-

[29]*New York Times*, Feb. 13, 1941. See also "H.R. 1776 as amended to Mar. 6, 1941," Calendar no. 51, 77th Cong., 1st sess., Report no. 45 (printed for the use of the Senate). This is a copy of the act as amended to March 6, showing the amendments made by the Foreign Relations Committee and by the Senate. I have a print in my possession and others may be seen in Senate, "file on H.R. 1776 (S. 275)."

Early in April, 1941, President Roosevelt sent a memo to the Attorney-General, Robert Jackson, in which he stated that, in his opinion, the clause was unconstitutional and that any attempt to end the powers granted by the Lend-Lease Bill would have to be in the form of a law that could be vetoed. It was published in the *Harvard Law Review*, LXVI, no.8 (June, 1953), 1357-58. See also Eugene C. Gerhart, *America's Advocate: Robert H. Jackson* (Indianapolis: The Bobbs-Merrill Co., 1958), pp. 227-28.

[30]*Senate Majority Report on H.R. 1776*, p. 3; *CR*, 77th Cong., 1st sess., LXXXVII, pt. 2, Feb. 19, 1941, p. 1167; Blum, *From the Morgenthau Diaries*, II, 226; Langer and Gleason, *The Undeclared War*, p. 282. See below in this chapter.

mittee vote of 13-9,[31] but it was to come back in a modified form and cause the Administration forces no end of trouble.

Unlike in the House of Representatives, where the major battle was in the Foreign Affairs Committee, in the Senate the opposition put forth its greatest effort during the floor fight. Initially some of those Senators most staunchly opposed to the bill claimed their intention was to defeat, not amend it, but they soon changed their minds as it became clear that the Administration had the votes to win any all-or-nothing contest. Even the President miscalculated the probable intensity of the Senate floor fight, for on February 12, the day before the bill was favorably reported out of the Foreign Relations Committee, he predicted that it would become law by March 1 or a little sooner. Nevertheless, there was never any question as to the ultimate fate of the bill. As early as February 18, Roosevelt informed the press that Averell Harriman would be leaving for England in ten days as "Defense Expediter," obviously for the purpose of administering Lend-Lease from London. During the same press conference the detailed questions reporters put to Roosevelt about the nature of the act's operations made it clear that they, as well as the President, assumed its passage was a foregone conclusion. An attempt by Senate Majority Leader Alben Barkley to speed up the process brought on the spectre of a filibuster. When, on February 19, he suggested longer sessions, Senator Burton Wheeler bluntly threatened stalling tactics that amounted to a filibuster. Barkley backed off and sessions continued as before.[32]

As the debate developed, it soon became apparent that the two amendments that stood the best chance of being adopted were the Byrnes amendment, which had been approved by the Foreign Relations Committee, and the Ellender amendment, which that committee had rejected. The Byrnes amendment, which limited Lend-Lease to those items purchased under a specific Lend-Lease appropriation or a Congressionally approved contract, also had vigorous support from Senator Harry F. Byrd of Virginia as well as the Republican opponents of the bill led by Senator Taft. As originally proposed and passed by the Foreign Relations Committee, the amendment would have required the President to get Congressional approval for any transfers,

[31] Senate, "file on H.R. 1776 (S. 275)."

[32] Senators Hiram Johnson, Gerald Nye, and Burton Wheeler spoke of defeating the bill according to an Associated Press dispatch. *New York Times*, Feb. 10, 1941. The same report stated that an Administration poll showed only twenty-three Senators opposed the bill. Roosevelt's confidence is evident in Roosevelt to William Phillips (Rome), Feb. 12, 1941, *F.D.R.: Personal Letters*, II, 1119; and transcript of press conference of Feb. 18, 1941, Roosevelt Papers, PPF 1-P, vol. 17, p. 128. The speedup attempt is recorded in *CR*, 77th Cong., 1st sess., LXXXVII, pt. 2, Feb. 19, 1941, pp. 1167-68. A similar incident occurred three days later. See *ibid.*, Feb. 22, 1941, pp. 1285-87; and the *New York Times*, Feb. 23, 1941.

even those falling under the "billion three" clause. Byrnes proposed applying the change only to future military purchases, but Senators Taft and Vandenberg immediately protested that it should apply to the "billion three" clause as well. In the debate that followed, it became clear that the Republicans hoped to use the amendment as a means of forcing the President to obtain Congressional approval for virtually every transfer, whereas Byrnes only intended to insure that military appropriations were spent on the American armed forces.[33]

The Administration's reaction was belated but strong. The Executive had planned to utilize the Lend-Lease Act freely to make legal transfers of new materials purchased out of military appropriations, and on February 28, Stimson, Morgenthau, and Acting Secretary of the Navy Forrestal criticized the amendment in a joint memorandum sent to the President with a copy to Harry Hopkins. They claimed that the change, which they said had been proposed by Byrd and Taft and approved in substance by Byrnes, cut "too close to the heart of the bill." By requiring such approval before transferring any articles purchased out of military appropriations, it would necessitate a virtually separate military and foreign aid program and eliminate joint procurement. Realizing that this was a political problem, they asked Roosevelt for suggestions. The President was then in bed with the grippe and in no mood to do battle with the Senate, while Cordell Hull, the Cabinet member with the greatest influence on Capitol Hill, found the protest vague and "a little hard . . . to get my teeth into." He further complained that the financial aspects of the bill had been taken care of in the past by Morgenthau, Stimson, and the President. Morgenthau called Harry Hopkins and asked him to get Roosevelt to give Hull a push, while Stimson, on March 1, met with the President and Hull in the White House. Hull wanted no part of the matter, but the President, still in bed with a cold, insisted that he meet with Senators George, Barkley, and Byrnes and work things out.[34]

The next day, a Sunday, Morgenthau, Stimson, and the three Senators met in Hull's rooms. Stimson did most of the talking and reiterated the arguments he had used with the President. His major emphasis was on the unification of British and American defense efforts. He stated that the President, in his "arsenal of democracy" speech, had frankly set out the principles to be followed and that the Lend-Lease Bill was designed to put those principles into practice by authorizing the maximum in flexibility and unification. Stimson com-

[33]*CR*, 77th Cong., 1st sess., LXXXVII, pt. 2, Feb. 19, 1941, pp. 1167-71, and March 5, 1941, pp. 1800-06. Byrd's amendment was somewhat more limiting and would have required all foreign aid to come out of an appropriation specifically passed for that purpose.

[34]Memo to Roosevelt from Stimson, Morgenthau, and Forrestal, Feb. 28, 1941, Hopkins Papers, box 302, "Book III: Background of Lend-Lease"; Stimson Diary, Feb. 28, March 1, 1941; Blum, *From the Morgenthau Diaries*, II, 226-27.

promised to the degree that Congress could make either over-all or specific appropriations, but he wanted no restrictions on switching between the two should a crisis arise. He plugged for central control over the entire defense program by claiming that putting it in the hands of American officers and advisers would result, not in "a loose, profligate spendthrift—but a skillful Yankee bargainer control in [sic] the direction of an intelligent guidance of war." Apparently their efforts had little effect, for that same evening Morgenthau called Hopkins and reported dejectedly that nothing had been accomplished. He bluntly surmised that the blame lay with the President, who had not given Cordell Hull the necessary push.[35]

On March 4, Stimson, Morgenthau, Forrestal, and Hull tried again, this time with the additional backing of Budget Director Harold Smith. John McCloy accompanied Stimson, and Edward Foley and Oscar Cox came with Morgenthau. When Senators Barkley, Byrnes, and George arrived, they were presented with a suggested counter-amendment drawn up by Foley and Smith. Senator George approved the idea and said that Senator Byrd would accept it; Barkley thought a substitute amendment was a bad idea and instead proposed just pointing out that Congress had all the control it needed over the purse strings via appropriation acts. Part way through the meeting, on arrangement by Secretary Stimson, General Marshall arrived and made a strong pitch for the fullest flexibility in the act. Stimson hoped that Marshall would be able to sway his old friend, Senator Byrnes.[36]

Byrnes had no problem living with the Foley-Smith amendment since it accomplished exactly what he had proposed back on February 19. Senator Byrd apparently found it palatable also, for he made no further attempt to push his more general requirement of a specific appropriation for any piece of foreign aid. The Republicans, who had obviously hoped to emasculate the President's authority under the bill, had no choice as their divide-and-conquer policy was circumvented. At any rate, on March 5, in a short series of votes, the Senate agreed to wording that clearly required the Administration to use only Lend-Lease funds to pay for any goods to be bought and transferred after the passage of the act. The pro-Lend-Lease forces, unable to muster the enthusiastic support of either the President or Secretary Hull, were able only to clarify the language of the restriction but

---

[35]The quote is from handwritten notes on Stimson's talk to the senators in Hull's rooms, March 2, 1941, Stimson Papers; See also Stimson Diary, March 2, 1941; Blum, *From the Morgenthau Diaries*, II, 226-27.

[36]Memo of conference in Secretary Hull's office, March 4, 1941, Hopkins Papers, box 302, "Book III: Background of Lend-Lease"; Stimson Diary, March 4, 1941; Blum, *From the Morgenthau Diaries*, II, 227; Langer and Gleason, *The Undeclared War*, pp. 282-83; Pogue, *Marshall*, p. 70.

could not retain the enormous discretion for the President which the original bill had granted.[37]

On February 18, Senator Allen Ellender of Louisiana reintroduced his amendment, already defeated in the Foreign Relations Committee, calling for a clause stating that nothing in the Lend-Lease Act gave the President any additional powers to employ United States military forces outside the Western Hemisphere, except in American possessions including the Philippine Islands. The amendment placed no legal obstruction in the path of the President, but as Senator George told reporters, it weakened the "moral effect" of the bill and, as a sign of internal disunity and lack of faith in the President, could give particular encouragement to Japan. Roosevelt was concerned enough to break his rule of no comments on amendments and stated in a press conference on February 25 that he opposed any change that would hinder the policy of aid to Britain, though he noted that the Ellender proposal was not mandatory. When a reporter commented that the suggested change jibed with everything Roosevelt had previously promised, the President called it largely a problem of geography and went on to give an extremely expansive definition of what he considered the Western Hemisphere. Time and again the Administration made its objections to the Ellender amendment clear—although the government had no intention of sending troops abroad, the modification might be interpreted as forbidding the President from sending the military overseas at all. From inside the State Department, the senior Far Eastern adviser, Stanley Hornbeck, sent a memo to Hull and Senator George which strongly criticized the amendment as psychologically and politically objectionable and capable of interpretation by Japan as a go-ahead signal.[38]

As much as the Administration disliked the Ellender amendment, it was difficult to attack it head-on. The pro-Lend-Lease, though anti-Roosevelt, *New York Herald-Tribune* epitomized the problem in an editorial on March 4 when it stated that the length of the Senate debate was largely due to the unreasonable attitute of the Administra-

[37]Roosevelt had a high estimation of Senator Byrnes's skills and value to the Administration. Ickes, *The Gathering Storm*, entry for Jan. 26, 1941, p. 417. This may account for some of the President's reluctance to have a head-on collision with Byrnes over the Senator's amendment. Blum, *From the Morgenthau Diaries*, II, 227, claims that the Foley amendment "provided that the President could dispose of defense articles abroad under Lend-Lease unless Congress imposed specific restrictions." Unless he referred to a Lend-Lease appropriation as a specific restriction, there is nothing in the amendments passed by the Senate which corresponds to what Blum says. Unhappily, because of the limitations on the use of the Morgenthau Diary, I cannot actually read the proposed modification as Foley and Smith drew it up.

[38]*CR*, 77th Cong., 1st sess., LXXXVII, pt. 1, Feb. 18, 1941, p. 1096; *New York Times*, Feb. 23, 26, 1941. *New York Herald-Tribune*, Feb. 24, 1941; transcript of press conference of Feb. 25, 1941, Roosevelt Papers, PPF 1-P, vol. 17, pp. 151-52 (Roosevelt's delineation of the Western Hemisphere included Greenland); memo to Hull from Hornbeck, Feb. 28, 1941, Hull Papers, box 48.

tion regarding amendments. It stated that so serious a decision as sending troops outside the Western Hemisphere or American possessions should properly be referred to Congress for approval, so why not write it into the bill. Besides, the editorial noted, the Ellender amendment did not change the existing powers of the President, and to top it off, Roosevelt had repeatedly denied any intention of sending American troops overseas. It closed by calling on the Democrats to avoid partisan politics. If the President and his cohorts flatly opposed the Ellender amendment without substituting something similar, they would be accused of planning to dispatch United States armed forces to fight in Europe, yet as Hull repeatedly told his friends on Capitol Hill, the over-all effect of the amendment was dangerous to American foreign policy. At the meeting in his office on March 4, Hull labelled the amendment a "fraud on the public," but Senator George noted that the opposition would argue that if the bill did not authorize the President to send troops outside the United States and the Western Hemisphere, why not say so.[39]

George, Barkley, Rayburn, and McCormack all agreed that the amendment was popular and met with Roosevelt and Vice-President Henry Wallace to work out a plan of action. Warned by John McCloy that Wendell Willkie might support the Ellender amendment, Stimson called his contact in the Willkie camp, Landon Thorne, and told him to tell Willkie that adoption of the proposal would probably start the Japanese toward Singapore. Willkie did not endorse the Ellender amendment, and the Administration came up with a substitute which legally said the same thing without mentioning any specific geographic areas. The new form of the amendment stated that nothing in the act changed existing law regarding the use of American military forces. On March 6, Senator Ellender himself introduced the new wording as a substitute for his original amendment. The opposition, led by Democratic Senators Bennett Clark of Missouri and Joseph O'Mahoney of Wyoming, attempted to change the wording so as to prohibit the use of any Lend-Lease goods to support American armed forces outside the United States, its possessions, or the Western Hemisphere except with the consent of Congress. After two days of long and tedious argument over a rash of amendments to the amendment and the like, their attack was defeated in a roll call vote, 63-28. Other attempts to beef up the revised Ellender amendment, including one by Senator Taft which was merely the original wording as proposed by Senator Ellender, were all beaten down by comparable margins, although the vote on Taft's reintroduction of the first Ellender amendment was a

[39]*New York Herald-Tribune*, March 4, 1941; Langer and Gleason, *The Undeclared War*, p. 282; memo of conference in Secretary Hull's office, March 4, 1941, Hopkins Papers, box 302, "Book III: Background of Lend-Lease."

relatively close 51-38. Finally, the tiring Senate approved the modified Ellender amendment by a vote of 65-24. [40]

As in the House of Representatives, the last two days of debate were filled with the submission and defeat of a series of amendments. None was really new, and their defeat was certain, but the opponents of Lend-Lease seemed unable to give up the fight and let a vote come on the legislation. The closest vote came on an amendment proposed by Robert Reynolds of North Carolina, the only Southern Democrat in the Senate to oppose the bill. Reynolds was primarily concerned with the question of Communist and Fascist infiltration of the government, and his primary objection to the Lend-Lease proposal was that it could be extended to the Soviet Union. Like its companion amendment in the House, the Tinkham amendment, Senator Reynolds' proposal that the Soviet Union be specifically excluded from Lend-Lease was supported largely by those who supported any amendment that limited or crippled the bill. Of those who voted for it, only 5 were true supporters of the Lend-Lease concept. It was defeated by a vote of 56-35, and from there on it was just a matter of time before the Senate passed the Lend-Lease Act. [41]

As the debate dragged on during March seventh and eighth, cries of "Vote! Vote!" were heard repeatedly from the floor, but the tide of repetitious amendments continued to flow. One of the few humorous interludes was provided by Senator Bennett Champ Clark of Missouri. He proposed as an amendment a portion of the Democratic Party platform of 1940 which flatly stated that the United States would not participate in any foreign wars. Laughter broke out as Senator Alva Adams of Colorado asked what the statute of limitations was on political platforms, and then the Senate easily defeated what was clearly a facetious amendment.[42]

The Senate rapidly lost interest in a Saturday debate over a bill whose passage was by then a foregone conclusion, and finally, after a speech by Senator Nye which bitterly criticized Roosevelt's foreign policy and, in particular, what he considered the President's lack of honesty in publicly stating his goals, the Senate cast its vote on the Lend-Lease Bill. All 95 Senators (one seat from West Virginia was vacant) either voted or announced what their vote would have been. The final count was 60 in favor and 31 opposed, with the 4 who did not vote splitting their announced positions, 2 in favor and 2 against.

The vote was again largely along partisan lines, although not surprisingly in the traditionally more independent Senate, the number of

[40]*CR*, 77th Cong., 1st sess., LXXXVII, pt. 2, March 6, 7, 1941, pp. 1884-1901, 1948-60, 1975, 1984.

[41]*Ibid.*, p. 1984. Dawson, *The Decision to Aid Russia*, p. 40.

[42]*CR*, 77th Cong., 1st sess., LXXXVII, pt. 2, March 8, 1941, pp. 2072-73.

defections from the party position was greater than in the House. Including the announced positions as if they were actual votes, 14 out of 65 Democrats voted against the bill, while 10 out of 28 Republicans supported it. The Senate's 2 Independents split on the vote. Wisconsin's Robert LaFollette, Jr., a Progressive, had opposed Lend-Lease from the beginning, while one of the Senate's grand old men, George Norris of Nebraska, then seated as an Independent, asserted that England was fighting America's war and voted for the bill. As in the House of Representatives, the defections occurred primarily in the Northeast and the Far West. Two Northeastern Democrats, Peter Gerry of Rhode Island and David Walsh of Massachusetts, opposed the bill, the latter largely out of the belief that it would interfere with American preparedness, primarily naval rearming. In the Far West, isolationism proved a stronger pull than party loyalty for seven of the fourteen Democrats from that area. Out of the Border, South, and Southwest areas, which sent only Democrats to the Senate, only one from each section voted against the bill: Robert Reynolds of North Carolina, Bennett Champ Clark of Missouri, who was a violent foe of Roosevelt's entire foreign policy, and Dennis Chavez of New Mexico, who mouthed many of the standard isolationist arguments but seemed primarily afraid that Lend-Lease would destroy good American-Latin-American relations. The Middle West led in both Republicans and votes against the bill, though surprisingly, three Republicans from that section voted for the legislation. In spite of the intensity of the floor

TABLE 2: SENATE VOTE ON THE LEND-LEASE BILL[a]

	Northeast	Border[b]	Middle West	South	Southwest	Far West	Total
total							
pro	12	10	8[c]	17	7	8	62
con	6	1	14[d]	1	1	10	33
						total vote	95[e]
Dems.							
pro	6	10	4	17	7	7	51
con	2	1	2	1	1	7	14
Reps.							
pro	6	0	3	0	0	1	10
con	4	0	11	0	0	3	18

[a]Breakdown of the vote on H.R. 1776 in the U.S. Senate by section and party. The vote is taken from CR, 77th Cong., 1st sess., LXXXVII, pt. 2, March 8, 1941, p. 2097. The party affiliation is from the Congressional Directory, 77th Cong., 1st sess., 1st ed., pp. 145-46.
[b]One seat for West Virginia was vacant.
[c]Includes the vote of Sen. George Norris, Independent from Nebraska.
[d]Includes the vote of Sen. Robert LaFollette, Jr., Progressive from Wisconsin.
[e]These statistics include the announced positions of four absent Senators as if they were actual votes. The number of votes actually cast on the floor of the Senate was 91.

debates in the Senate, the Administration garnered just short of a two to one margin for the bill, almost the same percentage as in the House. Again it was an impressive victory and one which created the atmosphere of unanimity which President Roosevelt so strongly desired.[43]

Again, determining what, if any, political pressure was applied by the President in the Senate is a difficult task. That such pressure was applied is indicated in two letters. One, from Senator James Byrnes to "Pa" Watson, noted that Senator Edwin Johnson of Colorado had changed his position after a conference at the White House. Byrnes said he could not account for the change but wrote: "I suspect a man named Roosevelt." The other indication was a request passed on to former Senator William H. King of Utah from the President asking King to tell "certain of his former colleagues" that he thought a filibuster would not be popular.[44] Such evidence, however, hardly qualifies as proof of serious arm-twisting.

Looking back at the Administration's handling of the Lend-Lease Bill in the Senate Foreign Relations Committee and in the Senate itself, one is quickly impressed by the hard work, long hours, and wise counsel contributed by Oscar Cox of the Treasury Department and John J. McCloy of the War Department. The Foreign Relations Committee file on H.R. 1776 is filled with memorandums from Cox suggesting tactics and giving useful rebuttals on the opposition amendments. Cox had been assigned by Morgenthau to the job of shepherding the bill through, and he performed his task expertly. McCloy was given a similar assignment by Secretary Stimson. In addition to being co-author of many of the Administration amendments that so successfully took the initiative away from the bill's opponents, he served as a liaison man between the War Department and the Senate leadership. During the Foreign Relations Committee hearings on the bill, McCloy went so far as to set up a cot in the Committee Office and sat with the page boys so as to be available at a moment's notice.[45] It is

---

[43]In his memoirs, Norris stated just that and further commented that whether the United States received compensation was of minor importance. George W. Norris, *Fighting Liberal: The Autobiography of George W. Norris* (New York: The Macmillan Co., 1945). Senator Gerry never stated to the Senate why he opposed the bill, but he voted down the line with the isolationists on every proposed amendment. The attitudes of Senators Clark and Reynolds show through clearly in the SFRC *Hearings*, since both were members of the Foreign Relations Committee. Senator Chavez's concern for the Good Neighbor Policy was stated but never clearly explained. See *CR*, 77th Cong., 1st sess., LXXXVII, pt. 2, Feb. 27, 1941, pp. 1480-91. The vote is fully broken down in Table 2.

[44]Byrnes to Watson, Feb. 15, 1941, Roosevelt Papers, OF 4193, Lend-Lease Agreement, 1940-43, box 1-2. Ironically, Johnson changed his mind again and eventually voted against the Lend-Lease Bill. Memo by Roosevelt to Stephen Early for King, March 5, 1941, *ibid*.

[45]Theodore Wyckoff, "The Office of Secretary of War Under Henry L. Stimson, 1940-1945," (Ph.D. diss., Princeton University, 1960, copy available in the office of the Chief of Military History, Washington, D.C.), pp. V-10 and V-11. For Cox's omnipresent memorandums, see Senate, "file on H.R. 1776 (S. 275)"; and the Cox Papers.

relatively easy to determine which people deserve the credit or blame for the broadest aspects of policy, but all too frequently historians ignore the work of the Oscar Coxes and John McCloys whose contributions, though smaller in quantity, were often just as crucial.

It is more difficult to pass out the credit in the Senate itself. The floor leader, Senator Alben Barkley, was harshly castigated in the press by Joseph Alsop and Robert Kintner for poor handling of the bill. They claimed that Senator Byrnes's efforts were the only thing that saved the bill from disaster and characterized Barkley as "well-liked and well-intentioned, . . . [but] unfortunately maladroit." Byrnes's amendment may have headed off the opposition, but the initial Administration reaction to it was very cold. On the other hand, Harold Ickes noted in his diary that John McCloy, who was in a position to know, told him that Barkley deserved much of the credit and was willing to stand up and oppose amendments that Byrnes was inclined to accept. Ickes, who was notoriously outspoken and partisan, criticized Byrnes for being so eager to get some sort of bill that he compromised unnecessarily. Nevertheless, as mentioned before, Roosevelt considered Byrnes's support in the Senate as critical, and contemporary press reports gave Byrnes the major share of the credit for getting the legislation through the Senate relatively unscathed.[46]

After passing the bill, the Senate routinely insisted upon its amendments and appointed a conference committee to work out a compromise with the House. The House leadership, so as to avoid reopening the debate as well as to hasten final passage of the bill, proposed a resolution agreeing to the Senate amendments. On Monday, March 10, the House, by unanimous consent, approved a two-hour debate on that resolution for the following day, with half the time controlled by Sol Bloom and the other half by Hamilton Fish.[47]

Bloom opened the debate on March 11 with a run-down of the meaning of each of the Senate amendments based on a memo probably given him by Oscar Cox. House Minority Leader Joe Martin set the tone for most of those who opposed the bill when he followed Bloom with a speech in which he called for speed in implementing the bill's provisions now that Congress had approved it, even though he was not fully convinced it was the best path to take. He then closed

[46]Alsop and Kintner in the *San Francisco Chronicle*, March 29, 1941. There is remarkably little scholarly material available on Barkley. His work as Senate Majority Leader during those critical years certainly entitles him to be remembered as more than just Harry Truman's Vice-President and the affable fellow who married a pretty widow while in that office. Other comments on Byrnes are in Ickes, *The Gathering Clouds*, entry for March 13, 1941, p. 456; Alsop and Kintner in the *San Francisco Chronicle*, March 29, 1941; Arthur Krock in the *New York Times*, March 11, 1941; Langer and Gleason, *The Undeclared War*, pp. 283-84; Sherwood, *Roosevelt and Hopkins*, p. 264.

[47]*CR*, 77th Cong., 1st sess., LXXXVII, pt. 2, March 8, 1941, p. 2098, and March 10, 1941, pp. 2142-43.

with a strong plea for national unity which must have been most pleasing to President Roosevelt: "We live, thank God, in a great country where we can debate these great questions and divide as our convictions direct us. But, once the decision is reached, we accept the verdict of the majority." Ham Fish noted that the vote that would soon come was not on the bill itself but only on the Senate amendments, and he asked the press to make that clear to the public. Almost every opposition speaker who followed Fish re-emphasized that point since most of them planned to vote for the amendments but did not want such a vote to be taken as one in favor of the bill. A few die-hards, such as Kansas' William Lambertson, proposed voting against the resolution so that the bill would be forced into a conference committee and they could have another full-fledged vote on the entire piece of legislation, but such a plan received little support. When the two-hour debate period ended, the House overwhelmingly accepted the bill as amended by the Senate in a vote of 317 in favor and only 71 opposed.[48]

Roosevelt signed the Lend-Lease Act into law at 3:50 that same afternoon. His famous grin, flashed at photographers during the signing ceremony, belied the long, hard struggle that had finally seen his promise of "all aid short of war" become a reality. The passing out of a number of pens used in signing the bill, a tradition that began with Roosevelt, not surprisingly was governed by political expediency. Instead of going to those members of the Administration who had played the key roles in developing the Lend-Lease Act, Roosevelt sent them to his Congressional allies. Senators Barkley, George, Byrnes, and Representatives Rayburn and McCormack received them, and one Republican, Senator Warren Austin of Vermont was similarly rewarded for supporting the bill.[49]

There were still some loose ends left to be tied. An Administrative organization had to be established to exercise the new authority the President had received, and Congress had to pass an appropriation, but Roosevelt had taken steps to handle those problems even while the Lend-Lease Bill was under debate.

Morgenthau had originally proposed to Roosevelt that the Treasury ought to keep in contact with the program, and the President had agreed, but by February 25, Roosevelt had changed his mind. In a

[48]Martin's statement is in *ibid.*, March 11, 1941, p. 2167. The debate follows on pp. 2168-78. The memo given Bloom is in HFAC, "file on H.R. 1776." It is unsigned and undated, but the style is that of Oscar Cox.

[49]See memo in Roosevelt Papers, OF 4193, Lend-Lease Agreement, 1940-43, box 1-2. Senator Tom Connally claimed in his memoirs that he received a pen, though his name is not on the list in the Roosevelt Papers. Connally, *My Name is Tom Connally*, p. 244. One enterprising New England boat salesman, knowing of Roosevelt's love of sailboating, wrote to suggest that Lord Halifax be given a pen and used one of his company's brochures as stationery. See Roosevelt Papers, OF 4193, Lend-Lease Affairs, 1941-44, box 8.

letter to Morgenthau, Hull, Stimson, and Knox, the President informed them that they would comprise an Advisory Committee on Lend-Lease, of which Harry Hopkins would be Secretary. He asked each of the four Secretaries to assign someone to work with Hopkins in developing the details. Clearly, Harry Hopkins was to be the man in charge of Lend-Lease. Morgenthau was initially a little hurt and jealous, but his man on Hopkins' staff, Philip Young, reassured him that Hopkins could handle the job. The Advisory Committee proved largely a figurehead, so that in essence, the passage of the Lend-Lease Bill signalled the end of Henry Morgenthau's remarkable role as unofficial co-ordinator of the aid to Britain program. Arthur Purvis, his British co-worker, after learning of the change in leadership, paid Morgenthau a compliment which obviously came from the heart: "You have from the start been a consistent and persistent friend 'in shade or shine' and this also at a time when such friends were few and far between. The fact that your guiding skill was available to us in the time of trial is far from the least of the debts we owe to the President."[50]

There was one small battle left to fight before the Administration could chalk up the Lend-Lease Act as a victory. Ironically, it was the one item that had started the entire chain of events—ready money. Purvis had given a working figure when he told Roosevelt on January fifth that Britain needed fifteen billion dollars as a start. Little more was done regarding the money problem until the Lend-Lease Bill cleared the House of Representatives. Then, on February 10, Morgenthau asked Purvis for detailed estimates on exactly what Britain needed and what it would cost. The British Supply Council in North America, which had replaced the old British Purchasing Commission, drew up the necessary statistics and came up with a grand total of $18,850,000,000 for 1941 and 1942. Two days later the War Department and representatives of the British Supply Council began drawing up a list of requirements, working on the assumption that the appropriation would have to be kept to a minimum so as to avoid problems with Congress.[51]

While the Army was compiling a co-ordinated set of requirements, Morgenthau held a meeting with one of his assistants, Dan Bell, who

[50]As quoted in Blum, *From the Morgenthau Diaries*, II, 234. The discussions regarding the initial Lend-Lease organization are treated in *ibid.*, pp. 228-34. Roosevelt's letter of Feb. 25 is in *F.D.R.: His Personal Letters*, II, 1128. Maj. Gen. J. H. Burns was assigned to Hopkins' staff by the War Department. See Stimson to Hopkins, Feb. 27, 1941, Hopkins Papers, box 302, "Book III: Background of Lend-Lease." There is a copy of Morgenthau's original proposal for the Lend-Lease organization in the Hopkins Papers; see Morgenthau to Roosevelt, Feb. 10, 1941, *ibid.* There is also substantial data on such plans in the Cox Papers. Cox went so far as to propose a cabinet-level position (Secretary of Supply) to handle such aid programs.

[51]Hall, *North American Supply*, pp. 265-66; Watson, *Chief of Staff*, pp. 323-24; memo to Gen. Moore from Lt. Col. Aurand, Feb. 12, 1941, Stimson Papers.

had been Director of the Budget, and Harold Smith, then in that position. They decided to recommend a lump sum appropriation that could then be distributed to the various Executive departments as necessary. Stimson and McCloy strongly disagreed, believing that Congress would never accept a blank check of eight or nine billion dollars, and Morgenthau accepted their arguments for itemized appropriations, although he recommended a contingency fund of 15 per cent of the total in case of unforeseen events. On February 17, Roosevelt met with Morgenthau, Stimson, Knox, Hopkins, and Claude Wickard, the Secretary of Agriculture, to discuss the appropriation. Roosevelt told the group that the Congressional leadership had also pressed strongly for a specific rather than a general appropriation, which, combined with the arguments of Stimson and Knox, persuaded the President to follow their recommendations.[52]

Shortly after the meeting, Morgenthau suggested to Harry Hopkins that he ask Prime Minister Churchill for some sort of public statement referring to the heavy tax burden Britons had shouldered, with particular emphasis on the tax increases made since the start of the war. This would serve two purposes for Morgenthau. Not only would it impress Congress during its consideration of the Lend-Lease appropriation, but it would also help prepare the American public for similar tax boosts. On March 3 Churchill responded with a cable providing some statistics and suggesting that the information "might be put in the hands of some of our friends." The figures were impressive. In addition to a wartime excess profits tax of 100 per cent for everything over a fixed prewar standard, personal income taxes had likewise been substantially raised. For a family with two children earning one thousand pounds a year, the prewar tax was one hundred twelve pounds, and the wartime tax almost doubled at two hundred eleven pounds. The increase was equally large all the way down the line.[53]

Morgenthau's major tactical maneuver in support of the Lend-Lease appropriation came in connection with the old problem of sales of

---

[52]Wickard's presence was probably designed to squelch talk among the opponents of Lend-Lease that agricultural products would not be included in the term "defense article." Eventually, the Senate tacked on an amendment that specifically mentioned agricultural goods as a "defense article." See CR, 77th Cong., 1st sess., LXXXVII, pt. 2, March 8, 1941, pp. 2050-52; transcript of the press conference of Feb. 4, 1941, Roosevelt Papers, PPF 1-P, vol. 17, p. 108; and the exchange of letters between Roosevelt and Rep. Cannon in ibid., OF 4193, Lend-Lease Agreement, 1940-43, box 1-2. The meeting is discussed in Blum, From the Morgenthau Diaries, II, 230. Blum makes no mention of Knox being present, but when Morgenthau had requested the meeting, Knox's name was included. See memo to the President of phone call from Morgenthau, Feb. 15, 1941, Roosevelt Papers, OF 21, Treasury, 1941.

[53]Hopkins to Churchill, Feb. 17, 1941, Roosevelt Papers, PPF 4096, Harry Hopkins; memo from Hopkins to Morgenthau, March 4, 1941, enclosing a telegram from Churchill to Hopkins, March 3, 1941, Hopkins Papers, box 302, "Book III: Background of Lend-Lease"; Blum, From the Morgenthau Diaries, II, 231.

British-owned direct investments in the United States. The question had arisen before the Lend-Lease Bill was even proposed, but the major significance of such sales was in connection with the first Lend-Lease appropriation. Though much of the pressure on the British government to force the sale of such investments grew out of the need to find cash for the "old commitments" and is thus integrally a part of the interim financing question discussed above, it was also part of the Administration's campaign to convince Congress and the public that Great Britain was doing the utmost to pay its own way. The nature of the opposition's attack on the Lend-Lease Bill made it essential to convince Americans that the wily British were not trying to fleece them.

Understandably reluctant to lose its profitable investments, the British government proved less than enthusiastic about effecting sales. By January, 1941, Purvis and Phillips began to feel that the Roosevelt Administration did not believe Britain was really trying to arrange sales of British-owned corporations in America, and they obtained permission from the British government to inform Morgenthau that negotiations were beginning immediately for the sale of over one hundred million dollars' worth of such assets. Purvis also agreed that Morgenthau should so inform Congress during the hearings on the Lend-Lease Bill. Even so, the British hoped to avoid the heavy losses caused by forcing the sale of investments that would lose a great portion of their earning power once ties with British parent corporations were broken. Some minor purchases of British-owned defense industries by the American government were made early in February, but no meaningful progress was made toward large-scale private sales.[54]

As it became increasingly clear, in mid-February, that the fight over Lend-Lease in the Senate would be a tough one, Morgenthau began to increase the pressure on Britain to divest some of the major British-owned investments. The British continued to view the scheme with a jaundiced eye. At a meeting between State and Treasury Department officials and members of the British Purchasing Commission, Phillips told the group that although it appeared Britain would run out of cash by the end of February, the liquidation of direct investments was proceeding slowly and should not be counted on as an immediate source of funds. Publicly, the British press complained that relatively little could be obtained by such sales of direct investments, and the *Financial News* commented that "there should certainly be other ways of putting up the necessary security, or at least of assuring that the

[54]Hall, *North American Supply*, pp. 273-75; Johnson (London) to Hull for the Treasury Dept., Feb. 3, 1941, State Dept., 841.5151/1772; Jesse H. Jones Papers (Library of Congress, Washington D.C.), box 30, Presidential correspondence, "Presidential series, Roosevelt, Franklin D., correspondence Jan.-Apr. 1941."

pledge of such assets as security for supplies does not involve an outright change of ownership." Prime Minister Churchill was himself not convinced that Britain had much more to gain than it would lose by selling the direct investments, but he finally agreed to a British Embassy plan to have the sales supervised by a joint committee in which the American government would have a final say. At the same time, Lord Halifax expressed the hope that the United States would see that extensive sales would be both bad business and morally unjustifiable. He also reported to London that the real problem was not Britain or the Roosevelt Administration but low bids from potential American buyers. Morgenthau wanted no part of the unpleasant task and left it up to the British to set the terms. All the Secretary wanted was sales, and soon.[55]

German comments, both public and private, dwelled constantly on the gentle but unmistakable hints by the British press and public officials that such sales might be motivated by the desire to take advantage of Great Britain's financial distress. The Germans were apparently convinced that the "leading Jewish intimates of the President" who authored the Lend-Lease Bill (unlike Congress, they had no doubts about the bill's authors) not only intended to remove all restrictions from the President's "all aid short of war" policy but would also demand significant concessions from England in the form of territory, oil, and the like, in return.[56] The campaign for the sale of direct investments only added some credibility to the German line.

Early in March, as the Lend-Lease debate finally began to draw to a close in the Senate, Morgenthau, worried about getting a Lend-Lease appropriation bill through Congress, firmly laid down the law to the British. On March 4, at Morgenthau's behest, Roosevelt sent a message to Churchill requesting some sort of spectacular sale so as to have something concrete to show Congress that Britain was doing her best. While awaiting a reply, Morgenthau bitterly complained about delaying tactics on the sale of direct investments and told his staff that he was "just boiling over." After his promises to Congress, Morgen-

---

[55]Memo from Feis to Hull and Welles, Feb. 6, 1941, State Dept., 841.24/469; the quote from the *Financial News* is in Johnson (London) to Hull for the Treasury Dept., Feb. 3, 1941, *ibid.*, 841.5151/1774; Hall, *North American Supply*, p. 275; Blum, *From the Morgenthau Diaries*, II, 235-36. Halifax succeeded Lothian as British Ambassador to the United States.

[56]Thomsen and Bötticher to the Foreign Ministry, Feb. 26, 1941, *DGFP*, XII, no. 88, pp. 161-64. Bötticher was the military attaché at Germany's Embassy in Washington. The mind boggles at the thought of what the German propagandists would have done with a memo written by Archibald MacLeish, the Librarian of Congress, which suggested using Lend-Lease to obtain British books and noted that Roosevelt agreed and believed rare books and manuscripts might be in the ultimate trade agreement. Considering the intensity of British national pride, publication of such a memo probably would have caused more ill-feeling than any economic demand. See memo by Archibald MacLeish, Feb. 19, 1941, Roosevelt Papers, OF 4193, Lend-Lease Agreement, 1940-43, box 1-2; and Roosevelt's favorable reply in a memo of March 17, 1941, Cox Papers, record group 90, box 85.

thau had to depend on Britain to be faithful to its commitments, and he angrily exclaimed: "I have reached the end of my rope. I have never been more outraged." On March 10, Morgenthau became sufficiently concerned to make an unannounced evening call on Ambassador Halifax at home. He told Halifax that something had to happen regarding sales of investments within the week or he would be put in an embarrassing position with Congress. The Secretary's New Deal beliefs showed through when, after he suggested replacing Sir Edward Peacock as Chief British negotiator for such sales, Lord Halifax warned that Peacock had powerful connections with the Bank of England and had strong political support. Morgenthau later noted that "they always think in terms of political affiliations."[57] An amusing comment for someone so closely connected with Franklin Roosevelt but not surprising considering Morgenthau's dislike of bankers in general and British bankers in particular.

The British government concluded finally that the best choice for the "spectacular sale" the Americans demanded was the Viscose Corporation of America, a firm that was 97 per cent owned by a British corporation, Messrs. Courtalds. Although British experts admitted there was a market for such a sale, they warned that forcing a quick sale would depress the price well below what otherwise might be obtained. Predictably, political expediency prevailed over profit, and on March 15, Ambassador Halifax told Morgenthau that the sale had been arranged. Morgenthau was pleased, and the Congressional appropriations committees were satisfied. The Secretary's private remarks following the announcement of the sale indicated both his political concern as well as his personal beliefs: "[It was] the most difficult fight I think I have waged against the vested interests and also the most significant, because the tie-up between the so-called "City" in London and our own Wall Street is terribly close. I consider this a great New Deal victory."[58]

The final conclusion of the direct investments question came long after the Lend-Lease Act became law. As the *Manchester Guardian* pointed out in March, the Viscose sale was a "sharp reminder that the Lease and Lend Bill has not solved our dollar problem." Eventually, largely under heavy pressure from Morgenthau, who wanted to redeem his earlier promise to Britain that America would assume the "old commitments," a loan from the Reconstruction Finance Corporation was arranged which virtually ended the need for Britain to sell her direct investments in America. Even so, a promise made by Budget

[57]Sayers, *Financial Policy*, p. 388. The quotations are from Blum, *From the Morgenthau Diaries*, II, 236-37.

[58]Sayers, *Financial Policy*, pp. 388-89. Morgenthau is quoted in Blum, *From the Morgenthau Diaries*, II, 238-39.

Director Harold Smith to Congress that the "old commitments" would be paid for in cash by Great Britain could not be ignored. Though Morgenthau still acknowledged his personal obligation in the matter of the United States assuming those liabilities, there was little he could do.[59]

Roosevelt took direct control of the appropriation measure during the Senate debate over the Lend-Lease Act itself, and on March 4, he told Budget Director Harold Smith that he wanted an estimate of the appropriation bill ready by the time he signed the Lend-Lease Act. Apparently the President left the drafting of the itemized appropriation up to Smith, Senator James Byrnes, and the Congressional leadership, for Smith complained to Roosevelt that he and Byrnes could not get together on a proposal and had decided to hold a conference with the leaders of the House and Senate Appropriations Committees. Stimson was displeased with the final product that came out of the Bureau of the Budget, and he and Hull redrafted the bill before it was sent to Congress. Although these two members of the Lend-Lease Advisory Committee put their touch on the legislation, the committee was never formally consulted nor did the President make any advance plans on how to handle the hearings that followed.[60]

As it turned out, Harold Smith and the military secretaries and chiefs provided the core of the testimony in the House hearings on the appropriation. Roosevelt had tried to get Morgenthau to testify, but the Treasury Secretary had demurred, saying that he did not want to talk about taxes for fear of shocking Congress nor did he want to give the opposition a chance to reopen the subject of Britain's finances. Besides, he told the President, in a comment mildly reminiscent of Hull's reaction to being eased out of the drafting of the Lend-Lease Bill, he could not explain the bill although Smith could and should. The House Committee agreed, and Morgenthau was excused from testifying.[61]

[59]The *Manchester Guardian* is quoted in Butterworth to the Treasury Dept., March 18, 1941, State Dept., 841.5151/1784; Sayers, *Financial Policy*, pp. 390-91, 396n. Blum, *From the Morgenthau Diaries*, II, 244-45. For additional data on this aspect of the direct investments question, see the two works just cited and also George Herring, "Experiment in Foreign Aid: Lend-Lease, 1941-1945" (Ph.D. diss., University of Virginia, 1965).

[60]Smith Papers, "Conferences with the President, 1941-1942," entry dated March 4, 1941; Burns to Hopkins, March 4, 1941, Hopkins Papers, box 302, "Book III: Background of Lend-Lease"; Blum, *From the Morgenthau Diaries*, II, 242. Stimson Diary, March 12, 1941. It is possible that Stimson and Hull cut down the size of the Lend-Lease appropriation as proposed by Smith. There is an unaddressed and unsigned memo in the Hopkins Papers, box 302, "Book III: Background of Lend-Lease," dated March 11, 1941, which shows that the seven-billion-dollar amount that was finally requested was originally 24 per cent higher. The memo also stated that seven billion dollars was the rock-bottom amount needed. The appropriation estimate and Roosevelt's covering letter are in *CR*, 77th Cong., 1st sess., LXXXVII, pt. 2, March 12, 1941, pp. 2192-93. It was ultimately designated H.R. 4050.

[61]Blum, *From the Morgenthau Diaries*, II, 242.

Since the real battle had already been fought, little of interest occurred during the House Appropriations Committee hearings. Stimson labelled them as "rather of a perfunctory character." Harold Smith explained the bill, and Secretaries Stimson and Knox and their subordinates presented arguments worked out largely in the War Department by McCloy and Lt. Col. Aurand. Although the appropriation was itemized, the categories into which it was divided, such as ordnance, aircraft, and vessels, were quite general. Stimson defended this as necessary, not only because of the changing world situation which required that the government be able to adapt quickly, but also because to be more specific would provide the enemy with valuable information about American defense production plans. He informed the House Committee that the British had supplied the United States with confidential lists of requirements months ago and that the War Department had worked up the estimates on that basis. He also noted that only 5 per cent of the goods they planned to purchase were purely British-type weapons. The rest were interchangable.[62]

Secretary of State Hull testified along the same lines as he had during the Lend-Lease hearings. He urged Congress to pass the appropriation with all possible speed because the world situation had become even more dangerous since he had testified before the House Foreign Affairs Committee. Hull closed with his strongest statement of support to date for the Lend-Lease Act, saying it was "the most effective step possible in the circumstances, to keep war away from our hemisphere, from our nation."[63]

The Appropriations Committee's report on the bill repeated the pleas made by the witnesses for the utmost speed in passing the bill, informed Congress that it had been given detailed secret data on allocations, and gave no indication of any serious differences of opinion among its members. It did attach a clause that prohibited using any of the appropriated funds for paying the wages of any person who advocated the violent overthrow of the American Con-

---

[62]Stimson Diary, March 13, 1941; transcript of Stimson's executive testimony before the Subcommittee of the Committee on Appropriations, U.S., House of Representatives, 77th Cong., 1st sess., "Defense Aid Supplemental Appropriation Bill, 1941," March 13, 1941, Stimson Papers, correspondence. Stimson's rough thoughts on his testimony can be found in a set of notes designated "appearance before House Committee in regard to aid to Britain, executive session," March, 1941, Stimson Papers. The open portions of the hearings are printed in U.S., House of Representatives, Subcommittee of the Committee on Appropriations, 77th Cong., 1st sess., *Hearings on H.R. 4050: Making a Supplemental Appropriation for the National Defense to Provide Aid to the Government of any Country Whose Defense the President Deems Vital to the Defense of the United States, and for Other Purposes* (Washington: U.S. Government Printing Office, 1941). Also see Watson, *Chief of Staff*, pp. 324-25.

[63]Copy of remarks made by Hull to the Deficiency Subcommittee of the House Appropriations Committee, March 13, 1941, Hull Papers, box 95. It was during these hearings that Budget Director Smith promised Congress that Britain would pay all the "old commitments" in cash and none of the Lend-Lease appropriation would go toward paying them.

stitution but noted that this type of restriction had been attached to most of the appropriation measures passed by Congress during that session.[64]

During the House debate over the bill, which was reported out of the committee after only three days of hearings, the unreconstructed opponents of Lend-Lease made some half-hearted attempts to gut or at least cut down the appropriation. William Lambertson of Kansas proposed cutting the total sum from seven to five billion dollars, and Edith Rogers of Massachusetts brought up the old argument that Britain should sign over her holdings in Latin America as collateral. Karl Mundt of South Dakota proposed that a tax increase to cover the new expenditure should accompany the appropriation but, like most of the opposition, felt bound to pass the appropriation after the majority had voted for the over-all policy. With the final outcome obvious to all, the House found it increasingly difficult to maintain a quorum during the debate, and the majority sharply restricted the amount of time given to discussing proposed amendments. In vote after vote the House rejected all attempts to cut the appropriation or to introduce new restrictions on the use of the money. Finally, in a sort of facetious frustration, Representative Robert Rich of Pennsylvania suggested that for five million dollars it would be easy to get someone to go over and "get Hitler," without a war or the death of a million men. The House rejected all attempts at amendment from the floor and passed the Lend-Lease appropriation by a vote of 336-55.[65]

The Senate Appropriations Committee went through the formality of holding hearings, and the Administration witnesses laboriously repeated the same things they had been saying since January when the Lend-Lease Bill was first proposed. The committee reported the bill out without change and then, acting with unusual dispatch, on the same day that the Senate received the bill, March 24, it passed it without amendment by a vote of 67-9. Senator Arthur Vandenberg, one of the program's most vigorous opponents, spoke for the majority of those who had voted against Lend-Lease when he said:

When H.R. 1776 became the law of the land, this issue of foreign policy was settled. It was settled within the interpretations of H.R. 1776, as given us by its sponsors. Certainly it was settled so far as this proposed $7,000,000,000 appropriation is concerned. The appropriation became inevitable, unless it be conceived that a wobbly Congress would sabotage its own solemn judgments in less than 3

---

[64]U.S., House of Representatives, Committee on Appropriations, 77th Cong., 1st sess., *Defense Aid Supplemental Appropriation Bill, 1941*, Report no. 276 (to accompany H.R. 4050; printed at the order of the House of Representatives, 1941). See pp. 2, 8-9.

[65]The brief two-day debate in the House over H.R. 4050 is in *CR*, 77th Cong., 1st sess., LXXXVII, pts. 2 and 3, March 18 and 19, 1941, pp. 2310-46, 2352-83. Rep. Rich's suggestion is on p. 2367. The vote is on p. 2384.

weeks, setting us before the world as contemptible vacillators whom none would respect and certainly none would fear. . . . It is this bill, or a spectacle of disunity which could easily jeopardize every aspiration of all our hearts and hopes, now that the die is cast.[66]

The speed with which the President moved to implement the Lend-Lease Act and its acccompanying appropriation has been told elsewhere and is not part of this story.[67] Historians can and have criticized both the Lend-Lease Act and the manner in which it was carried out, but no one can honestly challenge the fact that it fulfilled its major purpose—providing aid to Great Britain. As Harold Macmillan, later Prime Minister of the United Kingdom, wrote: "The provision of American aid in the shape of Lend-Lease saved us from something like disaster."[68]

[66]The brief Senate debate and vote are in *ibid.*, pt. 3, March 24, 1941, pp. 2499-2509. Senator Vandenberg's remarks are on pp. 2506-07. For the testimony before the Senate Appropriations Committee, see U.S., Senate, Committee on Appropriations, 77th Cong., 1st sess., *Hearings Before a Subcommittee on H.R. 4050: Making a Supplemental Appropriation for National Defense to Provide Aid to the Government of any Country Whose Defense the President Deems Vital to the Defense of the United States* (Washington: U.S. Government Printing Office, 1941). The committee report was strictly explanatory. See *ibid.*, *Defense Aid Supplemental Appropriation Act*, Report no. 135, Calendar no. 144 (to accompany H.R. 4050; printed at the order of the Senate, 1941). The report was submitted on March 22, but the Senate did not meet to receive it until March 24. Stimson claimed that the only opposition in the Senate came from the scrambling of various Senators for military patronage and spending in their own states; Stimson Diary, March 20, 1941.

[67]Sherwood, *Roosevelt and Hopkins*, pp. 264 ff., gives a good indication of the planning that had gone on even during the Lend-Lease debate so that the act could immediately be put into action. See also Blum, *From the Morgenthau Diaries*, II, 228-34, 248-55; and Herring, "Experiment in Foreign Aid: Lend-Lease, 1941-1945"; and the Stimson Diary. Fittingly, the first list of Lend-Lease goods to be transferred contained 900,000 feet of fire-hose. Rosenman, *Working With Roosevelt*, p. 272.

[68]Harold Macmillan, *Winds of Change*, as serialized in the London *Sunday Times*, July 31, 1966, p. 29.

CHAPTER VIII

"LIKE HITTING WADS OF COTTON WOOL": CONCLUSIONS

I n March, 1941, the British Ambassador, Lord Halifax, wrote Churchill concerning his frustrations in trying to deal with the American government. Although he admitted that the United States had made great strides in developing its defenses, he complained that the Roosevelt Administration was disorganized and loaded with loose ends. Trying to deal with them, he commented, "seems like hitting wads of cotton wool."[1]

The Englishman has my belated sympathies, for I find the job of drawing conclusions concerning Roosevelt and his foreign policy just as elusive as the fixed channels of authority Halifax futilely sought to find. Some of the events surrounding the Lend-Lease Act need no conclusions. The initial stimulation of Britain's financial crisis, combined with the President's clearcut belief that Britain had to be aided against Hitler, slowly but surely forced the Roosevelt Adminstration to provide financial aid. Once the disillusion following World War I plus the war debts problem were added to the brew, something akin to Lend-Lease became only a matter of time. The steps—from the Pittman Act, to the destroyers-bases deal, to the "fire-hose" analogy, and finally the bill itself—need no further recounting.

Though the bill was a product of many minds, the contributions of two individuals to its development and passage stand out. Henry Morgenthau, Jr., as the Administration official most directly concerned with the aid-to-Britain program before Lend-Lease, proved both a staunch ally and a stern taskmaster for the British. Convinced from the outset that Hitler and Nazi Germany were a threat to the United States and Western civilization, he constantly pushed for in-

---

[1] Lord Halifax to Churchill as quoted in Birkenhead, *Halifax*, p. 477.

creased aid to Britain and, what is more important, managed to keep such aid flowing in spite of administrative and political barriers.

The British role in the development of the Lend-Lease Act was dominated by Arthur Purvis. Displaying a remarkably sensitive feel for political realities on both sides of the Atlantic, he wielded the authority of a second British ambassador from the fall of 1939 until his untimely death on August 14, 1941, in a plane crash in Scotland. Probably his greatest contribution to Britain's war effort was his ability to gain and maintain the complete trust and respect of Secretary Morgenthau. On hearing of Purvis' death, Morgenthau, "shocked and grieved," commented: "It is my belief that Arthur did more here in Washington for the British Empire than anybody whom they have sent. He was worth a hundred generals. It will be impossible to replace him. I was devoted to him, and I like to think that my feeling was reciprocated."[2]

The story of the Lend-Lease Act is a fascinating case study in the legislative process, particularly as it functioned during the Roosevelt Administration. The broad concept was unmistakably Franklin Roosevelt's, but the initiative for the specific legislation remained almost exclusively with Henry Morgenthau, his staff, and the two Englishmen, Arthur Purvis and Sir Frederick Phillips.[3] Although Congress, other Cabinet members, and even the President himself managed to make modifications to the original draft of the act, the basic shape of the powers granted to the Executive remained the same as in the first rough proposal worked out by the Treasury and the B.P.C. on January 2, 1941.

The generally accepted picture of Franklin Roosevelt as a chaotic, haphazard, almost impulsive administrator is largely upheld, but that is not true of his political activities. He waited far too long before he finally proposed the badly needed consolidation of the aid to Britain program which the Lend-Lease Act provided, but the vote the bill received in Congress indicates that his sense of political timing was honed to a fine edge. In addition, his legislative tactics in and around Congress proved virtually errorless. The delay in proposing the Lend-Lease Act stemmed not only from his uncertainty about just how to solve the problem but also from a desire to avoid any large-scale debate over his foreign policy until he felt the time was right. Certainly any attempt to formalize the program of aiding Britain would

[2] As quoted in Blum, *From the Morgenthau Diaries*, II, 255. There is no biography of Arthur Blaikie Purvis, but H. Duncan Hall has written a sympathetic and perceptive sketch of his career in the *Dictionary of National Biography, 1941-1950*, pp. 700-702. In the same article Hall quotes Lord Woolton's description to the House of Lords of the Purvis mission: "Never have wider powers to commit this country been delegated to any mission."

[3] It is not entirely clear just how much Purvis and Phillips contributed to the original Lend-Lease draft. The only certain thing is that they were present at the first drafting session.

have brought on just such a debate; thus it was more convenient to leave it in the hands of an informal organization under Henry Morgenthau, who could be trusted to carry out the President's wishes faithfully.

The major controversy that still surrounds the Lend-Lease Act is where the historian begins to hit those "wads of cotton wool." What were the motives of President Franklin D. Roosevelt in proposing and pushing through what was most definitely an extraordinary grant of power to the Executive? This is, of course, only part of the broad problem of trying to analyze Roosevelt's entire foreign policy with respect to the European situation, but critic and friend alike agree that the Lend-Lease Act was the most significant of all the steps toward war taken before December 7, 1941.

Even the most ardent supporters of the Lend-Lease Act did not try to defend it in terms of traditional interpretations of international law. Cordell Hull, a devoted believer in the value of international law, told the Congressional committees during his testimony on the bill that one could not be expected to obey the law rigidly when the opponents of democracy did not. Anyone could see that the act gave Hitler an excuse to declare war on the United States, but that was not the question. The Roosevelt Administration maintained that Hitler had never worried about legitimate excuses for war in the past and assumed that if he wanted war with America he would not hesitate to manufacture a reason. The real question was not whether the Lend-Lease Act was a warlike action in terms of international law, but whether or not it would inevitably involve the sending of American military forces to Europe to fight against Germany.[4]

A more extreme corollary of that problem was the accusation that President Roosevelt consciously devised the Lend-Lease Act as a means of getting America into the war, in spite of public and Congressional objections. The more responsible members of the opposition concentrated on claiming that the legislation would force the United States to enter the war, but they usually stopped just short of actually accusing the President of planning it that way. Senator Arthur Vandenberg, in the privacy of his diary, condemned the bill and claimed it made Roosevelt "the Ace Power Politician of The World," turning the White House into the "G.H.Q. for all the wars of all the world," but he did not flatly assert that the President hoped for war. Henry Stimson, Roosevelt's Secretary of War, told his subordinates that the Lend-Lease Act was taking America into the war, and he may well have hoped for just that, but Stimson was notoriously more of a war-hawk than the President. General George Marshall, in an interview

---

[4]In terms of international law, the Lend-Lease Act, at the very least, was what Edward S. Corwin called "a qualified declaration of war." See his *Total War and the Constitution* (New York: Alfred A. Knopf, 1947), p. 29.

in 1957, admitted that the act made America's entry into the war a probability instead of a mere possibility but maintained that it did not guarantee active hostilities.[5] The Italians seemed the most certain that the bill presaged the sending of United States troops to Europe. They apparently planned to sink a large luxury liner in the Panama Canal if the bill passed, but the scheme was foiled by the United States Coast Guard.[6] The chief adviser in the German Foreign Ministry on American affairs, the perceptive Hans Dieckhoff, was more concerned with the broader scope of United States policy. His analysis was remarkably reasoned and logical and is worth quoting at length:

Essentially the development of public opinion in this matter will depend upon the progress of the war; if Germany succeeds in defeating the English decisively in the near future, then in all probability American public opinion will be in favor of staying out of the war; if the war continues undecided for a considerable time, then there is a considerable danger that public opinion will develop in the direction of a growing willingness to enter the war.[7]

Thus, as the Roosevelt Administration maintained, German actions would be the prime determinant of whether or not America would actively join the fight. Like Stimson, Dieckhoff believed the immediate effect of the Lend-Lease Act would be to boost the morale of the British.

Publicly and privately, as far as can be determined, Roosevelt stoutly maintained that the purpose of Lend-Lease was to keep America out of war, but the question remains, did he really believe that? Certainly he resented Senator Burton Wheeler and the other more caustic critics of the bill. The day after he signed the bill, he sat down after supper with Robert Sherwood and Toie Bachelder, two of his speechwriters, to write an address to be given to the White House Correspondents Association. As Sherwood recalled later, the President dictated "one of the most scathing, most vindictive speeches" the speechwriter had ever heard. He pulled out all the stops in attacking those who had accused him of the basest of motives in proposing the Lend-Lease Bill. Roosevelt never used that draft and was obviously just getting it off his chest, but the depth of his feelings was unmistakable.[8]

The accusation by Senator Wheeler and other contemporaries that the President's true foreign policy was consciously kept hidden from

[5] Vandenberg, *Private Papers*, entry of March 8, 1941, 7:10 P.M., pp. 9-11. Watson, *Chief of Staff*, pp. 325-26. See also the Stimson Diary, March 17, 1941. Pogue, *Marshall*, p. 71.

[6] On March 30, 1941, the Coast Guard seized all Italian ships in the area of the canal. Apparently it was just in time, for some had suffered self-inflicted damage although the largest, the *Biancamano*, was not harmed. See the Stimson Diary, March 7 and March 31, 1941.

[7] Memo by Dieckhoff, March 10, 1941, *DGFP*, XII, no. 146, pp. 258-59.

[8] Sherwood, *Roosevelt and Hopkins*, p. 266.

the American people has been echoed by his critics ever since. To charge Franklin Roosevelt with misleading the public during the election of 1940 is to accuse him of doing what virtually every presidential candidate has done since the Constitution went into effect. It is the nature of the system which causes what Winston Churchill so aptly termed America's "quadrennial madness." Like Woodrow Wilson in 1916, Roosevelt too was forced by political exigencies to advocate peace and preparedness, and like Wilson he was convinced that America's national interests were involved in the final outcome of the European struggle. Granted, Wilson firmly believed the United States could stay out of the war since he thought Britain and France could contain if not crush German militarism, whereas Roosevelt was not sure America could avoid the actual fighting—but a rather rational doubt does not indicate a desire. More to the point: must a candidate dwell on the possibility of war when doing so would probably elect people whose policies might, in his view, endanger national security? As much as one sympathizes with Roosevelt's dilemma, the national election is the one time every four years when the President should be obligated by his own conscience and the nature of the American political system to be totally honest and candid with the public. In that sense, democracy may be a suicide pact, which by its nature requires honesty regardless of the possible consequences. The Lend-Lease Act, however, was a post-election issue and thus poses a different set of questions.

Some of Roosevelt's motives in proposing Lend-Lease are obvious. The legislation began as a solution to a financial problem but quickly evolved into a solution for the equally important defense production tangle. Lack of co-ordination in defense purchasing among the American Army, Navy, and foreign buyers could be largely eliminated by Lend-Lease, and the act had the additional attraction of providing the Administration with a means of getting American industry converted more quickly to defense production. Convinced, as were most Americans, that Germany posed a threat to democratic institutions, the Administration designed the bill to permit Britain to keep on fighting, yet Roosevelt and his Cabinet were determined not to fight the war for British goals. Morgenthau insisted that Britain use every available source of dollars and gold, while Stimson rammed American-type weapons down the throats of the very reluctant British military. Hull maintained to the end that some sort of collateral should be posted by the United Kingdom, while Roosevelt's distrust of the British penchant for power politics and British colonialism has been amply demonstrated elsewhere.[9]

[9]A cogent presentation of this aspect of Roosevelt's attitude is in Gaddis Smith, *American Diplomacy During the Second World War, 1941-1945* (New York: John Wiley and Sons, 1965).

Churchill described the Lend-Lease Act, in a speech before Parliament, as "the most unsordid act in the history of any nation,"[10] but not all Englishmen have agreed. The suspicion that the United States was using the United Kingdom's financial crisis as a means of increasing America's share of the world market at Britain's expense lingered on throughout World War II. The *enfant terrible* of English historians, A. J. P. Taylor, bluntly asserted that Britain sacrificed her future in order to save the world. He believed Lend-Lease ruined Britain as an exporting power and ruthlessly stripped her of her remaining dollars. The British official historians were less harsh in their language and more understanding in their knowledge of the exigencies of American politics, but they nonetheless criticized the nature of the Lend-Lease Act. Although admitting that the Lend-Lease Bill pulled Britain out of absolute poverty, one described the new situation as the "poverty of the poor relation." Writing from hindsight, and obviously influenced by the abrupt termination of Lend-Lease at the end of World War II, they sadly complained that the barrier that existed between the dollar and the pound sterling was a man-made barrier which could have been eliminated had the United States been willing to pool fully its financial resources with those of Great Britain. Each country could then have met its own expenses with its own currency.[11] As one American student of history and semantics aptly pointed out, the Americans ignored the reality that money was a medium of exchange and instead concentrated on the mistaken notion that money was itself something of value.[12] Even Hitler voiced the accusation that the Americans intended to take advantage of Britain's woes. His public statements to that effect can be dismissed as propaganda, but similar private comments to Spanish and Russian diplomats indicate Hitler honestly believed that the British would have to satisfy America's imperialistic desires as a condition of aid.[13]

[10]Churchill, *Their Finest Hour*, p. 569.

[11]A. J. P. Taylor, *English History, 1914-1945* (New York and Oxford: Oxford University Press, 1965), pp. 469n. 533 (Note A), 513. The quotation is from Sayers, *Financial Policy*, p. 374. See also Hall, *North American Supply*, pp. 224-25. In general agreement with this position is D. F. McCurrach, "Britain's U.S. Dollar Problems, 1939-1945," *The Economic Journal*, LVIII, no. 231 (Sept., 1948), 368. A recent study by James McMillan and Bernard Harris, *The American Take-Over of Britain* (London: Leslie Frewin, 1968), pp. 24-27, implies that the United States had ulterior motives in setting up Lend-Lease.

[12]Catton, *Etc.*, VII (Spring, 1950), 180, 183. Catton claims that America went a long way toward eliminating the dollar sign during World War II but quickly lapsed into the old ways once the war was over.

[13]James V. Compton, *The Swastika and the Eagle: Hitler, the United States, and the Origins of World War II* (Boston: Houghton Mifflin Co., 1967), p. 32. Hans Dieckhoff, whose views were nationalistic rather than Nazi, emphasized the strength of America's drive toward imperial expansion in a propaganda treatise published in 1943. Silvanus [Hans H. Dieckhoff], *Zur Vorgeschichte des Roosevelt-Krieges* (Berlin: Junker und Dunnhaupt Verlag, 1943). The Russians apparently suspected the United States of similar perfidy. See the *Great Soviet Encyclopedia* as quoted in O. Lawrence Burnette, Jr., and William C. Haygood (eds.), *A Soviet View of the American Past* (Glenview, Ill.: Scott, Foresman and Co., 1964), p. 50.

It is misleading to state flatly that the American government used England's financial crisis as a means of substituting an American economic empire for the British one. Had this been a conscious policy of the Roosevelt Administration, far heavier pressures would have been applied. Although Morgenthau correctly accused the British of dragging their feet on the sale of British-owned investments in America, by the fall of 1940 the issue was largely forgotten since it would obviously be too late with too little. Morgenthau defended his hard bargaining on the grounds of political necessity, and that claim is partially supported by the fact that the only really strong Administration demands for such sales came in connection with the first Lend-Lease appropriation. Roosevelt's emphatic rejection of suggestions that the United States trade credits for Britain's Caribbean islands demonstrates the absence of any ambitions to acquire additional territory, and the periodic references to Britain's extensive economic holdings in Latin America were never coupled with any concrete proposals about how to transfer them to American hands. Individual American businessmen tried to use the wartime situation to force Britain to sell her American holdings at a discount, but the British government usually refused to submit to such blackmail, and the American government made no moves to force the issue. In fact, Morgenthau frequently condemned such actions.

Morgenthau's policy of forcing Great Britain to pay cash right to the end of their dollar resources found ample justification in the Congressional debate over Lend-Lease. The statistical evidence of Britain's dollar shortage overwhelmed opposition claims that the British could continue the fight against Hitler without aid from the United States. Nevertheless, the American belief in the fabled riches of the British Empire persisted. Many Americans, including Cordell Hull and Frank Knox, never really grasped the fact that Britain could run out of dollars without being bankrupt, and there are indications that even President Roosevelt remained skeptical of that fact. In spite of such doubts, the United States did adopt a policy that provided Britain with what was essentially a subsidy, not a loan. Thus, as one recent study of the economic aspects of Roosevelt's foreign policy points out, the nature of the Lend-Lease Act itself demonstrates that America had no intention of stripping England of her economic empire.[14] Although some Congressmen may have hoped that reverse Lend-Lease might result in the expansion of American business interests at the expense of British interests, nothing of the sort was ever hinted at by any of the members of the Administration.

Unquestionably, the notion of taking advantage of England came to the mind of many Americans. But in spite of the broad opportunities

[14]Lloyd C. Gardner, *Economic Aspects of New Deal Diplomacy* (Madison: University of Wisconsin Press, 1964), p. 276.

for doing just that, the Administration limited itself to occasional snatches of wishful thinking. Possibly Roosevelt and Morgenthau pushed Britain as far as they thought they could without causing the English to consider some sort of arrangement with Hitler, but if so, their success in hiding such a nefarious conspiracy is quite remarkable. If they were subject to such compelling greed, it appears highly unlikely that they would have been able to stop short of forcing Britain to divest herself of virtually all her American holdings. It is far more logical to assert that the hard bargain America drove rose initially out of the image of British opulence and continued because of the need to convince Congress that America had no choice but to provide the subsidy Britain required.

The Germans may have believed that England became a "paid vassal" of the United States with the enactment of Lend-Lease,[15] but neither the British nor the Americans saw it that way. Arthur Purvis, Britain's most successful representative in Washington during this trying time, expressed his heartfelt thoughts in a letter to President Roosevelt shortly after the Lend-Lease bill became law. In a handwritten note of thanks he told Roosevelt: "Apart entirely from what it means for the successful outcome of the struggle, I felt the ring of an understanding of human values—so rare in these days—which gives hope and inspiration for the future of men after the job is done."[16]

The crux of the debate over Roosevelt's foreign policy during this prewar period, including the Lend-Lease Act, is really just another facet of an age-old question that American democracy has never really answered: does the elected official have a responsibility to follow what he believes is desired by the electorate, or must his primary allegiance rest with his own conscience? To put it another way, must the leader in a democratic society first convince the public of the wisdom of his policies by open and above-board methods, or may he embark on a course of action and face the consequences at the next election? Do we trust our elected officials, or must they stand for election on every new policy decision?

A part of that question is answered by merely reading the United States Constitution. In this presidential form of government, no provisions are made for any sort of referendum by the public on major policy decisions. Unlike the parliamentary system, the American electorate is stuck with its choice of president. Thus, in terms of legal responsibility, the public debate over the Lend-Lease Act was interesting but not binding on the President or Congress. But legal responsibility is not what makes a democracy work. Rare indeed is the

---

[15]Thomsen to the Foreign Ministry, March 9, 1941, *DGFP*, XII, no. 141, pp. 251-52.

[16]Purvis to Roosevelt, March 16, 1941, Roosevelt Papers, PPF 7451.

Congressman or President who does not acknowledge, particularly at election time, that his aim is to represent the wishes of the people; thus, when those desires are expressed, most elected officials feel constrained to follow them. The conflict arises when the people indicate a course of action which directly disagrees with a representative's conscience. On many issues he is able to vote with his conscience and still avoid defeat at the polls; at other times resignation may be the only solution (though one rarely resorted to by politicians). To be sure, the promise that he would represent the wishes of the electorate is also an element to be considered by one's conscience, but often the crisis that faces the country will not allow the elected official to ignore his own reason and vote strictly as his constituents demand.

In the case of Franklin Roosevelt and a majority of the members of Congress, the conflict was acute. Roosevelt and most of Congress were convinced that Hitler's Germany was a direct and growing threat to the national security of the United States. The Administration believed that the British were fighting America's war, yet right down to the day of Pearl Harbor, American public opinion opposed entering the war. The argument over Roosevelt's foreign policy and more specifically, the Lend-Lease Act, thus revolves around a series of questions. First, was economic warfare with Germany in the national interest of the United States? If we assume that in the Presidential system it is the responsibility of the President to make that determination, then the only quarrel is with his judgment.[17] The answer to that question is far beyond the scope of this study, but if we assume that the national interest of the United States was involved, then new problems which are germane to the Lend-Lease Act are raised. A negative response, of course, ends the discussion, for Roosevelt stands condemned as of that point.

If one accepts the position that economic warfare against Germany was necessary, the question of the duties and limits of leadership in a democracy again occurs. This time it can be considered in the more restricted area of foreign policy. Even if one asserts that leadership in a democracy must be open and frank, is it necessary for a democratic nation to put itself at a disadvantage in its dealings with non-democratic nations that are not so limited? If the answer to that question is no, then Roosevelt seemingly worried far too much about public opinion and unanimity. If one carries this ultra-realist viewpoint to its logical conclusion, the President should have used his extensive powers as commander in chief to embroil the United States in the war with Germany as quickly as possible and then relied on

[17]That is the position taken by the United States Supreme Court in the Curtiss-Wright case. See Alfred H. Kelly and Winfred A. Harbison, *The American Constitution: Its Origins and Development*, 3d ed. (New York: W. W. Norton and Co., 1963), pp. 824, 827-28.

wartime patriotism to bring on national unity. On the other hand, if one still believes that the democratic leader should be democratic *so long as national security is not irreparably compromised*, then we can examine events surrounding the passage of the Lend-Lease Act to see if President Roosevelt followed that injunction.

Roosevelt was undoubtedly eager to obtain maximum public and Congressional support for the Lend-Lease Act. Since he had just been elected for a four-year term, his concern could hardly have been caused by a fear of defeat at the polls. The only logical assumption is that the President was attempting to work within the democratic structure as fully as he could without endangering American national security. The "dictator" charge is hard to substantiate. Roosevelt, most often accused by his own generation of being "King Franklin" and a potential dictator, actually took more care than any other President in similar circumstances to maintain the proper relationship between the executive and legislative branches. Abraham Lincoln and Woodrow Wilson both acted far more arbitrarily. Roosevelt was very leery of usurping Congressional prerogatives during the Lend-Lease debate and worked very closely with the Congressional leadership.

The basic criticism lodged against Roosevelt was the nature of the Lend-Lease debate, particularly during the hearings and on the floor of Congress. Charles Beard boiled it down to one bitter sentence: "At what point in time . . . did the President and the Secretary [Hull] decide that the policy of neutrality and isolation . . . was untenable and announce [it] to the public?"[18] Beard naïvely seems to be asking a professional politician openly to affront and insult a large group of voters by bluntly proclaiming that their ideas were totally wrong, yet in essence, that is just what the Roosevelt Administration did. The Lend-Lease debate was long and full. For the opposition to claim that the Administration avoided the key issue, namely the long-term implications of the act, is to confess their own inability to persuade the American public and other Congressmen that those implications were dangerous to the national security. In a democratic society it is the responsibility of the loyal opposition to point out to the public what it believes to be misguided actions on the part of the majority party. To expect the majority to make predictions that would, by their utterance, jeopardize their program is like demanding that a guilty man plead guilty in a court of law. When the opposition cannot convince the majority of the wisdom of their position and subsequently turns to verbal accusations of foul play and *ad hominem* arguments,

[18]Beard, *President Roosevelt and the Coming of the War*, p. 45.

one detects the pungent odor of sour grapes, or at the least, party politics.[19]

More importantly, a reading of the printed hearings on the Lend-Lease Bill and the newspaper accounts that dealt extensively with the legislation and its implications indicates without any doubt that nothing was left unsaid about the bill. If, with all the information available, the public could not clearly see the possible and probable results of the Lend-Lease Act, then they were hardly the ones to be trusted with major decisions. Time and again the bill's opponents warned that it meant war, yet Congress overwhelmingly approved it. There was no need for the Roosevelt Administration to point out the dangers and thereby weaken its case; the isolationists took care of that. Right or wrong, the Lend-Lease Act and the nature of the accompanying debate fell well within the basic practice of the American political system. Whether Roosevelt believed Lend-Lease would keep America out of war, or only wishfully hoped for that effect, is essentially a moot point. The legislation was fully discussed and resoundingly approved by Congress and thus, indirectly, by the people. Even so, although few can quarrel with the stated purpose of the Lend-Lease Act, one is still disturbed and even shocked by the lack of candor displayed by the Roosevelt Administration during the evolution of the legislation.

For better or for worse, regardless of the means or purpose, as of March, 1941, the United States of America had made the irrevocable commitment. Although actual war was nine months away, the Lend-Lease Act was a public announcement of the creation of the most productive and co-operative coalition of modern times—the Anglo-American alliance against Nazi Germany.

[19]Henry Morgenthau was party to an exaggeration when he forwarded to President Roosevelt a memo stating that the Lend-Lease victory left the fight against aid to Britain in the hands of the "fanatic fringe" and a "national political alliance of crackpots," all of whom bear the identifying marks of fascism—both far right and far left—but the labelling in the memo of the Lend-Lease Act as a watershed for American public opinion regarding the European war appears accurate. See Morgenthau to Roosevelt, March 14, 1941, enclosing a copy of a paper entitled "Evolution of the Minority," Roosevelt Papers, OF 21, Treasury, 1941. The author of this interesting document is not identified, but Morgenthau forwarded it with the terse comment, "This may interest you."

APPENDIX

The Lend-Lease Act, March 11, 1941

This is copied from a print of the act which is in my possession. The print was put out by the U.S. Government Printing Office in 1941.

[PUBLIC LAW 11–77TH CONGRESS]
[CHAPTER 11–1ST SESSION]
[H. R. 1776]
AN ACT

Further to promote the defense of the United States, and for other purposes.

Be it enacted by the Senate and House of Representatives of the United States of America in Congress assembled, That this Act may be cited as "An Act to Promote the Defense of the United States".

SEC. 2. As used in this Act—

(a) The term "defense article" means—

(1) Any weapon, munition, aircraft, vessel, or boat;

(2) Any machinery, facility, tool, material, or supply necessary for the manufacture, production, processing, repair, servicing, or operation of any article described in this subsection;

(3) Any component material or part of or equipment for any article described in this subsection;

(4) Any agricultural, industrial or other commodity or article for defense. Such term "defense article" includes any article described in this subsection: Manufactured or procured pursuant to section 3, or to which the United States or any foreign government has or hereafter acquires title, possession, or control.

(b) The term "defense information" means any plan, specification, design, prototype, or information pertaining to any defense article.

SEC. 3. (a) Notwithstanding the provisions of any other law, the President may, from time to time, when he deems it in the interest of national defense,

243

authorize the Secretary of War, the Secretary of the Navy, or the head of any other department or agency of the Government—

(1) To manufacture in arsenals, factories, and shipyards under their jurisdiction, or otherwise procure, to the extent to which funds are made available therefor, or contracts are authorized from time to time by the Congress, or both, any defense article for the government of any country whose defense the President deems vital to the defense of the United States.

(2) To sell, transfer title to, exchange, lease, lend, or otherwise dispose of, to any such government any defense article, but no defense article not manufactured or procured under paragraph (1) shall in any way be disposed of under this paragraph, except after consultation with the Chief of Staff of the Army or the Chief of Naval Operations of the Navy, or both. The value of defense articles disposed of in any way under authority of this paragraph, and procured from funds heretofore appropriated, shall not exceed $1,300,000,000. The value of such defense articles shall be determined by the head of the department or agency concerned or such other department, agency or officer as shall be designated in the manner provided in the rules and regulations issued hereunder. Defense articles procured from funds hereafter appropriated to any department or agency of the Government, other than from funds authorized to be appropriated under this Act, shall not be disposed of in any way under authority of this paragraph except to the extent hereafter authorized by the Congress in the Acts appropriating such funds or otherwise.

(3) To test, inspect, prove, repair, outfit, recondition, or otherwise to place in good working order, to the extent to which funds are made available therefor, or contracts are authorized from time to time by the Congress, or both, any defense article for any such government, or to procure any or all such services by private contract.

(4) To communicate to any such government any defense information, pertaining to any defense article furnished to such government under paragraph (2) of this subsection.

(5) To release for export any defense article disposed of in any way under this subsection to any such government.

(b) The terms and conditions upon which any such foreign government receives any aid authorized under subsection (a) shall be those which the President deems satisfactory, and the benefit to the United States may be payment or repayment in kind or property, or any other direct or indirect benefit which the President deems satisfactory.

(c) After June 30, 1943, or after the passage of a concurrent resolution by the two Houses before June 30, 1943, which declares that the powers conferred by or pursuant to subsection (a) are no longer necessary to promote the defense of the United States, neither the President nor the head of any department or agency shall exercise any of the powers conferred by or pursuant to subsection (a); except that until July 1, 1946, any of such powers may be exercised to the extent necessary to carry out a contract or agreement with such a foreign government made before July 1, 1943, or before the passage of such concurrent resolution, whichever is the earlier.

(d) Nothing in this Act shall be construed to authorize or to permit the authorization of convoying vessels by naval vessels of the United States.

(e) Nothing in this Act shall be construed to authorize or to permit the authorization of the entry of any American vessel into a combat area in violation of section 3 of the Neutrality Act of 1939.

SEC. 4. All contracts or agreements made for the disposition of any defense article or defense information pursuant to section 3 shall contain a clause by which the foreign government undertakes that it will not, without the consent of the President, transfer title to or possession of such defense article or defense information by gift, sale, or otherwise, or permit its use by anyone not an officer, employee, or agent of such foreign government.

SEC. 5. (a) The Secretary of War, the Secretary of the Navy, or the head of any other department or agency of the Government involved shall, when any such defense article or defense information is exported, immediately inform the department or agency designated by the President to administer section 6 of the Act of July 2, 1940 (54 Stat. 714), of the quantities, character, value, terms of disposition, and destination of the article and information so exported.

(b) The President from time to time, but not less frequently than once every ninety days, shall transmit to the Congress a report of operations under this Act except such information as he deems incompatible with the public interest to disclose. Reports provided for under this subsection shall be transmitted to the Secretary of the Senate or the Clerk of the House of Representatives, as the case may be, if the Senate or the House of Representatives, as the case may be, is not in session.

SEC. 6. (a) There is hereby authorized to be appropriated from time to time, out of any money in the Treasury not otherwise appropriated, such amounts as may be necessary to carry out the provisions and accomplish the purposes of this Act.

(b) All money and all property which is converted into money received under Section 3 from any government shall, with the approval of the Director of the Budget, revert to the respective appropriation or appropriations out of which funds were expended with respect to the defense article or defense information for which such consideration is received, and shall be available for expenditure for the purpose for which such expended funds were appropriated by law, during the fiscal year in which such funds are received and the ensuing fiscal year; but in no event shall any funds so received be available for expenditure after June 30, 1946.

SEC. 7. The Secretary of War, the Secretary of the Navy, and the head of the department or agency shall in all contracts or agreements for the disposition of any defense article or defense information fully protect the rights of all citizens of the United States who have patent rights in and to any such article or information which is hereby authorized to be disposed of and the payments collected for royalties on such patents shall be paid to the owners and holders of such patents.

SEC. 8. The Secretaries of War and of the Navy are hereby authorized to purchase or otherwise acquire arms, ammunition, and implements of war produced within the jurisdiction of any country to which section 3 is applicable, whenever the President deems such purchase or acquisition to be necessary in the interests of the defense of the United States.

SEC. 9. The President may, from time to time, promulgate such rules and regulations as may be necessary and proper to carry out any of the provisions of this Act; and he may exercise any power or authority conferred on him by this Act through such department, agency, or officer as he shall direct.

SEC. 10. Nothing in this Act shall be construed to change existing law relating to the use of the land and naval forces of the United States, except insofar as such use relates to the manufacture, procurement, and repair of defense articles, the communication of information and other noncombatant purposes enumerated in this Act.

SEC. 11. If any provision of this Act or the application of such provision to any circumstance shall be held invalid, the validity of the remainder of the Act and the applicability of such provision to other circumstances shall not be affected thereby.

Approved, March 11, 1941.

BIBLIOGRAPHY

The following bibliography is intended to cover only those materials that actually contributed to this study. The manuscript sources are discussed in a brief essay, and the printed materials are listed in the conventional manner. Annotations have been made regarding their usefulness and reliability. There are no annotations for items whose use is obvious or which were used for background material.

I. PRIMARY SOURCES

A. Manuscript Sources:

The official files of various United States government agencies provided the great bulk of the primary material for this study. Three files in the archives of the Department of the Army proved useful. The G-4 files and the AG Central files (AG400.3295) provided background materials, and the ASF, International Aid Division files supplied some interesting documents regarding defense production and priorities problems. In addition, the "History of the International Aid Division" in the files of the Office of the Chief of Military History (Washington, D.C.) was a useful narrative dealing with the same problems. The materials in the Department of the Navy were of no use in this study.

The files of the Department of State provided a great deal of valuable information. The "History of the Role of the State Department in Lend-Lease," written by George Fennemore for the Division of History and Research, was disappointingly vague. Of far greater use were the State Department's files in the National Archives. Decimal files 740.0011, 740.0011 EW 1939, 841.51, and 841.5151 contain a significant number of documents that deal with the formation of policy inside the State Department as well as reports from American government representatives in Great Britain. The following decimal files provided similar data though in smaller amounts: 121.841, 701.4151, 740.00111a, 800.24, 811.20, 841.20, 841.24, 841.248, 865.9111. The records of the Foreign Economic Administration, one of the now defunct World War II agencies, are presently under the custody of the State Department, although their use is restricted and permission to consult them must also be obtained from the originating agency of a document. The F.E.A. files contain some very valuable materials, but it is difficult to use them since they are not fully organized and catalogued. There is a "History of Lend-Lease," written for the Office of the Foreign Liquidation Commissioner at the end of World War II, which deals with the entire Lend-Lease program. Part One, Chapter One, entitled "Evolution of Lend-Lease," pertains to the background of the act. However, that chapter and the exhibits that accompany it provided very little data not available elsewhere. It was useful largely as a means of determining how contemporaries viewed the origins of the program. Of more value were the files of Philip Young which are included in the F.E.A. files. Young, as a member of Morgenthau's staff, was entrusted with substantial responsibility for the aid to Britain program, and his files reflect this. The files of the President's Liaison Committee, like the Young files, are spotty but highly valuable since they are one of the few sources of information concerning the activities of the organization that was responsible for aiding the British before the Lend-Lease Administration came into being. Unhappily, many of the documents are of British origin and thus remain classified under British government rules.

The Franklin D. Roosevelt Library (National Archives and Records Service, Hyde Park, New York) provided the greatest volume of the primary source materials for this study. The Presidential papers, which are organized into four files— the Official File, the President's Personal File, the President's Secretary's File, and Transcripts of Presidential Press Conferences—contain an enormous amount of data but are often frustratingly difficult to use. During the Roosevelt Administration filing was done by many different people, and as a result documents pertaining to the same subject are filed in many different places. Random sorting through various files of personal letters occasionally brought to light useful materials, but it is physically impossible to peruse every file in the collection. In addition, there are great, yawning gaps in the documentation available: answers to letters that are missing from the file and vice versa, references to memorandums and position papers that are not in the files, and so on. There is an almost total absence of meaningful memos or notes from the President to members of his official family, and diplomatic materials have obviously been carefully screened. As mentioned before in this study, only a tiny portion of the Roosevelt-Churchill correspondence is available, and there is nothing of value in the Felix Frankfurter file. The latter was admittedly "raided" at Mr. Frankfurter's request, but the other gaps are harder to explain. Newsman Arthur Krock bluntly stated that the Roosevelt Papers are highly selective and that documents were destroyed.[1] Even with these limitations, the papers are invaluable. The Harry L. Hopkins Papers, which are also in the Roosevelt Library, afforded very little that was not in Robert Sherwood's *Roosevelt and Hopkins*, and in fact the papers were organized by Mr. Sherwood in the process of writing his book. They are useful for additional details that were not included in Sherwood's broader study. The papers of Henry Morgenthau, Jr., were far and away the one indispensable source for this study. They are divided into three groups: his diary, transcripts of his press conferences, and Treasury Department press releases. The Morgenthau Diary was the key

---

[1] Krock interview, November 10, 1966.

source. It contains copies of virtually every official and quasi-official document that crossed Mr. Morgenthau's desk and thus provides the most valuable type of information for this sort of treatment—data on the development of policy. Documents that are of foreign government origin are closed, as are materials in which Mr. Morgenthau dwelled on personalities, but otherwise the restrictions are few. The index to each volume of the diary is very useful, although it can be tricky to use. References are often made to other volumes when the major portion of material on a subject is indexed, but that entry is not repeated in the volume that contains a smaller amount of data on that topic. In addition, the topic headings are somewhat cryptic and the pattern occasionally changes, apparently when different people took over the indexing task. The safest policy is to leaf through all major "group meetings" held between Morgenthau and his staff since the range of topics discussed at those meetings was very broad and the indexers usually included only those topics taken up at some length. This is a long and painstaking task, but worth the effort. One major restriction exists on the use of the Morgenthau Diary. The volumes are opened in four-year segments, twenty-five years after the close of each of Roosevelt's Administrations. Thus the period from January 20, 1941, through January 20, 1945, will not be available to scholars until that date in 1970. Diary volumes 259-347 were used in this study, along with volumes 12-16 of the Morgenthau press conferences and volumes 22 and 23 of the Treasury Department press releases. The papers of Harold D. Smith, Director of the Bureau of the Budget during this period, contained little of value. Files titled "White House Memoranda, 1939-1941," had nothing pertaining to Lend-Lease and two books labelled "Conferences with the President, 1939-1942," were even more disappointing. At the beginning of the entries for 1941, conferences regarding Lend-Lease are listed with the comment, "not dictated." I have been unable to find out why. The papers of Oscar Cox, which became available in 1968, added further details, although the bulk of the data concerning Lend-Lease is repeated in the Morgenthau Diary. The exception to that is material dealing with Cox's liaison duties with Congress during the debate over the bill.

The files of the United States House of Representatives, Committee on Foreign Affairs, 77th Congress, 1st Session, proved sparse but valuable. In the committee offices (Rayburn Building, Washington, D.C.) the closed file of committee correspondence with witnesses on H.R. 1776 provided a glimpse of the manner in which Sol Bloom organized the hearings, and the committee's "Minutes, 1940-1946," provided the roll call votes held in the committee on the amendments to the bill. That data is not available elsewhere. In the committee's files in the National Archives (Washington, D.C.) the "File on H.R. 1776" gave further information on the organization of the hearings plus some sampling of public opinion, and the "Docket" gave a concise legislative chronology of the bill.

Materials in the Library of Congress proved disappointing. The papers of Breckinridge Long occasionally gave a glimpse of the attitude of some of the State Department officials, but these have been published in a well-edited collection by Fred Israel. The papers of Norman H. Davis, Robert P. Patterson, and Thomas T. Connally were of no value whatsoever, and the papers of Secretary of the Navy Frank Knox are very spotty and to a great degree deal with personal rather than public matters. Knox carefully avoided mentioning controversial subjects in his private correspondence once he joined the Roosevelt Cabinet. Secretary of the Interior Jesse H. Jones's papers deal almost exclusively with domestic matters.

Cordell Hull's papers contain absolutely nothing of a controversial nature for this period. Sanitized or not, they are virtually useless in trying to determine how policy developed within the government. This may be rectified if additional papers held in the vault in the Manuscripts Division are made available to scholars. A typewritten transcript of Hull's testimony on H.R. 1776 before executive session of the Senate Committee on Foreign Relations, January 27, 1941, is in the Hull Papers.

The papers of Justice Felix Frankfurter, also in the Library of Congress, deserve special mention. At this writing those papers which have been turned over to the Library are open without restriction. This includes correspondence with all of the leading figures in the Roosevelt Administration. Unhappily, none of this material provided any meaningful information as to Frankfurter's influence on foreign policy or the Lend-Lease Act. Those papers that promise to be most valuable, his personal correspondence with President Roosevelt, are still held by Max Freedman. They are to be given to the Library of Congress at some unspecified future date. Mr. Freedman would not grant me access to them, nor has he answered my written queries.

The file of the United States Senate, 77th Congress, 1st Session, on H.R. 1776 (S. 275) in the National Archives (Washington, D.C.) provided only a small amount of correspondence, primarily from parties who wished to testify. The files of the Treasury Department were likewise quite sparse, although the file "Lend-Lease Bill (77th Congress)" in the legislative section files of the Office of the General Counsel provided some correspondence not available elsewhere. The records of the Bureau of Accounts, Record Group 39, Great Britain file, do contain some statistical data, but most of the important papers are included in the Morgenthau Diary.

The diary and papers of Secretary of War Henry L. Stimson, deposited in the Sterling Memorial Library at Yale University (New Haven, Connecticut), were very useful. Stimson was often very candid in his diary, and his papers provided some insights into the development of his thinking on various questions. Along with the Morgenthau Diary, Stimson's papers and diaries are the only reliable source of information on Roosevelt's Cabinet meetings.

The most unusual source of primary materials was the Sol Bloom Elementary School, PS No. 84, in New York City, New York. I am grateful to the principal of that school, Mr. Milton Forrest, for permitting me to see and copy the small collection of Sol Bloom materials which is held by the school. The collection is small, and a good portion of it is repeated in the House Foreign Affairs Committee files in the National Archives, but nevertheless it did prove interesting.

Stephen J. Spingarn and Ernest R. Feidler were kind enough to provide me with memorandums concerning the drafting of the Lend-Lease Act. Spingarn's memo is dated October 29, 1966, and Feidler's is dated November 2, 1966. Both are available in the Stephen J. Spingarn Papers at the Harry S Truman Library (Independence, Missouri). They also sent me a joint memorandum on the same subject dated July 10, 1968. A copy of that memo is in the Franklin D. Roosevelt Library.

The constituent correspondence file on H.R. 1776 of the Hon. Frances P. Bolton, M.C. (Washington, D.C.) provided a good indication of the attitude of Mid-Westerners regarding the Lend-Lease Bill. There was nothing regarding the Foreign Affairs Committee hearings on the bill in this file. The Sol Bloom Papers

in the New York Public Library (New York, New York) afforded similar information on New Yorkers, but again there was nothing regarding Bloom's official
relationship to the bill. The Sam Rayburn Library (Bonham, Texas) supplied a
copy of one of Speaker Rayburn's speeches in support of the bill but wrote that
there was no useful material on the bill in their files. A portion of the Sam
Rayburn Papers in the possession of Mr. D. B. Hardeman (Washington, D.C.), Mr.
Rayburn's former research assistant, provided some constituent correspondence
on the bill, but nothing else. Unhappily, Rayburn rarely made or kept records of
legislative or policy matters.

B. Published Documents:

Germany, Auswärtiges Amt. *Documents on German Foreign Policy, 1918-1945.*
Series D (1937-45), 13 vols. Washington: U.S. Government Printing Office,
1949-64.
  Volumes XI and XII were used in this study.

Documents on American Foreign Relations. Jones, S. Shepard, and Myers, Denys
P., eds. Vol. II (1939-40) and III (1940-41). Boston: World Peace Foundation,
1940-41.

U.S. Bureau of Demobilization, Civilian Production Administration. *Industrial
Mobilization for War: History of the War Production Board and Predecessor
Agencies, 1940-1945.* Vol. I, *Program and Administration.* Washington: U.S.
Government Printing Office, 1947.
  A deadly dull study, but loaded with material on the problem of defense
production. Proposed succeeding volumes were never published.

U.S., Congress, *Congressional Record.* Washington: U.S. Government Printing
Office. Vols. LXXXV-LXXXVII (1939-41).

U.S., Congress, Joint Committee on the Investigation of the Pearl Harbor Attack.
Hearings. 39 Parts. Washington: U.S. Government Printing Office, 1946-47. Part
XX.
  In addition to general background, this volume provided a memorandum by
Stimson regarding the general international situation and the Lend-Lease Bill.

U.S., Department of State. *Foreign Relations of the United States.* Washington:
U.S. Government Printing Office, 1862——.
  The following volumes were of direct use in this study: 1939, Vols. I, II; 1940,
Vols. I, III; 1941, Vol. III.

_____. *Peace and War: United States Foreign Policy, 1931-1941.* Washington:
U.S. Government Printing Office, 1943.

U.S., House of Representatives, Committee on Appropriations, 77th Cong., 1st
sess. *Defense Aid Supplemental Appropriation Bill, 1941,* Report no. 276 (to
accompany H.R. 4050). Washington: printed at the order of the House of
Representatives, 1941.

This is the report of the House Appropriations Committee on the initial Lend-Lease appropriation. No minority report was filed.

_____. *Hearings before a a Subcommittee on H.R. 4050: Making a Supplemental Appropriation for the National Defense to Provide Aid to the Government of any Country Whose Defense the President Deems Vital to the Defense of the United States, and for Other Purposes.* Washington: U.S. Government Printing Office, 1941.
These are the House Appropriations Committee hearings on the first Lend-Lease appropriation.

U.S., House of Representatives, Committee on Foreign Affairs, 77th Cong., 1st sess. *Hearings on H.R. 1776: A Bill Further to Promote the Defense of the United States, and for Other Purposes.* Washington: U.S. Government Printing Office, 1941.

_____. *To Promote the Defense of the United States,* Report no. 18 (to accompany H.R. 1776). 2 pts. Washington: printed at the order of the House of Representatives, 1941.

U.S., Senate, Committee on Appropriations, 77th Cong., 1st sess. *Defense Aid Supplemental Appropriation Act,* Report no. 135, Calendar no. 144 (to accompany H.R. 4050). Washington: printed at the order of the Senate, 1941.

_____. *Hearings before a Subcommittee on H.R. 4050: Making a Supplemental Appropriation for National Defense to Provide Aid to the Government of Any Country Whose Defense the President Deems Vital to the Defense of the United States.* Washington: U.S. Government Printing Office, 1941.
This, and the entry preceding, are the hearings and report of the Senate Appropriations Committee on the first Lend-Lease appropriation.

U.S., Senate, Committee on Foreign Relations, 77th Cong., 1st sess. *Promoting the Defense of the United States,* Report no. 45, Calendar no. 51 (to accompany H.R. 1776). 2 pts. Washington: printed at the order of the Senate, 1941.

_____. *Hearings on S. 275: A Bill Further to Promote the Defense of the United States, and for Other Purposes.* Washington: U.S. Government Printing Office, 1941.

C. Published Memoirs, Papers, and Speeches:

Bloom, Sol. *The Autobiography of Sol Bloom.* New York: G. P. Putnam's Sons, 1948.
Self-adulatory and lacking in detail, it is useful largely for color and human interest material on the period.

Blum, John Morton. *From the Morgenthau Diaries.* 3 vols. Vol. I, *Years of Crisis, 1928-1938.* Vol. II, *Years of Urgency, 1938-1941,* Boston: Houghton Mifflin Co., 1959-68.

This source, particularly vol. II, was of critical importance. Although the Morgenthau Diary is open to the public as far as January 20, 1941, Professor Blum had access to two other collections of Morgenthau materials; some papers of the Secretary's at the Roosevelt Library in Hyde Park, New York, and some personal papers still held by the Morgenthau heirs. The latter source was particularly valuable since it contained most of Morgenthau's memoranda of his conversations with the President. They are not available to scholars. Blum also had the advantage of Morgenthau's personal co-operation in writing these studies. Vol. II is also the only source of what the Morgenthau Diary says for the closed period beginning on January 20, 1941. Although they are written in a narrative style, they can essentially be used as a primary source.

Bullitt, William C. "How We Won the War and Lost the Peace." *Life*, August 20, 1948, 87 ff.
   A brief piece of "I told you so" historical hindsight by the American Ambassador in France during the early war years. Useful only for background and in determining the genesis of the "fire-hose" analogy.

Byrnes, James F. *All in One Lifetime*. New York: Harper and Brothers, 1958.

_____. *Speaking Frankly*. New York: Harper and Brothers, 1947.
   These two autobiographical studies by Byrnes provided surprisingly little information on his role in the Senate during the Lend-Lease debate.

Catton, Bruce. *The War Lords of Washington*. New York: Harcourt, Brace and Co., 1948.
   This famous historian of the Civil War was a member of the Office of Production Management during the early part of World War II and became convinced that the government-big business relationship was dangerous to American democracy. Useful only as a source of background material on the defense production tangle.

Churchill, Winston S. *Blood, Sweat, and Tears*. Compiled by Randolph Churchill. New York: G. P. Putnam's Sons, 1941.
   A collection of speeches delivered by Churchill in 1939 and 1940.

_____. *The Second World War*. 6 vols. Vol. I, *The Gathering Storm*, 1948. Vol. II, *Their Finest Hour*, 1949. Vol. III, *The Grand Alliance*, 1951. Boston: Houghton Mifflin Co., 1948-53.
   One of the few sources of British documentary materials for this period. In spite of some indications that Churchill occasionally wrote history as he wished it had happened, it is still an indispensable source of material for the entire war. There is surprisingly little concerning the Lend-Lease Act and the British financial crisis that preceded it. This may indicate that Churchill was more concerned with the war at that time and left such matters to his subordinates.

_____. *The Unrelenting Struggle; War Speeches*. Compiled by Charles Eade. Boston: Little, Brown and Co., 1942.
   Another collection of Churchill's speeches, this time covering the years 1941 and 1942.

Ciechanowski, Jan. *Defeat in Victory*. Garden City: Doubleday and Co., 1947.

Connally, Tom [Thomas Terry], with Steinberg, Alfred. *My Name is Tom Connally*. New York: Thomas Y. Crowell Co., 1954.
An uninformative memoir, primarily concerned with building up the image of the author.

Eden, Anthony (Earl of Avon), *The Memoirs of Anthony Eden, Earl of Avon*. 3 vols. Vol. II, *The Reckoning*, 1965. Boston: Houghton Mifflin Co., 1960-65.
Eden was concerned primarily with European affairs, thus there are relatively few comments regarding Lend-Lease or its origins.

Halifax, Lord. *Fullness of Days*. New York: Dodd, Mead and Co., 1957.
This, and a biography of Halifax listed below, were of peripheral value since Halifax was not concerned with American-British affairs until February, 1941.

Hull, Cordell. *The Memoirs of Cordell Hull*. 2 vols. New York: The Macmillan Co., 1948.
This virtually useless source consists largely of a long-winded defense of his and the Administration's policies. It is chronologically inaccurate and unreliable. Its value is restricted to those interested in examining Hull as viewed by Hull. It completely ignores most controversies and fails to give any indication of the way in which policy developed.

Ickes, Harold L. *The Secret Diary of Harold L. Ickes*. 3 vols. Vol. III, *The Lowering Clouds, 1939-1941*, 1954. New York: Simon and Schuster, 1953-54.
A highly opinionated view by one of the most cantankerous members of Roosevelt's Cabinet.

Ironside, General Sir William Edmund. *Time Unguarded: The Ironside Diaries, 1937-1940*. Edited by Colonel R. MacLeod and Denis Kelley. New York: David McKay Co., 1962.
This provided a glimpse into the British defense supply problem in the early stages of the war.

Krock, Arthur. *In the Nation: 1932-1966*. New York: McGraw-Hill Book Co., 1966.
This is merely a collection of Krock's columns.

Long, Breckinridge. *The War Diary of Breckinridge Long: Selections from the Years 1939-1944*. Edited by Fred L. Israel. Lincoln: University of Nebraska Press, 1966.
A highly representative selection that largely obviates the need to use the actual diaries which are in the Library of Congress.

Lothian, Philip H. Kerr; 11th Marquis of. *The American Speeches of Lord Lothian: July 1939 to December 1940*. London, New York, and Toronto: Oxford University Press, 1941.

Martin, Joseph W., Jr. *Joe Martin, My First Fifty Years in Politics*. As told to
Robert J. Donovan. New York: McGraw-Hill Book Co., 1960.

Moffat, Jay Pierrepont. *The Moffat Papers*. Edited by Nancy H. Hooker. Cambridge: Harvard University Press, 1956.
   Although Moffat was not directly concerned with the Lend-Lease Act, he was
a vigorous busybody whose diaries are often the major source of information
about squabbles inside the State Department.

Moran, Lord (Sir Charles Wilson). *Churchill: Taken from the Diaries of Lord
Moran: The Struggle for Survival, 1940-1965*. Boston: Houghton Mifflin Co.,
1966.
   This provided a few comments Churchill made later in the war concerning the
development of the Lend-Lease Act.

Morgenthau, Henry, Jr. "The Morgenthau Diaries: IV—The Story Behind Lend-
Lease." *Collier's*, October 18, 1947, 16 ff.
   One of a series of articles published by Morgenthau, it is quite incomplete and
chronologically confusing, but it does contain some data not available elsewhere.

_____. "Summary Report of the Secretary of the Treasury, 1945." Photocopy of
the original typecopy. Washington: July 21, 1945.
   This is an interesting summary written by Mr. Morgenthau of his stewardship
of the Treasury Department from 1934 to the time of his resignation in 1945.

Nelson, Donald M. *Arsenal of Democracy: The Story of American War Production*. New York: Harcourt, Brace and Co., 1946.

Nicolson, Harold. *The Diaries and Letters of Harold Nicolson*. Edited by Nigel
Nicolson. 3 vols. Vol. II, *The War Years*, 1967. New York: Atheneum, 1966-68.

Norris, George W. *Fighting Liberal: The Autobiography of George W. Norris*.
New York: The Macmillan Co., 1945.

Perkins, Frances. *The Roosevelt I Knew*. New York: The Viking Press, 1946.

Pickersgill, J. W. *The Mackenzie King Record*. Vol. I (1939-44). Toronto: The
University of Chicago Press and the University of Toronto Press, 1960.
   This proved occasionally illuminating because Canadian Prime Minister King
often acted as a go-between for various American officials and their English
counterparts.

Roosevelt, Franklin D. *F.D.R.: His Personal Letters, 1928-1945*. Edited by Elliott
Roosevelt. 3 vols. New York: Duell, Sloan and Pearce, Vol. II, 1950.
   This is a collection of some of the President's less controversial corre-
spondence.

_____. *The Public Papers and Addresses of Franklin D. Roosevelt*. Compiled by
Samuel I. Rosenman. 13 vols. London: Macmillan and Co., 1938-50.

This is a valuable collection but one which should be checked against the *New York Times* (or similar) transcript of Roosevelt's speeches since it does not include ad-libs and last-minute changes. The collection of press conferences is incomplete and must be supplemented by the press conference transcripts at the Roosevelt Library.

———. *Roosevelt and Frankfurter: Their Correspondence, 1928-1945.* Edited by Max Freedman. Boston: Little, Brown and Co., 1968.
Mr. Freedman did not respond to my queries about any materials not included in this volume regarding Frankfurter and Lend-Lease.

Rosenman, Samuel I. *Working With Roosevelt.* New York: Harper and Brothers, 1952.
This is useful primarily as a source of anecdotal material.

Sherwood, Robert E. *Roosevelt and Hopkins: An Intimate History.* Rev. ed. New York: Harper and Brothers, 1950.
This contains information on the *Tuscaloosa* cruise Roosevelt took in December, 1940, which is not available in either the Hopkins or Roosevelt Papers. Otherwise it is largely useful for background since Hopkins was not directly concerned with foreign affairs until December, 1940, and not until March, 1941, did he really get involved with Lend-Lease.

Stettinius, Edward R., Jr. *Lend-Lease: Weapon for Victory.* New York: The Macmillan Co., 1944.
Although this is primarily concerned with the Lend-Lease Administration's operations, there is a brief section on the origins of the act. The discussion is vague and lacks details. There may be additional data on the origins of the legislation in the Stettinius papers at the University of Virginia, but they are not yet open to scholars.

Stimson, Henry L., and Bundy, McGeorge. *On Active Service in Peace and War.* New York: Harper and Brothers, 1948.
This is an incomplete and apologetic set of memoirs which must be supplemented by the Stimson Diary and Papers.

Tully, Grace. *F.D.R. My Boss.* New York: Charles Scribner's Sons, 1949.
This is a largely anecdotal memoir written by one of Roosevelt's secretaries.

Vandenberg, Arthur. *The Private Papers of Senator Vandenberg.* Edited by Arthur H. Vandenberg, Jr. Boston: Houghton Mifflin Co., 1952.

Wheeler, Burton K., with Healy, Paul F. *Yankee From the West.* Garden City: Doubleday and Co., 1962.

D. Interviews:

Alsop, Joseph. Syndicated columnist, 1940–present. Washington, D.C., May 24, 1967.

Bolton, Hon. Frances P., M.C. Member, House Committee on Foreign Affairs, 1941-present. Washington, D.C., March 16, 1967.

Crawford, Boyd. Staff Administrator of the Committee on Foreign Affairs, U.S. House of Representatives (on the Committee staff in 1941). Telephone, October 31, 1966; November 4, 1966; various times in March, 1967.

Deschler, Lewis. Parliamentarian of the U.S. House of Representatives, 1928-present. Telephone, October 26, 1966; interview, August 1, 1967.

Feidler, Ernest R. Lawyer with the Treasury Department in 1941. Washington, D.C., September 5, 1968.

Foley, Edward. General Counsel, U.S. Department of the Treasury, 1940 and 1941. Washington, D.C., November 3, 1966.

Hall, H. Duncan. Author of *North American Supply* and attached to the British Embassy in Washington during World War II. Bethesda, Maryland, September 28, 1966.

Hardeman, D. B. Research Assistant to the Hon. Sam Rayburn, Speaker of the U.S. House of Representatives, 1957-November 16, 1961. Washington, D.C., various times, fall, 1966, and spring, 1967.

Krock, Arthur. Washington correspondent for the *New York Times* in 1940 and 1941. Washington, D.C., November 10, 1966.

McCormack, Hon. John. Speaker of the U.S. House of Representatives. Majority Leader of the House of Representatives in 1941. Washington, D.C., March 18, 1967.

Megill, H. Newton. Assistant Enrolling Clerk of the U.S. House of Representatives in 1940 and 1941. Telephone, Washington, D.C., June 29, 1966.

Mundt, Hon. Karl. United States Senator. Member of the House Committee on Foreign Affairs in 1941. Washington, D.C., April 29, 1967.

Pepper, Hon. Claude, M.C. Member of the Senate Foreign Relations Committee, 1939-41. Washington, D.C., March 6, 1967.

Rankin, Mrs. Jeannette. Member of Congress in 1941. Watkinsville, Georgia, February 23, 1968.

Spingarn, Stephen J. Lawyer with the Treasury Department in 1941. Washington, D.C., September 5, 1968.

E. Printed Contemporary Materials:

Alsop, Joseph, and Kintner, Robert. *American White Paper: The Story of American Diplomacy and the Second World War*. New York: Simon and Schuster, 1940.

This proved useful because the authors were given access to some of the official documents by a member of the State Department, Adolf Berle.

Cantrill, Hadley, ed. *Public Opinion, 1935-1946.* Princeton: Princeton University Press, 1951.
This is an invaluable collection of public opinion polls.

Council on Foreign Relations, comp. Clipping file, "Aid to Great Britain and Lend-Lease Act, 1940-1941." New York, New York.
A selection of newspaper clippings from throughout the country, although the New York newspapers are dominant.

Davis, Forrest, and Lindley, Ernest K. *How War Came: An American White Paper; From the Fall of France to Pearl Harbor.* New York: Simon and Schuster, 1942.
An "official" history written by two reporters who were friends of President Roosevelt.

Jay, Douglas, *Paying For the War.* n.p.: Labour Party (United Kingdom), April, 1940.
This pamphlet, put out by the British Labour Party, is interesting primarily because it does not predicate American financial aid. It is enclosed in Johnson to Hull, May 10, 1940, State Department, 841.51/1571.

Keynes, John Maynard. *How to Pay for the War.* London: Macmillan and Co., 1940.
A pamphlet available in State Department, 841.5151/1543.

[Murphy, Charles J. V.]. "Allied Purchasing: 'The Best Bargain We Can Jolly Well Make.' " *Fortune*, April, 1940, 68 ff.
A contemporary study of the British Purchasing Commission.

New York Herald-Tribune. January-March, 1941.

New York Times. 1939-41.

Shepardson, Whitney H., and Scroggs, William O. *The United States in World Affairs: An Account of American Foreign Relations, 1940.* New York and London: for the Council on Foreign Relations by Harper and Brothers, 1941.

The Times (London). 1939-41.

Washington Post. 1940-41.

Washington Times-Herald. 1940-41.

Wright, Quincy. "The Lend-Lease Bill and International Law." *American Journal of International Law,* XXXV (April, 1941), 305-14.

II. SECONDARY SOURCES

A. *Official Histories:*

The Army Air Forces in World War II (United States):

Cate, James L., and Williams, E. Kathleen. "The Air Corps Prepares for War, 1939-1941." In Vol. I, *Plans and Early Operations.* Edited by Wesley F. Craven and James L. Cate. Chicago: University of Chicago Press for the United States Air Force, Office of Air Force History, 1948.

History of the Second World War (United Kingdom):

Woodward, Sir Llewellyn. *British Foreign Policy in the Second World War.* London: Her Majesty's Stationery Office, 1962.
This is a broad study that provided only background material.

United Kingdom Military Series (Edited by J. R. M. Butler):

Butler, J. R. M. *Grand Strategy.* 6 vols. Vol. II, *September 1939-June 1941.* London: Her Majesty's Stationery Office, 1956.
Disappointingly lacking in detail, this afforded only background material.

Roskill, Captain S. W. *The War at Sea, 1939-1945.* 3 vols. Vol. I. *The Defensive,* 1954. London: Her Majesty's Stationery Office, 1954-61.

United Kingdom Civil Series (Edited by Sir Keith Hancock):

Hall, H. Duncan. *North American Supply.* London: Her Majesty's Stationery Office and Longmans, Green and Co., 1955.
This lucid and literate account of the role played by Canada and the United States in supplying Great Britain during the war is the single most informative source of details on British policy and policy formulation regarding financial and supply matters. If an official history can have heroes, Arthur Purvis and Henry Morgenthau, Jr., fit that label in this study. Although Mr. Hall claims not to be concerned with American policy, his insights into the workings of the American political system and policy-making are numerous and perceptive.

Hall, H. Duncan, and Wrigley, C. C. *Studies of Overseas Supply.* London: Her Majesty's Stationery Office and Longmans, Green and Co., 1956.
This is a series of case studies which grew out of Hall's work on *North American Supply.*

Hancock, W. K., and Gowing, M. M. *British War Economy.* London: His Majesty's Stationery Office, 1949.
This general survey contains some data on British policy formulation but is largely superseded in the area of Lend-Lease and the British financial crisis by later volumes in this series.

Sayers, R. S. *Financial Policy, 1939-1945.* London: Her Majesty's Stationery Office and Longmans, Green and Co., 1956.
This proved to be a valuable and readable study of a highly sophisticated question. As with the other volumes in this series, it is based on official British documents and along with its fellow volumes is the only extensive source of information concerning those documents.

History of United States Naval Operations in World War II:

Morison, Samuel E. Vol. I, *The Battle of the Atlantic, September 1939-May 1943.* Boston: Little, Brown and Co., 1947.
Useful only for background since Morison did not have access to policy documents.

United States Army in World War II. (Edited by Kent Roberts Greenfield):

The War Department:

Cline, Ray S. *Washington Command Post: The Operations Division.* Washington: Office of the Chief of Military History, 1951.
Primarily concerned with Army operations, this volume was of only slight value in determining the policy attitudes and influence of the War Department regarding the British financial crisis and its relationship to American defense. The three entries that follow this provided the bulk of that information.

Leighton, Richard M., and Coakley, Robert W. *Global Logistics and Strategy, 1940-1943.* Washington: Office of the Chief of Military History, 1955.

Matloff, Maurice, and Snell, Edwin M. *Strategic Planning for Coalition Warfare, 1941-1942.* Washington: Office of the Chief of Military History, 1953.

Watson, Mark S. *Chief of Staff: Prewar Plans and Preparations.* Washington: Historical Division, Department of the Army, 1950.

The Western Hemisphere:

Conn, Stetson, and Fairchild, Byron. *The Framework of Hemisphere Defense.* Washington: Office of the Chief of Military History, 1960.

B. Published Studies:

Adler, Selig. *The Isolationist Impulse: Its Twentieth Century Reaction.* New York: Collier Books, 1957.

_____. *The Uncertain Giant: 1921-1941; American Foreign Policy between the Wars.* New York and London: The Macmillan Co., 1965.

Bailey, Thomas A. *The Man in the Street: The Impact of American Opinion on Foreign Policy*. New York: The Macmillan Co., 1948.

Baker, Roscoe. *The American Legion and American Foreign Policy*. New York: Bookman Associates, 1954.

Barnard, Ellsworth. *Wendell Willkie: Fighter for Freedom*. Marquette: Northern Michigan University Press, 1966.
    In his bibliography Barnard states he did not consult a file in the Willkie Papers labelled "Lend-Lease." He wrote me that he was of the opinion that all of Willkie's correspondence with major government figures was in files designated with the official's name, and he believed the "Lend-Lease" file consisted of letters to Willkie from the general public concerning the bill.

Beard, Charles A. *President Roosevelt and the Coming of the War, 1941: A Study in Appearances and Realities*. New Haven: Yale University Press, 1948.
    A "revisionist" study that is highly critical of what the author considers to have been Roosevelt's conscious deception of the American public.

Beasley, Norman. *Knudsen: A Biography*. New York and London: Whittlesey House, McGraw-Hill Book Co., 1947.

Birkenhead, The Earl of. *Halifax: The Life of Lord Halifax*. London: Hamish Hamilton, 1965.

Brebner, John B. *North Atlantic Triangle: The Interplay of Canada, The United States and Great Britain*. New Haven: Yale University Press for the Carnegie Endowment for International Peace, 1945.

Broad, Lewis. *Winston Churchill: The Years of Achievement*. London: Sidgwick and Jackson, 1964.
    This is a relatively uninformative biography of Churchill based on published sources.

Buchanan, A. Russell. *The United States and World War II*. Vol. I, New American Nation Series, edited by Henry S. Commager and Richard B. Morris. New York, Evanston, and London: Harper and Row, 1964.

Burns, James MacGregor. *Roosevelt: The Lion and the Fox*. New York: Harcourt, Brace and Co., 1956.

Butler, J. R. M. *Lord Lothian (Philip Kerr), 1882-1940*. London: Macmillan and Co., 1960.
    A useful study based on Lothian's papers. Unhappily, it provides little information on British policy-formulation.

Chadwin, Mark L. *The Hawks of World War II*. Chapel Hill: University of North Carolina Press, 1968.
    A solid study of the interventionist movement prior to America's entry into World War II.

Chamberlin, William Henry. *America's Second Crusade.* Chicago: Henry Regnery Co., 1950.
A "revisionist" critique of Roosevelt's foreign policy.

Cole, Wayne S. *America First: The Battle Against Intervention, 1940-1941.* Madison: University of Wisconsin Press, 1953.

———. *Senator Gerald P. Nye and American Foreign Relations.* Minneapolis: University of Minnesota Press, 1962.
In addition to the title subject, this is an articulate explanation of the thesis of the agrarian roots of American isolationism.

Compton, James V. *The Swastika and the Eagle: Hitler, the United States, and the Origins of World War II.* Boston: Houghton Mifflin Co., 1967.

Cornwell, Elmer E., Jr. *Presidential Leadership of Public Opinion.* Bloomington: Indiana University Press, 1965.

Corwin, Edward S. *Total War and the Constitution.* New York: Alfred A. Knopf, 1947.

Current, Richard N. *Secretary Stimson: A Study in Statecraft.* New Brunswick: Rutgers University Press, 1954.
This is a provocative and persuasive criticism of Stimson's approach to foreign affairs. Current believes Stimson was virtually obsessed with the idea of power politics and the use of force.

Dahl, Robert A. *Congress and Foreign Policy.* New York: Norton and Co., 1964.
Dahl criticizes the dominance of the executive branch in foreign policy beginning in the late 1930's.

Davids, Jules. *America and the World of Our Time.* 2d ed. New York: Random House, 1962.

Davis, Kenneth S. *The Hero: Charles A. Lindbergh and the American Dream.* Garden City, N.Y.: Doubleday and Co., 1959.

Dawson, Raymond H. *The Decision to Aid Russia, 1941: Foreign Policy and Domestic Politics.* Chapel Hill: University of North Carolina Press, 1959.

Divine, Robert A. *The Illusion of Neutrality.* Chicago: University of Chicago Press, 1962.

———. *The Reluctant Belligerent: American Entry into World War II.* New York: John Wiley and Sons, 1965.

Dorough, C. Dwight. *Mr. Sam.* New York: Random House, 1962.
The scholarly, definitive biography of Sam Rayburn is yet to be written.

Drummond, Donald F. *The Passing of American Neutrality, 1937-1941.* Ann Arbor: University of Michigan Press, 1955.

Feiling, Keith. *The Life of Neville Chamberlain*. London: Macmillan and Co., 1946.

Feis, Herbert. *The Road to Pearl Harbor: Coming of the War between the United States and Japan*. New York: Atheneum, 1962. (Originally published in 1950.)

Friedländer, Saul. *Prelude to Downfall: Hitler and the United States, 1939-1941*. Translated by Aline B. and Alexander Werth. New York: Alfred A. Knopf, 1967.

Frye, Alton. *Nazi Germany and the American Hemisphere, 1933-1941*. New Haven and London: Yale University Press, 1967.

Gardner, Lloyd C. *Economic Aspects of New Deal Diplomacy*. Madison: University of Wisconsin Press, 1964.

Gerhart, Eugene C. *America's Advocate: Robert H. Jackson*. Indianapolis and New York: The Bobbs-Merrill Co., 1958.

Goodhart, Philip. *Fifty Ships That Saved the World: The Foundation of the Anglo-American Alliance*. Garden City, N.Y.: Doubleday and Co., 1965.
    Although it is overly dramatic and exaggerates the significance of the destroyer-bases deal, it is generally a useful study. It should, however, be supplemented by a more careful use of the papers in the Roosevelt Library and the State Department archives.

Hero, Alfred O., Jr. *The Southerner and World Affairs*. Baton Rouge: Louisiana State University Press, 1965.
    A good study of Southern public opinion and foreign affairs.

Israel, Fred L. *Nevada's Key Pittman*. Lincoln: University of Nebraska Press, 1965.
    Surprisingly, this contains virtually nothing on the Pittman Act of June, 1940, which was very important in the development of the Lend-Lease concept.

Johnson, Walter. *The Battle Against Isolation*. Chicago: University of Chicago Press, 1944.

Jonas, Manfred. *Isolationism in America, 1935-1941*. Ithaca: Cornell University Press, 1966.
    An unconvincing attempt to develop "new" categories in examining isolationism.

Langer, William L., and Gleason, S. Everett. *The Challenge to Isolation*. 2 vols. New York: Harper and Row, Torchbook ed., 1964.

_____. *The Undeclared War, 1940-1941*. New York: Harper and Brothers for the Council on Foreign Relations, 1953.
    This, and its companion volume cited immediately above, can, with caution, be used almost as a primary source since the authors had access to documents

that are still closed to the general scholar. The authors were clearly sympathetic to Roosevelt but valiantly strove to achieve objectivity, failing only occasionally. Their account of the development and passage of the Lend-Lease Act is full and informative.

Lash, Joseph P. *Eleanor Roosevelt: A Friend's Memoir*. Garden City, N.Y.: Doubleday and Co., 1964.
  Until Mr. Lash finishes a full multi-volume biography of Mrs. Roosevelt, her papers at the Roosevelt Library are closed. The footnoted manuscript that Mr. Lash claims he will deposit in the Roosevelt Library so that scholars can check his sources is apparently still just a promise.

Morison, Elting S. *Turmoil and Tradition: A Study of the Life and Times of Henry L. Stimson*. New York: Atheneum, 1964. (Originally published in 1960.)

Osgood, Robert E. *Ideals and Self-Interest in America's Foreign Relations.* Chicago: University of Chicago Press, Phoenix ed., 1964. (Originally published, 1953.)

Pogue, Forrest C. *George C. Marshall*. 2 vols. to date. Vol. II, *Ordeal and Hope, 1939-1942*; 1966. New York: The Viking Press, 1963——.
  Based primarily on War Department files, this adds little to the accounts of policy-formulation presented in the Army's official history of World War II.

Pratt, Julius W. *Cordell Hull, 1933-1944*. 2 vols. In *American Secretaries of State and Their Diplomacy*, edited by Robert Ferrell. New York: Cooper Square Publishers, 1964.
  A disappointing study based largely on printed sources.

Rauch, Basil. *Roosevelt: From Munich to Pearl Harbor*. New York: Creative Age Press, 1950.
  An unabashed and uncritical defense of Roosevelt's foreign policy.

Rogge, O. John. *The Official German Report: Nazi Penetration, 1924-42, Pan Arabism, 1939-Today*. New York: Thomas Yoseloff, 1961.
  Based on the author's work as an investigator and prosecutor for the Department of Justice following World War II, this disorganized and poorly written volume is loaded with undigested data.

Sanborn, Frederic R. *Design for War: A Study of Secret Power Politics, 1937-1941*. New York: The Devin-Adair Co., 1951.
  The title betrays the author's prejudices.

Schlauch, Wolfgang. *Rüstungshilfe der USA an die Verbündeten im Zweiten Weltkrieg*. Vol. XIII of *Beiträge zur Wehrforschung*. Darmstadt: Wehr und Wissen Verlagsgesellschaft mbH, 1967.
  An adequate summary based on published materials.

Snell, John L. *Illusion and Necessity: The Diplomacy of Global War, 1939-1945*. Boston: Houghton Mifflin Co., 1963.

Strout, Cushing. *The American Image of the Old World*. New York: Harper and Row, 1963.
A thought-provoking treatment of America's love-hate relationship with Europe.

Tansill, Charles C. *Back Door to War: The Roosevelt Foreign Policy, 1933-1941*. Chicago: Henry Regnery Co., 1952.
A "revisionist" study that is strongest for the years prior to 1939.

Taylor, A. J. P. *English History, 1914-1945*. New York and Oxford: Oxford University Press, 1965.

Thompson, Laurence. *1940*. New York: William Morrow and Co., 1966.

Tugwell, Rexford G. *The Democratic Roosevelt: A Biography of Franklin Delano Roosevelt*. Garden City, N.Y.: Doubleday and Co., 1957.

Tull, Charles J. *Father Coughlin and the New Deal*. Syracuse: Syracuse University Press, 1965.

Watt, D. C. *Personalities and Policies: Studies in the Formulation of British Foreign Policy in the Twentieth Century*. Notre Dame: University of Notre Dame Press, 1965.
A valuable bibliographical source.

Whalen, Richard J. *The Founding Father: The Story of Joseph P. Kennedy*. New York: New American Library, 1964.
This is a scholarly and persuasive "revisionist" look at Kennedy and the Roosevelt foreign policy.

Wheeler-Bennett, John W. *King George VI: His Life and Reign*. London: Macmillan and Co., 1958.
This study is based on materials not available to other scholars. Since George VI kept abreast of foreign affairs and exchanged personal letters with Roosevelt, it is a useful book.

Young, Kenneth. *Churchill and Beaverbrook*. London: Eyre and Spottiswoode, 1966.

C. Unpublished Studies:

Barber, Phillip M. "A Report . . . or How to Read Eighty-eight Newspapers Without Drawing a Breath." Appendix to Honors Thesis, University of Michigan, 1965.
Mr. Barber was kind enough to give this appendix to me. It is an interesting study of the type of coverage given to the Lend-Lease debate by the *Ann Arbor News*.

Chadwin, Mark L. "Warhawks: The Interventionists of 1940-1941." Ph.D. dissertation, Columbia University, 1966.

Dellinger, David W. "Destroyers for Bases: An End to the Illusion of Neutrality." Master's thesis, Georgetown University, 1967.
    Based largely on the papers in the Roosevelt Library, this is a solid, scholarly examination that fully covers the official aspects of the story. It is quite sketchy in the area of public opinion and the exchange.

Fleron, Frederic J., Jr. "The Isolationists and the Foreign Policy of FDR: A Study in Executive Leadership." Master's thesis, Brown University, 1961.
    The text of this study affords no new insights, but Mr. Fleron prepared some excellent graphs of public opinion from 1939 to 1941 based on public opinion polls.

Herring, George. "Experiment in Foreign Aid: Lend-Lease, 1941-1945." Ph.D. dissertation, University of Virginia, 1965.
    This picks up the story where I have left off. In addition to using the F.E.A. records in the National Archives, Mr. Herring had access to the Stettinius Papers at the University of Virginia Library. Those papers are still not available to most scholars.

Hodgkinson, H. D. "History of the Empire and Allied Requirements Division of the British Supply Council." Manuscript used in the preparation of the book, *North American Supply*.
    This unpublished manuscript was supplied to me through the courtesy of H. Duncan Hall. It concerned Lend-Lease and its origins only indirectly.

Kimball, Warren F. "Dieckhoff and America: A German's View of German-American Relations, 1937-1941." Master's thesis, Georgetown University, 1965.

Ragland, James F. "Franklin Roosevelt and Public Opinion, 1933-1940." Ph.D. dissertation, Stanford University, 1954.
    A blatantly pro-Roosevelt and virtually conclusionless treatment that was generally of very little use. The author obviously attempted far too broad a task.

Stickle, Warren. "New Jersey Politics—1940: An Acid Test of the Roosevelt Coalition." Master's thesis, Georgetown University, 1967.
    Primarily concerned with domestic affairs, this provided some idea of the effect of the foreign policy question on New Jersey voters in the 1940 election.

U.S., Department of the Army, International Aid Division, Army Service Forces. "Lend-Lease as of September 30, 1945." 2 vols. with a 10-vol. documentary supplement. Office of the Chief of Military History, Washington, D. C.
    This is primarily concerned with the operation of the Lend-Lease Act itself, and most of the material on the origins of the concept is available elsewhere.

Wyckoff, Theodore. "The Office of Secretary of War Under Henry L. Stimson, 1940-1945." Ph.D. dissertation, Princeton University, 1960.

There is a copy of this dissertation available in the Office of the Chief of Military History, Washington, D. C. In the area of Lend-Lease, it largely repeats material already presented in the Army's official history.

D. Articles and Essays:

Barnes, Harry Elmer. "Revisionism: A Key to Peace." *Rampart Journal*, II (Spring, 1966), 8-74.
  A long-winded but fascinating essay by the dean of "revisionist" historians. Its main use is as a historiographical survey of literature pertaining to World Wars I and II.

Billington, Ray Allen. "The Origins of Middle Western Isolationism." *Political Science Quarterly* LX (March, 1945), 44-64. Reprinted in Edward Saveth, ed., *Understanding the American Past*. 2d ed. Boston: Little, Brown and Co., 1965.

Carl, Joachim. "Das Amerikanische Leih- und Pacht-Gesetz." *Wehrwissenschaftlichen Rundschau*, Supplement 6 (May, 1957).
  A pedantic survey of the nature and origins of the Lend-Lease Act which depended completely upon secondary sources.

Catton, William R., Jr. "Origin and Establishment of Lend-Lease Policy: A Study in Symbolic Paralysis." *Etc.: A Review of General Semantics* VII (Spring, 1950), 180-88.
  Published in a now defunct journal, this interesting essay contends that the American public and government were paralyzed by their view of money as something of value in itself.

Cole, Wayne S. "America First and the South, 1940-1941." *Journal of Southern History* XXII (February, 1956), 36-47.

_____. "Senator Key Pittman and American Neutrality Policies, 1933-1940." *Mississippi Valley Historical Review* XLVI (March, 1960), 644-62.

DeConde, Alexander. "On Twentieth Century Isolationism." In *Isolation and Security*. Edited by A. DeConde. Durham: Duke University Press, 1957.
  A convincing attempt to analyze the various facets that made up American isolationism in the twentieth century.

_____. "The South and Isolationism." *Journal of Southern History* XXIV (August, 1958), 332-46.

Donovan, John C. "Congressional Isolationists and the Roosevelt Foreign Policy." *World Politics* III (April, 1951), 299-316.
  An interesting but outdated examination that concludes that Roosevelt moved as quickly as Congress would permit in the direction of aiding Great Britain.

Hall, H. Duncan. "Purvis, Arthur Blaikie." In the *Dictionary of National Biography, 1941-1950*, edited by L. G. Wickham Legg and E. T. Williams. Oxford: Oxford University Press, 1959.

Jonas, Manfred. "Pro-Axis Sentiment and American Isolationism." *Historian* XXIX (February, 1967), 221-37.
    Jonas erroneously claims that the isolationists sincerely wished to provide aid to Britain via a loan. Other than that, the article says little that has not been said before.

Kaufmann, William W. "Two American Ambassadors: Bullitt and Kennedy." In *The Diplomats, 1919-1939.* Edited by Gordon Craig and Felix Gilbert. New York: Atheneum, 1963. (Originally published 1953).

Kimball, Warren F. "Dieckhoff and America: A German's View of German-American Relations, 1937-1941." *Historian* XXVII (February, 1965), 218-43.

McCurrach, D. F. "Britain's U.S. Dollar Problems, 1939-1945." *Economic Journal* LVIII (September, 1948), 356-72.

Rieselbach, Leroy N. "The Demography of the Congressional Vote on Foreign Aid, 1939-1958." *American Political Science Review* LVIII (September, 1964), 577-88.

Stromberg, Roland N. "American Business and the Approach of War, 1935-1941." *Journal of Economic History* XIII (Winter, 1953), 58-78.

Whalen, Richard J. "The Strange Case of Tyler Kent." *Diplomat*, November, 1965, 17 ff.
    This journal is no longer being published and copies of it are difficult to obtain. I am grateful to the Metromedia Corporation of Washington, D. C., for obtaining a copy of the article for me.

INDEX

Acheson, Dean: consulted in drafting of Lend-Lease bill, 137
Adams, Sen. Alva B. (D-Colo.), 216
Adams, John: and monarchism, 172n
Advisory Committee on Lend-Lease. *See* Lend-Lease Advisory Committee
Agar, Herbert: accuses Roosevelt of misleading public, 11
Agnew, Sir Andrew: suggests sterling payments, 74
Aid to Britain. *See* United States, Coordination of aid to Britain
Aircraft industry: fears government control, 31
Aircraft purchasing: effect on U.S. production capabilities, 55
Alsop, Joseph: characterizes FDR, 100n
Alsop, Joseph, and Kintner, Robert: publicize British dollar shortage, 36; critical of Barkley, 219
America First Committee: criticizes Lend-Lease bill, 155; criticizes Lend-Lease concept, 127; Lend-Lease hearings, 192; organized, 75. *See also* Wood, Gen. Robert
American Aviation Daily: fears government control, 31
American Defense Society, 162
American Farm Bureau Federation, 115
American Federation of Labor, 162
American Legion: supports Lend-Lease bill, 172n
American Viscose. *See* Viscose Corporation of America
American White Paper: advocates aiding Britain, 36
American Youth Congress: opposes Lend-Lease bill, 193n
Anglo-French Purchasing Board: bypassed by buyers and sellers, 53-54; established, 25, 31. *See also* Monnet, Jean; Purvis, Arthur B.
Anti-Semitism: and Gerald L. K. Smith, 162
"A" Program. *See* Layton, Sir Walter
Arnold, Gen. Henry ("Hap"): accused of violating policy, 66; opposes giving military data to Great Britain, 36; supports expanded aircraft production goals, 67
Arnold, Rep. Laurence F. (D-Ill.): member, House Foreign Affairs Committee, 201n
"Arsenal of democracy" speech. *See* Roosevelt, Franklin D.
Aurand, Lt. Col. Henry F.: prepares testimony for use by Stimson, 227
Austin, Sen. Warren R. (R-Vt.): vote courted by Stimson, 199; mentioned, 147, 220

Bachelder, Toinette, 234
Bailey, Sen. Josiah (D-N.C.), 47
Bailey, Thomas A.: critique of Lend-Lease proposal, 12
"Balance sheet" technique, 131n
Ballantyne, Charles, 137
Bankhead, Rep. Walter (D-Ala.): does not vote on Lend-Lease bill, 207n
Bank of Canada, 149
Bank of England: reluctant to disclose financial data, 83; mentioned, 19
Barkley, Sen. Alben (D-Ky.): and amendments to Lend-Lease bill, 212-13, 215; effectiveness assessed, 219; introduces Lend-Lease bill, 153; legislative strategy for Lend-Lease bill, 141-47; and Lend-Lease debate, 178, 183, 190, 211; Pepper resolutions opposed by, 46-47; mentioned, 98, 207n, 220
Baruch, Bernard, 94
Batt, W. L., 94n
Battle of Britain: effect on U.S. aid to Britain, 74-75
Beaman, Middleton: and drafting of Lend-Lease bill, 136-37, 139; mentioned, 140
Beard, Charles A.: aid to Allies criticized by, 11; and British role in Lend-Lease concept, 124; and isolationism, 1; Lend-Lease debate studies by, 177; Roosevelt criticized by, 240
Beaverbrook, William M. Aitken, Lord: aircraft engine plans transferred to

 THE JOHNS HOPKINS PRESS

Designed by Arlene J. Sheer

*Composed in Press Roman with Times Roman display
by Jones Composition Company, Inc.*

*Printed offset by Universal Lithographers, Inc.,
on 60-lb Perkins and Squier, R*

Bound by L. H. Jenkins, Inc., in Columbia Riverside Chambray